SOLIDWORKS 2017
Tutorial with
Video Instruction

A Step-by-Step Project Based Approach
Utilizing 3D Solid Modeling

David C. Planchard
CSWP & SOLIDWORKS Accredited Educator

Publications

SDC Publications
P.O. Box 1334
Mission, KS 66222
913-262-2664
www.SDCpublications.com
Publisher: Stephen Schroff

Trademarks
SOLIDWORKS®, eDrawings®, SOLIDWORKS Simulation®, SOLIDWORKS Flow Simulation, and SOLIDWORKS Sustainability are registered trademarks of Dassault Systèmes SOLIDWORKS Corporation in the United States and other countries; certain images of the models in this publication courtesy of Dassault Systèmes SOLIDWORKS Corporation.

Microsoft Windows®, Microsoft Office® and its family of products are registered trademarks of the Microsoft Corporation. Other software applications and parts described in this book are trademarks or registered trademarks of their respective owners.

The publisher and the author make no representations or warranties with respect to the accuracy or completeness of the contents of this work and specifically disclaim all warranties, including without limitation warranties of fitness for a particular purpose. No warranty may be created or extended by sales or promotional materials. Dimensions of parts are modified for illustration purposes. Every effort is made to provide an accurate text. The author and the manufacturers shall not be held liable for any parts, components, assemblies or drawings developed or designed with this book or any responsibility for inaccuracies that appear in the book. Web and company information was valid at the time of this printing.

The Y14 ASME Engineering Drawing and Related Documentation Publications utilized in this text are as follows: ASME Y14.1 1995, ASME Y14.2M-1992 (R1998), ASME Y14.3M-1994 (R1999), ASME Y14.41-2003, ASME Y14.5-1982, ASME Y14.5-1999, and ASME B4.2. Note: By permission of The American Society of Mechanical Engineers, Codes and Standards, New York, NY, USA. All rights reserved.

Additional information references the American Welding Society, AWS 2.4:1997 Standard Symbols for Welding, Braising, and Non-Destructive Examinations, Miami, Florida, USA.

ISBN-13: 978-1-63057-074-3
ISBN-10: 1-63057-074-5

Printed and bound in the United States of America.

INTRODUCTION

SOLIDWORKS® 2017 Tutorial with video instruction is written to assist students, designers, engineers and professionals who are new to SOLIDWORKS. The text provides a step-by-step project based learning approach. It also contains information and examples on the five categories, to take and understand the Certified Associate - Mechanical Design (CSWA) exam.

The book is divided into three sections. Chapters 1 - 6 explore the SOLIDWORKS User Interface and CommandManager, Document and System properties, simple machine parts, simple and complex assemblies, proper design intent, design tables, configurations, equations, multi-sheet, multi-view drawings, BOMs, and Revision tables using basic and advanced features.

Chapters 7 - 10 prepare you for the Certified Associate - Mechanical Design (CSWA) exam. The certification indicates a foundation in and apprentice knowledge of 3D CAD and engineering practices and principles.

View Chapter 11 on Additive Manufacturing (3D printing) and its benefits and features. Understand the terms and technology used in low cost 3D printers.

Follow the step-by-step instructions and develop multiple assemblies that combine over 100 extruded machined parts and components. Formulate the skills to create, modify and edit sketches and solid features.

Learn the techniques to reuse features, parts and assemblies through symmetry, patterns, copied components, apply proper design intent, design tables and configurations. Learn by doing, not just by reading.

Desired outcomes and usage competencies are listed for each chapter. Know your objective up front. Follow the steps in each chapter to achieve your design goals.

Work between multiple documents, features, commands, custom properties and document properties that represent how engineers and designers utilize SOLIDWORKS in industry.

Redeem your code on the inside cover of the book. Download the models and videos to your hard drive. View the provided videos to enhance the user experience: Start a SOLIDWORKS session, Understand the SOLIDWORKS User Interface, Create 2D Sketches, Utilize various Sketch tools, Create 3D Features, Apply Design Intent, Create an Assembly and Create fundamental Drawings Part 1 & Part 2.

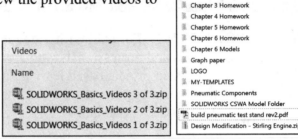

STEM final project

Create the final ROBOT assembly illustrated in chapter 6. The physical components and corresponding Science, Technology, Engineering and Math (STEM) curriculum are available from Gears Educational Systems. All assemblies and components for the final ROBOT assembly are provided.

About the Author

David Planchard is the founder of D&M Education LLC. Before starting D&M Education, he spent over 27 years in industry and academia holding various engineering, marketing, and teaching positions. He holds five U.S. patents. He has published and authored numerous papers on Machine Design, Product Design, Mechanics of Materials, and Solid Modeling. He is an active member of the SOLIDWORKS Users Group and the American Society of Engineering Education (ASEE). David holds a BSME, MSM with the following professional certifications: CCAI, CCNP, CSDA, CSWSA-FEA, CSWP, CSWP-DRWT and SOLIDWORKS Accredited Educator. David is a SOLIDWORKS Solution Partner, an Adjunct Faculty member and the SAE advisor at Worcester Polytechnic Institute in the Mechanical Engineering department. In 2012, David's senior Major Qualifying Project team (senior capstone) won first place in the Mechanical Engineering department at WPI. In 2014, 2015 and 2016 David's senior Major Qualifying Project team won the Provost award in Mechanical Engineering for design excellence.

David Planchard is the author of the following books:

- **SOLIDWORKS® 2017 Reference Guide with video instruction**, 2016, 2015, 2014, 2013, 2012, 2011, 2010, 2009 and 2008

- **Engineering Design with SOLIDWORKS® 2017 and video instruction**, 2016, 2015, 2014, 2013, 2012, 2011, 2010, 2009, 2008, 2007, 2006, 2005, 2004, and 2003

- **Engineering Graphics with SOLIDWORKS® 2017 and video instruction**, 2016, 2015, 2014, 2013, 2012, 2011, 2010

- **SOLIDWORKS® 2017 in 5 Hours with video instruction**, 2016, 2015, 2014

- **SOLIDWORKS® 2017 Tutorial with video instruction**, 2016, 2015, 2014, 2013, 2012, 2011, 2010, 2009, 2008, 2007, 2006, 2005, 2004, and 2003

- **Drawing and Detailing with SOLIDWORKS® 2014**, 2012, 2010, 2009, 2008, 2007, 2006, 2005, 2004, 2003, and 2002

- **Official Certified SOLIDWORKS® Professional (CSWP) Certification Guide with video instruction, Version 4: 2015 - 2017**, Version 3: 2012 - 2014, Version 2: 2012 - 2013, Version 1: 2010 - 2011

- **Official Guide to Certified SOLIDWORKS® Associate Exams: CSWA, CSDA, CSWSA-FEA Version 3: 2015 - 2017**, Version 2: 2012 - 2015, Version 1: 2012 – 2013

- **Assembly Modeling with SOLIDWORKS® 2012**, 2010, 2008, 2006, 2005-2004, 2003 and 2001Plus

Acknowledgements

Writing this book was a substantial effort that would not have been possible without the help and support of my loving family and of my professional colleagues. I would like to thank Professor John M. Sullivan Jr., Professor Jack Hall and the community of scholars at Worcester Polytechnic Institute who have enhanced my life, my knowledge and helped to shape the approach and content to this text.

The author is greatly indebted to my colleagues from Dassault Systèmes SOLIDWORKS Corporation for their help and continuous support: Avelino Rochino and Mike Puckett.

Thanks also to Professor Richard L. Roberts of Wentworth Institute of Technology, Professor Dennis Hance of Wright State University, Professor Jason Durfess of Eastern Washington University and Professor Aaron Schellenberg of Brigham Young University - Idaho who provided vision and invaluable suggestions.

SOLIDWORKS certification has enhanced my skills and knowledge and that of my students. Thank you to Ian Matthew Jutras (CSWE), who is a technical contributor and the creator of the videos, and Stephanie Planchard, technical procedure consultant.

Contact the Author

We realize that keeping software application books current is imperative to our customers. We value the hundreds of professors, students, designers, and engineers that have provided us input to enhance the book. Please contact me directly with any comments, questions or suggestions on this book or any of our other SOLIDWORKS books at dplanchard@msn.com or planchard@wpi.edu.

Note to Instructors

Please contact the publisher www.SDCpublications.com for classroom support materials (.ppt presentations, labs and more) and the Instructor's Guide with model solutions and tips that support the usage of this text in a classroom environment.

Trademarks, Disclaimer and Copyrighted Material

SOLIDWORKS®, eDrawings®, SOLIDWORKS Simulation®, SOLIDWORKS Flow Simulation, and SOLIDWORKS Sustainability are a registered trademark of Dassault Systèmes SOLIDWORKS Corporation in the United States and other countries; certain images of the models in this publication courtesy of Dassault Systèmes SOLIDWORKS Corporation.

Microsoft Windows®, Microsoft Office® and its family of products are registered trademarks of the Microsoft Corporation. Other software applications and parts described in this book are trademarks or registered trademarks of their respective owners.

The publisher and the author make no representations or warranties with respect to the accuracy or completeness of the contents of this work and specifically disclaim all warranties, including without limitation warranties of fitness for a particular purpose. No warranty may be created or extended by sales or promotional materials. Dimensions of parts are modified for illustration purposes. Every effort is made to provide an accurate text. The authors and the manufacturers shall not be held liable for any parts, components, assemblies or drawings developed or designed with this book or any responsibility for inaccuracies that appear in the book. Web and company information was valid at the time of this printing.

The Y14 ASME Engineering Drawing and Related Documentation Publications utilized in this text are as follows: ASME Y14.1 1995, ASME Y14.2M-1992 (R1998), ASME Y14.3M-1994 (R1999), ASME Y14.41-2003, ASME Y14.5-1982, ASME Y14.5-1999, and ASME B4.2. Note: By permission of The American Society of Mechanical Engineers, Codes and Standards, New York, NY, USA. All rights reserved.

Additional information references the American Welding Society, AWS 2.4:1997 Standard Symbols for Welding, Braising, and Non-Destructive Examinations, Miami, Florida, USA.

References

- SOLIDWORKS Help Topics and What's New, SOLIDWORKS Corporation, 2017.

- Beers & Johnson, <u>Vector Mechanics for Engineers</u>, 6th ed. McGraw Hill, Boston, MA.

- Jensen & Helsel, <u>Engineering Drawing and Design</u>, Glencoe, 1990.

- Lockhart & Johnson, <u>Engineering Design Communications</u>, Addison Wesley, 1999.

- Walker, James, <u>Machining Fundamentals</u>, Goodheart Wilcox, 1999.

- 80/20 Product Manual, 80/20, Inc., Columbia City, IN, 2012.

- Ticona Designing with Plastics - The Fundamentals, Summit, NJ, 2009.

- SMC Corporation of America, Product Manuals, Indiana, USA, 2012.

- Emerson-EPT Bearing Product Manuals and Gear Product Manuals, Emerson Power Transmission Corporation, Ithaca, NY, 2009.

- Emhart - A Black and Decker Company, On-line catalog, Hartford, CT, 2012.

During the initial SOLIDWORKS installation, you are requested to select either the ISO or ANSI drafting standard. ISO is typically a European drafting standard and uses First Angle Projection. This book is written using the ANSI (US) overall drafting standard and Third Angle Projection for drawings.

Screen shots in the book were made using SOLIDWORKS 2017 SP0 running Windows® 10.

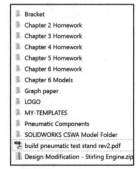

Redeem your code on the inside cover of the book. All templates, logos and model documents along with additional support materials for this book are available. View the video instruction files for additional information.

Instructor's information contains over 45 classroom presentations, along with helpful hints, what's new, sample quizzes, avi files of assemblies, projects and all initial and final SOLIDWORKS models.

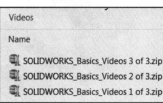

Additional projects are included in the exercise section of
Chapter 6. Copy the components from the Chapter 6 Homework
folder. View all components. Create an ANSI assembly document.
Insert and create all needed components and mates to assemble the
assembly and to simulate proper movement per the provided avi
file.

Chapter 6 Homework

Name

- Bench Vice Assembly Project
- Butterfly Valve Assembly Project
- Drill Guide Assembly Project
- Kant Twist Clamp Assembly Project
- Pipe Vice Assembly Project
- Pulley Assembly Project
- Quick Acting Clamp Assembly Project
- Radial Engine Assembly Project
- Shaper Tool Head Assembly Project
- Shock Assembly Project
- Welder Arm Assembly Project

TABLE OF CONTENTS

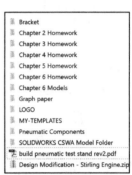

The Instructor's information contains over 45 classroom presentations along with helpful hints, What's new, sample quizzes, avi files of assemblies, projects and all initial and final SOLIDWORKS model files.

Redeem your code on the inside cover of the book. View the provided videos to enhance the user experience: Start a SOLIDWORKS session, Understand the SOLIDWORKS User Interface, Create 2D Sketches, Sketch Planes and utilize various Sketch tools, Create 3D Features and apply Design Intent, Create an Assembly and Create fundamental Drawings Part 1 & Part 2.

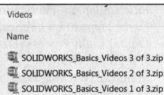

What is SOLIDWORKS?

SOLIDWORKS® is a mechanical design automation software package used to build parts, assemblies and drawings that takes advantage of the familiar Microsoft® Windows graphical user interface.

SOLIDWORKS is an easy to learn design and analysis tool (SOLIDWORKS Simulations, SOLIDWORKS Motion, SOLIDWORKS Flow Simulation etc.), which makes it possible for designers to quickly sketch 2D and 3D concepts, create 3D parts and assemblies and detail 2D drawings.

In SOLIDWORKS, you create 2D and 3D sketches, 3D parts, 3D assemblies and 2D drawings. The part, assembly and drawing documents are related. Additional information on SOLIDWORKS and its family of products can be obtained at their URL, www.SOLIDWORKS.com.

Features are the building blocks of parts. Use features to create parts, such as Extruded Boss/Base and Extruded Cut. Extruded features begin with a 2D sketch created on a Sketch plane.

The 2D sketch is a profile or cross section. Sketch tools such as lines, arcs and circles are used to create the 2D sketch. Sketch the general shape of the profile. Add Geometric relationships and dimensions to control the exact size of the geometry.

Create features by selecting edges or faces of existing features, such as a Fillet. The Fillet feature rounds sharp corners.

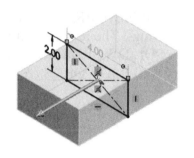

Dimensions drive features. Change a dimension, and you change the size of the part.

Apply Geometric relationships: Vertical, Horizontal, Parallel, etc. to maintain Design intent.

Create a hole that penetrates through a part. SOLIDWORKS maintains relationships through the change.

The step-by-step approach used in this text allows you to create parts, assemblies and drawings by doing, not just by reading.

The book provides the knowledge to modify all parts and components in a document. Change is an integral part of design.

Design Intent

What is design intent? All designs are created for a purpose. Design intent is the intellectual arrangement of features and dimensions of a design. Design intent governs the relationship between sketches in a feature, features in a part and parts in an assembly.

The SOLIDWORKS definition of design intent is the process in which the model is developed to accept future modifications. Models behave differently when design changes occur.

Design for change. Utilize geometry for symmetry, reuse common features, and reuse common parts. Build change into the following areas that you create:

- **Sketch**

- **Feature**

- **Part**

- **Assembly**

- **Drawing**

When editing or repairing geometric relations, it is considered best practice to edit the relation vs. deleting it.

Design Intent in a sketch

Build design intent in a sketch as the profile is created. A profile is determined from the Sketch Entities. Example: Rectangle, Circle, Arc, Point, Slot etc. Apply symmetry into a profile through a sketch centerline, mirror entity and position about the reference planes and Origin. Always know the location of the Origin in the sketch.

Build design intent as you sketch with automatic Geometric relations. Document the decisions made during the up-front design process. This is very valuable when you modify the design later.

A rectangle (Center Rectangle Sketch tool) contains Horizontal, Vertical and Perpendicular automatic Geometric relations.

Apply design intent using added Geometric relations if needed. Example: Horizontal, Vertical, Collinear, Perpendicular, Parallel, Equal etc.

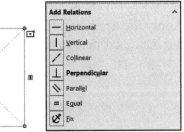

Example A: Apply design intent to create a square profile. Sketch a rectangle. Apply the Center Rectangle Sketch tool. Note: No construction reference centerline or Midpoint relation is required with the Center Rectangle tool. Insert dimensions to fully define the sketch.

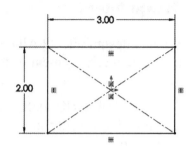

Example B: If you have a hole in a part that must always be 16.5mm≤ from an edge, dimension to the edge rather than to another point on the sketch. As the part size is modified, the hole location remains 16.5mm≤ from the edge as illustrated.

Design intent in a feature

Build design intent into a feature by addressing End Conditions (Blind, Through All, UpToVertex, etc.), symmetry, feature selection, and the order of feature creation.

Example A: The Extruded Base feature remains symmetric about the Front Plane. Utilize the Mid Plane End Condition option in Direction 1. Modify the depth, and the feature remains symmetric about the Front Plane.

Example B: Create 34 teeth in the model. Do you create each tooth separately using the Extruded Cut feature? No.

Create a single tooth and then apply the Circular Pattern feature. Modify the Circular Pattern from 32 to 24 teeth.

Design intent in a part

Utilize symmetry, feature order and reuse common features to build design intent into a part. Example A: Feature order. Is the entire part symmetric? Feature order affects the part.

Apply the Shell feature before the Fillet feature and the inside corners remain perpendicular.

Design intent in an assembly

Utilizing symmetry, reusing common parts and using the Mate relation between parts builds the design intent into an assembly.

Example A: Reuse geometry in an assembly. The assembly contains a linear pattern of holes. Insert one screw into the first hole. Utilize the Component Pattern feature to copy the machine screw to the other holes.

Design intent in a drawing

Utilize dimensions, tolerance and notes in parts and assemblies to build the design intent into a drawing.

Example A: Tolerance and material in the drawing. Insert an outside diameter tolerance +.000/-.002 into the TUBE part. The tolerance propagates to the drawing.

Define the Custom Property Material in the Part. The Material Custom Property propagates to your drawing.

Additional information on design process and design intent is available in SOLIDWORKS Help.

This book is designed to expose the new user to many tools, techniques and procedures. It may not always use the most direct tool or process.

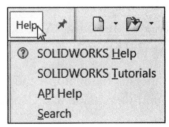

Overview of Chapters

Chapter 1: Overview of SOLIDWORKS and the SOLIDWORKS User Interface.

SOLIDWORKS is a design software application used to create 2D and 3D sketches, 3D parts and assemblies and 2D drawings.

Chapter 1 introduces the user to the SOLIDWORKS 2017 User Interface (UI) and CommandManager: Menu bar toolbar, Menu bar menu, Drop-down menus, Context toolbars, Consolidated drop-down toolbars, System feedback icons, Confirmation Corner, Heads-up View toolbar, Document Properties and more.

Start a new SOLIDWORKS Session. Create a new part. Open an existing part and view the created features and sketches using the Rollback bar. Design the part using proper design intent.

Chapter 2: Parts and Assembly Creation.

Create three parts: AXLE, SHAFT-COLLAR and FLATBAR

Understand and apply the following Sketch tools: Circle, Smart dimension and Centerpoint Straight Slot.

Insert geometric relations and dimensions: Equal, Vertical, Horizontal, Parallel, Perpendicular, Coincident and MidPoint.

Utilize the following features: Extruded Boss/Base, Extruded Cut and Linear Pattern.

Create the LINKAGE assembly. The LINKAGE assembly utilizes the provided AirCylinder assembly. Insert the following Standard mates: Coincident, Concentric and Parallel.

Utilize the Standard and Quick mate procedure.

Chapter 3: Front Support Assembly.

Chapter 3 introduces various Sketch planes to create parts. The Front, Top and Right Planes each contain the Extruded Boss/Base feature for the TRIANGLE, HEX-STANDOFF and ANGLE-13HOLE parts.

Utilize Geometric relationships in your sketch.

Create the SCREW part using the following features: Revolved Base, Extruded Cut, Fillet and Circular Pattern.

Create the FRONT-SUPPORT assembly.

Utilize additional parts from the Web or the provided components to create the RESERVOIR SUPPORT assembly in the chapter exercises.

Apply the following mate types: Concentric, Coincident, Parallel, Distance, Gear and Cam.

Chapter 4: Fundamentals of Drawing.

Chapter 4 covers the development of a customized Sheet format and Drawing template.

Review the differences between the Sheet and the Sheet format.

Develop a company logo from a bitmap or picture file.

Create a FLATBAR drawing.

Insert dimensions created from the part features.

Create a LINKAGE assembly drawing with multiple views.

Develop and incorporate a Bill of Materials into the drawing Custom Properties in the parts and assemblies.

Add information to the Bill of Materials in the assembly drawing.

Insert a Design Table to create multiple configurations of parts and assemblies.

Chapter 5: Advanced Features.

Chapter 5 focuses on creating six parts for the PNEUMATIC-TEST-MODULE Assembly: WHEEL, HOOK, WHEEL, HEX-ADAPTER, AXLE-3000 and SHAFTCOLLAR-500.

Obtain the ability to reuse geometry by modifying existing parts and to create new parts.

Knowledge of the following SOLIDWORKS features: Plane, Lofted Base, Extruded Cut, Swept Base, Dome, Thread, Extruded Boss/Base, Revolved Cut, Extruded Cut, Circular Pattern, Axis, Instant3D, Hole Wizard, Advanced Hole, Split Line and Thread Wizard.

Chapter 6: PNEUMATIC-TEST-MODULE Assembly and Final ROBOT Assembly.

Chapter 6 focuses on the PNEUMATIC-TEST-MODULE Assembly and the final ROBOT Assembly.

Create the WHEEL-AND-AXLE assembly. First, create the 3HOLE-SHAFTCOLLAR assembly and the 5HOLE-SHAFTCOLLAR assembly.

Insert the WHEEL part, AXLE 3000 part, HEX-ADAPTER part and SHAFTCOLLAR-500 part.

Insert the FLAT-PLATE part that was created in the Chapter 3 exercises. Insert the LINKAGE assembly and add components: HEX-STANDOFF, AXLE and SHAFT-COLLAR.

Insert the AIR-RESERVOIR-SUPPORT assembly. Insert the SCREW part. Utilize the Pattern Driven Component Pattern tool and the Linear Component Pattern tool.

Insert the FRONT-SUPPORT assembly and apply the Mirror Components tool to complete the Pneumatic Test Module Assembly.

Create the final ROBOT Assembly as illustrated with the Robot-platform sub-assembly, PNEUMATIC-TEST-MODULE sub-assembly, basic_integration sub-assembly and the HEX-ADAPTER component. Add additional components in the chapter exercises.

Learn the process to work with multiple documents between parts and assemblies and to apply the following Assembly tools: Insert Component, Standard Mates: Concentric, Coincident, and Parallel, Linear Component Pattern, Pattern Driven Component Pattern, Circular Component Pattern, Mirror Components and Replace Components.

Redeem your code on the inside cover of the book. All assemblies and components for the final ROBOT assembly are provided.

- Bracket
- Chapter 2 Homework
- Chapter 3 Homework
- Chapter 4 Homework
- Chapter 5 Homework
- Chapter 6 Homework
- Chapter 6 Models
- Graph paper
- LOGO
- MY-TEMPLATES
- Pneumatic Components
- SOLIDWORKS CSWA Model Folder
- build pneumatic test stand rev2.pdf
- Design Modification - Stirling Engine.zip

Additional projects are included in the exercise section of the chapter. Copy the components from the Chapter 6 Homework folders. View all components.

Create an ANSI assembly document. Insert and create all needed components and mates to assemble the assembly and to simulate proper movement per the provided avi file.

Chapter 6 Homework

Name

- Welder Arm Assembly Project
- Shock Assembly Project
- Quick Acting Clamp Assembly Project
- Radial Engine Assembly Project
- Shaper Tool Head Assembly Project
- Kant Twist Clamp Assembly Project
- Pipe Vice Assembly Project
- Pulley Assembly Project
- Bench Vice Assembly Project
- Butterfly Valve Assembly Project
- Drill Guide Assembly Project

Chapter 7 - 10: Introduction to the Certified Associate - Mechanical Design (CSWA) Exam.

DS SOLIDWORKS Corp. offers various stages of certification representing increasing levels of expertise in 3D CAD design as it applies to engineering: Certified SOLIDWORKS Associate CSWA, Certified SOLIDWORKS Professional CSWP and Certified SOLIDWORKS Expert CSWE along with specialty fields in Drawing, Simulation, Sheet Metal, Surfacing and more.

The CSWA certification indicates a foundation in and apprentice knowledge of 3D CAD design and engineering practices and principles. The main requirement for obtaining the CSWA certification is to take and pass the two part on-line proctored exams.

This first exam (part 1) is 90 minutes, minimum passing score is 80 with 6 questions. The second exam (part 2) is 90 minutes, minimum passing score is 80 with 8 questions.

The CSWA exam consists of 14 questions in the following five categories and subject areas:

- *Drafting Competencies*: (Three questions - multiple choice - 5 points each).

- *Basic Part Creation and Modification*: (Two questions - one multiple choice/one single answer - 15 points each).

- *Intermediate Part Creation and Modification*: (Two questions - one multiple choice/one single answer - 15 points each).

- *Advanced Part Creation and Modification:* (Three questions - one multiple choice/two single answers - 15 points each).

- *Assembly Creation and Modification*: (Two different assemblies - four questions - two multiple choice/two single answers - 30 points each).

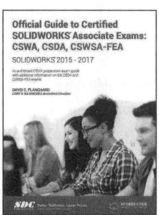

The **Official Guide to Certified SOLIDWORKS Associate Exams**: CSWA, CSDA, CSWSA-FEA book is written to assist the SOLIDWORKS user to pass the associate level exams. Information is provided to aid the user to pass the Certified Associate - Mechanical Design exam, the SOLIDWORKS Certified Associate - Sustainable Design exam, and the SOLIDWORKS Certified Associate - Simulation (FEA) exam. The primary goal of the book is not only to help you pass the exams but also to ensure that you understand and comprehend the concepts and implementation details of the process.

Chapter 11: Additive Manufacturing - 3D Printing.

Provide a basic understanding between the differences of Additive vs. Subtractive Manufacturing. Comprehend 3D printer terminology along with a working knowledge of preparing, saving, and printing a 3D CAD model on a low cost ($500 - $2,000) printer.

On the completion of this chapter, you will be able to:

- Discuss Additive vs Subtractive Manufacturing.

- Determine the differences between a Cartesian printer and a Delta printer.

- Create a STereoLithography (STL) file in SOLIDWORKS.

- 3D print directly from SOLIDWORKS using an Add-In.

  o Save an STL file to G-code.

- Discuss printer hardware.

- Select the correct filament type:

  o PLA (Polylactic acid), ABS (Acrylonitrile butadiene styrene) or Nylon.

- Prepare the G-code.

  o Address model setup, print orientation, extruder temperature, and bed temperature.

- Comprehend the following 3D printer terminology:

  o (STereoLithography) file - STL.

  o Fused Filament Fabrication - FFF.

  o Fused Deposition Model - FDM.

  o Digital Light Process - DLP.

  o Dissolvable Support System - DDS.

  o Fast Layer Deposition - FLD.

  o Raft, Skirt and Brim.

  o Support and Touching Buildplate.

  o Slicer, G-code.

- Address fit tolerance for interlocking parts.

- Define general 3D Printing tips.

About the Book

You will find a wealth of information in this book. The book is a project based step-by-step text written for new and intermediate users. The following conventions are used throughout this book:

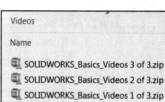

- The term document refers to a SOLIDWORKS part, drawing or assembly file.

- The list of items across the top of the SOLIDWORKS interface is the Menu bar menu or the Menu bar toolbar. Each item in the Menu bar has a pull-down menu. When you need to select a series of commands from these menus, the following format is used: Click **Insert, Reference Geometry, Plane** from the Menu bar. The Plane PropertyManager is displayed.

- The book is organized into chapters. Each chapter is focused on a specific subject or feature. Download all needed model files and folders.

- The ANSI overall drafting standard and Third Angle projection is used as the default setting in this text. IPS (inch, pound, second) and MMGS (millimeter, gram, second) unit systems are used.

- Redeem your code on the inside cover of the book. Download all folders and files to your hard drive. Work from your hard drive. All assemblies and components for the final ROBOT assembly are located in the Chapter 6 Models folder.

The following command syntax is used throughout the text. Commands that require you to perform an action are displayed in **Bold** text.

Format:	Convention:	Example:
Bold	• All commands actions. • Selected icon button. • Selected icon button. • Selected geometry: line, circle. • Value entries.	• Click **Options** ⚙ from the Menu bar toolbar. • Click **Corner Rectangle** ⬜ from the Sketch toolbar. • Click **Sketch** ▥ from the Context toolbar. • Select the **centerpoint**. • Enter **3.0** for Radius.
Capitalized	• Filenames. • First letter in a feature name.	• Save the **FLATBAR** assembly. • Click the **Fillet** ⬯ feature.

Windows Terminology in SOLIDWORKS

The mouse buttons provide an integral role in executing SOLIDWORKS commands. The mouse buttons execute commands, select geometry, display Shortcut menus and provide information feedback.

A summary of mouse button terminology is displayed below:

Item:	Description:
Click	Press and release the left mouse button.
Double-click	Double press and release the left mouse button.
Click inside	Press the left mouse button. Wait a second, and then press the left mouse button inside the text box. Use this technique to modify Feature names in the FeatureManager design tree.
Drag	Point to an object, press and hold the left mouse button down. Move the mouse pointer to a new location. Release the left mouse button.
Right-click	Press and release the right mouse button. A Shortcut menu is displayed. Use the left mouse button to select a menu command.
Tool Tip	Position the mouse pointer over an Icon (button). The tool name is displayed below the mouse pointer.
Large Tool Tip	Position the mouse pointer over an Icon (button). The tool name and a description of its functionality are displayed below the mouse pointer.
Mouse pointer feedback	Position the mouse pointer over various areas of the sketch, part, assembly or drawing. The cursor provides feedback depending on the geometry.

A mouse with a center wheel provides additional functionality in SOLIDWORKS. Roll the center wheel downward to enlarge the model in the Graphics window. Hold the center wheel down. Drag the mouse in the Graphics window to rotate the model.

Visit SOLIDWORKS website:
http://www.SOLIDWORKS.com/sw/support/hardware.html to view their supported
operating systems and hardware requirements.

The Instructor's
information contains over 45
classroom presentations, along
with helpful hints, What's new,
sample quizzes, avi files of
assemblies, projects, and all
initial and final SOLIDWORKS
model files.

The book is designed to expose
the new SOLIDWORKS user to
numerous tools and procedures.
It may not always use the
simplest and most direct
process.

Hardware & System Requirements
Research graphics cards hardware, system requirements, and other related topics.

SolidWorks System Requirements
Hardware and system requirements for SolidWorks
3D CAD products.

Data Management System Requirements
Hardware and system requirements for SolidWorks
Product Data Management (PDM) products.

SolidWorks Composer System Requirements
Hardware and system requirements for SolidWorks
Composer and other 3DVIA related products.

SolidWorks Electrical System Requirements
Hardware and system requirements for SolidWorks
Electrical products.

Graphics Card Drivers
Find graphics card drivers for your system to ensure
system performance and stability.

Anti-Virus
The following Anti-Virus applications have been
tested with SolidWorks 3D CAD products.

Hardware Benchmarks
Applications and references that can help determine
hardware performance.

The book does not cover starting a SOLIDWORKS session in detail for the first time. A
default SOLIDWORKS installation presents you with several options.

For additional information for an Education Edition, visit the following sites:
http://www.SOLIDWORKS.com/goedu and
http://www.SOLIDWORKS.com/sw/education/6443_ENU_HTML.htm.

Notes:

Chapter 1

Overview of SOLIDWORKS® 2017 and the User Interface

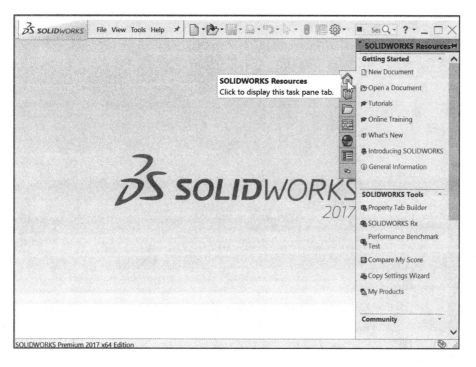

Below are the desired outcomes and usage competencies based on the completion of Chapter 1.

Desired Outcomes:	Usage Competencies:
• A comprehensive understanding of the SOLIDWORKS® 2017 User Interface (UI) and CommandManager.	• Ability to establish a SOLIDWORKS session. • Aptitude to utilize the following items: *Menu bar toolbar, Menu bar menu, Drop-down menus, Context toolbars, Consolidated drop-down toolbars, System feedback icons, Confirmation Corner, Heads-up View toolbar, Document Properties and more.* • Open a new and existing SOLIDWORKS part. • Knowledge to zoom, rotate and maneuver a three-button mouse in the SOLIDWORKS Graphics window.

Notes:

Chapter 1 - Overview of SOLIDWORKS® 2017 and the User Interface

Chapter Objective

Provide a comprehensive understanding of the SOLIDWORKS® default User Interface and CommandManager: Menu bar toolbar, Menu bar menu, Drop-down menu, Right-click Pop-up menus, Context toolbars/menus, Fly-out tool button, System feedback icons, Confirmation Corner, Heads-up View toolbar and more.

On the completion of this chapter, you will be able to:

- Establish a SOLIDWORKS session.

- Comprehend the SOLIDWORKS 2017 User Interface.

- Recognize the default Reference Planes in the FeatureManager.

- Open a new and existing SOLIDWORKS part.

- Utilize SOLIDWORKS Help and SOLIDWORKS Tutorials.

- Zoom, rotate and maneuver a three-button mouse in the SOLIDWORKS Graphics window.

What is SOLIDWORKS®?

- SOLIDWORKS® is a mechanical design automation software package used to build parts, assemblies and drawings that takes advantage of the familiar Microsoft® Windows graphical user interface.

- SOLIDWORKS is an easy to learn design and analysis tool (SOLIDWORKS Simulation, SOLIDWORKS Motion, SOLIDWORKS Flow Simulation, Sustainability, etc.), which makes it possible for designers to quickly sketch 2D and 3D concepts, create 3D parts and assemblies and detail 2D drawings.

- Model dimensions in SOLIDWORKS are associative between parts, assemblies and drawings. Reference dimensions are one-way associative from the part to the drawing or from the part to the assembly.

- This book is written for the beginner to intermediate user.

Start a SOLIDWORKS 2017 Session

Start a SOLIDWORKS session and familiarize yourself with the SOLIDWORKS User Interface. As you read and perform the tasks in this chapter, you will obtain a sense of how to use the book and the structure. Actual input commands or required actions in the chapter are displayed in bold.

This book does not cover starting a SOLIDWORKS session in detail for the first time. A default SOLIDWORKS installation presents you with several options. For additional information, visit http://www.SOLIDWORKS.com.

🔆 Redeem your code on the inside face of the book. Download the models and videos to your hard drive. View the provided videos to enhance the user experience.

Activity: Start a SOLIDWORKS 2017 Session

Start a SOLIDWORKS 2017 session.

1) Click **Start** on the Windows Taskbar.

2) Click **All Programs**.

3) Click the **SOLIDWORKS 2017** folder.

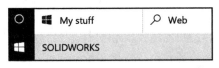

4) Click **SOLIDWORKS 2017** application. The SOLIDWORKS program window opens. Note: Do not open a document at this time.

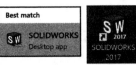

🔆 If available, double-click the SOLIDWORKS 2017 icon on your desktop to start a SOLIDWORKS session.

Read the Tip of the Day dialog box.

If you do not see this screen, click the SOLIDWORKS Resources 🏠 icon on the right side of the Graphics window located in the Task Pane.

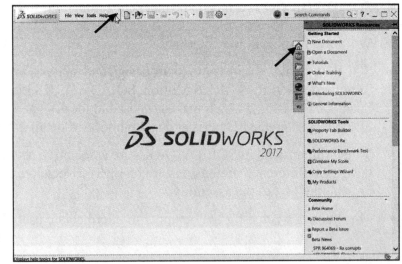

5) **Hover** the mouse pointer over the SOLIDWORKS icon as illustrated.

6) **Pin** the Menu Bar toolbar. View your options.

Menu Bar toolbar

The SOLIDWORKS 2017 (UI) is designed to make maximum use of the Graphics window. The Menu Bar toolbar contains a set of the most frequently used tool buttons from the Standard toolbar.

These are the available default tools:

- **New** □ - Creates a new document; **Open** ☝ - Opens an existing document; **Save** 🖫 - Saves an active document; **Print** 🖨 - Prints an active document; **Undo** ↻ - Reverses the last action; **Select** ☖ - Selects Sketch entities, components and more; **Rebuild** ◉ - Rebuilds the active part, assembly or drawing; **File Properties** ▤ - Shows the summary information on the active document; and **Options** ⚙ - Changes system options and Add-Ins for SOLIDWORKS.

Menu Bar menu

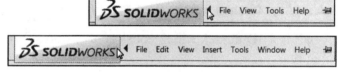

Click SOLIDWORKS in the Menu Bar toolbar to display the Menu Bar menu. SOLIDWORKS provides a context-sensitive menu structure. The menu titles remain the same for all three types of documents, but the menu items change depending on which type of document is active.

Example: The Insert menu includes features in part documents, mates in assembly documents, and drawing views in drawing documents. The display of the menu is also dependent on the workflow customization that you have selected. The default menu items for an active document are *File, Edit, View, Insert, Tools, Window, Help* and *Pin*.

The Pin ☍ option displays the Menu bar toolbar and the Menu bar menu as illustrated. Throughout the book, the Menu bar menu and the Menu bar toolbar are referred to as the Menu bar.

Drop-down menu

SOLIDWORKS takes advantage of the familiar Microsoft®
Windows user interface. Communicate with SOLIDWORKS
through drop-down menus, Context sensitive toolbars,
Consolidated toolbars or the CommandManager tabs.

A command is an instruction that informs
SOLIDWORKS to perform a task.

To close a SOLIDWORKS drop-down menu, press the Esc
key. You can also click any other part of the SOLIDWORKS
Graphics window or click another drop-down menu.

Create a New Part Document

In the next section create a new part document.

> **Activity: Create a new Part Document**

A part is a 3D model, which consists of features. What are
features?

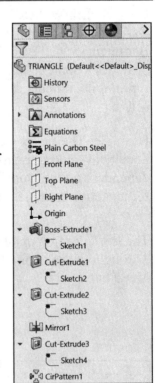

- Features are geometry building blocks.

- Most features either add or remove material.

- Some features do not affect material (Cosmetic Thread).

- Features are created either from 2D or 3D sketched profiles or
  from edges and faces of existing geometry.

- Features are individual shapes that, combined with other
  features, makes up a part or assembly. Some features, such as
  bosses and cuts, originate as sketches. Other features, such as
  shells and fillets, modify a feature's geometry.

- Features are displayed in the FeatureManager as illustrated
  (Boss-Extrude1, Cut-Extrude1, Cut-Extrude2, Mirror1,
  Cut-Extrude3 and CirPattern1).

The first sketch of a part is called the Base Sketch. The Base
sketch is the foundation for the 3D model. In this book, we focus
on 2D sketches and 3D features.

There are two modes in the New SOLIDWORKS Document dialog box: *Novice* and *Advanced*. The *Novice* option is the default option with three templates. The *Advanced* mode contains access to additional templates and tabs that you create in system options. Use the *Advanced* mode in this book.

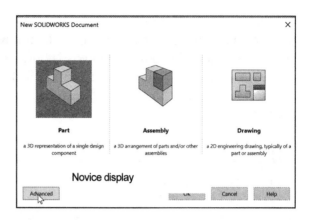

Create a new part.

7) Click **New** 📄 from the Menu bar. The New SOLIDWORKS Document dialog box is displayed.

Select the Advanced mode.

8) Click the **Advanced** button as illustrated. The Advanced mode is set.

9) Click the **Templates** tab.

10) Click the **Part** icon. Part is the default template from the New SOLIDWORKS Document dialog box.

11) Click **OK** from the New SOLIDWORKS Document dialog box.

🔆 Illustrations may vary depending on your SOLIDWORKS version and operating system.

🔆 Redeem your code on the inside face of the book. View the provided videos and models to enhance the user experience.

The Advanced mode remains selected for all new documents in the current SOLIDWORKS session. When you exit SOLIDWORKS, the Advanced mode setting is saved.

The default SOLIDWORKS installation contains two tabs in the New SOLIDWORKS Document dialog box: *Templates* and *Tutorial*. The *Templates* tab corresponds to the default SOLIDWORKS templates. The *Tutorial* tab corresponds to the templates utilized in the SOLIDWORKS Tutorials.

Part1 is displayed in the FeatureManager and is the name of the document. Part1 is the default part window name.

The Part Origin ⊥ is displayed in blue in the center of the Graphics window. The Origin represents the intersection of the three default reference planes: *Front Plane*, *Top Plane* and *Right Plane*. The positive X-axis is horizontal and points to the right of the Origin in the Front view. The positive Y-axis is vertical and points upward in the Front view. The FeatureManager contains a list of features, reference geometry, and settings utilized in the part.

Edit the document units directly from the Graphics window as illustrated.

Dynamic Annotation Views : Only available with SOLIDWORKS MBD (Model Based Definition). Provides the ability to control how annotations are displayed when you rotate models.

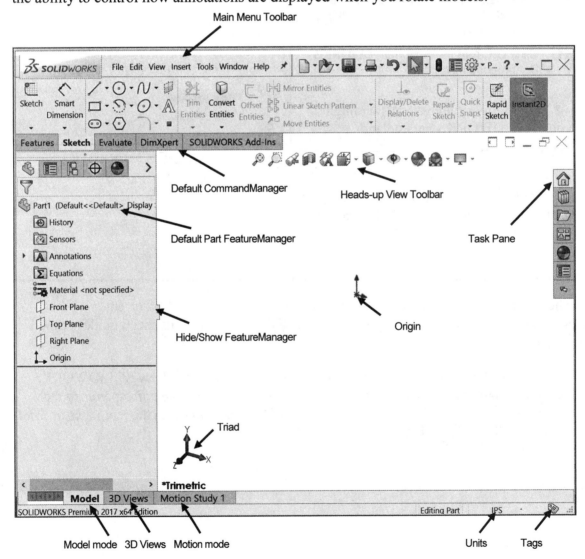

View the Default Sketch Planes.

12) Click the **Front Plane** from the FeatureManager.

13) Click the **Top Plane** from the FeatureManager.

14) Click the **Right Plane** from the FeatureManager.

15) Click the **Origin** from the FeatureManager. The Origin is the intersection of the Front, Top and Right Planes.

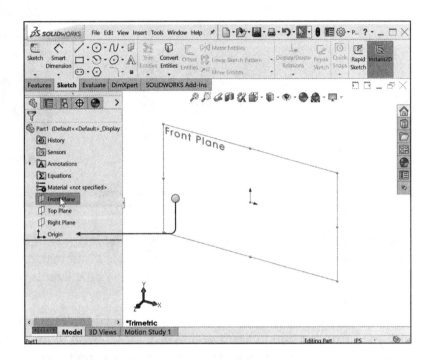

Redeem your code on the inside cover of the book. In the next section, download the SW-TUTORIAL-2017 folder to your hard drive. Open the Bracket part. Review the features and sketches in the Bracket FeatureManager. Work directly from your hard drive.

Activity: Download the provided SW-TUTORIAL folder. Open a Part.

Download the provided SW-TUTORIAL 2017 folder. Open an existing SOLIDWORKS part.

16) **Download** the SW-TUTORIAL 2017 folder to a local hard drive.

17) Click **Open** from the Menu bar menu.

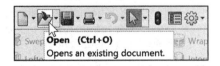

18) Browse to the **SW-TUTORIAL-2017\Bracket** folder.

19) Double-click the **Bracket** part. The Bracket part is displayed in the Graphics window.

Part FeatureManager

The FeatureManager design tree is located on the left side of the SOLIDWORKS Graphics window. The FeatureManager provides a summarized view of the active part, assembly, or drawing document. The tree displays the details on how the part, assembly or drawing document was created.

Use the FeatureManager rollback bar to temporarily roll back to an earlier state, to absorbed features, roll forward, roll to previous, or roll to the end of the FeatureManager design tree. You can add new features or edit existing features while the model is in the rolled-back state. You can save models with the rollback bar placed anywhere.

In the next section, review the features in the Bracket FeatureManager using the Rollback bar.

Activity: Use the FeatureManager Rollback Bar option

Apply the FeatureManager Rollback Bar. Revert to an earlier state in the model.

20) Place the **mouse pointer** over the rollback bar in the FeatureManager design tree as illustrated. The pointer changes to a hand 🖐. Note the provided information on the feature. This is called Dynamic Reference Visualization.

21) Drag the **rollback bar** up the FeatureManager design tree until it is above the features you want rolled back, in this case Diameter Hole1.

22) **Release** the mouse button.

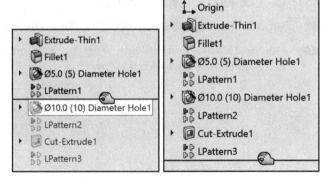

View the first feature in the Bracket Part.

23) Drag the **rollback bar** up the FeatureManager above Fillet1. View the results in the Graphics window.

Return to the original Bracket Part FeatureManager.

24) Right-click **Extrude-Thin1** in the FeatureManager. The Pop-up Context toolbar is displayed.

25) Click **Roll to End**. View the results in the Graphics window.

Heads-up View toolbar

SOLIDWORKS provides the user with numerous view options. One of the most useful tools is the Heads-up View toolbar displayed in the Graphics window when a document is active.

☀️ Dynamic Annotation Views 🔍: Only available with SOLIDWORKS MBD (Model Based Definition). Provides the ability to control how annotations are displayed when you rotate models.

In the next section, apply the following tools: Zoom to Fit, Zoom to Area, Zoom out, Rotate and select various view orientations from the Heads-up View toolbar.

Activity: Utilize the Heads-up View toolbar

Zoom to Fit the model in the Graphics window.

26) Click the **Zoom to Fit** 🔍 icon. The tool fits the model to the Graphics window.

Zoom to Area on the model in the Graphics window.

27) Click the **Zoom to Area** 🔍 icon. The Zoom to Area 🔍 icon is displayed.

Zoom in on the top left hole.
28) **Window-select** the top left corner as illustrated. View the results.

De-select the Zoom to Area tool.

29) Click the **Zoom to Area** 🔍 icon.

Fit the model to the Graphics window.
30) Press the **f** key.

Rotate the model.
31) Hold the **middle mouse button** down. Drag **upward** ↻, **downward** ↻, to the **left** ↻ and to the **right** ↻ to rotate the model in the Graphics window.

Display a few Standard Views.

32) Click **inside** the Graphics window.

33) Click **Front** from the drop-down Heads-up view toolbar. The model is displayed in the Front view.

34) Click **Right** from the drop-down Heads-up view toolbar. The model is displayed in the Right view.

35) Click **Top** from the drop-down Heads-up view toolbar. The model is displayed in the Top view.

Display a Trimetric view of the Bracket model.

36) Click **Trimetric** from the drop-down Heads-up view toolbar as illustrated. Note your options. View the results in the Graphics window.

SOLIDWORKS Help

Help in SOLIDWORKS is context-sensitive and in HTML format. Help is accessed in many ways, including Help buttons in all dialog boxes and PropertyManager (or press F1) and Help ⓘ tool on the Standard toolbar for SOLIDWORKS Help.

37) Click **Help** from the Menu bar.

38) Click **SOLIDWORKS Help**. The SOLIDWORKS Help Home Page is displayed by default. View your options.

☀ SOLIDWORKS Web Help is active by default under Help in the Main menu.

Close Help. Return to the SOLIDWORKS Graphics window.

39) **Close** ☒ SOLIDWORKS Home.

SOLIDWORKS Tutorials

Display and explore the SOLIDWORKS tutorials.

40) Click **Help** from the Menu bar.

41) Click **SOLIDWORKS Tutorials**. The SOLIDWORKS Tutorials are displayed. The SOLIDWORKS Tutorials are presented by category.

42) Click the **Getting Started** category. The Getting Started category provides three 30 minute lessons on parts, assemblies, and drawings.

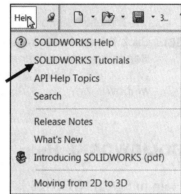

In the next section view the additional User Interface tools.

Activity: Close all Tutorials and Models

Close SOLIDWORKS Tutorials and open models.

43) **Close** ☒ SOLIDWORKS Tutorials.

44) Click **Window, Close All** from the Menu bar menu.

SOLIDWORKS Icon Style

SOLIDWORKS provides a new icon style. It allows vector-based scaling for superior support of high resolution, high pixel density displays. The new icon style standardized the perspective of icons; it also removes non-essential details and emphasizes primary elements. Consistent visual styling applies to all icons.

Additional User Interface Tools

This book utilizes additional areas of the SOLIDWORKS User Interface. Explore an overview of these tools in the next section.

Right-click

Right-click in the Graphics window on a model, or in the FeatureManager on a feature or sketch to display the Context-sensitive toolbar. If you are in the middle of a command, this toolbar displays a list of options specifically related to that command.

Right-click an empty space in the Graphics window of a part or assembly, and a selection context toolbar above the shortcut menu is displayed. This provides easy access to the most commonly used selection tools.

Consolidated toolbar

Similar commands are grouped together in the CommandManager. Example: Variations of the Rectangle sketch tool are grouped in a single fly-out button as illustrated.

If you select the Consolidated toolbar button without expanding:

For some commands such as Sketch, the most commonly used command is performed. This command is the first listed and the command shown on the button.

For commands such as rectangle, where you may want to repeatedly create the same variant of the rectangle, the last used command is performed. This is the highlighted command when the Consolidated toolbar is expanded.

System feedback icon

SOLIDWORKS provides system feedback by attaching a symbol to the mouse pointer cursor.

The system feedback symbol indicates what you are selecting or what the system is expecting you to select.

As you move the mouse pointer across your model, system feedback is displayed in the form of a symbol, riding next to the cursor as illustrated. This is a valuable feature in SOLIDWORKS.

Confirmation Corner

When numerous SOLIDWORKS commands are active, a symbol or a set of symbols are displayed in the upper right hand corner of the Graphics window. This area is called the Confirmation Corner.

When a sketch is active, the confirmation corner box displays two symbols. The first symbol is the sketch tool icon. The second symbol is a large red X. These two symbols supply a visual reminder that you are in an active sketch. Click the sketch symbol icon to exit the sketch and to save any changes that you made.

When other commands are active, the confirmation corner box provides a green check mark and a large red X. Use the green check mark to execute the current command. Use the large red X to cancel the command.

Confirm changes you make in sketches and tools by using the D keyboard shortcut to move the OK and Cancel buttons to the pointer location in the Graphics window.

Heads-up View toolbar

SOLIDWORKS provides the user with numerous view options from the Standard Views, View and Heads-up View toolbar.

For a drawing document

The Heads-up View toolbar is a transparent toolbar that is displayed in the Graphics window when a document is active.

You can hide, move or modify the Heads-up View toolbar. To modify the Heads-up View toolbar, right-click on a tool and select or deselect the tools that you want to display.

The following views are available: Note: The available views are document dependent.

- *Zoom to Fit* : Zooms the model to fit the Graphics window.

- *Zoom to Area* : Zooms to the areas you select with a bounding box.

- *Previous View* : Displays the previous view.

- *Section View* : Displays a cutaway of a part or assembly, using one or more cross section planes.

- *Dynamic Annotation Views* : Only available with SOLIDWORKS MBD. Provides the ability to control how annotations are displayed when you rotate models.

The Orientation dialog has an option to display a view cube (in-context View Selector) with a live model preview. This helps the user to understand how each standard view orientates the model. With the view cube, you can access additional standard views. The views are easy to understand and they can be accessed simply by selecting a face on the cube.

To activate the Orientation dialog box, press (Ctrl + spacebar) or click the View Orientation icon from the Heads up View toolbar. The active model is displayed in the View Selector in an Isometric orientation (default view).

As you hover over the buttons in the Orientation dialog box, the corresponding faces dynamically highlight in the View Selector. Select a view in the View Selector or click the view from the Orientation dialog box. The Orientation dialog box closes and the model rotates to the selected view.

Click the View Selector icon in the Orientation dialog box to show or hide the in-context View Selector.

Press **Ctrl + spacebar** to activate the View Selector.

Press the **spacebar** to activate the Orientation dialog box.

- *View Orientation box* : Provides the ability to select a view orientation or the number of viewports. The available options are *Top, Left, Front, Right, Back, Bottom, Single view, Two view - Horizontal, Two view - Vertical, Four view.* Click the drop-down arrow to access Axonometric views: Isometric, Dimetric and Trimetric.

- *Display Style* : Provides the ability to display the style for the active view. The available options are *Wireframe, Hidden Lines Visible, Hidden Lines Removed, Shaded, Shaded With Edges.*

- *Hide/Show Items* 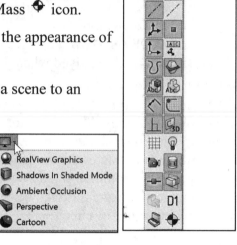 ˙: Provides the ability to select items to hide or show in the Graphics window. The available items are document dependent. Note the View Center of Mass ⊕ icon.

- *Edit Appearance* ●: Provides the ability to edit the appearance of entities of the model.

- *Apply Scene* ● ˙: Provides the ability to apply a scene to an active part or assembly document. View the available options.

- *View Setting* ▭ ˙: Provides the ability to select the following settings: *RealView Graphics*, *Shadows In Shaded Mode*, *Ambient Occlusion*, *Perspective* and *Cartoon*.

- *Rotate view* ↻ : Provides the ability to rotate a drawing view. Input Drawing view angle and select the ability to update and rotate center marks with view.

- *3D Drawing View* ⬟: Provides the ability to dynamically manipulate the drawing view in 3D to make a selection.

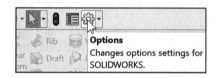

🔆 To display a grid for a part, click Options ⚙, Document Properties tab. Click Grid/Snaps, check the Display grid box.

🔆 Add a custom view to the Heads-up View toolbar. Press the space key. The Orientation dialog box is displayed. Click the New View 🔭 tool. The Name View dialog box is displayed. Enter a new named view. Click OK.

🔆 SOLIDWORKS provides the ability to click directly on the triad in the Graphic window to modify the part orientation. Hold the Ctrl key down, click an axis of the triad; it rotates about that axis 90 degrees.

*Front

SOLIDWORKS CommandManager

The SOLIDWORKS CommandManager is a Context-sensitive toolbar that automatically updates based on the toolbar you want to access. By default, it has toolbars embedded in it based on your active document type. When you click a tab below the CommandManager, it updates to display that toolbar. For example, if you click the Sketch tab, the Sketch toolbar is displayed.

⚡ For commercial users, SOLIDWORKS Model Based Definition (MBD) is a separate application. For education users, SOLIDWORKS MBD is included in the SOLIDWORKS Education Edition as an Add In.

Below is an illustrated CommandManager for a default Part document.

⚡ Button sizes. You can set sizes for buttons from the Toolbars tab of the Customize dialog box. To facilitate element selection on touch interfaces such as tablets, you can set up the larger Size buttons and text from the Options menu (Standard toolbar).

The SOLIDWORKS CommandManager is a Context-sensitive toolbar that automatically updates based on the toolbar you want to access. By default, it has toolbars embedded in it based on your active document type.

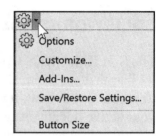

For commercial users, SOLIDWORKS Model Based Definition (MBD) is a separate application. For education users, SOLIDWORKS MBD is included in the SOLIDWORKS Education Edition as an Add In.

Below is an illustrated CommandManager for a default Drawing document.

To add a custom tab to your CommandManager, right-click on a tab and click Customize CommandManager from the drop-down menu. The Customize dialog box is displayed. You can also select to add a blank tab as illustrated and populate it with custom tools from the Customize dialog box.

The SOLIDWORKS CommandManager is a Context-sensitive toolbar that automatically updates based on the toolbar you want to access. By default, it has toolbars embedded in it based on your active document type.

🔅 For commercial users, SOLIDWORKS Model Based Definition (MBD) is a separate application. For education users, SOLIDWORKS MBD is included in the SOLIDWORKS Education Edition as an Add In.

Below is an illustrated CommandManager for a default Assembly document.

By default, the illustrated options are selected in the Customize box for the CommandManager. Right-click on an existing tab and click Customize CommandManager to view your options.

Float the CommandManager. Drag the Features, Sketch or any CommandManager tab. Drag the CommandManager anywhere on or outside the SOLIDWORKS window.

To dock the CommandManager, perform one of the following:

While dragging the CommandManager in the SOLIDWORKS window, move the pointer over a docking icon -

Dock above , Dock left , Dock right and click the needed command.

Double-click the floating CommandManager to revert the CommandManager to the last docking position.

Screen shots in the book were made using SOLIDWORKS 2017 SP0 running Windows® 10 Professional.

An updated color scheme for certain icons makes the SOLIDWORKS application more accessible to people with color blindness. Icons in the active PropertyManager use blue to indicate what you must select on the screen: faces, edges, and so on.

Selection Enhancements

Right-click an empty space in the Graphics window of a part or assembly; a selection context toolbar above the shortcut menu provides easy access to the most commonly used selection tools.

- **Box Selection** ▢. Provides the ability to select entities in parts, assemblies, and drawings by dragging a selection box with the pointer.

- **Lasso Selection** ⌇. Provides the ability to select entities by drawing a lasso around the entities.

- **Selection Filters** 🖗. Displays a list of selection filter commands.

- **Select Other** ⊡. Displays the Select Other dialog box.

- **Select** ⬚. Displays a list of selection commands.

- **Magnified Selection** ⬚. Displays the magnifying glass, which gives you a magnified view of a section of a model.

🔅 Save space in the CommandManager, right-click in the CommandManager and un-check the Use Large Buttons with Text box. This eliminates the text associated with the tool.

🔅 DimXpert provides the ability to graphically check if the model is fully dimensioned and toleranced. DimXpert automatically recognizes manufacturing features. Manufacturing features are not SOLIDWORKS features. Manufacturing features are defined in 1.1.12 of the ASME Y14.5M-1994 Dimensioning and Tolerancing standard. See SOLIDWORKS Help for additional information.

FeatureManager Design Tree

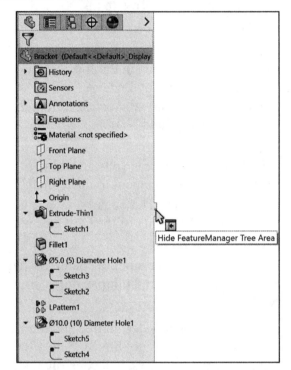

The FeatureManager consists of five default tabs:

- *FeatureManager design tree* 📦 tab.

- *PropertyManager* 📧 tab.

- *ConfigurationManager* 🔢 tab.

- *DimXpertManager* ⊕ tab.

- *DisplayManager* ● tab.

Select the Hide FeatureManager Tree Area arrows as illustrated to enlarge the Graphics window for modeling.

🔅 The Sensors tool 📷 located in the FeatureManager monitors selected properties in a part or assembly and alerts you when values deviate from the specified limits. There are five sensor types: Simulation Data, Mass properties, Dimensions, Measurement and Costing Data.

Various commands provide the ability to control what is displayed in the FeatureManager design tree:

1. Show or Hide FeatureManager items.

Click **Options** ⚙ from the Menu bar. Click **FeatureManager** from the System Options tab. **Customize** your FeatureManager from the Hide/Show Tree Items dialog box.

2. Filter the FeatureManager design tree. Enter information in the filter field. You can filter by *Type of features, Feature names, Sketches, Folders, Mates, User-defined tags* and *Custom properties*.

Tags are keywords you can add to a SOLIDWORKS document to make them easier to filter and to search. The Tags 🏷 icon is located in the bottom right corner of the Graphics window.

Collapse all items in the FeatureManager, **right-click** and select **Collapse items**, or press the **Shift** + **C** keys.

The FeatureManager design tree and the Graphics window are dynamically linked. Select sketches, features, drawing views, and construction geometry in either pane.

Split the FeatureManager design tree and either display two FeatureManager instances, or combine the FeatureManager design tree with the ConfigurationManager or PropertyManager.

Move between the FeatureManager design tree, PropertyManager, ConfigurationManager and DimXpertManager by selecting the tabs at the top of the menu.

Split line

The ConfigurationManager is located to the right of the FeatureManager. Use the ConfigurationManager to create, select and view multiple configurations of parts and assemblies.

The icons in the ConfigurationManager denote whether the configuration was created manually or with a design table.

The DimXpertManager tab provides the ability to insert dimensions and tolerances manually or automatically. The DimXpertManager provides the following selections: **Auto**

Dimension Scheme ⊕, Basic Location Dimension ⊢□⊣,

Basic Size Dimension □↘ **Show Tolerance Status** ±☉,

Copy Scheme ⊕ and **TolAnalyst Study** ⊠.

Fly-out FeatureManager

The fly-out FeatureManager design tree provides the ability to view and select items in the PropertyManager and the FeatureManager design tree at the same time.

Throughout the book, you will select commands and command options from the drop-down menu, fly-out FeatureManager, Context toolbar or from a SOLIDWORKS toolbar.

Another method for accessing a command is to use the accelerator key. Accelerator keys are special key strokes which activate the drop-down menu options. Some commands in the menu bar and items in the drop-down menus have an underlined character.

Press the Alt or Ctrl key followed by the corresponding key to the underlined character activates that command or option.

Illustrations may vary depending on your SOLIDWORKS version and operating system.

Task Pane

The Task Pane is displayed when a SOLIDWORKS session starts. The Task Pane can be displayed in the following states: *visible or hidden, expanded or collapsed, pinned or unpinned, docked or floating*.

The Task Pane contains the following default tabs:

- *SOLIDWORKS Resources* ⌂.

- *Design Library* 📖 .

- *File Explorer* 🗀 .

- *View Palette* ▦.

- *Appearances, Scenes and Decals* ●.

- *Custom Properties* 🗏.

- *SOLIDWORKS Forum* 🗨.

💡 Additional tabs are displayed with Add-Ins.

Use the **Back** and **Forward** buttons in the Design Library tab and the Appearances, Scenes, and Decals tab of the Task Pane to navigate in folders.

SOLIDWORKS Resources

The basic SOLIDWORKS Resources ⌂ menu displays the following default selections:

- *Getting Started.*

- *SOLIDWORKS Tools.*

- *Community.*

- *Online Resources.*

- *Subscription Services.*

- *Tip of the Day.*

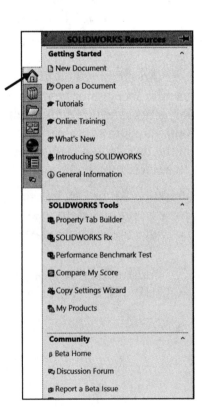

Other user interfaces are available during the initial software installation selection: *Machine Design, Mold Design* or *Consumer Products Design*.

Design Library

The Design Library 🗄 contains reusable parts, assemblies, and other elements including library features.

The Design Library tab contains four default selections. Each default selection contains additional sub categories.

These are the default selections:

- *Design Library.*

- *Toolbox.*

- *3D ContentCentral (Internet access required).*

- *SOLIDWORKS Content (Internet access required).*

🔆 Activate the SOLIDWORKS Toolbox. Click Tools, Add-Ins.., from the Main menu. Check the SOLIDWORKS Toolbox Library from the Add-ins dialog box or click SOLIDWORKS Toolbox from the SOLIDWORKS Add-Ins tab.

To access the Design Library folders in a non-network environment, click Add File Location 🗄 and browse to the needed path. Paths may vary depending on your SOLIDWORKS version and window setup. In a network environment, contact your IT department for system details.

File Explorer

File Explorer 🗀 duplicates Windows Explorer from your local computer and displays the following:

- *Resent Documents.*

- *Directories.*

- *Open in SOLIDWORKS and Desktop folders.*

Search

The SOLIDWORKS Search box is displayed in the upper right corner of the SOLIDWORKS Graphics window (Menu Bar toolbar). Enter the text or key words to search.

New search modes have been added to SOLIDWORKS Search as illustrated.

View Palette

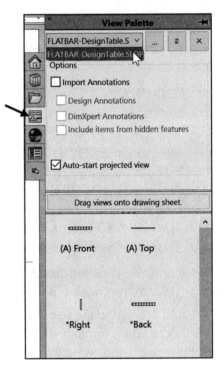

The View Palette tool located in the Task Pane provides the ability to insert drawing views of an active document, or click the Browse button to locate the desired document.

Click and drag the view from the View Palette into an active drawing sheet to create a drawing view.

The selected model is FLATBAR in the illustration.

Appearances, Scenes and Decals

Appearances, Scenes and Decals 🌑 provide a simplified way to display models in a photo-realistic setting using a library of Appearances, Scenes, and Decals.

An appearance defines the visual properties of a model, including color and texture. Appearances do not affect physical properties, which are defined by materials.

Scenes provide a visual backdrop behind a model. In SOLIDWORKS they provide reflections on the model. PhotoView 360 is an Add-in. Drag and drop a selected appearance, scene or decal on a feature, surface, part or assembly.

Custom Properties

The Custom Properties 📇 tool provides the ability to enter custom and configuration specific properties directly into SOLIDWORKS files.

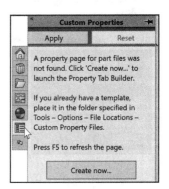

SOLIDWORKS Forum

Click the SOLIDWORKS Forum 💬 icon to search directly within the Task Pane. An internet connection is required. You are required to register and to log in for postings and discussions.

User Interface for Scaling High Resolution Screens

The SOLIDWORKS software supports high-resolution, high-pixel density displays. All aspects of the user interface respond to the Microsoft Windows® display scaling setting. In dialog boxes, PropertyManagers, and the FeatureManager design tree, the SOLIDWORKS software uses your display scaling setting to display buttons and icons at an appropriate size. Icons that are associated with text are scaled to a size appropriate for the text. In addition, for toolbars, you can display Small, Medium, or Large buttons. Click the **Options drop-down arrow** from the Standard Menu bar, and click Button size to size the icons.

Motion Study tab

Motion Studies are graphical simulations of motion for an assembly. Access the MotionManager from the Motion Study tab. The Motion Study tab is located in the bottom left corner of the Graphics window.

Incorporate visual properties such as lighting and camera perspective. Click the Motion Study tab to view the MotionManager. Click the Model tab to return to the FeatureManager design tree.

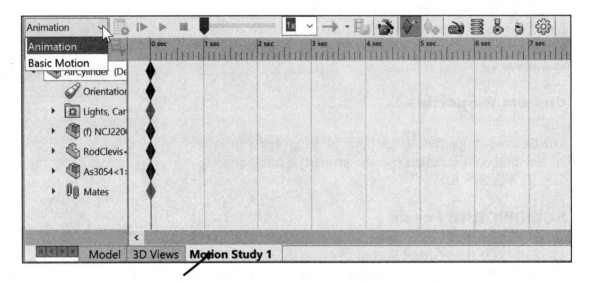

The MotionManager displays a timeline-based interface and provides the following selections from the drop-down menu as illustrated:

- *Animation:* Apply Animation to animate the motion of an assembly. Add a motor and insert positions of assembly components at various times using set key points. Use the Animation option to create animations for motion that do **<u>not</u>** require accounting for mass or gravity.

- *Basic Motion:* Apply Basic Motion for approximating the effects of motors, springs, collisions and gravity on assemblies. Basic Motion takes mass into account in calculating motion. Basic Motion computation is relatively fast, so you can use this for creating presentation animations using physics-based simulations. Use the Basic Motion option to create simulations of motion that account for mass, collisions or gravity.

If the Motion Study tab is not displayed in the Graphics window, click **View, MotionManager** from the Menu bar.

3D Views tab

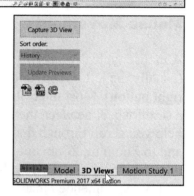

SOLIDWORKS MBD (Model Based Definition) lets you create models without the need for drawings giving you an integrated manufacturing. MBD helps companies define, organize, and publish 3D product and manufacturing information (PMI), including 3D model data in industry standard file formats.

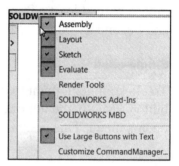

Create 3D drawing views of your parts and assemblies that contain the model settings needed for review and manufacturing. This lets users navigate back to those settings as they evaluate the design.

Use the tools in the SOLIDWORKS MBD CommandManager to set up your model with selected configurations, including explodes and abbreviated views, annotations, display states, zoom level, view orientation and section views. Capture those settings so that you and other users can return to them at any time using the 3D view palette.

To access the 3D View palette, click the 3DViews tab at the bottom of the SOLIDWORKS window or the SOLIDWORKS MBD tab in the CommandManager. The Capture 3D View button opens the Capture 3D View PropertyManager, where you specify the 3D view name, and the configuration, display state and annotation view to capture. See SOLIDWORKS help for additional information.

Dynamic Reference Visualization

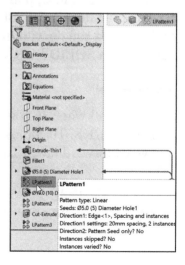

Dynamic Reference Visualization provides the ability to view the parent relationships between items in the FeatureManager design tree. When you hover over a feature with references in the FeatureManager design tree, arrows display showing the relationships. If a reference cannot be shown because a feature is not expanded, the arrow points to the feature that contains the reference and the actual reference appears in a text box to the right of the arrow. Use Dynamic reference visualization for a part, assembly and ever mates.

To display the Dynamic Reference Visualization, click
**View ➢ User Interface ➢ Dynamic Reference
Visualization** from the Main menu bar.

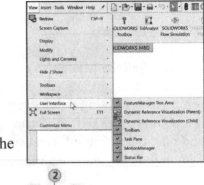

Mouse Movements

A mouse typically has two buttons: a primary button
(usually the left button) and a secondary button (usually the
right button). Most mice also include
a scroll wheel between the buttons to
help you scroll through documents
and to Zoom in, Zoom out and rotate
models in SOLIDWORKS. It is
highly recommended that you use a
mouse with at least a Primary, Scroll
and Secondary button.

① Primary button   ② Scroll wheel   ③ Secondary button

Single-click

To click an item, point to the item on the screen, and then press and release the primary
button (usually the left button). Clicking is most often used to select (mark) an item or
open a menu. This is sometimes called single-clicking or left-clicking.

Double-click

To double-click an item, point to the item on the screen, and then click twice quickly. If
the two clicks are spaced too far apart, they might be interpreted as two individual clicks
rather than as one double-click. Double-clicking is most often used to open items on your
desktop. For example, you can start a program or open a folder by double-clicking its
icon on the desktop.

Right-click

To right-click an item, point to the item on the screen, and then press and release the
secondary button (usually the right button). Right-clicking an item usually displays a list
of things you can do with the item. Right-click in the open Graphics window or on a
command in SOLIDWORKS, and additional pop-up context is displayed.

Scroll wheel

Use the scroll wheel to zoom-in or to zoom-out of the Graphics window in
SOLIDWORKS. To zoom-in, roll the wheel backward (toward you). To zoom-out, roll
the wheel forward (away from you).

Summary

The SOLIDWORKS 2017 User Interface and CommandManager consist of the following main options: Menu bar toolbar, Menu bar menu, Drop-down menus, Context toolbars, Consolidated fly-out menus, System feedback icons, Confirmation Corner and Heads-up View toolbar.

The default CommandManager Part tabs control the display of the *Features*, *Sketch*, *Evaluate*, *DimXpert* and *SOLIDWORKS Add-Ins* toolbars.

The FeatureManager consists of five default tabs:

- FeatureManager design tree.

- PropertyManager.

- ConfigurationManager.

- DimXpertManager.

- DisplayManager.

You learned about creating a new SOLIDWORKS part and opening an existing SOLIDWORKS part along with using the Rollback bar to view the sketches and features.

You also learned about SOLIDWORKS Help, SOLIDWORKS Tutorials and basic mouse movements to manipulate your SOLIDWORKS model.

Templates are part, drawing and assembly documents which include user-defined parameters. Open a new part, drawing or assembly. Select a template for the new document.

- *Parts*. The Parts default template is located in the C:\ProgramData\SolidWorks\\SOLIDWORKS 2017\templates\Part.prtdot folder.

- *Assemblies*. The Assemblies default template is located in the C:\ProgramData\SolidWorks\\SOLIDWORKS 2017\templates\Assembly.asmdot folder.

- *Drawings*. The Drawings default template is located in the C:\ProgramData\SolidWorks\\SOLIDWORKS 2017\templates\Drawing.drwdot folder.

For commercial users, SOLIDWORKS Model Based Definition (MBD) is a separate application. For education users, SOLIDWORKS MBD is included in the SOLIDWORKS Education Edition as an Add In.

Redeem your code on the inside face of the book. View the provided videos and models to enhance the user experience.

In Chapter 2, obtain the working familiarity of the following SOLIDWORKS sketch and feature tools: *Line, Circle, Centerpoint Straight Slot, Smart Dimension, Extruded Boss/Base, Extruded Cut and Linear Pattern.*

Create three individual parts: AXLE, SHAFT-COLLAR and FLATBAR.

Create the assembly, LINKAGE using the three created parts and the downloaded sub-assembly - AirCylinder.

Chapter 2

Parts and Assembly Creation

Below are the desired outcomes and usage competencies based on the completion of Chapter 2.

Desired Outcomes:	Usage Competencies:

• Create three parts:
 	
   o AXLE
 	
   o SHAFT-COLLAR
 	
   o FLATBAR
	• Create 2D sketch profiles on the correct Sketch plane.
	
	• Apply the following 3D features: Extruded Boss/Base, Extruded Cut and Linear Pattern.

• Create an assembly:
 	
   o LINKAGE assembly
 	
   o Apply Standard mates
 	
   o Motion Study
	• Understand the Assembly toolbar.
	
	• Insert components into an assembly.
	
	• Apply the following Standard mates: Concentric, Coincident and Parallel.
	
	• Understand the Quick mate procedure.

Notes:

Chapter 2 - Parts and Assembly Creation

Chapter Objective

SOLIDWORKS is a design software application used to model and create 2D and 3D sketches, 3D parts, 3D assemblies and 2D drawings. The chapter objective is to obtain the working familiarity of the following SOLIDWORKS sketch and feature tools: Line, Circle, Centerpoint Straight Slot, Smart Dimension, Extruded Boss/Base, Extruded Cut and Linear Pattern.

Create three individual parts: AXLE, SHAFT-COLLAR and FLATBAR.

Create the assembly, LINKAGE using the three created parts and the downloaded sub-assembly, AirCylinder.

On the completion of this chapter, you will be able to:

- Set units and dimensioning standards for a SOLIDWORKS Part and Assembly document.

- Create a 2D sketch.

- Understand and apply the following Sketch tools:

  o Circle, Smart dimension and Centerpoint Straight Slot.

- Identify the correct Sketch plane for the 2D sketch:

  o Front, Top, Right.

- Insert geometric relations and dimensions:

  o Equal, Vertical, Horizontal, Parallel, Perpendicular, Coincident and MidPoint.

- Modify sketch dimensions and geometric relations.

- Create a 3D model.

- Understand and apply the following SOLIDWORKS features:

  o Extruded Boss/Base, Extruded Cut and Linear Pattern.

- Download an assembly document (with references) in SOLIDWORKS.

- Create an assembly document.

- Insert components:

  o Download and create components.

- Understand and know the various features in the Assembly toolbar.

- Apply the following Standard mates: Coincident, Concentric and Parallel.

- Apply the Quick mate procedure.

☼ View the provided videos on creating 2D sketches, 3D Features and Assembly to enhance your experience in this chapter.

Chapter Overview

SOLIDWORKS is a 3D solid modeling CAD software package used to produce and model parts, assemblies, and drawings.

SOLIDWORKS provides design software to create 3D models and 2D drawings.

Create three parts in this chapter:

- AXLE

- SHAFT-COLLAR

- FLATBAR

Create the LINKAGE assembly. Download the AirCylinder assembly from the Pneumatic Components folder.

Combine the created parts with the AirCylinder sub-assembly to create the LINKAGE assembly.

Illustrations in this book display the default SOLIDWORKS user interface for 2017 SP0.

AXLE

SHAFT-COLLAR

FLATBAR

AirCylinder assembly

LINKAGE assembly

AXLE Part

The AXLE is a cylindrical rod. The AXLE
supports the two FLATBAR parts.

Tangent edges and origins are displayed for
educational purposes in this book.

The AXLE rotates about its axis. The
dimensions for the AXLE are determined from
other components in the LINKAGE assembly.

AXLE

FLATBAR

Start a new SOLIDWORKS session.

Create the AXLE part.

AXLE

Apply the feature to create the part. Features are the building
blocks that add or remove material.

Utilize the Extruded Boss/Base 🗐 tool from the Features
toolbar to create a Boss-Extrude1 feature. The Extruded
Boss/Base feature adds material. The Base feature (Boss-
Extrude1) is the first feature of the part. The Base feature is the
foundation of the part. Keep the Base feature <u>simple!</u>

The Base feature geometry for the AXLE is a simple
extrusion. How do you create a solid Extruded
Boss/Base feature for the AXLE?

- Select the Front Plane as the Sketch plane.

- Sketch a circular 2D profile on the Front Plane,
  centered at the Origin as illustrated.

Origin

- Apply the Extruded Boss/Base Feature. Extend the
  profile perpendicular (⊥) to the Front Plane.

Utilize symmetry. Extrude the sketch with the Mid
Plane End Condition in Direction 1. The Extruded
Boss/Base feature is centered on both sides of the Front
Plane.

Start a SOLIDWORKS session. The SOLIDWORKS
application is located in the Programs folder.

Origin

SOLIDWORKS displays the Tip of the Day box. Read the Tip of the Day to obtain additional knowledge on SOLIDWORKS.

Create a new part. Select File, New from the Menu bar toolbar or click New ⬜ from the Menu bar menu. There are two options for new documents: Novice and Advanced. Select the Advanced option. Select the default Part document.

Activity: Start a SOLIDWORKS Session and Create a New Part Document

Start a SOLIDWORKS 2017 session.

1)   Type **SOLIDWORKS** in the Search Window.

2)   Click **All Programs**.

3)   Click the **SOLIDWORKS 2017** application. The SOLIDWORKS program window opens. Note: Do not open a document at this time.

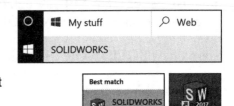

4)   If you do not see the below screen, click the SOLIDWORKS **Resources** 🏠 tab on the right side of the Graphics window location in the Task Pane as illustrated.

5)   **Hover** the mouse pointer over the SOLIDWORKS icon as illustrated.

6)   **Pin** the Menu Bar toolbar. View your options.

🔆 If available, double-click the SOLIDWORKS icon on the Windows Desktop to start a SOLIDWORKS session.

There are two modes in the New
SOLIDWORKS Document dialog box:
Novice and Advanced. The *Novice*
option is the default option with three
templates. The *Advanced* mode contains
access to additional templates and tabs
that you create in system options. Use
the *Advanced* mode in this book.

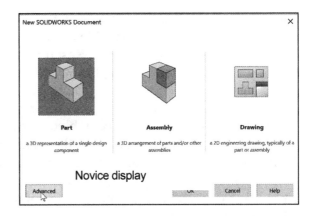

Create a New part.

7) Click **New** ⬜ from the Menu bar. The
New SOLIDWORKS Document dialog
box is displayed.

Select Advanced Mode.

8) Click the **Advanced** button to display
the New SOLIDWORKS Document
dialog box in Advance mode.

9) Click the **Templates** tab.

10) Click **Part**. Part is the default template
from the New SOLIDWORKS
Document dialog box.

11) Click **OK**.

SOLIDWORKS Web Help is active by
default under Help in the Main menu bar.

The *Advanced* mode remains selected for all new documents in the current
SOLIDWORKS session. When you exit SOLIDWORKS, the *Advanced* mode setting is
saved.

The default SOLIDWORKS installation contains two tabs in the New SOLIDWORKS
Document dialog box: *Templates* and *Tutorial*. The *Templates* tab corresponds to the
default SOLIDWORKS templates. The *Tutorial* tab corresponds to the templates utilized
in the SOLIDWORKS Tutorials.

☀ During the initial SOLIDWORKS installation, you are requested to select either the
ISO or ANSI drafting standard. ISO is typically a European drafting standard and uses
First Angle Projection. This book is written using the ANSI (US) overall drafting
standard and Third Angle Projection for all drawing documents.

Part1 is displayed in the FeatureManager and is the name of the document. Part1 is the default part window name. The Menu bar, CommandManager, FeatureManager, Heads-up View toolbar, SOLIDWORKS Resources, SOLIDWORKS Search, Task Pane and the Origin are displayed in the Graphics window.

The Part Origin ⊥ is displayed in blue in the center of the Graphics window. The Origin represents the intersection of the three default reference planes: *Front Plane*, *Top Plane* and *Right Plane*. The positive X-axis is horizontal and points to the right of the Origin in the Front view. The positive Y-axis is vertical and points upward in the Front view. The FeatureManager contains a list of features, reference geometry, and settings utilized in the part.

Edit the document units directly from the Graphics window as illustrated.

Grid/Snaps are deactivated in the Graphics window for improved modeling clarity.

The CommandManager is document dependent. The tabs are located on the bottom left side of the CommandManager and display the available toolbars and features for each corresponding tab. The default tabs for a Part are Features, Sketch, Evaluate, DimXpert and SOLIDWORKS Add-Ins.

The Features icon and Features toolbar should be selected by default in Part mode.

The CommandManager is utilized in this text. Control the CommandManager display.

Right-click in the gray area to the right of the Options ⚙ icon in the Menu bar toolbar. A complete list of toolbars is displayed. Check CommandManager if required.

Select individual toolbars from the View, Toolbars list to display in the Graphics window.

💡 Click **View**, **Hide/Show**, **Origins** from the Menu bar menu to display the Origin in the Graphics window.

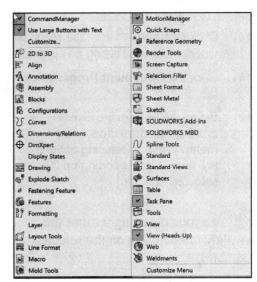

View the provided videos in the book to enhance the user experience: *Start a SOLIDWORKS session, Understand the SOLIDWORKS Interface, Create 2D Sketches, Sketch Planes and use various Sketch tools, Create 3D Features and apply Design Intent, Create an Assembly*, and *Create fundamental Drawings Part 1 & Part2.*

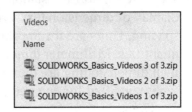

SOLIDWORKS allows vector-based scaling for superior support of high resolution high pixel density displays. The new icon style standardized the perspective of icons; it also removes non-essential details and emphasizes primary elements. Consistent visual styling applies to all icons.

Activity: Create the AXLE Part

If needed, set the Menu bar toolbar and Menu bar menu.

12) Click **SOLIDWORKS** to expand the Menu bar menu.

13) Pin 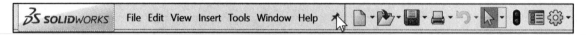 the Menu bar as illustrated. Use both the Menu bar menu and the Menu bar toolbar in this book.

The SOLIDWORKS Help Topics contains step-by-step instructions for various commands. The Help ⑦ icon is displayed in the dialog box or in the PropertyManager for each feature.

Set the Document Properties.

14) Click **Options** ⚙ from the Menu bar. The System Options General dialog box is displayed.

15) Click the **Document Properties** tab.

16) Select **ANSI** from the Overall drafting standard drop-down menu. Various Detailing options are available depending on the selected standard.

💡 Various detailing options are available depending on the selected standard.

The Overall drafting standard determines the display of dimension text, arrows, symbols, and spacing. Units are the measurement of physical quantities. Millimeter dimensioning and decimal inch dimensioning are the two most common unit types specified for engineering parts and drawings.

The primary units in this book are provided in IPS (inch, pound, second). The optional secondary units are provided in MMGS (millimeters, grams, second) and are indicated in brackets [ ].

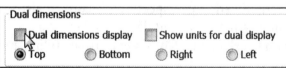

Most illustrations are provided in both inches and millimeters.

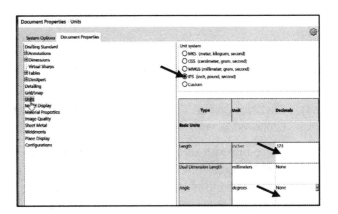

Set the document units.

17)   Click **Units**.

18)   Click **IPS** (inch, pound, second) **[MMGS]** for Unit system.

19)   Select **.123, [.12]** (three decimal places) for Length basic units.

20)   Select **None** for Angle decimal places.

21)   Click **OK** from the Document Properties - Units dialog box. The Part FeatureManager is displayed.

Activity: AXLE Part-Extruded Base Feature

Insert a new sketch for the Extruded Base feature.

22)   Right-click **Front Plane** from the FeatureManager. This is your Sketch plane. The Context toolbar is displayed.

23)   Click **Sketch** from the Context toolbar as illustrated.

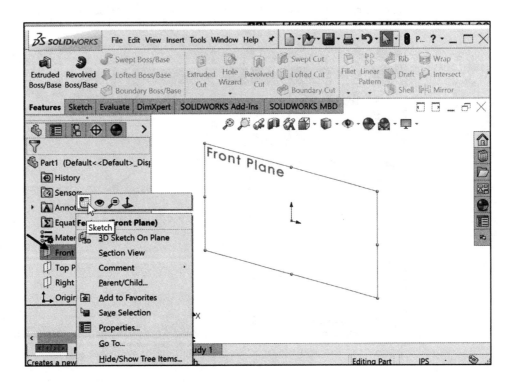

The Sketch toolbar is displayed. Front Plane is your Sketch plane. Note: the grid is deactivated for picture clarity.

You can also click the Front Plane from the FeatureManager and click the Sketch tab from the CommandManager.

24)   Click the **Circle** ⊙ tool from the Sketch toolbar. The Circle PropertyManager is displayed.

The Circle-based tool uses a Consolidated Circle PropertyManager. The SOLIDWORKS application defaults to the last used tool type.

25)   Drag the **mouse pointer** into the Graphics window. The cursor displays the Circle icon.

26)   Click the **Origin** ↳ of the circle. The cursor displays the Coincident to point feedback symbol.

27)   Drag the **mouse pointer** to the right of the Origin to create the circle as illustrated. The center point of the circle is positioned at the Origin.

28) Click a **position** to create the circle. The activated
circle is displayed in blue.

Add a dimension.

29) Click **Smart Dimension** from the Sketch toolbar.

The cursor displays the Smart Dimension icon

30) Click the **circumference** of the circle.

31) Click a **position** diagonally above the circle in the
Graphics window.

32) Enter **.188**in, **[4.78]** in the Modify dialog box. Note the
Dimension Modify dialog box provides the ability to select
a unit drop-down menu to directly modify units in a sketch
or feature from the document properties.

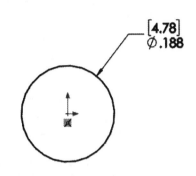

33) Click the **Green Check mark** ✔ in the Modify dialog box.
The diameter of the circle is .188 inches.

The circular sketch is centered at the Origin. The
dimension indicates the diameter of the circle. Sketch
Relations are displayed in the model.

Press the f key to fit the part document to the
Graphics window.

Add relations, then dimensions. This keeps the user
from having too many unnecessary dimensions. This
also helps to show the design intent of the model.
Dimension what geometry you intend to modify or
adjust.

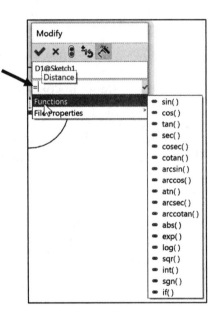

The Dimension Modify dialog box provides the
ability to create an equation driven dimension relative
to a function or File Property. To create an equation in
a numeric input field, start by entering = (equal sign).

Extrude the sketch to create the Base Feature.

34) Click the **Features** tab from the CommandManager.

35) Click the **Extruded Boss/Base** Features tool. The Boss-Extrude PropertyManager is displayed. Blind is the default End Condition in Direction 1.

36) Select **Mid Plane** for End Condition in Direction 1.

37) Enter **1.375**in, [**34.93**] for Depth in Direction 1. Accept the default conditions.

38) Click **OK** ✔ from the Boss-Extrude PropertyManager. Boss-Extrude1 is displayed in the FeatureManager.

Fit the model to the Graphics window.

39) Press the **f** key. Note the location of the Origin in the model.

Origin

Use Symmetry. When possible and if it makes sense, model objects symmetrically about the origin.

🔅 Rename a feature or sketch.
Slowly click the feature or sketch name twice and enter the new name when the old one is highlighted.

🔅 Display an Isometric view of the model. Press the **space bar** to display the Orientation dialog box. Click the **Isometric view** 🔲 icon.

The Boss-Extrude PropertyManager displays the parameters utilized to define the feature. The Mid Plane End Condition in the Direction 1 box extrudes the sketch equally on both sides of the Sketch plane. The depth defines the extrude distance.

The Boss-Extrude1 feature name is displayed in the FeatureManager. The FeatureManager lists the features, planes, and other geometry that constructs the part. Extrude features add material. Extrude features require the following: *Sketch Plane, Sketch* and *depth*.

The Sketch plane is the Front Plane. The Sketch is a circle with the diameter of .188in, [4.76]. The Depth is 1.375in, [34.93].

For many features (Extruded Boss/Base, Extruded Cut, Simple Hole, Revolved Boss/Base, Revolved Cut, Fillet, Chamfer, Scale, Shell, Rib, Circular Pattern, Linear Pattern, Curve Driven Pattern, Revolved Surface, Extruded Surface, Fillet Surface, Edge Flange and Base Flange) you can enter and modify equations directly in the PropertyManager fields that allow numerical inputs.

In this example, you can enter equations in:

- Depth fields for Direction 1 and Direction 2

- Draft fields for Direction 1 and Direction 2

- Thickness fields for a Thin Feature with two direction types

- Offset Distance field

To create an equation in a numeric input field, start by entering = (equal sign). A drop-down list displays options for Global Variables, functions, and file properties. Numeric input fields that contain equations can display either the equation itself or its evaluated value. You can toggle between the equation and the value by clicking the Equations or Global Variable button that appears at the beginning of the field.

Activity: AXLE Part-Save

Save the part.

40) Click **Save As** from the drop-down Menu bar.

41) Click the **Documents** file folder. The procedure will be different depending on your Operating System.

Create a new folder if needed.

42) Click **New** Folder.

43) Enter **SW-TUTORIAL-2017** for the file folder name. In this book all models, assemblies and drawings are saved to the SW-TUTORIAL-2017 folder.

44) Double-click the **SW-TUTORIAL-2017** file folder. SW-TUTORIAL-2017 is the Save in file folder name.

45) Enter **AXLE** for the File name.

46) Enter **AXLE ROD** for the Description.

47) Click **Save**. The AXLE FeatureManager is displayed.

 Organize parts, assemblies and drawings into
folders. All documents for this book are saved in the SW-TUTORIAL-2017 folder.

Activity: AXLE Part - Edit Appearance

Modify the color of the part.

48) Right-click the **AXLE** icon at the top of the FeatureManager.

49) Click the **Appearances** drop-down arrow.

50) Click the **Edit color** box as illustrated. The Color PropertyManager is displayed. AXLE is displayed in the Selection box.

51)   Select a **light blue** color from the Color box. View your options.

52)   Click **OK** ✔ from the Color PropertyManager. View the AXLE in the Graphics window.

Use the Appearances PropertyManager to apply colors, material appearances, and transparency to parts and assembly components. For sketches or curves only, use the Sketch/Curve Color PropertyManager to apply colors.

🔆 The Advanced tab includes the Illumination and Surface Finish tabs, and additional options in the Color/Image and Mapping tabs. To display the simplified Color/Image or Mapping interfaces, click the Basic tab.

Sketching in SOLIDWORKS is the basis for creating features. Features are the basis for creating parts, which can be put together into assemblies.

The sketch status appears in the window status bar and in the FeatureManager. Colors indicate the state of individual sketch entities. Sketches are generally in one of the following states:

1.) *(+) Over defined.* The sketch is displayed in orange - red.

2.) *(-) Under defined.* The sketch is displayed in blue.

3.) *No prefix.* The sketch is fully defined. This is the ideal sketch state. A fully defined sketch has complete information (manufacturing and inspection) and is displayed in black.

The SketchXpert PropertyManager provides the ability to diagnose an over defined sketch to create a fully defined sketch. If you have an over defined sketch, click Over Defined at the bottom of the Graphics window toolbar. The SketchXpert PropertyManager is displayed. Click the Diagnose button.

Select the desired solution and click the Accept button from the Results box.

Activity: AXLE Part-View Modes

Orthographic projection is the process of projecting views onto Parallel planes with ⊥ projectors.

The default reference planes are the Front, Top and Right Planes.

The Isometric view displays the part in 3D with two equal projection angles.

Click **View**, **Hide/Show**, **Origins** from the Menu bar menu to display the Origin in the Graphics window.

Origin

Display the various view modes using the Heads-up View toolbar.

53) **Deactivate** the View Selector. Hide the in-context View Selector box.

Display a Front view.

54) Click **Front view** from the Heads-up View toolbar.

Display a Top view.

55) Click **Top view** from the Heads-up View toolbar.

Display a Right view.

56) Click **Right view** from the Heads-up View toolbar.

Display an Isometric view.

57)   Click **Isometric view** from the Heads-up View toolbar.

View modes manipulate the model in the Graphics window.

Zoom out/Zoom in.

58)   Press the lower case **z** key to zoom out. Note: you can also use the middle mouse button.

59)   Press the upper case **Z** key to zoom in. Note: you can also use the middle mouse button.

View the available view tools in the Graphics window.

60)   **Right-click** in the Graphics window. View the available view tools.

Deselect the view menu.

61)   Click **inside** the Graphics window.

Rotate the model.

62)   Click the **middle mouse** button and move your mouse. The model rotates. The Rotate icon ↻ is displayed.

63)   Press the **up arrow** on your key board. The arrow keys rotate the model in 15 degree increments.

🔅 View modes remain active until deactivated from the View toolbar or unchecked from the pop-up menu.

🔅 Utilize the center wheel of the mouse to Zoom In/Zoom Out and Rotate the model in the Graphics window.

View the various Display Styles.

64)   Click **Isometric view** from the Heads-up View toolbar.

65)   Click the **drop-down arrow** from the Display Styles box from the Heads-up Views toolbar as illustrated. SOLIDWORKS provides five key Display Styles:

- *Shaded* 🔲. Displays a shaded view of the model with no edges.

- *Shaded With Edges* 🔲. Displays a shaded view of the model with edges.

- *Hidden Lines Removed* ⬠. Displays only those model edges that can be seen from the current view orientation.

- *Hidden Lines Visible* ⬡. Displays all edges of the model. Edges that are hidden from the current view are displayed in a different color or font.

- *Wireframe* ⬡. Displays all edges of the model.

Save the AXLE part.

66) Click **Save** 💾. The AXLE part is complete.

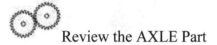 Review the AXLE Part

The AXLE part utilized the Extruded Boss/Base feature. The Extruded Boss/Base feature adds material. The Extruded feature required a Sketch Plane, sketch and depth. The AXLE Sketch plane was the Front Plane. The 2D circle was sketched centered at the Origin. A dimension defined the overall size of the sketch based on the dimensions of mating parts in the LINKAGE assembly.

The default name of the Base feature is Boss-Extrude1. Boss-Extrude1 utilized the Mid Plane End Condition. The Boss-Extrude1 feature is symmetrical about the Front Plane.

The Edit Color option modified the part color. Select the Part icon in the FeatureManager to modify the color of the part. Color and a prefix define the sketch status. A blue sketch is under defined. A black sketch is fully defined. A red sketch is over defined.

The default Reference planes are the Front, Top, and Right Planes. Utilize the Heads-up View toolbar to display the principle views of a part. The View Orientation and Display Style tools manipulate the model in the Graphics windows.

💡 Instant3D provides the ability to click and drag geometry and dimension manipulator points to resize features in the Graphics window, and to use on-screen rulers to measure modifications. In this book, you will primarily use the PropertyManager and dialog boxes to create and modify model dimensions. Explore Instant3D as an exercise.

SHAFT-COLLAR Part

The SHAFT-COLLAR part is a hardened steel ring fastened to the AXLE part.

Two SHAFT-COLLAR parts are used to position the two FLATBAR parts on the AXLE.

Create the SHAFT-COLLAR part.

Utilize the Extruded Boss/Base 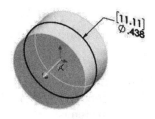 feature. The Extruded Boss/Base feature requires a 2D circular profile.

Utilize symmetry. Sketch a circle on the Front Plane centered at the Origin.

Extrude the sketch with the Mid Plane End Condition. The Extruded Boss/Base feature (Boss-Extrude1) is centered on both sides of the Front Plane.

SHAFT-COLLAR

The Extruded Cut feature removes material. Utilize an Extruded Cut feature to create a hole. The Extruded Cut feature requires a 2D circular profile. Sketch a circle on the front face centered at the Origin.

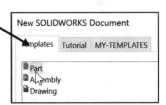

The Through All End Condition extends the Extruded Cut feature from the front face through all existing geometry.

💡 This book is designed to expose the new SOLIDWORKS user to many different tools, techniques and procedures. It may not always use the most direct tool or process.

Activity: SHAFT-COLLAR Part-Extruded Boss/Base Feature

Create a New part.

67)   Click **New** ⬜ from the Menu bar. The New SOLIDWORKS Document dialog box is displayed.

68)   Click the **Templates** tab. Part is the default template from the New SOLIDWORKS Document dialog box.

69)   Double-click **Part**. The Part FeatureManager is displayed.

New SOLIDWORKS Document

Templates   Tutorial   MY-TEMPLATES

Part
Assembly
Drawing

Save the part.

70) Click **Save As** from the drop-down Menu bar.

71) Enter **SHAFT-COLLAR** for File name in the SW-TUTORIAL-2017 folder.

72) Enter **SHAFT-COLLAR** for Description.

73) Click **Save**. The SHAFT-COLLAR FeatureManager is displayed.

Set the Dimension standard and part units.

74) Click **Options** ⚙ from the Main menu.

75) Click the **Document Properties** tab from the dialog box.

76) Select **ANSI** from the Overall drafting standard drop-down menu.

77) Click **Units**.

78) Click **IPS** (inch, pound, second), [**MMGS**] for Unit system.

79) Select **.123**, [**.12**] (three decimal places) for Length units Decimal places.

80) Select **None** for Angular units Decimal places.

81) Click **OK** from the Document Properties - Units dialog box.

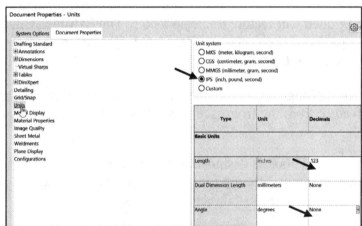

When you create a new part or assembly, the three default Planes (Front, Right and Top) are aligned with specific views.

The Plane you select for the Base sketch determines the orientation of the part.

Insert a new sketch for the Extruded Base feature.

82) Right-click **Front Plane** from the FeatureManager. This is the Sketch plane. The Context toolbar is displayed.

83) Click **Sketch** 📇 from the Context toolbar as illustrated. The Sketch toolbar is displayed.

84) Click the **Circle** ⊙ tool from the Sketch toolbar. The Circle PropertyManager is displayed.

85) Click the **Origin** ⊥. The cursor displays the Coincident to point feedback symbol.

86) Drag the **mouse pointer** to the right of the Origin as illustrated.

87) Click a **position** to create the circle.

Add a dimension.

88) Click **Smart Dimension** ↖ from the Sketch toolbar.

89) Click the **circumference** of the circle. The cursor displays the diameter feedback symbol.

90) Click a **position** diagonally above the circle in the Graphics window.

91) Enter **.4375**in, **[11.11]** in the Modify dialog box.

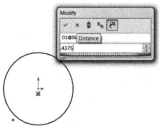

92) Click the **Green Check mark** ✔ in the Modify dialog box. The black sketch is fully defined.

Note: Three decimal places are displayed. The diameter value .4375 rounds to .438.

Extrude the sketch to create the Base feature.

93) Click the **Features** tab from the CommandManager.

94) Click the **Extruded Boss/Base** 🗔 features tool. The Boss-Extrude PropertyManager is displayed.

95) Select **Mid Plane** for End Condition in Direction 1.

96) Enter .250in, [6.35] for Depth. Accept the default conditions. View the location of the Origin.

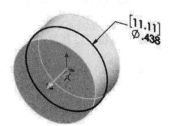

97) Click **OK** ✔ from the Boss-Extrude PropertyManager. Boss-Extrude1 is displayed in the FeatureManager.

Fit the model to the Graphics window. Display a trimetric view.

98)　Press the **f** key.

99)　Click **Trimetric** from the Heads-Up View toolbar.

Save the model.

100)　Click **Save** .

Activity: SHAFT-COLLAR Part-Extruded Cut Feature

Insert a new sketch for the Extruded Cut feature.

101)　Right-click the **front circular face** of the Boss-Extrude1 feature for the Sketch plane. The mouse pointer displays the face feedback icon.

🔆 View the mouse pointer feedback icon for the correct geometry: line, face, point or vertex.

102)　Click **Sketch** from the Context toolbar as illustrated. The Sketch toolbar is displayed. This is your Sketch plane.

103)　Click **Hidden Lines Removed** from the Heads-up View toolbar.

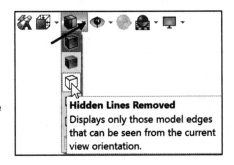

104)　Click the **Circle** tool from the Sketch toolbar. The Circle PropertyManager is displayed.

105)　Click the red **Origin** . The cursor displays the Coincident to point feedback symbol.

106)　Drag the **mouse pointer** to the right of the Origin.

107)　Click a **position** to create the circle as illustrated.

Add a dimension.

108)　Click the **Smart Dimension** Sketch tool.

109)　Click the **circumference** of the circle.

110)　Click a **position** diagonally above the circle in the Graphics window.

111)　Enter **.190**in, **[4.83]** in the Modify dialog box.

112)　Click the **Green Check mark** in the Modify dialog box.

Insert an Extruded Cut feature.

113) Click the **Features** tab from the CommandManager.

114) Click **Extruded Cut** from the Features toolbar. The Cut-Extrude PropertyManager is displayed.

115) Select **Through All** for End Condition in Direction 1. The direction arrow points to the back. If needed, click the Reverse Direction button. Accept the default conditions.

116) Click **OK** ✔ from the Cut-Extrude PropertyManager. Cut-Extrude1 is displayed in the FeatureManager.

The Extruded Cut feature is named Cut-Extrude1. The Through All End Condition removes material from the Front Plane through the Boss-Extrude1 geometry.

 Model about the origin; this provides a point of reference.

 Press the **spacebar** to activate the Orientation dialog box.

Activity: SHAFT-COLLAR-Modify Dimensions and Edit Color

Modify the dimensions.

117) Click **Trimetric view** from the Heads-up View toolbar.

118) Click the **z** key a few times to Zoom in.

119) Double-click the **outside cylindrical face** of the SHAFT-COLLAR. The Boss-Extrude1 dimensions are displayed. Sketch dimensions are displayed in black. The Extrude depth dimensions are displayed in blue.

120) Double-click the **.250**in, **[6.35]** depth dimension.

121) Enter **.500**in, **[12.70]**.

Rebuild the model.

122) Click **Rebuild** from the Menu bar.

The Boss-Extrude1 feature and Cut-Extrude1 feature are modified.

Return to the original dimensions.

123) Click the **Undo** tool from the Menu bar.

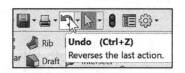

Display Shaded With Edges.

124) Click **Shaded With Edges** from the Heads-up View toolbar. Modify the part color.

125) Right-click the **SHAFT-COLLAR Part** icon at the top of the FeatureManager.

126) Click the **Appearances** drop-down arrow.

127) Click the **Edit color** box as illustrated. The Color PropertyManager is displayed. SHAFT-COLLAR is displayed in the Selection box.

128) Click the **Basic** tab.

129) Select a **light green** color from the Color box.

130) Click **OK** ✔ from the Color PropertyManager. View the SHAFT-COLLAR in the Graphics window.

Save the SHAFT-COLLAR part.

131) Click **Save** 💾. The SHAFT-COLLAR part is complete. All sketches should be fully defined.

 Review the SHAFT-COLLAR Part

The SHAFT-COLLAR utilized an Extruded Boss/Base feature. The Extruded Boss/Base feature adds material. An Extruded feature required a Sketch Plane, sketch and depth.

The Sketch plane was the Front Plane. The 2D circle was sketched centered at the Origin. A dimension fully defined the overall size of the sketch. The default name of the feature was Boss-Extrude1. Boss-Extrude1 utilized the Mid Plane End Condition. The Boss-Extrude1 feature was symmetric about the Front Plane.

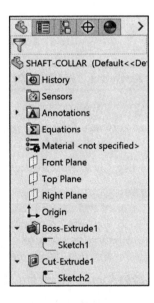

The Extruded Cut 🔲 feature removed material to create the hole. The Extruded Cut feature default named was Cut-Extrude1. The Through All End Condition option created the Cut-Extrude1 feature. Feature dimensions were modified. The Edit Color option was utilized to modify the part color.

🔆 Click **Options, Document Properties** tab, **Dimension** and click the **Smart** box to have the dimension leader arrowhead point inwards for ANSI.

FLATBAR Part

The FLATBAR part fastens to the AXLE. The
FLATBAR contains nine, ∅.190in holes spaced
0.5in apart.

The FLATBAR part is manufactured from .090inch
6061 alloy.

Create the FLATBAR part. Utilize the Centerpoint
Straight Slot Sketch ⊂⊃ tool with an Extruded

Boss/Base feature. The Extruded feature requires
a 2D profile sketched on the Front Plane.

The Centerpoint Straight Slot Sketch tool
automatically applies design symmetry (Midpoint and
Equal geometric relations). Create the 2D profile
centered about the Origin. Relations control the size
and position of entities with constraints.

First Point   Second Point

Utilize an Extruded Cut feature to create
the first hole. This is the seed feature for the
Linear Pattern.

Utilize a Linear Pattern feature to create
the remaining holes. A Linear Pattern creates
an array of features in a specified direction.

Add relations, then dimensions. This
keeps the user from having too many
unnecessary dimensions. This also helps to
show the design intent of the model.

Activity: FLATBAR Part-Extruded Base Feature

Create a New part.
132) Click **New** from the Menu bar. The New SOLIDWORKS
Document dialog box is displayed.

133) Click the **Templates** tab.

134) Double-click **Part**. The Part FeatureManager is
displayed.

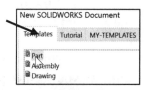

Save the part.
135) Click **Save As** from the drop-down Menu bar.

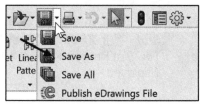

136) Enter **FLATBAR** for File name in the SW-TUTORIAL-2017 folder.

137) Enter **FLAT BAR 9 HOLES** for Description.

138) Click **Save**. The FLATBAR FeatureManager is displayed.

Set the Dimension standard and part units.

139) Click **Options** from the Main menu.

140) Click the **Document Properties** tab from the dialog box.

141) Select **ANSI** from the Overall drafting standard drop-down menu.

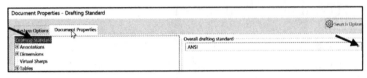

142) Click **Units**.

143) Click **IPS**, [**MMGS**] for Unit system.

144) Select **.123**, [**.12**] for Length units Decimal places.

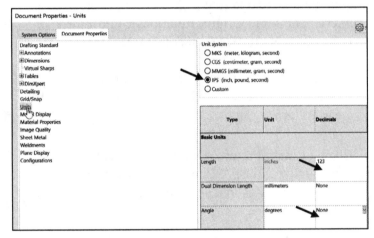

145) Select **None** for Angular units Decimal places.

146) Click **OK** to set the document units.

Insert a new sketch for the Extruded Base feature.

147) Right-click **Front Plane** from the FeatureManager. This is the Sketch plane.

148) Click **Sketch** from the Context toolbar as illustrated. The Sketch toolbar is displayed.

Utilize the Consolidated Slot Sketch toolbar. Apply the Centerpoint Straight Slot Sketch tool. The Straight Slot Sketch tool provides the ability to sketch a straight slot from a center point. In this example, use the origin as your center point.

149) Click the **Centerpoint Straight Slot** tool from the Sketch toolbar. The Slot PropertyManager is displayed.

Create the Straight Slot with three points.

150) Click the **Origin**. This is your first point.

151) Click a **point** directly to the right of the Origin. This is your second point.

152) Click a **point** directly above the second point. This is your third point. The Straight Slot is displayed.

First Point   Second Point

153) Click **OK** ✔ from the Slot PropertyManager.

View the Sketch relations.

154) Click **View**, **Hide/Show**, **Sketch Relations** from the Menu bar menu. View the sketch relations in the Graphics window.

Deactivate the Sketch relations.

155) Click **View**, **Hide/Show**, un-check **Sketch Relations** from the Menu bar. The Straight Slot Sketch tool provides a midpoint relation with the Origin and Equal relations between the other sketch entities.

Add dimensions.

156) Click the **Smart Dimension** ✎ tool from the Sketch toolbar.

157) Click the **horizontal centerline**.

158) Click a **position** above the top horizontal line in the Graphics window.

159) Enter **4.000**in, [**101.6**] in the Modify dialog box.

160) Click the **Green Check mark** ✔ in the Modify dialog box.

161) Click the **right arc** of the FLATBAR.

162) Click a **position** diagonally to the right in the Graphics window.

163) Enter **.250**in, [**6.35**] in the Modify dialog box.

164) Click the **Green Check mark** ✔ in the Modify dialog box. The black sketch is fully defined.

🔅 Model about the Origin; this provides a point of reference for your dimensions to fully define the sketch.

🔅 It's considered best practice to fully define all sketches in the model. However, there are times when this is not practical, generally when using the Spline tool to create a freeform shape.

[101.60]
4.000

[6.35]
R.250

Extrude the sketch to create the Base (Boss-Extrude1) feature.

165) Click **Extruded Boss/Base** from the Features toolbar. The Boss-Extrude PropertyManager is displayed.

166) Enter **.090**in, **[2.29]** for Depth. Accept the default conditions.

167) Click **OK** from the Boss-Extrude PropertyManager. Boss-Extrude1 is displayed in the FeatureManager.

Fit the model to the Graphics window.
168) Press the **f** key.

Save the FLATBAR part.
169) Click **Save**.

This book is designed to expose the new SOLIDWORKS user to many different tools, techniques and procedures. It may not always use the most direct tool or process.

Activity: FLATBAR Part-Extruded Cut Feature

Insert a new sketch for the Extruded Cut Feature.
170) Right-click the **front face** of the Boss-Extrude1 feature in the Graphics window. This is the Sketch plane. Boss-Extrude1 is highlighted in the FeatureManager.

171) Click **Sketch** from the Context toolbar as illustrated. The Sketch toolbar is displayed.

Display a Front view - Hidden Lines Removed.
172) Click **Front view** from the Heads-up View toolbar.

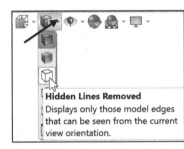

173) Click **Hidden Lines Removed** from the Heads-up View toolbar.

The process of placing the mouse pointer over an existing arc to locate its center point is called "wake up."

Wake up the Center point.

174) Click the **Circle** ⊙ Sketch tool from the Sketch toolbar. The Circle PropertyManager is displayed.

175) Place the **mouse pointer** on the left arc. Do not click. The center point of the slot arc is displayed.

176) Click the **center point** of the arc.

177) Click a **position** to the right of the center point to create the circle as illustrated.

Center point of the arc

Add a dimension.

178) Click the **Smart Dimension** ✎ Sketch tool.

179) Click the **circumference** of the circle.

180) Click a **position** diagonally above and to the left of the circle in the Graphics window.

181) Enter **.190**in, [**4.83**] in the Modify box.

182) Click the **Green Check mark** ✔ in the Modify dialog box.

R = 0.137

[4.83]
Ø.190

Display an Isometric view - Shaded With Edges.

183) Click **Isometric view** 🧊 from the Heads-up View toolbar.

184) Click **Shaded With Edges** 🧊 from the Heads-up View toolbar.

Insert an Extruded Cut feature.

185) Click the **Features** tab from the CommandManager.

186) Click **Extruded Cut** 🗔 from the Features toolbar. The Cut- Extrude PropertyManager is displayed.

187) Select **Through All** for End Condition in Direction 1. The direction arrow points to the back. Accept the default conditions.

188) Click **OK** ✔ from the Cut-Extrude PropertyManager. The Cut-Extrude1 feature is displayed in the FeatureManager.

Save the FLATBAR part.

189) Click **Save** 💾.

💡 Think design intent. When do you use various End Conditions? What are you trying to do with the design? How does the component fit into an Assembly?

The blue Cut-Extrude1 icon indicates that the feature is selected.

Select features by clicking their icons in the FeatureManager or by selecting their geometry in the Graphics window.

When you create a new part or assembly, the three default Planes (Front, Right and Top) are aligned with specific views. The Plane you select for the Base sketch determines the orientation of the part.

Activity: FLATBAR Part-Linear Pattern Feature

Create a Linear Pattern feature.

190) Click the **Linear Pattern** tool from the Features toolbar. The Linear Pattern PropertyManager is displayed. Cut-Extrude1 is displayed in the Features to Pattern box. Note: If Cut-Extrude1 is not displayed, click inside the Features to Pattern box. Click Cut-Extrude1 from the fly-out FeatureManager.

191) Click **inside** the Pattern Direction box. Click the **top edge** of the Boss-Extrude1 feature for Direction1 in the Graphics window. Edge<1> is displayed in the Pattern Direction box.

192) Enter **0.5**in, [**12.70**] for Spacing.

193) Enter **9** for Number of Instances. Instances are the number of occurrences of a feature.

194) The Direction arrow points to the right. Click the **Reverse Direction** button if required.

195) Check **Geometry pattern** from the Options box.

196) Click **OK** from the Linear Pattern PropertyManager. The LPattern1 feature is displayed in the FeatureManager.

Save the FLATBAR part.

197) Click **Save** 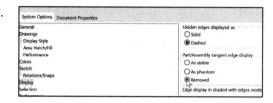. The FLATBAR part is complete.

Close all documents.

198) Click **Windows, Close All** from the Menu bar.

To remove Tangent edges, click **Display** from the Options menu, and check the **Removed** box.

 Review the FLATBAR Part

The FLATBAR part utilized an Extruded Boss/Base feature as the first feature. The Sketch plane was the Front Plane. The 2D sketch utilized the Straight Slot Sketch tool to create the slot profile.

You added linear and radial dimensions to define your sketch. You applied the Extruded Boss/Base feature with a Blind End Condition in Direction 1. Boss-Extrude1 was created.

You created a circle sketch for the Extruded Cut feature on the front face of Boss-Extrude1. The front face was your Sketch plane for the Extruded Cut feature. The Extruded Cut feature removed material to create the hole. The Extruded Cut feature default name was Cut-Extrude1. The Through All End Condition option in Direction 1 created the Cut-Extrude1 feature. The Cut-Extrude1 feature is the seed feature for the Linear Pattern of holes.

The Linear Pattern feature created an array of 9 holes, equally spaced along the length of the FLATBAR part.

LINKAGE Assembly

An assembly is a document that contains two or more parts. An assembly inserted into another assembly is called a sub-assembly. A part or sub-assembly inserted into an assembly is called a component. The LINKAGE assembly consists of the following components: AXLE, SHAFT-COLLAR, FLATBAR and AirCylinder sub-assembly.

Establishing the correct component relationship in an assembly requires forethought on component interaction. Mates are geometric relationships that align and fit components in an assembly. Mates remove degrees of freedom from a component.

Mate Types

Mates reflect the physical behavior of a component in an assembly. The components in the LINKAGE assembly utilize Standard mate types. Review Standard, Advanced and Mechanical mate types.

Standard Mates:

Components are assembled with various mate types. These are the Standard mate types:

Coincident Mate: Locates the selected faces, edges, or planes so they use the same infinite line. A Coincident mate positions two vertices for contact.

Parallel Mate: Locates the selected items to lie in the same direction and to remain a constant distance apart.

Perpendicular Mate: Locates the selected items at a 90 degree angle to each other.

Tangent Mate: Locates the selected items in a tangent mate. At least one selected item must be either a conical, cylindrical, or spherical face.

Concentric Mate: Locates the selected items so they can share the same center point.

Lock Mate: Maintains the position and orientation between two components.

Distance Mate: Locates the selected items with a specified distance between them. Use the drop-down arrow box or enter the distance value directly.

Angle Mate: Locates the selected items at the specified angle to each other. Use the drop-down arrow box or enter the angle value directly.

There are two Mate Alignment options. The Aligned option positions the components so that the normal vectors from the selected faces point in the same direction. The Anti-Aligned option positions the components so that the normal vectors from the selected faces point in opposite directions.

Advanced Mates:

The following are the Advanced mate types:

Profile Center: Mate to Center automatically center-aligns common component types such as rectangular and circular profiles to each other and fully defines the components.

Symmetric Mate: Positions two selected entities to be symmetric about a plane or planar face. A Symmetric Mate does not create a Mirrored Component.

Width Mate: Centers a tab within the width of a groove.

Path Mate: Constrains a selected point on a component to a path.

Linear/Linear Coupler Mate: Establishes a relationship between the translation of one component and the translation of another component.

Distance (Limit) Mate: Locates the selected items with a specified distance between them. Use the drop-down arrow box or enter the distance value directly.

Angle Mate: Locates the selected items at the specified angle to each other. Use the drop-down arrow box or enter the angle value directly.

Mechanical Mates:

The following are the Mechanical mate types:

Cam Mate: Forces a plane, cylinder, or point to be tangent or coincident to a series of tangent extruded faces.

Slot Mate: Mate bolts to straight or arced slots and you can mate slots to slots. Select an axis, cylindrical face, or a slot to create slot mates.

Hinge Mate: Limits the movement between two components to one rotational degree of freedom.

Gear Mate: Forces two components to rotate relative to one another around selected axes.

Rack Pinion Mate: Provides the ability to have Linear translation of a part; rack causes circular rotation in another part, pinion, and vice versa.

Screw Mate: Constrains two components to be concentric, and adds a pitch relationship between the rotation of one component and the translation of the other.

Universal Joint Mate: The rotation of one component (the output shaft) about its axis is driven by the rotation of another component (the input shaft) about its axis.

Example: Utilize a Concentric mate between the AXLE cylindrical face and the FLATBAR Extruded Cut feature (hole). Utilize a Coincident mate between the SHAFT-COLLAR back face and the FLATBAR front flat face.

The LINKAGE assembly requires the AirCylinder assembly. The AirCylinder assembly is located in the Pneumatic Components folder.

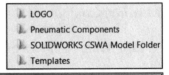

Activity: AirCylinder Assembly-Open and Save As option

Download all needed folders and files to your local hard drive.

199) Download the folders and files to your SW-TUTORIAL-2017 folder. Work from your hard drive.

Create a new assembly.

200) Click **New** from the Menu bar. The New SOLIDWORKS Document dialog box is displayed.

201) Click the **Templates** tab.

202) Double-click **Assembly** from the New SOLIDWORKS Document dialog box. The Begin Assembly PropertyManager is displayed.

203) Click the **Browse** button.

204) Browse to the **SW-TUTORIAL-2017\Pneumatic Components** folder on your hard drive. Note: Open models are displayed in the Open documents box.

205) Double-click the **AirCylinder** assembly from the SW-TUTORIAL-2017\Pneumatic Components folder. The AirCylinder assembly is displayed in the Graphics window.

Mate to the first component added to the assembly. If you mate to the first component or base component of the assembly and decide to change its orientation later, all the components will move with it.

💡 Determine the static and dynamic behavior of mates in each sub-assembly before creating the top level assembly.

206) Click **OK** ✔ from the Begin Assembly PropertyManager to fix the AirCylinder assembly in the Graphics window. The (f) symbol is placed in front of the AirCylinder name in the FeatureManager.

207) If required, click **Yes** to Rebuild.

208) Click **Save As** from the Menu bar.

209) Select **SW-TUTORIAL-2017** on your hard drive for Save in folder.

210) Enter **LINKAGE** for file name.

211) Click the **Include all referenced components** box.

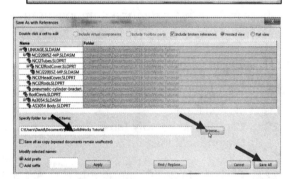

212) Click the **Advanced** button. An assembly and drawing document has part\component references. You must save the assembly document and all of the reference components to the same folder.

213) Click the **Browse** button from the Specify folder for selected items.

214) Select the **SW-TUTORIAL-2017** folder on your hard drive.

215) Click **OK** from the Browse For Folder dialog box.

216) Click **Save All**. The LINKAGE assembly FeatureManager is displayed.

You can also use the Pack and Go option to save an assembly or drawing document with references, toolbox components, studies, etc.

💡 This book is designed to expose the SOLIDWORKS user to numerous tools and procedures. It may not always use the simplest and most direct process.

Assemble the AXLE to the RodClevis using the Standard and Quick mate procedure. No command (click Mate from the Assembly CommandManager) is required using the Quick mate procedure. Hold the Ctrl key down, and make your selections. Release the Ctrl key; a Quick Mate pop-up is displayed below the context toolbar. Select your mate and you are finished.

Utilize the Quick mate procedure on Standard mates, Cam mate, Profile Center mate, Slot mate, Symmetric mate and Width mate. To activate the Quick mate functionality, click Tools, Customize. On the toolbars tab, under Context toolbar settings, select Show Quick Mate. Quick Mate is selected by default.

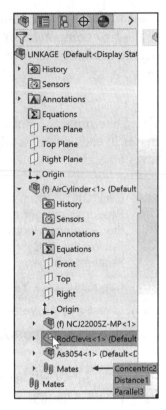

Use the Quick mate procedure for reference geometry (such as planes, axes, and points) along with model geometry (such as faces, edges and vertices).

Display the RodClevis component in the FeatureManager.
217) **Expand** the AirCylinder assembly in the FeatureManager.

218) Click **RodClevis<1>** from the FeatureManager. The RodClevis is highlighted in the Graphics window.

If required hide the Origins.
219) Click **View**, **Hide/Show**, un-check **Origins** from the Menu bar.

The AirCylinder is the first component in the LINKAGE assembly and is fixed (f) to the LINKAGE assembly Origin.

Display an Isometric view.
220) Click **Isometric view** .

Insert the AXLE part.
221) Click the **Assembly** tab in the CommandManager.

222) Click the **Insert Components** Assembly tool. The Insert Component PropertyManager is displayed.

223) Click the **Browse** button.

224) Browse to the **SW-TUTORIAL-2017** folder. Note if AXLE is active, double-click AXLE from the Open documents box.

225) Double-click **AXLE** from the SW-TUTORIAL-2017 folder.

226) Click a **position** to the front of the AirCylinder assembly as illustrated.

Enlarge the view.
227) **Zoom in** on the RodClevis and the AXLE.

Insert a Concentric mate. Use the Quick mate procedure.
228) Click the **inside front hole face** of the RodClevis.
The cursor displays the face feedback symbol.

229) Hold the **Ctrl** key down.

230) Click the **long cylindrical face** of the AXLE. The
cursor displays the face feedback symbol.

231) Release the **Ctrl** key. The Mate pop-up menu is
displayed.

232) Click **Concentric** from the Mate pop-up menu. The
AXLE is positioned concentric to the RodClevis hole.

Move the AXLE.
233) Click and drag the **AXLE** left to right. The AXLE
translates in and out of the RodClevis holes.

☼ Position the mouse pointer in the middle of the
face to select the entire face. Do not position the
mouse pointer near the edge of the face. If the wrong
face or edge is selected, click inside the Graphics
window to deselect the entity.

☼ This book is designed to expose the
SOLIDWORKS user to numerous tools and
procedures. It may not always use the simplest and
most direct process.

Display a Top view.
234) Click **Top view** ⬛.

Insert a Coincident mate.
235) Click the **Mate** ✎ tool from the Assembly
toolbar. The Mate PropertyManager is
displayed. If required, right-click **Clear
Selections** inside the Mate Selections box.

Expand the LINKAGE assembly and components in the
fly-out FeatureManager.
236) **Expand** the LINKAGE assembly from the fly-
out FeatureManager.

237) **Expand** the AirCylinder assembly from the fly-out FeatureManager.

238) Click the **Front Plane** of the AirCylinder assembly from the fly-out FeatureManager.

239) **Expand** the AXLE part from the fly-out FeatureManager.

240) Click the **Front Plane** of the AXLE part from the fly-out FeatureManager. The selected planes are displayed in the Mate Selections box. Coincident mate is selected by default.

241) Click **OK** ✔ from the Mate PropertyManager.

The AirCylinder Front Plane and the AXLE Front Plane are Coincident. The AXLE is centered in the RodClevis.

Display the Mates in the FeatureManager to check that the components and the mate types correspond to the design intent. If you delete a mate and then recreate it, the mate numbers will be in a different order.

Display an Isometric view.

242) Click **Isometric view** .

Display the Mates in the folder.
243) **Expand** the Mates folder in the FeatureManager.

244) **View** the created mates.

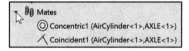

Activity: LINKAGE Assembly-Insert FLATBAR Part

Insert the FLATBAR part.

245) Click the **Insert Components** Assembly tool. The Insert Component PropertyManager is displayed.

246) Click the **Browse** button.

247) Browse to the **SW-TUTORIAL-2017** folder.

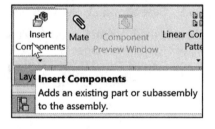

248) Click the **Filter Parts (*.prt;*sldprt)** button in the Open dialog box to view part documents.

249) Double-click **FLATBAR**.

Place the component in the assembly.
250) Click a **position** in the Graphics window as illustrated. Use the z key to Zoom out if required.

Enlarge the view.
251) Zoom in on the AXLE and the left side of the FLATBAR to enlarge the view.

Insert a Concentric mate.
252) Click the inside **left hole face** of the FLATBAR.

253) Hold the **Ctrl** key down.

254) Click the **long cylindrical face** of the AXLE.

255) Release the **Ctrl** key. The Mate pop-up menu is displayed.

256) Click **Concentric** from the Mate pop-up menu.

Fit the model to the Graphics window.
257) Press the **f** key.

Move the FLATBAR.
258) Click and drag the **FLATBAR**. The FLATBAR translates and rotates along the AXLE.

Insert a Coincident mate.
259) Click the **front face** of the FLATBAR.

260) Rotate the model to view the back face of the RodClevis.

261) Hold the **Ctrl** key down.

262) Click the **back face** of the RodClevis as illustrated.

263) Release the **Ctrl** key. The Mate pop-up menu is displayed.

264) Click **Coincident** from the Mate pop-up menu.

Display an Isometric view.

265) Click **Isometric view** .

Insert the second FLATBAR component.

266) Click the **Insert Components** Assembly tool. The Insert Component PropertyManager is displayed.

267) Click the **Browse** button.

268) Browse to the **SW-TUTORIAL-2017** folder.

269) Click the **Filter Parts (*.prt;*sldprt)** button in the Open dialog box to view part documents.

270) Double-click **FLATBAR**.

271) Click a **position** to the front of the AirCylinder in the Graphics window as illustrated.

Enlarge the view.

272) **Zoom in** on the second FLATBAR and the AXLE.

Insert a Concentric mate.

273) Click the **left inside hole face** of the second FLATBAR.

274) Hold the **Ctrl** key down.

275) Click the **long cylindrical face** of the AXLE.

276) Release the **Ctrl** key. The Mate pop-up menu is displayed.

277) Click **Concentric** from the Mate pop-up menu.

278) Click and drag the **second FLATBAR** to the front.

Fit the model to the Graphics window.

279) Press the **f** key.

This book is designed to expose the new SOLIDWORKS user to many different tools, techniques and procedures. It may not always use the most direct tool or process.

Insert a Coincident mate.

280) Press the **left arrow key** approximately 5 times to rotate the model to view the back face of the second FLATBAR.

281) Click the **back face** of the second FLATBAR.

282) Press the **right arrow key** approximately 5 times to rotate the model to view the front face of the RodClevis.

283) Hold the **Ctrl** key down.

284) Click the **front face** of the RodClevis.

285) Release the **Ctrl** key. The Mate pop-up menu is displayed.

286) Click **Coincident** from the Mate pop-up menu.

Insert a Parallel mate.

287) Press the **Shift-z** keys to Zoom in on the model.

288) Click the **top narrow face** of the first FLATBAR.

289) Hold the **Ctrl** key down.

290) Click the **top narrow face** of the second FLATBAR.

291) Release the **Ctrl** key.

292) Click **Parallel** ＼ from the Mate pop-up menu.

Display an Isometric view.

293) Click **Isometric view** ⬛.

Move the two FLATBAR parts.

294) Click and drag the **second FLATBAR**. Both FLATBAR parts move together.

View the Mates folder.

295) **Expand** the Mates folder from the FeatureManager. View the created mates.

Determine the static and dynamic behavior of mates in each sub-assembly before creating the top level assembly.

Mates
- ◎ Concentric1 (AirCylinder<1>,AXLE<1>)
- ⩘ Coincident1 (AirCylinder<1>,AXLE<1>)
- ◎ Concentric2 (AXLE<1>,FLATBAR<1>)
- ⩘ Coincident2 (AirCylinder<1>,FLATBAR<1>)
- ◎ Concentric3 (AXLE<1>,FLATBAR<2>)
- ⩘ Coincident3 (AirCylinder<1>,FLATBAR<2>)
- ＼ Parallel1 (FLATBAR<1>,FLATBAR<2>)

💡 Utilize the Search feature in the Systems Options dialog box to quickly locate information for System Options or Document Properties.

Activity: LINKAGE Assembly-Insert SHAFT-COLLAR Part

Insert the first SHAFT-COLLAR.

296) Click the **Insert Components** Assembly tool. The Insert Component PropertyManager is displayed.

297) Click the **Browse** button.

298) Browse to the **SW-TUTORIAL-2017** folder.

299) Click the **Filter Parts (*.prt;*sldprt)** button in the Open dialog box to view part documents.

300) Double-click **SHAFT-COLLAR**.

301) Click a **position** to the back of the AXLE as illustrated.

Enlarge the view.

302) Click the **Zoom to Area** tool.

303) **Zoom-in** on the SHAFT-COLLAR and the AXLE component.

Deactivate the tool.

304) Click the **Zoom to Area** tool.

Insert a Concentric mate.
305) Click the **inside hole face** of the SHAFT-COLLAR.

306) Hold the **Ctrl** key down.

307) Click the **long cylindrical face** of the AXLE.

308) Release the **Ctrl** key. The Mate pop-up menu is displayed.

309) Click **Concentric** from the Mate pop-up menu.

Insert a Coincident mate.
310) Press the **Shift-z** keys to Zoom in on the model.

311) Click the **front face** of the SHAFT-COLLAR as illustrated.

312) **Rotate** the model to view the back face of the first FLATBAR.

313) Hold the **Ctrl** key down.

314) Click the **back face** of the first FLATBAR.

315) Release the **Ctrl** key. The Mate pop-up menu is displayed.

316) Click **Coincident** from the Mate pop-up menu.

Display an Isometric view.

317) Click **Isometric view** .

Insert the second SHAFT-COLLAR.

318) Click the **Insert Components** Assembly tool. The Insert Component PropertyManager is displayed.

319) Click the **Browse** button.

320) Browse to the **SW-TUTORIAL-2017** folder.

321) Click the **Filter Parts (*.prt;*.sldprt)** button in the Open dialog box to view part documents.

322) Double-click **SHAFT-COLLAR**.

323) Click a **position** near the AXLE as illustrated.

Enlarge the view.

324) Click the **Zoom to Area** tool.

325) **Zoom-in** on the second SHAFT-COLLAR and the AXLE to enlarge the view.

326) Click the **Zoom to Area** tool to deactivate the tool.

Insert a Concentric mate.
327) Click the **inside hole face** of the second SHAFT-COLLAR.

328) Hold the **Ctrl** key down.

329) Click the **long cylindrical face** of the AXLE.

330) Release the **Ctrl** key. The Mate pop-up menu is displayed.

331) Click **Concentric** from the Mate pop-up menu.

Insert a Coincident mate.
332) Click the **back face** of the second SHAFT-COLLAR.

333) **Rotate** to view the front face of the second FLATBAR.

334) Hold the **Ctrl** key down.

335) Click the **front face** of the second FLATBAR.

336) Release the **Ctrl** key. The Mate pop-up menu is displayed.

337) Click **Coincident** from the Mate pop-up menu.

View the created Mates.
338) Expand the Mates folder. View the created mates.

Display an Isometric view.
339) Click **Isometric view** .

Fit the model to the Graphics window.
340) Press the **f** key.

Save the LINKAGE assembly.

341) Click **Save** . Click **Rebuild and Save** the document. The LINKAGE assembly is complete.

Use the Pack and Go option to save an assembly or drawing with references. The Pack and Go tool saves either to a folder or creates a zip file to e-mail. View SOLIDWORKS help for additional information.

Review the LINKAGE Assembly

An assembly is a document that contains two or more parts. A part or sub-assembly inserted into an assembly is called a component. You created the LINKAGE assembly. The AirCylinder sub-assembly was the first component inserted into the LINKAGE assembly. The AirCylinder assembly was obtained from the Pneumatic Components folder.

The AirCylinder assembly was fixed to the Origin. The Concentric and Coincident mates added Geometric relationships between the inserted components in the LINKAGE assembly.

Quick Mate is a procedure to mate components together. No command (click Mate from the Assembly CommandManager) is required. Hold the Ctrl key down, make your selections. Release the Ctrl key; a Quick Mate pop-up is displayed below the context toolbar. Select your mate and you are finished.

Utilize the Quick Mate procedure for Standard mates, Cam mate, Profile Center mate, Slot mate, Symmetric mate and Width mate. To activate the Quick Mate functionality, click Tools, Customize. On the toolbars tab, under Context toolbar settings, select Show Quick Mates. Quick Mate is selected by default.

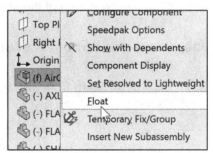

To remove the fixed state, Right-click a component name in the FeatureManager. Click Float. The component is free to move.

The AXLE part was the second component inserted into the LINKAGE assembly. The AXLE required a Concentric mate between the two cylindrical faces and a Coincident mate between two the Front Planes.

The FLATBAR part was the third component inserted into the LINKAGE assembly. The FLATBAR required a Concentric mate between the two cylindrical faces and a Coincident mate between the two flat faces.

A second FLATBAR was inserted into the LINKAGE assembly. A Parallel mate was added between the two FLATBARs.

Two SHAFT-COLLAR parts were inserted into the LINKAGE assembly. Each SHAFT-COLLAR required a Concentric mate between the two cylindrical faces and a Coincident mate between the two flat faces.

Motion Study - Basic Motion Tool

Motion Studies are graphical simulations of motion for assembly models. You can incorporate visual properties such as lighting and camera perspective into a motion study. Motion studies do not change an assembly model or its properties. They simulate and animate the motion you prescribe for your model. Use SOLIDWORKS mates to restrict the motion of components in an assembly when you model motion.

Create a Motion Study. Select the Basic Motion option from the MotionManager. The Basic Motion option provides the ability to approximate the effects of motors, springs, collisions and gravity on your assembly. Basic Motion takes mass into account in calculating motion. Note: The Animation option does not!

Activity: LINKAGE Assembly-Basic Motion

Insert a Rotary Motor using the Motion Study tab.

342) Click the **Motion Study 1** tab located in the bottom left corner of the Graphics window. The MotionManager is displayed.

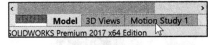

343) Select **Basic Motion** for Type of study from the MotionManager drop-down menu as illustrated.

344) Click **Motor** from the MotionManager. The Motor PropertyManager is displayed.

345) Click the **Rotary Motor** box.

346) Click the **FLATBAR front face** as illustrated. A red Rotary Motor icon is displayed. The red direction arrow points counterclockwise.

347) Enter **150 RPM** for speed in the Motion box.

348) Click **OK** from the Motor PropertyManager.

Record the Simulation.

349) Click **Calculate**. The FLATBAR rotates in a counterclockwise direction for a set period of time.

350) Click **Play**. View the simulation.

LINKAGE Assembly Basic Simulation

Save the simulation in an AVI file to the SW-TUTORIAL-2017
folder.

351) Click **Save Animation**.

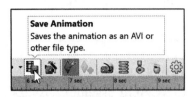

352) Click **Save** from the Save Animation to File dialog box.
View your options.

353) Click **OK** from the Video Compression box.

Close the Motion Study and return to SOLIDWORKS.

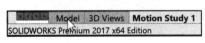

354) Click the **Model** tab location in the bottom left corner of
the Graphics window.

Fit the assembly to the Graphics window.

355) Press the **f** key.

Save the LINKAGE assembly.

356) Click **Save**.

Exit SOLIDWORKS.

357) Click **Windows**, **Close All** from the Menu bar.

The LINKAGE assembly chapter is complete.

Rename a feature or sketch for clarity. Slowly click the feature
or sketch name twice and enter the new name when the old one is
highlighted.

Use the Pack and Go option to save an assembly or drawing
with references. The Pack and Go tool saves either to a folder or
creates a zip file to e-mail. View SOLIDWORKS help for additional
information.

 Review the Motion Study

The Rotary Motor Basic Motion tool combined Mates and Physical Dynamics to rotate
the FLATBAR components in the LINKAGE assembly. The Rotary Motor was applied
to the front face of the FLATBAR. You utilized the Calculate option to play the
simulation. You saved the simulation in an .avi file.

Additional details on Motion Study, Assembly, mates, and Simulation are available
in SOLIDWORKS help. Keywords: Motion Study and Basic Motion.

Chapter Summary

In this chapter, you created three parts (AXLE, SHAFT-COLLAR and FLATBAR), downloaded the AirCylinder assembly from the Pneumatic Components folder and created the LINKAGE assembly using the Standard and Quick mate procedure.

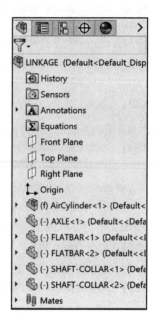

You developed an understanding of the SOLIDWORKS User Interface: Menus, Toolbars, Task Pane, CommandManager, FeatureManager, System feedback icons, Document Properties, Parts and Assemblies.

You created 2D sketches and addressed the three key states of a sketch: *Fully Defined*, *Over Defined* and *Under Defined*. Note: Always review your FeatureManager for the proper sketch state.

You obtained the knowledge of the following SOLIDWORKS features: Extruded Boss/Base, Extruded Cut, and Linear Pattern. Features are the building blocks of parts. The Extruded Boss/Base feature required a Sketch plane, sketch, and depth.

The Extruded Boss/Base feature added material to a part. The Boss-Extruded1 feature was utilized in the AXLE, SHAFT-COLLAR and FLATBAR parts.

The Extruded Cut feature removed material from the part. The Extruded Cut feature was utilized to create a hole in the SHAFT-COLLAR and FLATBAR parts. Note: Both were Through All holes. We will address the Hole Wizard later in the book. The Linear Pattern feature was utilized to create an array of holes in the FLATBAR part.

When parts are inserted into an assembly, they are called components. You created the LINKAGE assembly by inserting the AirCylinder assembly, AXLE, SHAFT-COLLAR and FLATBAR parts.

Mates are geometric relationships that align and fit components in an assembly. Concentric, Coincident and Parallel mates were utilized to assemble the components.

You created a Motion Study. The Rotary Motor Basic Motion tool combined Mates and Physical Dynamics to rotate the FLATBAR components in the LINKAGE assembly.

View the provided videos on creating 2D Sketches, 3D Features and Assemblies to enhance your experience in this chapter.

Questions

1. Explain the steps in starting a SOLIDWORKS session.

2. Describe the procedure to begin a new 2D sketch.

3. Explain the steps required to modify units in a part document from inches to millimeters.

4. Describe the procedure to create a simple 3D cylinder on the Front Plane with an Extruded Boss/Base (Boss-Extrude1) feature.

5. Identify the three default Reference planes in SOLIDWORKS.

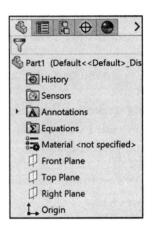

6. Describe a Base feature. Provide two examples from this chapter.

7. Describe the differences between an Extruded Boss/Base feature and an Extruded Cut feature.

8. The sketch color black indicates a sketch is _____ defined.

9. The sketch color blue indicates a sketch is _____ defined.

10. The sketch color red indicates a sketch is _____ defined.

11. Describe the procedure to "wake up" a center point in a sketch.

12. Define a Geometric relation. Provide three examples.

13. Describe the procedure to create a Linear Pattern feature.

14. Describe an assembly or sub-assembly.

15. What are mates and why are they important in assembling components?

16. In an assembly, each component has_____# degrees of freedom. Name them.

17. True or False. A fixed component cannot move in an assembly.

18. Review the Design Intent section in the book. Identify how you incorporated design intent into a part or assembly document.

Exercises

Exercise 2.1: Identify the Sketch plane for the Boss-Extrude1 (Base) feature as illustrated. Simplify the number of features.

A: Top Plane

B: Front Plane

C: Right Plane

D: Left Plane

Correct answer _____.

Create the part. Dimensions are arbitrary.

Origin

Exercise 2.2: Identify the Sketch plane for the Boss-Extrude1 (Base) feature as illustrated. Simplify the number of features.

A: Top Plane

B: Front Plane

C: Right Plane

D: Left Plane

Correct answer _____.

Create the part. Dimensions are arbitrary.

Origin

Exercise 2.3: Identify the Sketch plane for the Boss-Extrude1 (Base) feature as illustrated. Simplify the number of features.

A: Top Plane

B: Front Plane

C: Right Plane

D: Left Plane

Correct answer _____.

Create the part. Dimensions are arbitrary.

Origin

Exercise 2.4: FLATBAR - 3HOLE Part

Create an ANSI, IPS FLATBAR - 3HOLE part document.

- Utilize the Front Plane for the Sketch plane. Insert an Extruded Base (Boss-Extrude1) feature. Do not display Tangent Edges.

- Create an Extruded Cut feature. This is your seed feature. Apply the Linear Pattern feature. The FLATBAR - 3HOLE part is manufactured from 0.06in., [1.5mm] 6061 Alloy.

Exercise 2.5: FLATBAR - 5HOLE Part

Create an ANSI, IPS, FLATBAR - 5HOLE part as illustrated.

- Utilize the Front Plane for the Sketch plane. Insert an Extruded Base (Boss-Extrude1) feature.

- Create an Extruded Cut feature. This is your seed feature. Apply the Linear Pattern feature. The FLATBAR - 5HOLE part is manufactured from 0.06in, [1.5mm] 6061 Alloy.

- Calculate the required dimensions for the FLATBAR - 5HOLE part. Use the following information: Holes are .500in. on center, Radius is .250in., and hole diameter is .190in.

- Do not display Tangent edges in the final model.

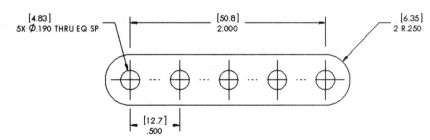

Think design intent. When do you use the various End Conditions and Geometric sketch relations? What are you trying to do with the design? How does the component fit into an assembly?

Exercise 2.6: Simple Block Part

Create the illustrated ANSI part. Note the location of the Origin in the illustration.

- Calculate the overall mass of the illustrated model.

- Apply the Mass Properties tool.

- Think about the steps that you would use to build the model.

- Review the provided information carefully.

- Units are represented in the IPS (inch, pound, second) system.

- A = 3.50in, B = .70in

Given:
A = 3.50
B = .70
Material: 1060 Alloy
Density = 0.0975 lb/in^3
Units: IPS
Decimal places = 2

Origin

Exercise 2.7: Simple Block Part

Create the illustrated ANSI part. Note the location of the Origin in the illustration.

Create the sketch symmetric about the Front Plane. The Front Plane in this problem is **not** your Sketch Plane. Utilize the Blind End Condition in Direction 1.

Given:
A = 3.00
B = .75
Material: Copper
Density = 0.321 lb/in^3
Units: IPS
Decimal places = 2

- Calculate the overall mass of the illustrated model.

- Apply the Mass Properties tool.

- Think about the steps that you would use to build the model.

- Review the provided information carefully. Units are represented in the IPS (inch, pound, second) system.

- A = 3.00in, B = .75in

Note: Sketch1 is symmetrical.

Origin

Exercise 2.8: Simple Block Part

Create an ANSI part from the illustrated model. Note the location of the Origin in the illustration.

- Calculate the volume of the part and locate the Center of mass with the provided information.

- Apply the Mass Properties tool.

- Think about the steps that you would use to build the model.

- Review the provided information carefully.

Given:
A = 3.30
B = 2.00
Material: 2014 Alloy
Density = .101 lb/in^3
Units: IPS
Decimal places = 2

Exercise 2.9: Simple Block Part

Create an ANSI, MMGS part from the illustrated drawing: Front, Top, Right and Isometric views.

Note the location of the Origin in the illustration. The drawing views are displayed in Third Angle Projection.

- Apply 1060 Alloy for material.

- Calculate the Volume of the part.

- Locate the Center of mass.

Think about the steps that you would use to build the model. The part is symmetric about the Front Plane.

Origin

Exercise 2.10: Simple Block Part

Create the ANSI, MMGS part from the illustrated drawing:
Front, Top, Right and Isometric views.

- Apply 1060 Alloy for
  material.

- The part is symmetric about
  the Front Plane.

- Calculate the Volume of
  the part and locate the
  Center of mass.

Think about the steps that you
would use to build the model.

The drawing views are
displayed in Third Angle
Projection.

Exercise 2.11: LINKAGE-2 Assembly

Create the LINKAGE-2
assembly.

- Copy the LINKAGE assembly from the Chapter 2
  Homework folder to your local hard drive.

- Open the assembly.

- Select Save As from the drop-down Menu bar.

- Check the Save as copy and open check box.

- Enter LINKAGE-2 for file
  name. LINKAGE-2
  ASSEMBLY for
  description.

The FLATBAR-3HOLE part was created in
Exercise 2.4. Utilize two AXLE parts, four
SHAFT COLLAR parts, and two FLATBAR-
3HOLE parts to create the LINKAGE-2 assembly
as illustrated.

- Insert the first AXLE part.

- Insert a Concentric mate.

- Insert a Coincident mate.

- Insert the first FLATBAR-3HOLE part.

- Insert a Concentric mate.

- Insert a Coincident mate.

- Perform the same procedure for the second
  FLATBAR-3HOLE part.

- Insert a Parallel mate between the 2 FLATBAR-
  3HOLE parts. Note: The 2 FLATBAR-3HOLE
  parts move together.

When a component is in the Lightweight
state, only a subset of its model data is loaded into
memory. The remaining model data is loaded on an
as-needed basis.

When a component is fully resolved, all its
model data is loaded into memory.

- Insert the second AXLE part.

- Insert a Concentric mate.

- Insert a Coincident mate.

- Insert the first SHAFT-COLLAR part.

- Insert a Concentric mate.

- Insert a Coincident mate.

- Perform the same tasks to insert the other three required SHAFT-COLLAR parts as illustrated.

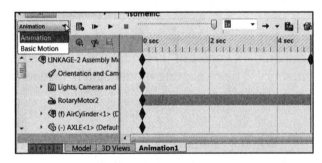

Exercise 2.12: LINKAGE-2 Assembly Motion Study

Create a Motion Study using the LINKAGE-2 Assembly that was created in the previous exercise.

- Create a Basic Motion Study.

- Apply a Rotary Motor to the front FLATBAR-3HOLE as illustrated.

- Play and Save the Simulation.

Exercise 2.13: ROCKER Assembly

Create a ROCKER assembly. The ROCKER assembly consists of two AXLE parts, two FLATBAR-5HOLE parts, and two FLATBAR-3HOLE parts.

The FLATBAR-3HOLE parts are linked together with the FLATBAR-5HOLE.

The three parts rotate clockwise and counterclockwise, above the Top Plane. Create the ROCKER assembly.

- Insert the first FLATBAR-5HOLE part. The FLATBAR-5HOLE is fixed to the Origin of the ROCKER assembly.

- Insert the first AXLE part.

- Insert a Concentric mate.

- Insert a Coincident mate.

- Insert the second AXLE part.

- Insert a Concentric mate.

- Insert a Coincident mate.

- Insert the first FLATBAR-3HOLE part.

- Insert a Concentric mate.

- Insert a Coincident mate.

- Insert the second FLATBAR-3HOLE part.

- Insert a Concentric mate.

- Insert a Coincident mate.

- Insert the second FLATBAR-5HOLE part.

- Insert the required mates.

Note: The end holes of the second FLATBAR-5HOLE are concentric with the end holes of the FLATBAR-3HOLE parts.

Note: In mechanical design, the ROCKER assembly is classified as a mechanism. A Four-Bar Linkage is a common mechanism comprised of four links.

Link1 is called the Frame.

The AXLE part is Link1.

Link2 and Link4 are called the Cranks.

The FLATBAR-3HOLE parts are Link2 and Link4. Link3 is called the Coupler. The FLATBAR-5HOLE part is Link3.

If an assembly or component is loaded in a Lightweight state, right-click the assembly name or component name from the FeatureManager. Click Set Lightweight to Resolved.

Determine the static and dynamic behavior of mates in each sub-assembly before creating the top level assembly.

Exercise 2.14: 4 Bar linkage

Create the 4 bar linkage assembly as illustrated. Create the five components. Assume dimensions.

View the avi file for proper movement in the Chapter 2 Homework folder.

In an assembly, fix (f) the first component to the origin or fully define it to the three default reference planes.

Insert all needed mates to simulate the movement of a 4 bar linkage assembly.

Read the section on Coincident, Concentric and Distance mates in SOLIDWORKS help and in the SOLIDWORKS 2017 Tutorial book.

Create a base with text for extra credit.

Below are a few sample models from my Freshman Engineering class.

Note the different designs to maintain the proper movement of a 4 bar linkage using a base.

Exercise 2.15: Fill Pattern 2-1

Create a Polygon Layout Fill Pattern feature.
Apply the seed cut option.

1. Open **Fill Pattern 2-1** from the Chapter 2 Homework folder.

2. Click the **Fill Pattern** 🐚 Features tool. The Fill Pattern PropertyManager is displayed.

3. Click the **Front face** of Extrude1. Face<1> is displayed in the Fill Boundary box. The direction arrow points to the right.

4. Click **Polygon** for Pattern Layout.

5. Click **Target spacing**.

6. Enter **15**mm for Loop Spacing.

7. Enter **6** for Polygon sides.

8. Enter **10**mm for Instances Spacing.

9. Enter **10**mm for Margins. View the direction arrow.

10. Click **Create seed cut**.

11. Click **Circle** for Features to Pattern.

12. Enter **4**mm for Diameter.

13. Click **OK** ✔ from the Fill Pattern PropertyManager. Fill Pattern1 is created and is displayed in the FeatureManager.

14. **View** the results.

Exercise 2.16: Fill Pattern 2-2

Create a Circular Layout Fill Pattern feature.

1. **Copy** the Chapter 2 Homework folder to your hard drive.

2. Open **Fill Pattern 2-2** from the Chapter 2 Homework folder.

3. Click the **Fill Pattern** Features tool. The Fill Pattern PropertyManager is displayed.

4. Click the **top face** of Boss-Extrude1. Face<1> is displayed in the Fill Boundary box. The direction arrow points to the back. Click **Circular** for Pattern Layout.

5. Enter **.10**in for Loop Spacing.

6. Click **Target spacing**.

7. Enter .10in Instance Spacing.

8. Enter **.05**in for Margins. Edge<1> is selected for Pattern Direction.

9. Click **inside** the Features to Pattern box.

10. Click **Boss-Extrude2** from the fly-out FeatureManager. Boss-Extrude2 is displayed in the Features to Pattern box.

11. Click **OK** from the Fill Pattern PropertyManager. Fill Pattern1 is created and is displayed in the FeatureManager.

12. **View** the results.

Exercise 2.17: Tangent Mate

Create a Tangent mate between the roller-wheel and the cam on both sides to simulate movement per the avi file.

1. **Copy** the Chapter 2 Homework folder to your hard drive.

2. Open **Tangent** from the Chapter 2 Homework\Tangent folder. The assembly is displayed.

Create a Tangent mate between the roller-wheel and the cam on both sides. The cam was created with imported geometry (curve).

💡 A Tangent mate places the selected items tangent to each other. At least one selected item must be either a conical, cylindrical,or spherical face. An Angle mate places the selected items at the specified angle to each other.

3. Click the **Mate** 🖇 tool from the Assembly tab.

4. **Pin** the Mate PropertyManager.

Create the first Tangent mate.
5. Click the **contact face** of the left cam as illustrated.

6. Click the **contact face** of the left roller-wheel as illustrated.

7. Click **Tangent** ⟲ mate from the PropertyManager.

8. Click **OK** ✔ from the Tangent1 PropertyManager.

You can set an option in the Mate PropertyManager so that the first component you select from becomes transparent. Then selecting from the second component is easier, especially if the second component is behind the first. The option is supported for all mate types except those that might have more than one selection from the first component (width, symmetry, linear coupler, cam, and hinge).

Create the second Tangent mate.
9. Click the **contact face** of the left cam.

10. Click the **contact face** of the left roller-wheel.

11. Click **Tangent** ⟲ mate from the PropertyManager.

12. Click **OK** ✔ from the Tangent2 PropertyManager.

13. **Un-Pin** the Mate PropertyManager.

14. Click **OK** ✔ from the Mate PropertyManager.

15. Display an **Isometric** view.

16. **Move** the cam. View the results.

Exercise 2.18: Motion Study 1

Apply a motor to move components in an assembly. Set up an animation motion study. Use the motion study time line and the MotionManager design tree to suppress mates in the motion study.

1. **Copy** the Chapter 2 Homework folder to your hard drive.

2. Open **Motion Study 1** from the Chapter 2 Homework\Motion Study folder.

3. Click the **Motion Study 1** tab at the bottom of the Graphics window.

4. Select **Basic Motion** for Study type.

5. Click the **Motor** 🖼 tool from the MotionManager toolbar. The Motor PropertyManager is displayed.

6. Click **Rotary Motor** for Motor Type.

7. Select **Face<1>@Part2-1** for Motor Direction in the Graphics window as illustrated. The direction arrow points counterclockwise.

8. Select **Constant speed** for Motor Type.

9. Enter **30** for Constant Speed Motor.

10. Click **OK** ✔ from the Motor PropertyManager.

Set the duration and run your animation on the 4bar-Linkage.

11. Drag the key to **6** seconds as illustrated.

12. Click **Play from Start** ▷ from the MotionManager. View the results.

In the next section, suppress a Concentric mate on a component. View the results in the Motion Study.

13. **Expand** the Mate folder in the
    MotionManager Design tree.

14. Right-click at 2 seconds and select
    Place Key ◆⁺ for the Concentric2
    mate.

15. Right-click at 4 seconds and select
    Place Key ◆⁺ for the Concentric2
    mate.

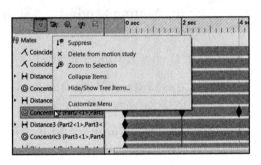

16. Set the time bar to **2 seconds**.

17. Right-click **Concentric2** in the
    MotionManager design tree.

18. Click **Suppress**. The mate is suppressed
    between the 2 and 4 second marks.

19. Click the **Calculate** 📇 tool. After calculating
    a motion study, you can view it again.

20. Click **Play from Start** ▷ from the
    MotionManager toolbar. View the results.
    Explore your options and the
    available tools. View
    SOLIDWORKS Help for
    additional information on a
    Motion Study.

Return to the FeatureManager.

21. Click the **Model** tab to return
    to SOLIDWORKS.

22. **Close** the model.

Chapter 3

FRONT-SUPPORT Assembly

Below are the desired outcomes and usage competencies based on the completion of Chapter 3.

Desired Outcomes:	Usage Competencies:

• Create four parts:
 	
  o HEX-STANDOFF
 	
  o ANGLE-13HOLE
 	
  o TRIANGLE
 	
  o SCREW
	• Apply the following model features: Extruded Boss/Base, Extruded Thin, Extruded Cut, Revolved Boss/Base, Hole Wizard, Linear Pattern, Circular Pattern, Mirror, Fillet and Chamfer.
	
	• Apply sketch techniques with various sketch tools and Construction geometry.

• Create an assembly: o FRONT-SUPPORT assembly	• Comprehend the assembly process and insert the following mate types: Concentric, Coincident, Parallel, Distance, Gear, Screw, Hinge and Cam.

Notes:

Chapter 3 - FRONT-SUPPORT Assembly

Chapter Objective

Create four new parts utilizing the Top, Front and Right Planes. Determine the Sketch plane for each feature. Obtain the knowledge of the following SOLIDWORKS features: Extruded Boss/Base, Extruded Thin, Extruded Cut, Revolved Boss/Base, Hole Wizard, Linear Pattern, Circular Pattern, Fillet and Chamfer.

Apply sketch techniques with various Sketch tools: Line, Circle, Corner Rectangle, Centerline, Dynamic Mirror, Straight Slot, Trim Entities, Polygon, Tangent Arc, Sketch Fillet, Offset Entities and Convert Entities.

Create four new parts:

1. HEX-STANDOFF

2. ANGLE-13HOLE

3. TRIANGLE

4. SCREW

Create the FRONT-SUPPORT assembly.

On the completion of this chapter, you will be able to:

- Select the correct Sketch plane.

- Generate a 2D sketch.

- Insert the required dimensions and Geometric relations.

- Apply the following SOLIDWORKS features:
  - Extruded Boss/Base
  - Extruded Cut
  - Extruded Thin
  - Revolved Base
  - Linear and Circular Pattern
  - Mirror
  - Fillet
  - Hole Wizard
  - Chamfer

- Apply the following mate types: Concentric, Coincident, Parallel, Distance, Gear and Cam.

Chapter Overview

The FRONT-SUPPORT assembly supports various pneumatic components and is incorporated into the PNEUMATIC-TEST-MODULE.

Create four new parts in this chapter:

1. HEX-STANDOFF

2. ANGLE-13HOLE

3. TRIANGLE

4. SCREW

ANGLE-13HOLE

HEX-STANDOFF

Create the FRONT-SUPPORT assembly using the four new created parts.

The FRONT-SUPPORT assembly is used in the exercises at the end of this chapter and in later chapters of the book.

TRIANGLE   Simplified SCREW

Think design intent. When do you use various End Conditions and Geometric sketch relations? What are you trying to do with the design? How does the component fit into an assembly?

FRONT-SUPPORT

Redeem the code on the inside cover of the book. Download the Model folder and videos to your local hard drive. View the provided videos to enhance the user experience: Start a SOLIDWORKS Session, Understand the SOLIDWORKS User Interface, Create 2D Sketches, Sketch Planes and use various Sketch tools, Create 3D Features and apply Design Intent, Create an Assembly and Create Fundamental Drawings Part 1 & Part 2.

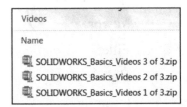

Videos

Name

SOLIDWORKS_Basics_Videos 3 of 3.zip
SOLIDWORKS_Basics_Videos 2 of 3.zip
SOLIDWORKS_Basics_Videos 1 of 3.zip

Reference Planes and Orthographic Projection

The three default ⊥ Reference planes represent infinite 2D planes in 3D space:

- Front
- Top
- Right

Planes have no thickness or mass.

Orthographic projection is the process of projecting views onto parallel planes with ⊥ projectors.

These are the default ⊥ datum planes:

- Primary
- Secondary
- Tertiary

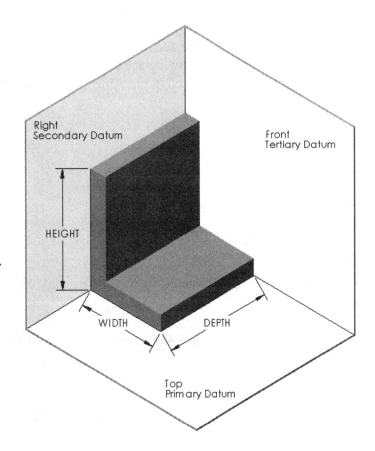

These are the planes used in manufacturing:

- Primary datum plane contacts the part at a minimum of three points.
- Secondary datum plane contacts the part at a minimum of two points.
- Tertiary datum plane contacts the part at a minimum of one point.

The part view orientation depends on the Base feature Sketch plane.

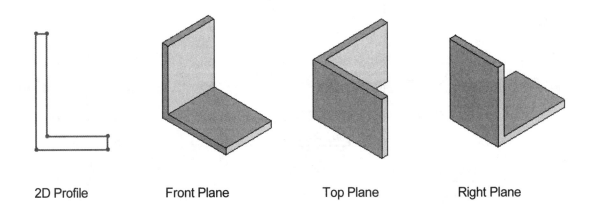

2D Profile   Front Plane   Top Plane   Right Plane

The part view orientation is dependent on the Base feature Sketch plane. Compare the available default Sketch planes in the FeatureManager: Front, Top and Right Plane.

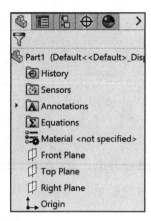

Each Boss-Extrude1 feature above was created with an L-shaped 2D Sketch profile. The following are the six principle views of Orthographic projection listed in the ASME Y14.3 standard:

- Top

- Front

- Right side

- Bottom

- Rear (Back)

- Left side

SOLIDWORKS Standard view names correspond to these Orthographic projection view names.

ASME Y14.3M Principle View Name:	SOLIDWORKS Standard View:
Front	Front
Top	Top
Right side	Right
Bottom	Bottom
Rear	Back
Left side	Left

These are the standard drawing views in Third Angle Orthographic projection:

- Front

- Top

- Right

- Isometric

There are two Orthographic projection drawing systems. The first Orthographic projection system is called the Third Angle projection. The second Orthographic projection system is called the First Angle projection. The systems are derived from positioning a 3D object in the third or first quadrant.

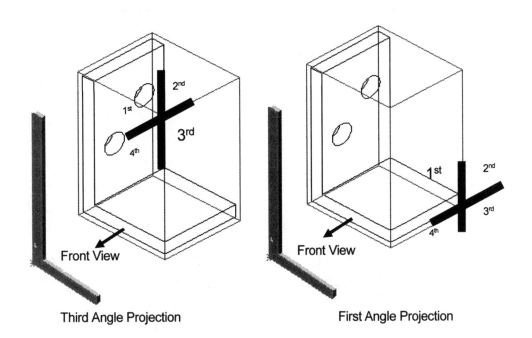

Third Angle Projection   First Angle Projection

Third Angle Projection

The part is positioned in the third quadrant in third angle projection. The 2D projection planes are located between the viewer and the part. The projected views are placed on a drawing.

First Angle Projection

The part is positioned in the first quadrant in First Angle projection. Views are projected onto the planes located behind the part. The projected views are placed on a drawing. First Angle projection is primarily used in Europe and Asia.

Third Angle projection is primarily used in the U.S. & Canada and is based on the ASME Y14.3M Multi and Sectional View Drawings standard. Designers should have knowledge and understanding of both systems.

There are numerous multi-national companies. Example: A part is designed in the U.S., manufactured in Japan and destined for a European market.

Third Angle projection is used in this text. A truncated cone symbol appears on the drawing to indicate the Projection System:

Third Angle Projection Symbol

First Angle Projection Symbol

Select the Sketch plane based on symmetry and orientation of the part in the FRONT-SUPPORT assembly. Utilize the standard views: *Front, Back, Right, Left, Top, Bottom* and *Isometric* to orient the part. Create the 2D drawings for the parts in Chapter 4.

HEX-STANDOFF Part

The HEX-STANDOFF part is a hexagonal shaped part utilized to elevate components in the FRONT-SUPPORT assembly. Machine screws are utilized to fasten components to the HEX-STANDOFF.

Create the HEX-STANDOFF part with the Extruded Boss/Base 🗐 feature. The Sketch plane for the HEX-STANDOFF Boss-Extrude1 feature is the Top Plane.

HEX-STANDOFF

Create the HEX-STANDOFF in the orientation utilized by the FRONT-SUPPORT assembly.

Origin　　　　　　　　Origin　　　Origin

Note the location of the origin in the model. When you create a new part, the three default Planes (Front, Right and Top) are aligned with specific views. The Plane you select for the Base sketch determines the orientation of the part.

All sketches should be fully defined in the FeatureManager.

Insert Geometric relations first then dimensions in a sketch to maintain design intent.

The Boss-Extrude1 feature sketch consists of two profiles. The first sketch is a circle centered at the Origin on the Top Plane.

The second sketch is a polygon with 6 sides centered at the Origin. The polygon utilizes an inscribed circle to construct the geometry.

Geometric relations are constraints that control the size and position of the sketch entities. Apply a Horizontal relation in the polygon sketch.

Origin

Extrude the sketch perpendicular to the Top Plane. Utilize the Edit Sketch tool to modify the sketch.

The Hole Wizard feature creates complex and simple Hole features. Utilize the Hole Wizard feature to create a Tapped Hole.

The Tapped Hole depth and diameter are based on drill size and screw type parameters. Apply a Coincident relation to position the Tapped Hole aligned with the Origin.

Activity: HEX-STANDOFF Part-Extruded Boss/Base Feature

Create a New part.

1) Click **New** 🗋 from the Menu bar.

2) Click the **Templates** tab.

3) Double-click **Part**. The Part FeatureManager is displayed.

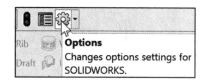

Set the dimensioning standard and part unit.

4) Click **Options** ⚙ from the Main menu.

5) Click the **Document Properties** tab from the dialog box.

6) Select **ANSI** from the Overall drafting standard box.

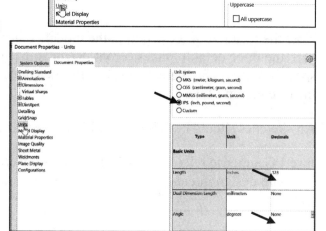

Set document unit and decimal places.

7) Click **Units**.

8) Select **IPS**, **[MMGS]** for Unit system.

9) Select **.123**, **[.12]** for Length units Decimal places. Select **None** for Angular units Decimal places.

10) Click **OK**. The Part FeatureManager is displayed.

The primary units are provided in IPS (inch, pound, seconds). The optional secondary units are provided in MMGS (millimeter, gram, second) and are indicated in brackets [ ]. Illustrations are provided in inches and millimeters.

Save the part.

11)   Click **Save As** from the drop-down Menu bar.

12)   Select the **SW-TUTORIAL-2017** folder.

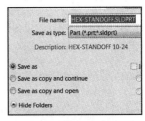

13)   Enter **HEX-STANDOFF** for File name.

14)   Enter **HEX-STANDOFF 10-24** for Description.

15)   Click **Save**. The HEX-STANDOFF FeatureManager is displayed.

Select the Sketch plane.

16)   Right-click **Top Plane** from the FeatureManager. This is the Sketch plane.

Insert a Boss-Extrude1 feature (Base feature) sketched on the Top Plane. Note: A plane is an infinite 2D area. The blue boundary is for visual reference.

Insert a new sketch.

17)   Click **Sketch** from the Context toolbar. The Sketch toolbar is displayed.

18)   Click the **Circle** Sketch tool. The Circle PropertyManager is displayed.

19)   Drag the **mouse pointer** into the Graphics window. The cursor displays the Circle icon.

20)   Click the **Origin**.

21)   Drag the **mouse pointer** to the right of the Origin.

22)   Click a **position** to create the circle as illustrated.

Insert a Polygon.

23)   Click the **Polygon** Sketch tool. The Polygon PropertyManager is displayed. The cursor displays the Polygon icon.

24)   Click the **Origin** as illustrated.

25) Drag the **mouse pointer** horizontally to the right.

26) Click a **position** to the right of the circle to create the hexagon as illustrated. **Display** Geometric relations.

Add a dimension.

27) Click the **Smart Dimension** Sketch tool.

28) Click the **circumference** of the first circle.

29) Click a **position** diagonally above the hexagon to locate the dimension.

30) Enter **.150**in, **[3.81]** in the Modify box.

31) Click the **Green Check mark** in the Modify dialog box.

32) Click the **circumference** of the inscribed circle. Click a **position** diagonally below the hexagon to locate the dimension.

33) Enter **.313**in, **[7.95]** in the Modify box.

34) Click the **Green Check mark** in the Modify dialog box. The black sketch is fully defined.

35) **Deactivate** the Geometric relations.

Fit the model to the Graphics window.
36) Press the **f** key to fit the model to the Graphics window.

If required, click the arrowhead dot to toggle the direction of the dimension arrow.

37) Click **OK** from the Dimension PropertyManager.

Add a Horizontal relation.

38) Click the **Origin** . Hold the **Ctrl** key down.

39) Click the right most **point** of the hexagon. The Properties PropertyManager is displayed.

40) Release the **Ctrl** key. Click **Horizontal** from the Add Relations box. Click **OK** from the Properties PropertyManager.

 You can also right-click and click **Make Horizontal** from the Context toolbar.

Extrude the sketch.

41) Click the **Features** tab in the CommandManager.

42) Click **Extruded Boss/Base** from the Features toolbar. The Boss-Extrude PropertyManager is displayed. Blind is the default End Condition in Direction1. The direction arrow points upward.

43) Enter .735in, [**18.67**] for Depth.

44) Click **OK** from the Boss-Extrude PropertyManager. Boss-Extrude1 is displayed in the FeatureManager.

Fit the model to the Graphics window.

45) Press the **f** key.

The Boss-Extrude1 feature (Base feature) was sketched on the Top Plane. Changes occur in the design process. Edit the sketch of Boss-Extrude1. Delete the circle and close the sketch. Apply the Hole Wizard feature to create a Tapped Hole.

Edit Sketch1.

46) **Expand** Boss-Extrude1 in the FeatureManager.

47) Right-click **Sketch1** in the FeatureManager.

48) Click **Edit Sketch** from the Context toolbar.

Delete the inside circle.

49) Click the **circumference** of the inside circle as illustrated. The Circle PropertyManager is displayed.

50) Press the **Delete** key.

51) Click **Yes** to the Sketcher Confirm Delete message. Both the circle geometry and its dimension are deleted.

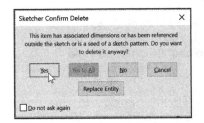

Save and close the sketch.

52) Click **Save**.

53) Click **Rebuild and Save**. The Boss-Extrude1 feature is updated. Note: Sketch1 is fully defined.

Fit the model to the Graphics window.

54) Press the **f** key.

Activity: HEX-STANDOFF Part-Hole Wizard Feature

Insert a Tapped Hole with the Hole Wizard feature tool. Create a 2D Sketch.

55) Click **Hidden Lines Visible** ⬚ from the Heads-up View toolbar.

56) Click **Hole Wizard** 🕳 from the Features toolbar. The Hole Specification PropertyManager is displayed.

Note: For metric, utilize ANSI Metric and M5x0.8 for size.

57) Click **Straight Tap** for Hole Specification.

58) Select **ANSI Inch, [ANSI Metric]** for Standard.

59) Select **Bottoming Tapped Hole** for Type.

60) Select **#10-24, [Ø5]** for Size.

61) Select **Through All** for End Condition.

62) Click the **Cosmetic thread** box. Accept the default conditions.

63) Click the **Positions** tab.

64) Click the **top face** of Boss-Extrude1 to the right of the origin. Do not select the center of the part.

65) Click the **center of the part** to locate the center point of the hole as illustrated. The Tapped Hole is displayed in yellow. Yellow is a preview color. The Point Sketch tool is automatically selected. No other holes are required. You created a Coincident relation to the center point of the Tapped Hole in the Top view.

66) Right-click **Select** in the Graphics window to deselect the Point Sketch tool. Do not right-click on the model.

67) Click **OK** ✔ from the Hole Position PropertyManager.

The #10-24 Tapped Hole1 feature is displayed in the
FeatureManager. Sketch2 determines the center point location of
the Tapped Hole. Sketch3 is the profile of the
Tapped Hole.

Save the HEX-STANDOFF part.

68) Click **Shaded With Edges** 🗍 from the Heads-
up View toolbar.

69) Click **inside** the Graphics window.

70) Click **Save** 🖫. The HEX-STANDOFF is
complete. View the threads.

 To view the thread, right-click the
Annotations folder, and click Details. Check the Cosmetic thread
box and the Shaded cosmetic threads box. Click OK.

 Review the HEX-STANDOFF Part.

The HEX-STANDOFF part utilized the Extruded Boss/Base feature. The
Boss-Extrude1 feature required a sketch on the Top Plane. The first profile
was a circle centered at the Origin on the Top Plane. The second profile
used the Polygon Sketch tool. You utilized the Edit Sketch tool to modify
the Sketch profile and to delete the circle.

The Hole Wizard feature created a Tapped Hole. The Hole Wizard feature
required the Boss-Extrude1 top face as the Sketch plane.

A Coincident relation located the center point of the Tapped Hole aligned
with respect to the Origin.

ANGLE-13HOLE Part

The ANGLE-13HOLE part is an L-shaped support
bracket. The ANGLE-13HOLE part is
manufactured from 0.090in, [2.3] aluminum.

The ANGLE-13HOLE part contains fillets, holes,
and slot cuts.

ANGLE-13HOLE

Simplify the overall design into seven features. Utilize symmetry and Linear Patterns.

The open L-Shaped profile is sketched on the Right Plane.

Utilize an Extruded Thin feature with the Mid Plane option to locate the part symmetrical to the Right Plane.

Insert the first Extruded Cut feature for the first hole. This is the seed feature for the Linear Pattern. The hole sketch is located on the top face of the Extruded Thin feature.

Insert a Linear Pattern feature to create an array of 13 holes along the bottom horizontal edge.

Insert a Fillet ⬦ feature to round the four corners.

🔆 Model about the origin; this provides a point of reference.

Insert the second Extruded Cut feature on the front face of the Extruded Thin feature. This is the seed feature for the second Linear Pattern.

Insert a Linear Pattern feature to create an array of 3 holes along the top horizontal edge.

Utilize the Sketch Mirror tool to create the slot profile. Use the Slot Sketch tool.

Insert the third Extruded Cut feature to create the two slots.

☀ Select the Sketch plane for the Base feature that corresponds to the parts' orientation in the assembly.

Activity: ANGLE-13HOLE Part-Documents Properties

Create a New part.

71) Click **New** ☐ from the Menu bar.

72) Double-click **Part**. The Part FeatureManager is displayed.

Set the dimensioning standard and part unit.

73) Click **Options** ⚙ from the Main menu.

74) Click the **Document Properties** tab from the dialog box.

75) Select **ANSI** from the Overall drafting standard drop-down menu.

76) Click **Units**.

77) Select **IPS**, **[MMGS]** for Unit system.

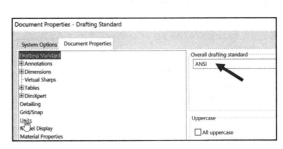

78) Select **.123**, **[.12]** for Length units Decimal places.

79) Select **None** for Angular units Decimal places. Click **OK**.

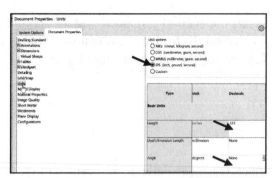

Save the part.

80) Click **Save As** from the Menu bar. Select the **SW-TUTORIAL-2017** file folder.

81) Enter **ANGLE-13 HOLE** for File name.

82) Enter **ANGLE BRACKET-13 HOLE** for Description.

83) Click **Save**. The ANGLE-13 Hole FeatureManager is displayed.

Activity: ANGLE-13HOLE Part-Extruded Thin Feature

Insert an Extruded Thin feature sketched on the Right Plane.

Select the Sketch plane.

84) Right-click **Right Plane** from the FeatureManager.

Sketch a horizontal line.

85) Click **Sketch** from the Context toolbar. The Sketch toolbar is displayed.

86) Click the **Line** Sketch tool from the Sketch toolbar.

87) Click the **Origin** as illustrated.

88) Click a **position** to the right of the Origin.

Sketch a vertical line.

89) Click a **position** directly above the right end point.

De-select the Line Sketch tool.

90) Right-click **Select** in the Graphics window.

Add an Equal relation.

91) Click the **vertical** line.

92) Hold the **Ctrl** key down.

93) Click the **horizontal line**.

94) Release the **Ctrl** key.

95) Right-click **Make Equal** = from the Context toolbar.

96) Click **OK** ✔ from the Properties PropertyManager.

Add a dimension.

97) Click the **Smart Dimension** ✎ Sketch tool.

98) Click the **horizontal** line.

99) Click a **position** below the profile.

100) Enter .700in, [17.78] in the Modify box.

101) Click the **Green Check mark** ✔. The black sketch is fully defined.

🔆 Save rebuild time. Add relations and dimensions to fully define a sketch. Fully defined sketches are displayed in black.

Extrude the sketch.

102) Click **Extruded Boss/Base** 🗍 from the Features toolbar. The Boss-Extrude PropertyManager is displayed.

103) Select **Mid Plane** for End Condition in Direction 1.

104) Enter **7.000**in, [177.8] for Depth. Note: Thin Feature is checked.

105) If needed, click the **Reverse Direction Arrow** button for One-Direction. Material thickness is created above the Origin.

106) Enter .090in, [2.3] for Thickness.

107) Check the **Auto-fillet corners** box.

108) Enter .090in, [2.3] for Fillet Radius.

109) Click **OK** ✔ from the Boss-Extrude PropertyManager. Extrude-Thin1 is displayed in the FeatureManager. Sketch1 is fully defined.

Fit the model to the Graphics window.
110) Press the **f** key.

🔆 Think design intent. When do you use the various End Conditions and Geometric sketch relations? What are you trying to do with the design? How does the component fit into an assembly?

💡 Clarify the Extrude-Thin1 feature direction and thickness options. Utilize multiple view orientations and Zoom In before selecting OK ✔ from the Boss-Extrude PropertyManager.

Modify feature dimensions.

111) Click **Extrude-Thin1** in the FeatureManager.

112) Click the **7.000**in, **[177.80]** dimension in the Graphics window.

113) Enter **6.500**in, **[165.10]**.

114) Click **inside** the Graphics window.

Save the model.

115) Click **Save** 💾.

Activity: ANGLE-13HOLE Part-Extruded Cut Feature

Insert a new sketch for the Extruded Cut feature.

116) Right-click the **top face** of Extrude-Thin1 as illustrated. This is the Sketch plane.

117) Click **Sketch** 🗒 from the Context toolbar. The Sketch toolbar is displayed.

118) Click **Top view** 🔲 from the Heads-up View toolbar.

119) Click the **Circle** ⊙ Sketch tool.

120) Sketch a **circle** on the left side of the Origin as illustrated.

Add dimensions.

121) Click the **Smart Dimension** 🖋 Sketch tool.

122) Click the **Origin** .

123) Click the **center point** of the circle.

124) Click a **position** below the horizontal profile line.

125) Enter **3.000**in, [**76.2**]. Click the **Green Check mark** .

126) Click the **bottom horizontal line**.

127) Click the **center point** of the circle.

128) Click a **position** to the left of the profile.

129) Enter **.250**in, [**6.35**].

130) Click the **Green Check mark** .

131) Create a diameter dimension. Click the **circumference** of the circle. Click a **position** diagonally above the profile.

132) Enter **.190**in, [**4.83**].

133) Click the **Green Check mark** .

Insert an Extruded Cut Feature.

134) Click **Extruded Cut** from the Features toolbar. The Cut-Extrude PropertyManager is displayed. Select **Through All** for End Condition in Direction 1. Accept the default conditions.

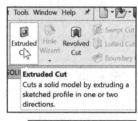

135) Click **OK** from the Cut-Extrude PropertyManager. Cut-Extrude1 is displayed in the FeatureManager. Cut-Extrude1 is the seed feature for the Linear Pattern feature of holes.

Display an Isometric view.

136) Click **Isometric view** from the Heads-up View toolbar.

Save the model.

137) Click **Save** .

Activity: ANGLE-13HOLE Part-Linear Pattern Feature

Insert a Linear Pattern feature.

138) Click **Top View** ⬚ from the Heads-up View toolbar.

139) Click **Linear Pattern** ⬚⬚ from the Features toolbar. The Linear Pattern PropertyManager is displayed. Cut-Extrude1 is displayed in the Features to Pattern box.

140) Click the **bottom horizontal edge** of the Extrude-Thin1 feature for Direction1. Edge<1> is displayed in the Pattern Direction box. The direction arrow points to the right. If required, click the Reverse Direction button.

141) Enter **0.5**in, **[12.70]** for Spacing.

142) Enter **13** for Number of Instances. If needed, click inside the **Features and Faces** box. Click **Cut-Extrude1** from the fly-out FeatureManager.

143) Check the **Geometry pattern** box under Options.

144) Click **OK** ✔ from the Linear Pattern PropertyManager. LPattern1 is displayed in the FeatureManager.

Display an Isometric view.

145) Click **Isometric view** ⬛ from the Heads-up View toolbar.

Save the ANGLE-13HOLE part.

146) Click **Save** 💾. Note: All sketches should be fully defined in the FeatureManager.

🔆 Use Symmetry. When possible and if it makes sense, model objects symmetrically about the origin. Even if the part is not symmetrical, the way it attaches or is manufactured could have symmetry.

Activity: ANGLE-13HOLE Part - Fillet Feature

Insert a Constant Radius Fillet Feature.
147) Zoom in on the right top edge as illustrated.

148) Click the **right top edge** of the Extrude-Thin1 feature.

149) Click **Fillet** 🗍 from the Features toolbar. The Fillet PropertyManager is displayed.

150) Click the **Manual** tab.

151) Click **Constant Radius Fillet** Type.

152) Enter **.250 [6.35]** for Radius.

153) Click the **right bottom edge**. Edge<1> and Edge<2> are displayed in the Items To Fillet box. Note the new fillet pop-up menu.

154) Click **OK** ✔ from the Fillet PropertyManager. Fillet1 is displayed in the FeatureManager.

🔅 Two Fillet PropertyManager tabs are available. Use the Manual tab to control features for all Fillet types. Use the FilletXpert tab when you want SOLIDWORKS to manage the structure of the underlying features only for a Constant radius Fillet type. Click the ⑦ button for additional information.

Fit the model to the Graphics window.
155) Press the **f** key.

Edit the Fillet feature.
156) Zoom in on the left side of the Extrude-Thin1 feature.

157) Right-click **Fillet1** from the FeatureManager.

158) Click **Edit Feature** from the Context toolbar. The Fillet1 PropertyManager is displayed.

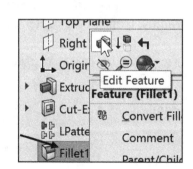

159) Click the **left top edge** and **left bottom edge**. Edge<3> and Edge <4> are added to the Items To Fillet box.

160) Click **OK** ✔ from the Fillet1 PropertyManager. The four edges have a Fillet feature with a .250in radius.

Display an Isometric view.

161) Click **Isometric view** ⬡ from the Heads-up View toolbar.

Save the ANGLE-13HOLE part.

162) Click **Save** 💾.

💡 This book is designed to expose the new SOLIDWORKS user to many different tools, techniques and procedures. It may not always use the most direct tool or process.

Activity: ANGLE-13HOLE Part-Second Extruded Cut/Linear Pattern

Insert a new sketch for the second Extruded Cut feature.

163) Right-click the **front face** of the Extrude-Thin1 feature in the Graphics window. The front face is the Sketch plane.

164) Click **Sketch** 🖊 from the Context toolbar. The Sketch toolbar is displayed.

165) Click **Front view** ⬛ from the Heads-up View toolbar.

166) Click **Wireframe** ⬚ from the Heads-up View toolbar to display LPattern1.

Note: Do not align the center point of the circle with the center point of the LPattern1 feature. Do not align the center point of the circle with the center point of the Fillet radius. Control the center point position with dimensions.

167) Click the **Circle** ⊙ Sketch tool. The cursor displays the Circle icon.

168) Sketch a **circle** on the left side of the Origin between the two LPattern1 holes as illustrated.

Add dimensions.

169) Click the **Smart Dimension** Sketch tool.

170) Click the **Origin**.

171) Click the **center point** of the circle.

172) Click a **position** below the horizontal profile line. Enter **3.000**in, [**76.20**].

173) Click the **Green Check mark**.

174) Click the **top horizontal line**.

175) Click the **center point** of the circle.

176) Click a **position** to the left of the profile.

177) Enter **.250**in, [**6.35**]. Click the **Green Check mark**.

178) Click the **circumference** of the circle.

179) Click a **position** above the profile.

180) Enter **.190**in, [**4.83**].

181) Click the **Green Check mark**.

Insert an Extruded Cut Feature.

182) Click **Extruded Cut** from the Features toolbar. The Cut-Extrude PropertyManager is displayed.

183) Select **Through All** for End Condition in Direction1. Accept the default conditions.

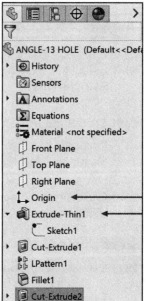

184) Click **OK** from the Cut-Extrude PropertyManager. Cut-Extrude2 is displayed in the FeatureManager.

Create the second Linear Pattern Feature.

185) Click **Linear Pattern** from the Features toolbar. The Linear Pattern FeatureManager is displayed. Cut-Extrude2 is displayed in the Features to Pattern box.

186) Click inside the **Pattern Direction** box.

187) Click the **top horizontal edge** of the Extrude-Thin1 feature for Direction1. Edge<1> is displayed in the Pattern Direction box. The Direction arrow points to the right. If required, click the **Reverse Direction** button.

188) Enter **3.000**in, **[76.20]** for Spacing.

189) Enter **3** for Number of Instances. Note: Cut-Extrude2 (Seed feature) is displayed in the Features to Pattern box. Check the **Geometry pattern** box under Options.

190) Click **OK** ✔ from the Linear Pattern PropertyManager. LPattern2 is displayed in the FeatureManager.

Display an Isometric view - Shaded With Edges.

191) Click **Isometric view** 🔲 from the Heads-up View toolbar.

192) Click **Shaded With Edges** 🔲 from the Heads-up View toolbar.

Save the ANGLE-13HOLE part.

193) Click **Save** 🔲.

Activity: ANGLE-13HOLE Part-Third Extruded Cut

Insert a new sketch for the third Extruded Cut Feature.

194) Select the Sketch plane. Right-click the **front face** of Extrude-Thin1.

195) Click **Sketch** 🔲 from the Context toolbar. The Sketch toolbar is displayed. Click **Front view** 🔲 from the Heads-up View toolbar.

196) Click **Hidden Lines Removed** 🔲 from the Heads-up View toolbar.

Sketch a vertical centerline.

197) Click the **Centerline** ⌀ Sketch tool. The Insert Line PropertyManager is displayed.

198) Click the **Origin** ⌀.

199) Click a **vertical position** above the top horizontal line as illustrated.

200) Click **Tools, Sketch Tools, Dynamic Mirror** from the Menu bar.

201) Click the **centerline** in the Graphics window.

Sketch a rectangle.

202) Click **Wireframe** ⊞ from the Heads-up View toolbar.

Apply the Straight Slot Sketch tool. Sketch a straight slot using two end points and a point for height.

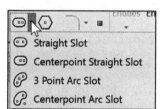

203) Click the **Straight Slot** ⬭ Sketch tool from the Consolidated Slot toolbar. Do not align the rectangle first point and second point to the center points of Lpattern1.

204) Click the **first point** of the rectangle to the left of the Origin as illustrated.

205) Click the **second point** directly to the right.

206) Click the **third point** to create the slot as illustrated. View the two slots on the model.

207) Click **OK** ✔ from the Slot PropertyManager.

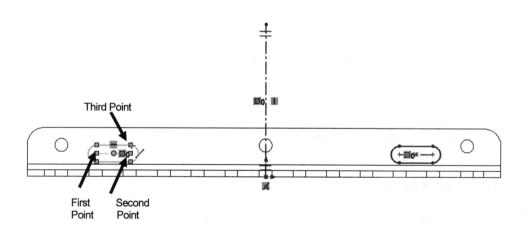

Deactivate the Dynamic Mirror tool.
208) Click **Tools**, **Sketch Tools**, **Dynamic Mirror** from the Menu bar.

Add a Concentric relation.
209) **Zoom in** on the centerline.

210) Click the **top end point** of the centerline.

211) Hold the **Ctrl** key down.

212) Click the **circumference** of the circle.

213) Release the **Ctrl** key.

214) Click **Concentric** from the Add Relations box.

The endpoint of the centerline is positioned in the center of the circle. Note: Right-click Clear Selections to remove selected entities from the Add Relations box.

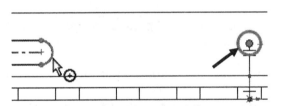

Add an Equal relation.
215) Click the circumference of the **circle**.

216) Hold the **Ctrl** key down.

217) Click the **left arc** of the first rectangle.

218) Release the **Ctrl** key.

219) Click **Equal** ＝ from the Add Relations box. The arc radius is equal to the circle radius.

Add a Horizontal relation.
220) Click the **top end point** of the centerline as illustrated.

221) Hold the **Ctrl** key down.

222) Click the **center point** of the left arc of the first rectangle.

223) Release the **Ctrl** key.

224) Click **Horizontal** ― from the Add Relations box.

225) Click **OK** ✓ from the Properties PropertyManager.

The right arc is horizontally aligned to the left arc due to symmetry from the Sketch Mirror tool.

Add dimensions. Dimension the distance between the two slots.

226) Click the **Smart Dimension** Sketch tool.

227) Click the **right arc center point** of the left slot.

228) Click the **left arc center point** of the right slot.

229) Click a **position** above the top horizontal line.

230) Enter **1.000**in, **[25.40]** in the Modify dialog box.

231) Click the **Green Check mark** .

232) Click the **left center point** of the left arc.

233) Click the **right center point** of the left arc.

234) Click a **position** above the top horizontal line.

235) Enter **2.000**in, **[50.80]** in the Modify dialog box.

236) Click the **Green Check mark** . The black sketch is fully defined.

Display an Isometric view.

237) Click **Isometric view** .

Origin and Tangent edges are displayed for educational purposes.

Insert an Extruded Cut Feature.

238) Click **Extruded Cut** from the
Features toolbar. The
Cut-Extrude PropertyManager is
displayed.

239) Select **Through All** for End
Condition in Direction1. The
direction arrow points to the back.

240) Click **OK** ✔ from the Extrude
PropertyManager. Cut-Extrude3 is
displayed in the FeatureManager.

Display Shaded With Edges.

241) Click **Shaded With Edges** 🔲 from
the Heads-up View toolbar.

Save the ANGLE-13HOLE part.

242) Click **Save** 💾. The ANGLE-
13HOLE is complete. All sketches
in the FeatureManager should be
fully defined.

 Model about the origin; it provides a point of reference.

The dimension between the two slots is over-defined if the arc center points are aligned
to the center points of the LPattern1 feature. An over-defined sketch is displayed in red,
in the FeatureManager.

The mouse pointer displays a blue dashed line when horizontal
and vertical sketch references are inferred.

Add relations, then dimensions. This will
keep the user from having too many
unnecessary dimensions. This helps to show
the design intent of the model.

Right-click and drag in the Graphics area to
display the mouse gesture wheel. Customize
the default commands for a sketch, part,
assembly or drawing document.

Review the ANGLE-13HOLE Part

The ANGLE-13HOLE part utilized an open L-Shaped profile sketched on the Right Plane. The Extruded Thin feature with the Mid Plane option located the part symmetrical to the Right Plane. The first Extruded Cut feature created the first hole sketched on the top face of the Extruded Thin feature.

The first Linear Pattern feature created an array of 13 holes along the bottom horizontal edge. The Fillet feature rounded the four corners. The second Extruded Cut feature created a hole on the Front face. The second Linear Pattern feature created an array of 3 holes along the top horizontal edge. The third Extruded Cut feature created two slot cuts using the Straight Slot Sketch tool.

Additional details on Extruded Base/Thin, Extruded Cut, Linear Pattern, Fillet, Mirror Entities, Add Relations, Slot, Straight Slot, Centerline, Line, Rectangle, and Smart Dimensions are available in Help. Keywords: Extruded Boss/Base - Thin, Extruded Cut, Patterns, Fillet, Sketch Entities, Sketch tools, and dimensions.

TRIANGLE Part

The TRIANGLE part is a multipurpose supporting plane.

The TRIANGLE is manufactured from .090in, [2.3] aluminum. The TRIANGLE contains numerous features.

Utilize symmetry and Sketch tools to simplify the geometry creation.

The center points of the slots and holes locate key geometry for the TRIANGLE.

Utilize sketched construction geometry to locate the center points.

☀ Construction geometry is not calculated in the extruded profile.

Utilize the Sketch Offset tool and Sketch Fillet to create the sketch profile for the Extruded Boss/Base 🗍 (Boss-Extrude1) feature.

Utilize the Dynamic Mirror Sketch tool and the Circle Sketch tool to create the first Extruded Cut 🗔 feature.

Utilize the Corner Rectangle, Trim, and the Tangent Arc Sketch tools to create the second Extruded Cut 🗔 feature left bottom slot.

Note: A goal of this book is to expose the new user to different tools and methods. You can also apply the Straight Slot Sketch tool and eliminate steps.

Utilize the Mirror 🕮 feature to create the right bottom slot.

Utilize the Straight Slot Sketch tool to create the third Extruded Cut 🗔 feature.

Utilize the Circular Pattern feature to create the three radial slot cuts.

Activity: TRIANGLE Part-Mirror, Offset and Fillet Sketch Tools

Create a New part.

243) Click **New** ⬜ from the Menu bar. Click the **Templates** tab.

244) Double-click **Part**. The Part FeatureManager is displayed.

Save the part.

245) Click **Save As** from the drop-down Menu bar.

246) Select **SW-TUTORIAL-2017** for the Save in file folder.

247) Enter **TRIANGLE** for File name.

248) Enter **TRIANGLE** for Description.

249) Click **Save**. The TRIANGLE FeatureManager is displayed.

Set the dimensioning standard and part unit.

250) Click **Options** ⚙ from the Main menu.

251) Click the **Document Properties** tab from the dialog box.

252) Select **ANSI** from the Overall drafting standard box.

253) Click **Units**.

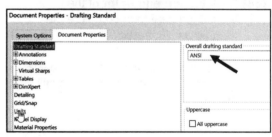

254) Click **IPS**, [**MMGS**] for Unit system.

255) Select **.123**, [**.12**] for Length units Decimal places.

256) Select **None** for Angular units Decimal places.

257) Click **OK** to set the document units.

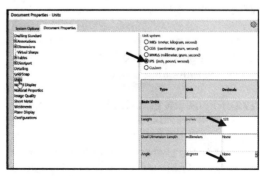

Insert a new sketch for the Extruded Base feature.
258) Right-click **Front Plane** from the FeatureManager.

259) Click **Sketch** ⌐ from the Context toolbar. The Sketch toolbar is displayed.

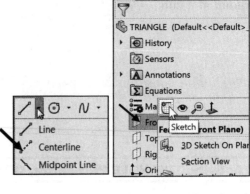

Sketch a vertical centerline.
260) Click the **Centerline** ⌐ Sketch tool.

261) Click the **Origin** ↳. Click a vertical **position** above the Origin as illustrated.

Deselect the Centerline Sketch tool.
262) Right-click **Select**.

Sketch a Mirrored profile.
263) Click **Tools**, **Sketch Tools**, **Dynamic Mirror** from the Menu bar.

264) Click the **centerline** in the Graphics window.

265) Click the **Centerline** ⌐ Sketch tool.

266) Click the **Origin** ↳.

267) Click a **position** to the left of the Origin to create a horizontal line.

268) Click the **top end point** of the vertical centerline to complete the triangle as illustrated.

269) Right-click **End Chain** to end the line segment. The Centerline tool is still active.

270) Click the **Origin** ↳.

271) Click a **position** coincident with the right-angled centerline. *Do not select the Midpoint.*

272) Right-click **End Chain** to end the line segment.

Deactivate the Dynamic Mirror Sketch tool.
273) Click **Tools**, **Sketch Tools**, **Dynamic Mirror** from the Menu bar.

Add a dimension.

274) Click **Smart Dimension** from the Sketch toolbar.

275) Click the **right horizontal** centerline.

276) Click the **inside right** centerline.

277) Click a **position** between the two lines.

278) Enter **45**deg in the Modify dialog box for the angular dimension.

279) Click the **Green Check mark** in the Modify dialog box.

280) Click the **horizontal centerline**.

281) Click a position **below** the centerline.

282) Enter **3.000**in, **[76.20]**.

283) Click the **Green Check mark** in the Modify dialog box.

284) Click the **left angled** centerline.

285) Click **position** aligned to the left angled centerline.

286) Enter **2.120**in, **[53.85]**.

287) Click the **Green Check mark** in the Modify dialog box.

Offset the sketch.
288) Right-click **Select** in the Graphics window.

289) Hold the **Ctrl** key down.

290) Click the **three outside centerlines**: Line2, Line4, and Line5 are displayed in the Selected Entities box.

291) Release the **Ctrl** key.

292) Click the **Offset Entities** Sketch tool.

293) Enter **.250**in, **[6.35]** for Offset Distance. The yellow Offset direction is outward.

294) Click **OK** ✔ from the Offset Entities PropertyManager. If needed, deactivate the Sketch relations in the Graphics window.

Three profile lines are displayed. The centerlines are on the inside.

Insert the Sketch Fillet.

295) Click **Sketch Fillet** ⌐ from the Sketch toolbar. The Sketch Fillet PropertyManager is displayed.

296) Enter **.250**in, **[6.35]** for Radius.

297) Click the **three outside corner** points.

298) Click **OK** ✔ from the Sketch Fillet PropertyManager.

299) Click **OK** ✔ from the Sketch Fillet PropertyManager.

Activity: TRIANGLE Part-Extruded Boss/Base Feature

Extrude the sketch. Create the Boss-Extrude1 feature.

300) Click **Extruded Boss/Base** 🗊 from the Features toolbar. Blind is the default End Condition in Direction1.

301) Enter **.090**in, **[2.3]** for Depth in Direction 1. The direction arrow points to the front.

302) Click **OK** ✔ from the Boss-Extrude PropertyManager. Boss-Extrude1 is displayed in the FeatureManager.

Display an Isometric view. Save the TRIANGLE part.

303) Click **Isometric view** 🗗 from the Heads-up View toolbar.

304) Click **Save** 💾.

🔆 Insert centerlines and relations to build sketches that are referenced by multiple features.

Display Sketch1.

305) Expand Boss-Extrude1 in the FeatureManager.

306) Right-click **Sketch1**.

307) Click **Show**.

Activity: TRIANGLE Part-First Extruded Cut Feature

Insert a new sketch for the first Extruded Cut.

308) Right-click the **front face** of Boss-Extrude1. This is your Sketch plane.

309) Click **Sketch** ⬚ from the Context toolbar. The Sketch toolbar is displayed.

310) Click **Front view** 🔲 from the Heads-up View toolbar.

311) Display **Hidden Lines Removed**.

312) Click the **Circle** ⊙ Sketch tool. The Circle PropertyManager is displayed.

313) Sketch a **circle** centered at the Origin.

314) Sketch a **circle** centered at the endpoint of the vertical centerline as illustrated.

Sketch a vertical centerline.

315) Click the **Centerline** ✏ Sketch tool.

316) Click the **Origin** ⤫.

317) Click the **center point** of the top circle.

Deselect the Centerline Sketch tool.

318) Right-click **Select**.

Sketch a Mirrored profile.

319) Click **Tools**, **Sketch Tools**, **Dynamic Mirror** from the Menu bar.

320) Click the **centerline** in the Graphics window.

321) Click the **Circle** ⊙ Sketch tool. The Circle PropertyManager is displayed.

322) Sketch a **circle** on the left side of the centerline, coincident with the left centerline, in the lower half of the triangle.

323) Sketch a **circle** on the left side of the centerline, coincident with the left centerline, in the upper half of the triangle. Right-click **Select.**

324) Deactivate the Dynamic Mirror tool. Click **Tools, Sketch Tools, Dynamic Mirror** from the Menu bar.

Add an Equal relation.
325) Click a **circle**. Hold the **Ctrl** key down.

326) Click the five other **circles**. Release the **Ctrl** key.

327) Click **Make Equal** = from the Pop-up menu.

Add a dimension.
328) Click the **Smart Dimension** Sketch tool.

329) Click the circumference of the **top circle**.

330) Click a **position** off the TRIANGLE.

331) Enter **.190**in, **[4.83]**. Click the **Green Check mark** in the Modify dialog box.

Create the aligned dimensions.
332) Click the bottom **left point**. Click the **center point** of the bottom left circle.

333) Click a **position** aligned to the angled centerline.

334) Enter **.710**in, **[18.03]**.

335) Click the **Green Check mark** in the Modify dialog box. Click the **bottom left point**.

336) Click the **center point** of the top left circle as illustrated.

337) Click a **position** aligned to the angled centerline. Enter **1.410**in, **[35.81]**.

338) Click the **Green Check mark** in the Modify dialog box. The sketch is fully defined.

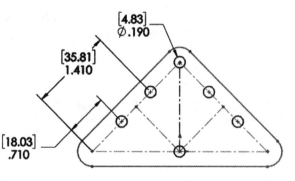

Insert an Extruded Cut Feature.

339) Click **Extruded Cut** from the
Features toolbar. The Cut-Extrude
PropertyManager is displayed.

340) Select **Through All** for the End
Condition in Direction1.

341) Click **OK** ✔ from the Cut-Extrude
PropertyManager. Cut-Extrude1 is
displayed in the FeatureManager.

Display an Isometric view. Save the model.

342) Click **Isometric view** 🧊 from the Heads-up View toolbar.

343) Click **Save** 💾.

Activity: TRIANGLE Part-Second Extruded Cut Feature

Insert a new slot sketch for the second Extruded Cut.

344) Right-click the **front face** of Boss-Extrude1 for the Sketch
plane.

345) Click **Sketch** 🖊 from the Context toolbar. The Sketch
toolbar is displayed.

346) Click **Front view** 🔲 from the Heads-up View toolbar.

347) Click the **Corner Rectangle** ▭ tool from the Consolidated
Sketch toolbar. Note: The purpose of this book
is to teach you different tools and methods. You
can also apply the Straight Slot Sketch tool and
eliminate many of the next steps.

348) Sketch a **rectangle** to the left of the Origin as
illustrated.

Trim the vertical lines.

349) Click the **Trim Entities** ✂ Sketch tool. The Trim
PropertyManager is displayed.

350) Click **Trim to closest** in the Options box. The Trim to
closest ✂ icon is displayed. Click the **left vertical** line
of the rectangle.

351) Click the **right vertical** line of the rectangle.

352) Click **OK** ✔ from the Trim PropertyManager.

Sketch the Tangent Arcs.

353) Click the **Tangent Arc** Sketch tool from the Consolidated Sketch toolbar. The Arc PropertyManager is displayed.

354) Sketch a **180° arc** on the left side.

355) Sketch a **180° arc** on the right side.

356) Click **OK** from the Arc PropertyManager.

Add an Equal relation.
357) Click the **right arc**. Hold the **Ctrl** key down.

358) Click the **left arc**. Click the **bottom center circle**. Release the **Ctrl** key.

359) Click **Make Equal** = from the Pop-up menu. Click **OK** from the Properties PropertyManager.

Add a Coincident relation.
360) Press the **f** key to fit the model to the Graphics window.

361) Click the **center point** of the left arc.

362) Hold the **Ctrl** key down.

363) Click the **left lower point** as illustrated.

364) Release the **Ctrl** key.

365) Click **Coincident** from the Add Relations box.

Add a Tangent relation.
366) Click the bottom horizontal line.

367) Hold the **Ctrl** key down. Click the **first arc tangent**.

368) Release the **Ctrl** key.

369) Click **Tangent** from the Add Relations box.

370) Click **OK** from the Properties PropertyManager.

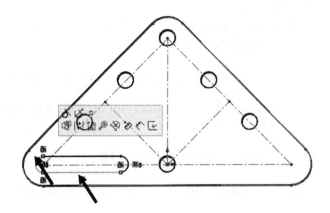

Add a dimension.

371) Click the **Smart Dimension** Sketch tool.

372) Click the **left center point** of the left arc.

373) Click the **right center point** of the right arc.

374) Click a **position** below the horizontal line.

375) Enter **1.000**in, **[25.40]** in the Modify dialog box.

376) Click the **Green Check mark** ✔.

Insert an Extruded Cut feature.

377) Click **Isometric view** 🔲.

378) Click **Extruded Cut** 🔲 from the Features toolbar. The Cut-Extrude PropertyManager is displayed.

379) Select **Through All** for End Condition in Direction 1.

380) Click **OK** ✔ from the Cut-Extrude PropertyManager.

Save the model.

381) Click **Save** 💾. Cut-Extrude2 is highlighted in the FeatureManager.

Activity: TRIANGLE Part-Mirror Feature

Mirror the Cut-Extrude2 feature.

382) Click **Mirror** ⊨⊧ from the Features toolbar. The Mirror PropertyManager is displayed. Cut-Extrude2 is displayed in the Feature to Mirror box.

383) Click **Right Plane** from the fly-out TRIANGLE FeatureManager. Right Plane is displayed in the Mirror Face/Plane box.

384) Check the **Geometry Pattern** box.

385) Click **OK** ✔ from the Mirror PropertyManager. Mirror1 is displayed in the FeatureManager.

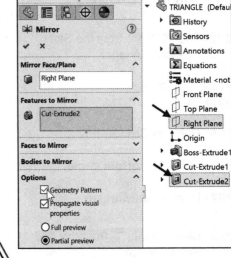

Activity: TRIANGLE Part-Third Extruded Cut Feature

Insert a new sketch for the third Extruded Cut feature.
386) Right-click the **front face** of Boss-Extrude1 for the Sketch
plane.

387) Click **Sketch** from the Context toolbar. The Sketch toolbar is
displayed.

388) Click **Front view** .

Sketch a Straight Slot.
389) Click the **Straight Slot** Sketch tool from the Consolidated
Rectangle toolbar. The Straight Slot icon is displayed.

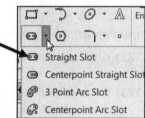

390) Click a **position** coincident with the left angled centerline as
illustrated.

Sketch the second point.
391) Click a **position** aligned to the centerline.
A dashed line is displayed.

Sketch the third point.
392) Click a **position** above the inside left
centerline. The Straight Slot sketch is
displayed.

Click the Question mark ⑦ in the
PropertyManager to obtain additional
information on the tool.

393) Click **OK** from the Slot
PropertyManager.

First point

Second point

Add an Equal relation.
394) Click the **left arc**.

395) Hold the **Ctrl** key down.

396) Click the **bottom circle**.

397) Release the **Ctrl** key.

398) Click **Equal** = from the Add
Relations box.

Add a dimension.

399) Click the **Smart Dimension** ✎ Sketch tool.

400) Click the **left center point** of the left arc.

401) Click the **right center point** of the right arc.

402) Click a **position** below the horizontal line.

403) Enter **.560**in, **[14.22]** in the Modify dialog box.

404) Click the **Green Check mark** ✔. The sketch is fully defined.

Insert an Extruded Cut Feature.

405) Click **Isometric view** 🔳.

406) Click **Extruded Cut** 🔳 from the Features toolbar. The Cut-Extrude PropertyManager is displayed.

407) Select **Through All** for the End Condition in Direction 1.

408) Click **OK** ✔ from the Cut-Extrude PropertyManager. Cut-Extrude3 is displayed in the FeatureManager.

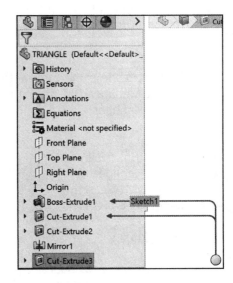

Save the model.

409) Click **Save** 💾.

Display the Temporary Axis.

410) Click **View, Hide/Show, check Temporary Axes** from the Menu bar.

This book is designed to expose the new SOLIDWORKS user to many different tools, techniques and procedures. It may not always use the most direct tool or process.

Activity: TRIANGLE Part-Circular Pattern Feature

Insert a Circular Pattern feature.

411) Click **Circular Pattern** from the Features Consolidated toolbar. The Circular Pattern PropertyManager is displayed. Cut-Extrude3 is displayed in the Features to Pattern box.

412) Click the **Temporary Axis** displayed through the center hole located at the Origin. The Temporary Axis is displayed as Axis <1> in the Pattern Axis box.

413) Enter **90**deg for Angle.

414) Enter **3** for Number of Instances.

415) Check the **Equal spacing** box. If required, click **Reverse Direction**. Click the **Geometry pattern** box.

416) Click **OK** from the Circular Pattern PropertyManager. CirPattern1 is displayed in the FeatureManager.

Hide Sketch1.
417) Expand Boss-Extrude1 from the FeatureManager.

418) Right-click **Sketch1**.

419) Click **Hide**.

Display an Isometric view. Deactivate the Temporary Axes. Save the TRIANGLE part.
420) Click **Isometric view**.

421) Click **View**, **Hide/Show**, un-check **Temporary Axes** from the Menu bar.

422) Display **Shaded with Edges**.

423) Click **Save**. The TRIANGLE part is complete.

 Model about the origin; it provides a point of reference.

Review the TRIANGLE Part

The TRIANGLE part utilized a Boss-Extrude1 feature. A triangular shape profile was sketched on the Front Plane. Symmetry and construction geometry sketch tools located center points for slots and holes.

The Sketch Fillet tool created rounded corners for the profile. The Sketch Mirror and Circle Sketch tools were utilized to create the Extruded Cut features.

The Corner Rectangle, Sketch Trim, and Tangent Arc tools were utilized to create the second Extruded Cut feature, left bottom slot. The Mirror feature was utilized to create the right bottom slot.

The Parallelogram and Tangent Arc Sketch tools were utilized to create the third Extruded Cut feature. The Circular Pattern feature created the three radial slot cuts. The following Geometric relations were utilized: *Equal, Parallel, Coincident* and *Tangent*.

Additional details on Rectangle, Circle, Tangent Arc, Parallelogram, Mirror Entities, Sketch Fillet, Offset Entities, Extruded Boss/Base, Extruded Cut, Mirror and Circular Pattern are available in SOLIDWORKS Help.

SCREW Part

The SCREW part is a simplified model of a 10-24 x 3/8 Machine screw. Screws, nuts and washers are classified as fasteners. An assembly contains hundreds of fasteners. Utilize simplified versions to conserve model and rebuild time.

Machine screws are described in terms of the following:
- Nominal diameter - Size 10.

- Threads per inch - 24.

Simplified version

- Length - 3/8.

Screw diameter, less than ¼ inch, is represented by a size number. Size 10 refers to a diameter of .190 inch. Utilize the SCREW part to fasten components in the FRONT-SUPPORT assembly.

The SCREW part utilizes a Revolved Base feature to add material. The Revolved Boss/Base feature requires a centerline and sketch on a Sketch plane. A Revolved feature requires an angle of revolution. The sketch is revolved around the centerline.

Sketch a centerline on the Front Sketch plane.

Sketch a closed profile.

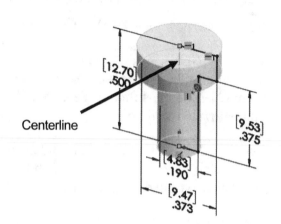

Revolve the sketch 360 degrees.

Utilize the Edit Sketch tool to modify the sketch. Utilize the Sketch Trim and Tangent Arc tool to create a new profile.

Utilize an Extruded Cut feature sketched on the Front Plane. This is the seed feature for the Circular Pattern.

Utilize the Circular Pattern feature to create four instances.

Apply the Fillet feature to round edges and faces. Utilize the Fillet feature to round the top edge.

Apply the Chamfer feature to bevel edges and faces. Utilize a Chamfer feature to bevel the bottom face.

Note: Utilize an M5 Machine screw for metric units.

Activity: SCREW Part-Documents Properties

Create a New part.

424) Click **New** 📄 from the Menu bar.

425) Click the **Templates** tab. Double-click **Part**.

Save the part.

426) Click **Save As** from the drop-down Menu bar. Select **SW-TUTORIAL-2017** for the Save in file folder.

427) Enter **SCREW** for File name. Enter **MACHINE SCREW 10-24x3/8** for Description.

428) Click **Save**. The SCREW FeatureManager is displayed.

Set the dimensioning standard and part unit.

429) Click **Options** ⚙ from the Main menu.

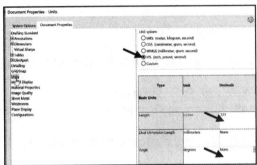

430) Click the **Documents Properties** tab from the dialog box. Select **ANSI** from the Overall drafting standard box.

431) Click **Units**. Select **IPS**, **[MMGS]** for Unit system. Select **.123**, **[.12]** for Length units Decimal places. Select **None** for Angular units Decimal places. Click **OK**.

Activity: SCREW Part-Revolved Feature

Insert a Revolved feature sketched on the Front Plane. The Front Plane is the default Sketch plane.

Insert a new sketch.

432) Right-click **Front Plane** from the FeatureManager.

433) Click **Sketch** 📝 from the Context toolbar. The Sketch toolbar is displayed.

434) Click the **Centerline** ⟋ Sketch tool. The Insert Line PropertyManager is displayed.

Sketch a vertical centerline.

435) Click the **Origin** ⊥ .

436) Click a **position** directly above the Origin as illustrated.

Origin

437) Right-click **End Chain** to end the centerline.

Add a dimension.
438) Click the **Smart Dimension** ✎ Sketch tool.

439) Click the **centerline**. Click a **position** to the left.

440) Enter .500in, [12.70]. Click the **Green Check mark** ✓.

Fit the sketch to the Graphics Window.
441) Press the **f** key.

Sketch the profile.
442) Click the **Line** ✐ Sketch tool.

Sketch the first horizontal line.

443) Click the **Origin** ↧.

444) Click a **position** to the right of the Origin.

Sketch the first vertical line.
445) Click a position **above** the horizontal line endpoint.

446) Sketch the second **horizontal line**.

447) Sketch the second **vertical line**. The top point of the vertical line is collinear with the top point of the centerline.

Origin

448) Sketch the third **horizontal line**. The left endpoint of the horizontal line is coincident with the top point of the centerline.

449) Right-click **Select** to deselect the Line Sketch tool.

Add a Horizontal relation.
450) Click the **top** most right point. Hold the **Ctrl** key down.

451) Click the **top** most left point. Release the **Ctrl** key.

452) Click **Horizontal** ▬ from the Add Relations box.

453) Click **OK** ✓ from the Properties PropertyManager.

Add a dimension.
454) Click the **Smart Dimension** ✎ Sketch tool. Create the first diameter dimension.

455) Click the **centerline** in the Graphics window. Click the **first vertical line**.

456) Click a **position** to the left of the Origin to create a diameter dimension.

457) Enter **.190**in, **[4.83]**.

458) Click the **Green Check mark** ✔.

A diameter dimension for a Revolved sketch requires a centerline, profile line, and a dimension position to the left of the centerline.

A dimension position directly below the bottom horizontal line creates a radial dimension.

Create the second diameter dimension.
459) Click the **centerline** in the Graphics window.

460) Click the **second vertical line**.

461) Click a **position** to the left of the Origin to create a diameter dimension.

462) Enter **.373**in, **[9.47]**.

Create a vertical dimension.
463) Click the **first vertical line**.

464) Click a **position** to the right of the line.

465) Enter **.375**in, **[9.53]**.

Center the dimension text.
466) Click the **.190**in, **[4.83]** dimension.

467) Drag the **text** between the two extension lines.

468) Click the **.373**in, **[9.47]** dimension.

469) Drag the **text** between the two extension lines. If required, click the **blue arrow dots** to flip the arrows inside the extension lines.

470) Right-click **Select** to deselect the Smart Dimension Sketch tool.

Select the Centerline for axis of revolution.
471) Click the **vertical centerline** as illustrated.

Revolve the sketch.

472) Click **Revolved Boss/Base** 🍥 from the Features toolbar.

473) Click **Yes**. The Revolve PropertyManager is displayed.

The "Yes" button causes a vertical line to be automatically sketched from the top left point to the Origin. The Graphics window displays the Isometric view and a preview of the Revolved Base feature.

The Revolve PropertyManager displays 360 degrees for the Angle of Revolution.

474) Click **OK** ✔ from the Revolve PropertyManager.

The FeatureManager displays the Revolve1 name for the first feature. The Revolved Boss/Base feature requires a centerline, sketch, and an angle of revolution. A solid Revolved Boss/Base feature requires a closed sketch. Draw the sketch on one side of the centerline.

The SCREW requires a rounded profile. Edit the Revolved Base sketch. Insert a Tangent Arc.

Edit the Revolved Base sketch.
475) Right-click **Revolve1** in the FeatureManager.

476) Click **Edit Sketch** ✎ from the Context toolbar.

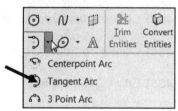

477) Click **Front view** ▱.

478) Click the **Tangent Arc** ⌐ Sketch tool.

479) Click the **top centerline** point as illustrated.

480) Drag the **mouse pointer** to the right and downward.

481) Click a **position** collinear with the right vertical line, below the midpoint. The arc is displayed tangent to the top horizontal line.

Deselect the Tangent Arc Sketch tool.
482) Right-click **Select**.

Delete unwanted geometry.
483) Click the **Trim Entities** ⛌ Sketch tool. The Trim PropertyManager is displayed.

484) Click **Trim to closest** from the Options box. The Trim to closest icon is displayed.

485) Click the **right top vertical line** as illustrated.

486) Click the **top horizontal line** as illustrated. The two lines are removed.

487) Click **OK** ✔ from the Trim PropertyManager. Note: You may still view lines until you exit the sketch.

Add a dimension.
488) Click the **Smart Dimension** ◄ Sketch tool.

489) Click the **arc**.

490) Click a **position** above the profile.

491) Enter **.304**in, [**7.72**].

492) Click the **Green Check mark** ✔ . The sketch should be fully defined; if not, add a .05 inch dimension as illustrated.

Exit the Sketch. Save the model.
493) Click **Exit Sketch** from the Sketch toolbar.

494) Click **Save** 🖫 .

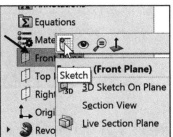

The SCREW requires an Extruded Cut feature on the Front Plane. Utilize the Convert Entities Sketch tool to extract the Revolved Base top arc edge for the profile of the Extruded Cut.

Activity: SCREW Part-Extruded Cut Feature

Insert a new sketch for the Extruded Cut feature.
495) Right-click **Front Plane** from the FeatureManager.

496) Click **Sketch** 🖉 from the Context toolbar. The Sketch toolbar is displayed.

497) Click the **top arc** as illustrated. The mouse pointer displays the silhouette edge icon for feedback.

498) Click the **Convert Entities** 🗊 Sketch tool.

499) Click the **Line** ╱ Sketch tool.

500) Sketch a **vertical line**. The top endpoint of the line is coincident with the arc, vertically aligned to the Origin.

501) Sketch a **horizontal line**. The right end point of the line is coincident with the arc. Do not select the arc midpoint. Right-click **Select**.

502) Click **Isometric view** .

503) Click the **Trim Entities** Sketch tool. The Trim PropertyManager is displayed.

504) Click **Power trim** from the Options box.

505) Click and drag the mouse pointer to **intersect** the **right** arc line as illustrated.

506) If needed, click and drag the mouse pointer to **intersect** the **left** arc line as illustrated.

507) Click **OK** from the Trim PropertyManager.

Add a dimension.

508) Click the **Smart Dimension** Sketch tool.

509) Click the **vertical line**.

510) Click a **position** to the right of the profile.

511) Enter .030in, [0.76].

512) Click the **Green Check mark** .

Insert an Extruded Cut Feature.

513) Click **Isometric view** .

514) Click **Extruded Cut** from the Features toolbar. The Cut-Extrude PropertyManager is displayed.

515) Select **Mid Plane** for the End Condition in Direction 1.

516) Enter .050in, [1.27] for Depth.

517) Click **OK** from the Cut-Extrude PropertyManager. Cut-Extrude1 is displayed in the FeatureManager.

Activity: SCREW Part-Circular Pattern Feature

Insert the Circular Pattern feature.
518) Click **View**, **Hide/Show,** check **Temporary Axes**
from the Menu bar. The Temporary Axis is required
for the Circular Pattern feature.

519) Click **Circular Pattern** from the Features
Consolidated toolbar. Cut-Extrude1 is displayed in
the Features to Pattern box.

520) Click the **Temporary Axis** in the Graphics window.
Axis<1> is displayed in the Pattern Axis box.

521) Check the **Equal spacing** box.

522) Enter **360**deg for Angle.

523) Enter **4** for Number of Instances. Check the **Geometry pattern**
box.

524) Click **OK** from the Circular Pattern PropertyManager.
CirPattern1 is displayed in the FeatureManager.

Save the model.
525) Click **Save** .

Use Symmetry. When possible and if it makes sense,
model objects symmetrically about the origin.

Activity: SCREW Part-Fillet Feature

Insert a Constant Radius Fillet Type feature.
526) Click the **top circular edge** as illustrated.

527) Click **Fillet** from the Features
toolbar. The Fillet
PropertyManager is displayed.

528) Click the **Manual** tab. Edge<1> is
displayed in the Items to Fillet box.

529) Click the **Constant Radius Fillet**
icon for Fillet Type.

530) Enter **.010**in, [.**25**] for Radius.

531) Click **OK** from the Fillet
PropertyManager. Fillet1 is displayed in the FeatureManager.

Activity: SCREW Part-Chamfer Feature

Insert the Chamfer feature.
532) Click the **bottom circular edge**.

533) Click **Chamfer** from the Features
Consolidated toolbar. Edge<1> is
displayed in the Items to Chamfer box.

534) Click **Angle distance** for type.

535) Enter .**050**in, [**1.27**] for Distance. View
the direction of the arrow.

536) Click **OK** ✔ from the Chamfer
PropertyManager. Chamfer1 is
displayed in the FeatureManager.

💡 Simplify the part. Save rebuild time.
Suppress features that are not required in the assembly.

A suppressed feature is not displayed in the Graphics window. A
suppressed feature is removed from any rebuild calculations.

Suppress the Fillet and Chamfer feature.
537) Hold the **Ctrl** key down.

538) Click **Fillet1** and **Chamfer1** from the FeatureManager.

539) Release the **Ctrl** key.

540) Right-click **Suppress** from the Context toolbar. Note:
Suppressed features are displayed in light gray in the
FeatureManager.

Deactivate the Temporary Axes in the Graphics window.
541) Click **View**, **Hide/Show,** un-check **Temporary Axes** from the
Menu bar.

Display an Isometric view. Save the SCREW part.
542) Click **Isometric view** from the Heads-up View toolbar.

543) Click **Save** .

Close all open documents.
544) Click **Window**, **Close All** from the Menu bar.

Review the SCREW Part.

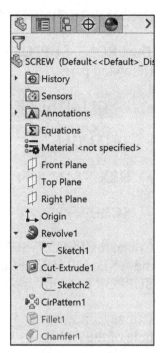

The Revolved Boss/Base feature was utilized to create the simplified SCREW part. The Revolved Boss/Base feature required a centerline sketched on the Front Sketch plane and a closed profile. The sketch was revolved 360 degrees to create the Base feature for the SCREW part.

Edit Sketch was utilized to modify the sketch. The Sketch Trim and Tangent Arc tools created a new profile.

The Extruded Cut feature was sketched on the Front Plane. The Circular Pattern feature created four instances. The Fillet feature rounded the top edges.

The Chamfer feature beveled the bottom edge. The Fillet and Chamfer are suppressed to save rebuild time in the assembly. Note: suppressed features are displayed in light gray in the FeatureManager.

Additional details on Convert Entities, Silhouette Edge, Revolved Boss/Base, Circular Pattern, Fillet, and Chamfer are available in SOLIDWORKS Help. Keywords: Sketch tools, silhouette, features, Pattern, Revolve, Fillet and Chamfer.

The Origin and Tangent edges are displayed for educational purposes.

Think design intent. When do you use the various End Conditions and Geometric sketch relations? What are you trying to do with the design? How does the component fit into an assembly?

Mate to the first part added to the assembly. If you mate to the first part or base part of the assembly and decide to change its orientation later, all the parts will move with it.

View the provided videos on creating 2D Sketches, 3D Features and Assemblies to enhance your experience in the chapter.

FRONT-SUPPORT Assembly

The FRONT-SUPPORT assembly consists of the
following parts:

- ANGLE-13HOLE

- TRIANGLE

- HEX-STANDOFF

- SCREW

Create the FRONT-SUPPORT assembly. Insert
the ANGLE-13HOLE part. The ANGLE-13HOLE part is fixed to the FRONT-
SUPPORT Origin. Insert the first HEX-STANDOFF part.

Utilize Concentric and Coincident mates to assemble the HEX-STANDOFF to the left
hole of the ANGLE-13HOLE part. Insert the second HEX-STANDOFF part.

Utilize Concentric and Coincident mates to assemble the HEX-STANDOFF to the third
hole from the right side. Insert the TRIANGLE part. Utilize Concentric, Distance, and
Parallel mates to assemble the TRIANGLE. Utilize Concentric/Coincident SmartMates to
assemble the four SCREWS. Note: Other mate types can be used.

Determine the static and dynamic behavior of mates in each sub-assembly before
creating the top level assembly.

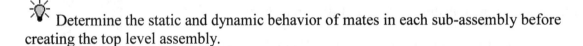

Activity: FRONT-SUPPORT Assembly-Insert ANGLE-13HOLE

Create a new assembly.

545) Click **New** ⬜ from the Menu bar.

546) Double-click **Assembly** from the Templates tab. The Begin Assembly
PropertyManager is displayed. The Begin Assembly PropertyManager is
displayed if the Start command when creating new assembly box is
checked.

547) Click the **Browse** button.

548) Browse to the **SW-TUTORIAL-2017** folder on your hard drive.

549) Double-click the **ANGLE-13HOLE** part.

Fix the first component to the Origin.

550) Click **OK** ✔ from the Begin Assembly PropertyManager. The first component is fixed to the Origin (f).

Save the assembly.

551) Click **Save As** from the drop-down Menu bar.

552) Select **SW-TUTORIAL-2017** for the Save in file folder.

553) Enter **FRONT-SUPPORT** for File name.

554) Enter **FRONT SUPPORT ASSEMBLY** for Description.

555) Click **Save**. The FRONT-SUPPORT assembly FeatureManager is displayed.

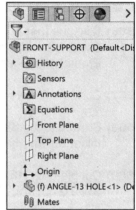

Set the dimensioning standard and assembly unit.

556) Click **Options** ⚙ from the Main menu.

557) Click the **Document Properties** tab from the dialog box.

558) Select **ANSI** from the Overall drafting standard box.

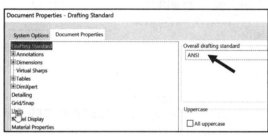

Set document units.

559) Click **Units**.

560) Select **IPS**, [**MMGS**] for Unit system.

561) Select **.123**, [**.12**] for Length units Decimal places.

562) Select **None** for Angular units Decimal places.

563) Click **OK**.

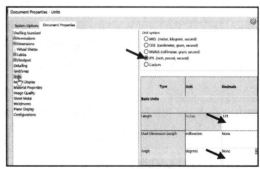

The ANGLE-13HOLE name in the FeatureManager displays an (f) symbol. The (f) symbol indicates that the ANGLE-13HOLE component is fixed to the FRONT-SUPPORT assembly Origin. The component cannot move or rotate.

🔅 To remove the fixed state, Right-click a component name in the FeatureManager. Click **Float**. The component is free to move.

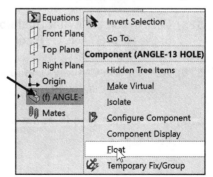

Display an Isometric view.

564) Click **Isometric view** 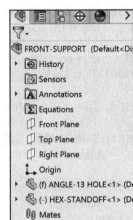 from the Heads-up View toolbar.

Save the assembly.

565) Click **Save** .

Activity: FRONT-SUPPORT Assembly-Insert HEX-STANDOFF

Insert the HEX-STANDOFF part.

566) Click the **Insert Components**
　　　Assembly tool. The Insert Component
　　　PropertyManager is displayed.

567) Click the **Browse** button.

568) Browse to the **SW-TUTORIAL-2017**
　　　folder on your hard drive.

569) Double-click **HEX-STANDOFF** from the
　　　SW-TUTORIAL 2017 folder.

570) Click a **position** near the left top front
　　　hole as illustrated.

Enlarge the view.
571) **Zoom in** on the front left side of the assembly.

Move the component.
572) Click and drag the **HEX-STANDOFF** component below the ANGLE-
　　　13HOLE left hole.

The HEX-STANDOFF name in the FeatureManager
displays a (-) minus sign. The minus sign indicates that
the HEX-STANDOFF part is free to move.

Insert a Concentric mate.
573) Click the **left inside cylindrical hole face** of the
　　　ANGLE-13HOLE component.

574) Hold the **Ctrl** key down.

575) Click inside the **cylindrical hole face**
　　　of the HEX-STANDOFF component.

576) Release the **Ctrl** key. The Mate pop-
　　　up menu is displayed.

577) Click **Concentric** from the Mate pop-
　　　up menu.

578) Click and drag the **HEX-STANDOFF** component below the ANGLE-13HOLE component until the top face is displayed.

Insert a Coincident mate.
579) Click the **HEX-STANDOFF top face**.

580) Press the **Up Arrow key** approximately 5 times to view the bottom face of the ANGLE-13HOLE component.

581) Hold the **Ctrl** key down.

582) Click the **ANGLE-13HOLE bottom face**.

583) Release the **Ctrl** key. The Mate pop-up menu is displayed.

584) Click **Coincident** from the Mate pop-up menu.

Display an Isometric view.
585) Click **Isometric view** .

586) Click and drag the **HEX-STANDOFF** component. The HEX-STANDOFF rotates about its axis.

Insert a Parallel mate.
587) Click **Front view** .

588) Click the **HEX-STANDOFF front face**.

589) Hold the **Ctrl** key down.

590) Click the **ANGLE-13HOLE front face**.

591) Release the **Ctrl** key. The Mate pop-up menu is displayed.

592) Click **Parallel** from the Mate pop-up menu.

Display the created mates.
593) Expand the Mates folder in the FRONT-SUPPORT FeatureManager. Three mates are displayed between the ANGLE-13HOLE component and the HEX-STANDOFF component. The HEX-STANDOFF component is fully defined.

Save the FRONT-SUPPORT assembly.
594) Click **Save** 💾.

Insert the second HEX-STANDOFF part.
595) Hold the **Ctrl** key down.

596) Click and drag the **HEX-STANDOFF<1>**
🔩 HEX-STANDOFF<1> name from the FeatureManager into
the FRONT-SUPPORT assembly Graphics window.

597) Release the **mouse pointer** below the far right hole of the
ANGLE-13HOLE component.

598) Release the **Ctrl** key. HEX-STANDOFF<2> is displayed in
the Graphics window and listed in the FeatureManager.

💡 The number <2> indicates the second instance or copy
of the same component. The instance number increments
every time you insert the same component. If you delete a
component and then reinsert the component in the same
SOLIDWORKS session, the instance number increments
by one.

Enlarge the view.
599) **Zoom in** on the right side of the assembly.

Insert a Concentric mate.
600) Click the **third hole
cylindrical face** from the right
ANGLE-13HOLE component.

601) Hold the **Ctrl** key down.

602) Click inside the **cylindrical
hole face** of the second HEX-
STANDOFF component.

603) Release the **Ctrl** key. The
Mate pop-up menu is
displayed.

604) Click **Concentric** from the Mate pop-up menu.

Move the second HEX-STANDOFF part.
605) Click and drag the **HEX-STANDOFF** component
below the ANGLE-13HOLE component until its top
face is displayed.

Insert a Coincident mate.
606) Click the **second HEX-STANDOFF** top face.

607) Press the **up arrow key** approximately 5 times to view the bottom face of the ANGLE-13HOLE component.

608) Hold the **Ctrl** key down.

609) Click the **ANGLE-13HOLE bottom face**.

610) Release the **Ctrl** key.

611) Click **Coincident** from the Mate pop-up menu.

Insert a Parallel mate.
612) Click **Front view** .

613) Click the **front face** of the second HEX-STANDOFF.

614) Hold the **Ctrl** key down.

615) Click the **front face** of the ANGLE-13HOLE.

616) Release the **Ctrl** key. The Mate pop-up menu is displayed.

617) Click **Parallel** ⟍ from the Mate pop-up menu.

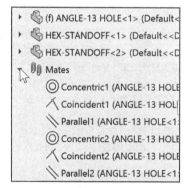

Display the created mates.
618) **Expand** the Mates folder in the FRONT-SUPPORT FeatureManager. Three mates are displayed between the ANGLE-13HOLE component and the second HEX-STANDOFF component. The second HEX-STANDOFF is fully defined.

Activity: FRONT-SUPPORT Assembly-Insert the TRIANGLE

Insert the TRIANGLE part.
619) Click **Isometric view** .

620) Click the **Insert Components** Assembly tool. The Insert Component PropertyManager is displayed.

621) Click the **Browse** button.

622) Browse to the **SW-TUTORIAL-2017** folder on your hard drive.

623) Double-click **TRIANGLE**.

624) Click a **position** in back of the ANGLE-13HOLE component as illustrated.

Enlarge the view.
625) **Zoom in** on the right side of the TRIANGLE and the ANGLE-13HOLE.

Insert a Concentric mate.
626) Click the **inside right arc face** of the TRIANGLE.

627) Hold the **Ctrl** key down.

628) Click the **inside right arc face** of the ANGLE-13HOLE slot.

629) Release the **Ctrl** key. The Mate pop-up menu is displayed.

630) Click **Concentric** from the Mate pop-up menu.

Fit the model to the Graphics window.
631) Press the **f** key.

Insert a Distance mate.
632) Click the **front face** of the TRIANGLE.

633) Press the **left Arrow key** approximately 5 times to view the back face of the ANGLE-13HOLE component.

634) Hold the **Ctrl** key down. Click the **back face** of the ANGLE-13HOLE component.

635) Release the **Ctrl** key. The Mate pop-up menu is displayed.

636) Click **Distance** |↔| from the Mate pop-up menu.

637) Enter **0**.

638) Click the **Green Check mark** ✔.

💡 A Distance Mate of 0 provides additional flexibility compared to a Coincident mate. A Distance mate value can be modified.

Insert a Parallel mate.

639) Click **Bottom view** ⬚.

640) Click the **narrow bottom face** of the TRIANGLE.

641) Hold the **Ctrl** key down.

642) Click the **bottom face** of the ANGLE-13HOLE.

643) Release the **Ctrl** key.

644) Click **Parallel** ⬊ from the Mate pop-up menu.

Display the Isometric view.

645) Click **Isometric view** ⬠.

View the created mates.

646) Expand the Mates folder. View the created mates.

Save the FRONT-SUPPORT assembly.

647) Click **Save** 🖫.

Assemble the four SCREW parts with SmartMates.

A SmartMate is a mate that automatically occurs when a component is placed into an assembly.

The mouse pointer displays a SmartMate feedback symbol when common geometry and relationships exist between the component and the assembly.

SmartMates are Concentric, Coincident, or Concentric and Coincident.

A Concentric SmartMate assumes that the geometry on the component has the same center as the geometry on an assembled reference.

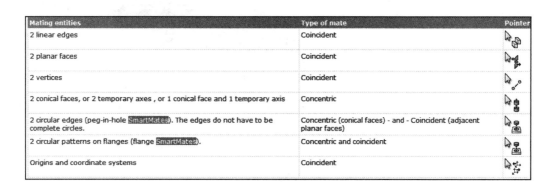

Mating entities	Type of mate	Pointer
2 linear edges	Coincident	
2 planar faces	Coincident	
2 vertices	Coincident	
2 conical faces, or 2 temporary axes , or 1 conical face and 1 temporary axis	Concentric	
2 circular edges (peg-in-hole SmartMates). The edges do not have to be complete circles.	Concentric (conical faces) - and - Coincident (adjacent planar faces)	
2 circular patterns on flanges (flange SmartMates).	Concentric and coincident	
Origins and coordinate systems	Coincident	

As the component is dragged into place, the mouse pointer provides various feedback icons. The SCREW utilizes a Concentric and Coincident SmartMate. Assemble the first SCREW. The circular edge of the SCREW mates Concentric and Coincident with the circular edge of the right slot of the TRIANGLE.

Activity: FRONT-SUPPORT Assembly-Insert the SCREW

Insert the SCREW part.

648) Click **Open** 📂 from the Menu bar.

649) Double-click **SCREW** from the SW-TUTORIAL-2017 folder. The SCREW PropertyManager is displayed.

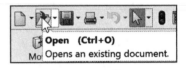

Display the SCREW part and the FRONT-SUPPORT assembly.
650) Click **Window, Tile Horizontally** from the Menu bar.

651) **Zoom in** on the right side of the FRONT-SUPPORT assembly. Note: Work between the two tile windows.

Insert the first SCREW.
652) Click and drag the **circular edge** of the SCREW part into the FRONT-SUPPORT assembly Graphic window.

653) Release the mouse pointer on the **top 3ʳᵈ circular hole edge** of the ANGLE-13HOLE. The mouse pointer displays the Coincident/Concentric circular edges icon.

Reference geometry defines the shape or form of a surface or a solid. Reference geometry includes planes, axes, coordinate systems and points.

Use the Pack and Go option to save an assembly or drawing with references. The Pack and Go tool saves either to a folder or creates a zip file to email. View SOLIDWORKS help for additional information.

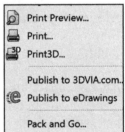

Insert the second SCREW.
654) Zoom in on the right side of the FRONT-SUPPORT assembly.

655) Click and drag the **circular edge** of the SCREW part into the FRONT-SUPPORT assembly Graphic window.

656) Release the mouse pointer on the **right arc edge** of the ANGLE-13HOLE. The mouse pointer displays the Coincident/Concentric circular edges icon.

Insert the third SCREW part.
657) Zoom in on the left side of the FRONT-SUPPORT assembly.

658) Click and drag the **circular edge** of the SCREW part into the FRONT-SUPPORT Assembly Graphic window.

659) Release the mouse pointer on the **left arc edge** of the ANGLE-13HOLE. The mouse pointer displays the Coincident/Concentric circular edges icon.

Insert the fourth SCREW part.
660) Zoom in on the bottom circular edge of the ANGLE-13HOLE.

661) Click and drag the **circular edge** of the SCREW part into the FRONT-SUPPORT Assembly Graphic window.

662) Release the mouse pointer on the **bottom circular edge** of the ANGLE-13HOLE. The mouse pointer displays the Coincident/Concentric circular edges icon.

663) Close the SCREW part window.

664) Maximize the FRONT-SUPPORT assembly window.

Display an Isometric view.
665) Click **Isometric view** . View the results in the Graphics window.

Save the FRONT-SUPPORT assembly.
666) Click **Save** 💾.

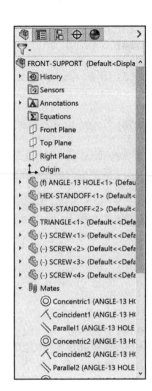

Select the Ctrl-Tab keys to quickly alternate between open
SOLIDWORKS documents.

Close all open parts and assemblies.
667) Click **Windows**, **Close All** from the Menu bar.

The FRONT-SUPPORT assembly is complete.

Display the Mates in the FeatureManager to check that the
components and the mate types correspond to the design intent.

When a component is in the Lightweight 🪶 state, only a
subset of its model data is loaded in memory. The remaining
model data is loaded on an as-needed basis.

 Review the FRONT-SUPPORT Assembly.

The ANGLE-13HOLE part was the first part inserted into the FRONT-SUPPORT
assembly. The ANGLE-13HOLE part was fixed to the FRONT-SUPPORT Origin.

Concentric, Coincident, and Parallel mates were utilized to assemble the HEX-
STANDOFF to the ANGLE-13HOLE. *Concentric*, *Distance*, and *Parallel* mates were
utilized to assemble the TRIANGLE to the ANGLE-13HOLE. The
Concentric/Coincident SmartMate was utilized to mate the four SCREW parts to the
FRONT-SUPPORT assembly.

Chapter Summary

In this chapter you created four parts, HEX-STANDOFF, ANGLE-13HOLE,
TRIANGLE and SCREW, utilizing the Top, Front, Right Planes and the FRONT-
SUPPORT assembly.

You obtained the knowledge of the following SOLIDWORKS features: Extruded
Boss/Base, Extruded Thin, Extruded Cut, Revolved Boss/Base, Hole Wizard, Linear
Pattern, Circular Pattern, Fillet, and Chamfer. You also applied sketch techniques with
various Sketch tools: Line, Circle, Corner Rectangle, Centerline, Dynamic Mirror,
Straight Slot, Trim Entities, Polygon, Tangent Arc, Sketch Fillet, Offset Entities and
Convert Entities.

You utilized centerlines as construction geometry to reference dimensions and relationships. You incorporated the four new parts to create the FRONT-SUPPORT assembly. Concentric, Distance, and Parallel mates were utilized to assemble the TRIANGLE to the ANGLE-13HOLE.

You applied the Quick mate procedure in the FRONT-SUPPORT assembly. Quick mate is a procedure to mate components together. No command (click Mate from the Assembly CommandManager) is required. Hold the Ctrl key down, and make your selections. Release the Ctrl key; a Quick Mate pop-up is displayed below the context toolbar. Select your mate and you are finished.

Utilize Quick mate on Standard mates, Cam mate, Profile Center mate, Slot mate, Symmetric mate and Width mate. To activate the Quick Mates functionality, click Tools, Customize. On the toolbars tab, under Context toolbar settings, select Show quick mates. Quick Mates should be selected by default.

Use the Quick mate procedure for reference geometry (such as planes, axes, and points) along with model geometry (such as faces, edges and vertices).

The Concentric/Coincident SmartMate was utilized to mate the four SCREW parts to the FRONT-SUPPORT assembly.

Questions

1. Identify the three default Reference planes used in SOLIDWORKS.

2. True or False. Sketches are created only on the Front Plane.

3. Identify the sketch tool required to create a hexagon.

4. Describe the profile required for an Extruded Thin feature.

5. Mirror Entities, Offset Entities, Sketch Fillet, and Trim Entities are located in the _____ toolbar.

6. List the six standard principle orthographic views in a drawing: _____, _____, _____, _____, _____, _____,

7. Identify the type of Geometric relations that can be added to a sketch.

8. Describe the difference between a Circular Pattern feature and a Linear Pattern feature.

9. Describe the difference between a Fillet feature and a Chamfer feature.

10. Identify the function of the Hole Wizard feature.

11. Four 10-24x3/8 Machine Screws are required for an assembly. The diameter is _____. The threads per inch is _____. The length is _____.

12. Describe the difference between a Distance mate and a Coincident mate.

13. True or False. A fixed component cannot move in an assembly.

14. Describe the procedure to remove the fix state (f) of a component in an assembly.

15. Determine the procedure to rotate a component in an assembly.

16. Describe the procedure to resolve a Lightweight component in an assembly.

17. Describe the procedure to resolve a Lightweight assembly.

Exercises

Exercise 3.1: HEX-NUT Part

Create an ANSI, IPS HEX-NUT part. Apply 6061 Alloy material. Apply the following dimensions:

- Depth: .125 in, [3.18].

- Inside hole diameter: .190in, [4.83].

- Outside diameter: .375in, [9.53].

Use the Top Plane as the Sketch plane.

Exercise 3.2: FRONT-SUPPORT-2 Assembly

Create an ANSI, IPS FRONT-SUPPORT-2 assembly.

- Name the new assembly FRONT-SUPPORT-2.

- Insert the FRONT-SUPPORT assembly. The FRONT-SUPPORT assembly was created in this Chapter. Note: The FRONT-SUPPORT assembly is provided in the Chapter 3 Homework folder.

- Fix the FRONT-SUPPORT assembly to the Origin.

- Insert the first HEX-NUT (Exercise 3.1) into the FRONT-SUPPORT-2 assembly.

- Insert a Concentric mate and Coincident mate.

- Insert the second HEX-NUT part.

- Insert a Concentric mate and Coincident mate.

You can also insert a Parallel mate between the HEX-NUT parts and the FRONT-SUPPORT assembly.

Exercise 3.3: Weight-Hook Assembly

Create an ANSI, IPS Weight-Hook assembly. The Weight-Hook assembly has two components: WEIGHT and HOOK.

- Create a new assembly document.

- Copy and insert the WEIGHT part from the Chapter 3 Homework folder.

- Fix the WEIGHT to the Origin in the Assem1 FeatureManager.

- Insert the HOOK part from the Chapter 3 Homework folder into the assembly.

- Insert a Concentric mate between the inside top cylindrical face of the WEIGHT and the cylindrical face of the thread. Concentric is the default mate.

- Insert the first Coincident mate between the top edge of the circular hole of the WEIGHT and the top circular edge of Sweep1, above the thread.

- Coincident is the default mate. The HOOK can rotate in the WEIGHT.

- Fix the position of the HOOK. Insert the second Coincident mate between the Right Plane of the WEIGHT and the Right Plane of the HOOK. Coincident is the default mate.

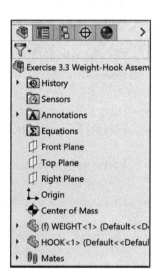

- Expand the Mates folder and view the created mates. Note: Tangent edges and origins are displayed for educational purposes.

- Calculate the Mass and Volume of the assembly.

- Identify the Center of Mass for the assembly.

Exercise 3.4: Weight-Link Assembly

Create an ANSI, IPS Weight-Link assembly. The Weight-Link assembly has two components and a sub-assembly: Axle component, FLATBAR component, and the Weight-Hook sub-assembly that you created in a previous exercise. Note: Tangent edges and origins are displayed for educational purposes.

- Create a new assembly document.

- Copy and insert the Axle part from the Chapter 3 Homework folder.

- Fix the Axle component to the Origin.

- Copy and insert the FLATBAR part from the Chapter 3 Homework folder. Rotate as needed.

- Insert a Concentric mate between the Axle cylindrical face and the FLATBAR inside face of the top circle.

- Insert a Coincident mate between the Front Plane of the Axle and the Front Plane of the FLATBAR.

- Insert a Coincident mate between the Right Plane of the Axle and the Top Plane of the FLATBAR. Position the FLATBAR as illustrated.

- Insert the Weight-Hook sub-assembly that you created in Exercise 3.3.

- Identify the Center of Mass for the assembly.

Determine the static and dynamic behavior of mates in each sub-assembly before creating the top level assembly.

Use the Pack and Go option to save an assembly or drawing with references. The Pack and Go tool saves either to a folder or creates a zip file to e-mail. View SOLIDWORKS help for additional information.

- Insert a Tangent mate between the inside bottom cylindrical face of the FLATBAR and the top circular face of the HOOK, in the Weight-Hook assembly. Tangent mate is selected by default. Click Flip Mate Alignment if needed.

- Insert a Coincident mate between the Front Plane of the FLATBAR and the Front Plane of the Weight-Hook sub-assembly. Coincident mate is selected by default. The Weight-Hook sub-assembly is free to move in the bottom circular hole of the FLATBAR.

Exercise 3.5: Binder Clip

Create a simple Gem® binder clip.

Create an ANSI - IPS assembly. Create two components - Binder and Binder Clip.

Apply material (plan carbon steel) to each component and address all needed mates. Think about where you would start.

Note: The cuts in the main body are made before folding the metal and strengthening the material during manufacturing. You do not need to model this exactly. The key to this exercise is to apply Advance distance mates (Limit mates) to limit the movement of the handle.

What is the Base Sketch for each component?

What are the dimensions? Measure all dimensions (approximately) from a small or large Gem binder clip.

View SOLIDWORKS Help or Chapter 5 on the Swept Base feature to create the Binder Clip handle.

☀ Determine the static and dynamic behavior of mates in each sub-assembly before creating the top level assembly.

Exercise 3.6: Limit Mate (Advanced Mate)

- Copy the Chapter 3 Homework\Limit Mate folder to your hard drive.

- Open the Limit Mate (Advanced distance mate) assembly.

- Insert a Limit Mate to restrict the movement of the Slide Component - lower and upper movement. (Use the Measure tool to obtain maximum and minimum distances.)

- Use SOLIDWORKS Help for additional information.

A Limit Mate is an Advanced Mate type. Limit mates allow components to move within a range of values for distance and angle mates. You specify a starting distance or angle as well as a maximum and minimum value.

- Save the model and move the Slide to view the results in the Graphics window. Think about how you would use this mate type in other assemblies.

☀ Use the Pack and Go option to save an assembly or drawing with references. The Pack and Go tool saves either to a folder or creates a zip file to e-mail. View SOLIDWORKS help for additional information.

Exercise 3.7: Screw Mate (Mechanical Mate)

- Copy the Chapter 3 Homework\Screw Mate folder to your hard drive.

- Open the Screw Mate assembly.

- Insert a Screw mate between the inside Face of the Base and the Face of the vice and any other mates that are required. A Screw is a Mechanical Mate type. View the avi file for proper movement.

- Calculate the total mass and volume of the assembly.

A Screw mate constrains two components to be concentric and also adds a pitch relationship between the rotation of one component and the translation of the other. Translation of one component along the axis causes rotation of the other component according to the pitch relationship. Likewise, rotation of one component causes translation of the other component. Use SOLIDWORKS Help if needed.

Note: Use the Select Other tool (See SOLIDWORKS Help if needed) to select the proper inside faces and to create the Screw mate for the assembly.

- Rotate the handle and view the results. Think about how you would use this mate type in other assemblies.

Exercise 3.8: Angle Mate

- Copy the Chapter 3 Homework\Angle Mate folder to your hard drive.

- Open the Angle Mate assembly.

- Move the Handle in the assembly. The Handle is free to rotate.

- Set the angle of the Handle.

- Insert an Angle mate (165 degree) between the Handle and the Side of the valve using Planes. An Angle mate places the selected items at the specified angle to each other. The Handle has a 165 degree Angle mate to restrict flow through the valve.

- Think about how you would use this mate type in other assemblies.

Exercise 3.8A: Angle Mate (Cont:)

Create two end caps (lids) for the ball valve using the Top-down Assembly method. Note: The Reference-In-Content symbols in the FeatureManager.

- Modify the Appearance of the body to observe the change, and enhance visualization.

- Apply the Select-other tool to obtain access to hidden faces and edges.

▸   (f) Side<1> (Standard<<Stai

▸   Side<2> (Standard<<Standa

▸   Ball1<1> (Standard<<Stand

▸   Handle<1> (Standard<<Stai

▸   [Part1^Angle Mate]<1> ->

▸   [Part2^Angle Mate]<1> ->

▸   Mate

  (-) Sketch1

Exercise 3.9: Symmetric Mate (Advanced Mate)

- Copy the Chapter 3 Homework\Symmetric Mate folder to your hard drive.

- Open the Symmetric Mate assembly.

- Insert a Symmetric Mate between the two Guild Rollers.

- Think about how you would use this mate type in other assemblies.

Exercise 3.10: Gear Mate (Mechanical mate)

View the ppt presentation and avi file on Gears located in the Chapter 3 Homework\Gears folder.

Create the Gear assembly as illustrated below.

All needed information is provided in the ppt.

Create all needed components and mates. Use the SOLIDWORKS Toolbox. The SOLIDWORKS Toolbox is an add-in.

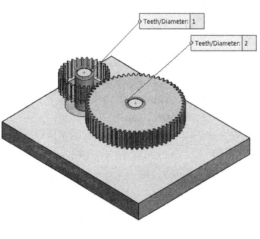

Exercise 3.10A: Slot Mate (Center in Slot option)

Copy the Chapter 3 Homework\Slot Mate folder to your hard drive.

Open the Slot Mate assembly.

Insert a Slot mate (center in slot option) between the Flange bolt and the right side slot.

Insert a second Flange bolt into the assembly.

Insert the second slot mate (center in slot option) between the second Flange bolt and the left side slot.

Insert a Coincident mate between the top face of the GUIDE and the bottom face of the second Flange bolt cap.

Expand the Mates folder. View the created mates.

Exercise 3.11: Slider Part

Create the part from the illustrated A-ANSI - MMGS Third Angle Projection drawing below: Front, Top, Right and Isometric view.

Note: The location of the Origin (Shown in an Isometric view).

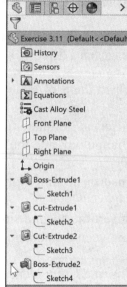

- Apply Cast Alloy steel for material.

- The part is symmetric about the Front Plane.

- Apply Mid Plane for End Condition in Boss-Extrude1.

- Apply Through All for End Condition in Cut-Extrude1.

- Apply Through All for End Condition in Cut-Extrude2.

- Apply Up to Surface for End Condition in Boss Extrude2

- Calculate the Volume of the part and locate the Center of mass.

Think about the steps that you would take to build the model. Do you need the Right view for manufacturing? Does it add any important information?

Exercise 3.12: Cosmetic Thread Part

Apply a Cosmetic thread: 1/4-20-2 UNC 2A. A cosmetic thread represents the inner diameter of a thread on a boss or the outer diameter of a thread.

Copy the Cosmetic thread part from the Chapter 3 Homework folder to your hard drive.

Open the part.

Create a Cosmetic thread. Produce the geometry of the thread.

Click the bottom edge of the part as illustrated.

Click Insert, Annotations, Cosmetic Thread from the Menu bar menu. View the Cosmetic Thread PropertyManager. Edge<1> is displayed.

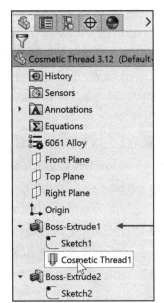

Select Blind for End Condition.

Enter 1.00 for depth.

Enter .200 for min diameter.

Enter ¼-20-2 UNC 2A in the Thread Callout box.

Click OK ✔ from the Cosmetic Thread FeatureManager.

Expand the FeatureManager. View the Cosmetic Thread feature. If needed, right-click the Annotations folder, and click Details.

Check the Cosmetic threads and Shaded cosmetic threads box.

Click OK. View the cosmetic thread on the model.

The Thread Callout: ¼-20-2 UNC 2A is automatically inserted into a drawing document, if the drawing document is in the ANSI drafting standard.

Exercise 3.13: Hole - Block

Create the Hole-Block ANSI - IPS part using the Hole Wizard feature as illustrated. Create the Hole-Block part on the Front Plane.

The Hole Wizard feature creates either a 2D or 3D sketch for the placement of the hole in the FeatureManager.

You can consecutively place multiple holes of the same type. The Hole Wizard creates 2D sketches for holes unless you select a non-planar face or click the 3D Sketch button in the Hole Position PropertyManager.

Hole Wizard creates two sketches: a sketch of the revolved cut profile of the selected hole type and the other sketch of the center placement for the profile. Both sketches should be fully defined.

Create a rectangular prism 2 inches wide by 5 inches long by 2 inches high. On the top surface of the prism, place four holes, 1 inch apart.

- Hole #1: Simple Hole Type: Fractional Drill Size, 7/16 diameter, End Condition: Blind, 0.75 inch deep.

- Hole #2: Counterbore hole Type: for 3/8 inch diameter Hex bolt, End Condition: Through All.

- Hole #3: Countersink hole Type: for 3/8 inch diameter Flat head screw, 1.5 inch deep.

- Hole #4: Tapped hole Type, Size ¼-20, End Condition: Blind - 1.0 inch deep.

Exercise 3.14: Hole Wizard Part

Apply the 3D sketch placement method as illustrated in the FeatureManager. Insert and dimension a hole on a cylindrical face.

Copy the Hole Wizard 3-14 part from the Chapter 3 Homework folder to your hard drive.

Open the Hole Wizard 3-14 part.

Note: With a 3D sketch, press the Tab key to move between planes.

Click the Hole Wizard Features tool. The Hole Specification PropertyManager is displayed.

Select the Counterbore Hole Type.

Select ANSI Inch for Standard.

Select Socket Head Cap Screw for fastener Type.

Select 1/4 for Size. Select Normal for Fit.

Select Through All for End Condition.

Enter .100 for Head clearance in the Options box.

Click the Positions Tab. The Hole Position PropertyManager is displayed.

Click the 3D Sketch button. SOLIDWORKS displays a 3D

interface with the Point ^{XY} tool active.

When the Point tool is active, wherever you click you will create a point.

Click the cylindrical face of the model as illustrated. The selected face is displayed in blue.

Insert a dimension between the top face and the Sketch point.

Click the Smart Dimension Sketch tool.

Click the top flat face of the model and the sketch point.

Enter .25in.

Locate the point angularly around the cylinder. Apply construction geometry.

Activate the Temporary Axes. Click View, Hide/show, check the Temporary Axes box from the Menu bar toolbar.

Click the Line ⟋ Sketch tool. Note: 3D sketch is still activated.

Ctrl+click the top flat face of the model. This moves the red space handle origin to the selected face. This also constrains any new sketch entities to the top flat face.

Note the mouse pointer ⟲ 𝙰 icon.

Move the mouse pointer near the center of the activated top flat face as illustrated. View the small black circle. The circle indicates that the end point of the line will pick up a Coincident relation.

Click the center point of the circle.

Sketch a line so it picks up the **AlongZ sketch relation**. The cursor displays the relation to be applied. **This is a very important step.** The line should be black.

Create an AlongY sketch relation between the centerpoint of the hole on the cylindrical face and the endpoint of the sketched line as illustrated. The sketch is fully defined.

Click OK ✔ from the Properties PropertyManager.

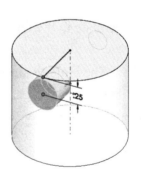

Click OK ✔ from the Hole Position PropertyManager.

Expand the FeatureManager and view the results. The two sketches are fully defined. One sketch is the hole profile; the other sketch is to define the position of the feature.

Close the model.

Exercise 3.15: Counter Weight Assembly

Create the Counter Weight assembly as illustrated using SmartMates and Standard mates.

Copy the Chapter 3 Homework\Counter-Weight folder to your local hard drive.

Create a new assembly. The Counter Weight assembly consists of the following items:

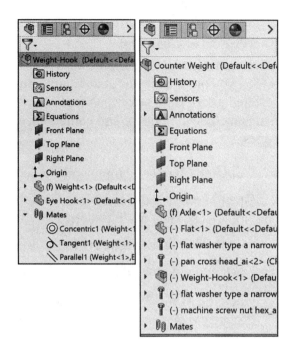

- Weight-Hook sub-assembly.

- Weight.

- Eye Hook.

- Axle component (f). Fixed to the origin.

- Flat component.

- Flat Washer Type A (from the SOLIDWORKS Toolbox).

- Pan Cross Head Screw (from the SOLIDWORKS Toolbox).

- Flat Washer Type A (from the SOLIDWORKS toolbox).

- Machine Screw Nut Hex (from the SOLIDWORKS Toolbox).

Apply SmartMates with the Flat Washer Type A Narrow_AI, Machine Screw Nut Hex_AI and the Pan Cross Head_AI components.

Use a Distance mate to fit the Axle in the middle of the Flat. Note a Symmetric mate could replace the Distance mate. Think about the design of the assembly. Apply all needed Lock mates.

The symbol (f) represents a fixed component. A fixed component cannot move and is locked to the assembly Origin.

Exercise 3.16: Gear Mate

Insert a Mechanical Gear mate between two gears. Gear mates force two components to rotate relative to one another about selected axes. Valid selections for the axis of rotation for gear mates include cylindrical and conical faces, axes, and linear edges.

1. **Copy** the Chapter 3 Homework folder to your hard drive.

2. Open **Mechanical Gear Mate** from the Chapter 3 Homework\Gear Mate folder.

3. Click and drag the **right gear**.

4. Click and drag the **left gear**. The gears move independently.

5. Click the **Mate** ✎ tool from the Assembly tab. The Mate PropertyManager is displayed.

6. **Clear** all selections.

7. **Align the components** before adding the Mechanical mate. To align the two components, select a Front view and move them manually.

8. Select the **inside cylindrical face** of the left hole.

9. Select the **inside cylindrical face** of the right hole.

10. **Expand** the Mechanical Mates box from the Mate PropertyManager.

11. Click **Gear** 🜚 mate from the Mechanical Mates box. The GearMate1 PropertyManager is displayed. Accept the default settings.

12. Click **OK** ✔ from the GearMate1 PropertyManager.

13. **Expand** the Mates folder. View the created GearMate1.

14. **Rotate** the Gears in the Graphics window.

15. **View** the results.

Exercise 3.17: Cam Mate

Create a Tangent Cam follower mate and a Coincident Cam follower mate. A cam-follower mate is a type of Tangent or Coincident mate. It allows you to mate a cylinder, plane or point to a series of tangent extruded faces, such as you would find on a cam.

Create the profile of the cam from lines, arcs and splines as long as they are tangent and form a closed loop.

1. **Copy** the Chapter 3 Homework folder to your hard drive.

2. Open **Cam Mate** from the from the Chapter 3 Homework\Cam Mate folder. View the model. The model contains two cams.

3. **Expand** the Mates folder to view the existing mates.

Insert a tangent Cam follower mate.

4. Click the **Mate** ✎ tool from the Assembly tab.

5. **Pin** the Mate PropertyManager.

6. **Expand** the Mechanical Mates box from the Mate PropertyManager.

7. Click **Cam Follower** ⌀ mate.

8. Click inside of the **Cam Path** box.

9. Click the **outside face** of cam-s<1> as illustrated.

10. Click the **face of Link-c<1>** as illustrated. Face<2>@Link-c-1 is displayed.

11. Click **OK** ✔ from the CamMateTangent1 PropertyManager.

Insert a Coincident Cam follower mate.

12. Click **Cam Follower** ⌀ mate from the Mechanical Mates box.

13. Click the **outside face** of cam-s2<1>.

14. Click the vertex of **riser<1>** as illustrated. Vertex<1>@riser-1 is displayed.

15. Click **OK** ✔ from the CamMateCoincident1 PropertyManager.

16. **Un-pin** the Mate PropertyManager.

17. Click **OK** ✔ from the Mate PropertyManager.

18. **Expand** the Mates folder. View the new created mates.

19. Display an **Isometric** view.

20. **Rotate** the cams.

21. **View** the results in the Graphics window.

When creating a cam follower mate, make sure that your Spline or Extruded Boss/Base feature, which you use to form the cam contact face, does nothing but form the face.

In the next exercise of the spur gear and rack, the gear's pitch circle must be tangent to the rack's pitch line, which is the construction line in the middle of the tooth cut.

Exercise 3.18: Rack Pinion Mate

The Spur gear and rack components for this exercise were obtained
from the SOLIDWORKS Toolbox folder marked Power
Transmission. Insert a Mechanical Rack Pinion mate.

1. **Copy** the Chapter 3 Homework folder to your hard drive.

2. Open **Rack Pinion Mate** from the Chapter 3 Homework\Rack
    Pinion Mate folder.

3. View the displayed: (TooCutSkeSim and
    ToothCutSim). If needed, display the illustrated
    sketches to mate the assembly.

The Diametral Pitch, Pressure Angle and Face Width
values should be the same for the spur gear as the rack.

Tangency is required between the spur gear and
rack.

4. **Expand** the Mates folder to view the existing
    mates. Four Coincident mates and a Distance mate
    were created in the assembly.

Insert a Rack Pinion mate.

5. Click the **Mate** ✎ tool from the Assembly tab.

6. **Expand** the Mechanical Mates box from the Mate
    PropertyManager.

7. Click **Rack Pinion** ⚙ mate from the Mechanical
    Mates box.

8. Mate the rack. Make sure the teeth of the spur gear
    and rack are **meshing
    properly**; they are not
    interfering with each
    other. It is important to
    create a starting point
    were the gear and rack
    have no interference.

9. Click the **bottom linear edge of the rack** in the direction of travel. Any linear edge that runs in the direction of travel is acceptable.

10. Click the **spur gear pitch circle** as illustrated. The Pinion pitch diameter, 1in, is taken from the sketch geometry. Accept the default settings.

11. Click **OK** ✔ from the RackPinionMate1 PropertyManager.

12. **Rotate** the spur gear on the rack. View the results.

13. **Hide** the sketches in the model.

14. **Close** the model.

The Pitch Diameter is the diameter of an imaginary pitch circle on which a gear tooth is designed. Pitch circles of the two spur gears are required to be tangent for the gears to move and work properly.

The distance between the center point of the gear and the pitch line of the rack represents the theoretical distance required.

💡 Diametral Pitch is the ratio equal to the number of teeth on a gear per inch of pitch diameter.

💡 Before applying the Rack Pinion mate, make sure the teeth of the spur gear and rack are meshing properly.

Pressure Angle is the angle of direction of pressure between contacting teeth. Pressure angle determines the size of the base circle and the shape of the involute teeth. It is common for the pressure angle to be 20 or 14 1/2 degrees.

Exercise 3.19: Hinge Mate

Create a Mechanical Hinge mate. The two components in this tutorial were obtained from the SOLIDWORKS What's New section.

1. **Copy** the Chapter 3 Homework folder to your hard drive.

2. Open **Hinge Mate** from the Chapter 3 Homework\Hinge Mate folder. Two components are displayed.

A Hinge mate has the same effect as adding a Concentric mate plus a Coincident mate. You can also limit the angular movement between the two components.

3. Click the **Mate** ✎ tool from the Assembly tab.

4. **Expand** the Mechanical Mates box from the Mate PropertyManager.

5. Click **Hinge** ▦ mate from the Mechanical Mates box.

Set two Concentric faces.

6. Click the **inside cylindrical face** of the first component as illustrated.

7. Click the **outside cylindrical face** of the second component as illustrated. The two selected faces are displayed.

Set two Coincident faces.

8. Click the **front flat face** of the first component as illustrated.

9. Click the **bottom flat face** of the second component as illustrated. View the results in the Graphics window.

You can specify a limit angle for rotation by checking the **Specify angle limits** box and selecting the required faces.

10. Click **OK** ✔ from the Hinge1 PropertyManager.

11. **Rotate** the flap component about the pin.

12. **Close** the model.

A Hinge mate limits the movement between two components to one rotational degree of freedom.

Similar to other mate types, Hinge mates do not prevent interference or collisions between components. To prevent interference, use Collision Detection or Interference Detection.

Exercise 3.20: Exploded View
Use the Exploded View tool. Insert an Exploded View into an assembly.

1. **Copy** the Chapter 3 Homework folder to your hard drive.

2. Activate **SOLIDWORKS Toolbox**.

3. Open **ExplodedView** from the Chapter 3 Homework\Exploded view folder.

4. Click the **Exploded View** tool. The Explode PropertyManager is displayed. The rotation and translation handles appear.

5. Click each of the **8 Hex bolts** in the Graphics window and drag upward using the triad. Explode Step1 - 8 are created in the Explode Steps box.

6. Click the **SF_plate1** in the Graphics window and drag the plate backwards using the triad as illustrated. Explode Step9 is created.

7. Click each of the **8 Hex Flange Nuts** and drag them downward using the triad from the Graphics window as illustrated.

8. Click **OK** from the Explode PropertyManager.

9. Click the **ConfigurationManager** tab.

10. **Expand** the Default configuration.

11. Right-click **ExplView1**.

12. Click **Animate collapse**. View the Animation.

13. Click **Loop** from the Animation Controller. The model will continue to play until you stop it.

14. Click **Play** from the Animation Controller.

15. Click **Stop** from the Animation Controller.

Click End from the Animation Controller. The End option brings the model to the end point in the animation.

16. **Close** the Animation Controller. **Return** to the FeatureManager. **Close** the model.

Exercise 3.21: Collision Detection

Apply the Collision Detection tool to an assembly.

1. **Copy** the Chapter 3 Homework folder to your hard drive.

2. Open **Collision Detection** from the Chapter 3 Homework\Collision Detection folder.

3. Click the **Move Component** tool from

4. the Assembly tab in the CommandManager. View the Move Component PropertyManager.

5. Click the **Collision Detection** box.

6. Click the **All components** box. The **These components** option provides the ability to select individual components for collision detection.

7. Check the **Stop at collision** box.

8. Check the **Dragged part only** box. View the defaults.

9. Click and drag the **Collar downward** towards the base as illustrated. The Collision Detection tool informs the user when there is a collision between the components.

10. Click **OK** ✔ from the Move Component PropertyManager.

11. **Close** the model.

🔅 **Physical Dynamics** is an option in Collision Detection that allows you to see the motion of assembly components in a realistic way. With Physical Dynamics enabled, when you drag a component, the component applies a force to components that it touches and moves the components if they are free to move.

Exercise 3.22: AIR RESERVOIR SUPPORT AND PLATE Assembly

The project team developed a concept sketch of the PNEUMATIC TEST MODULE assembly. Develop the AIR RESERVOIR SUPPORT AND PLATE assembly.

PNEUMATIC TEST MODULE Assembly Layout

Create three new parts:

- FLAT-PLATE

- IM15-MOUNT

- ANGLE-BRACKET

The Reservoir is a purchased part. The assembly file is located in the Chapter 3 Homework folder.

AIR RESERVOIR SUPPORT Assembly
Courtesy of Gears Educational Systems & SMC
Corporation of America

- Create a new assembly named AIR RESERVOIR SUPPORT AND PLATE.

- Two M15-MOUNT parts and two ANGLE-BRACKET parts hold the SMC AIR RESERVOIR.

- The ANGLE-BRACKET parts are fastened to the FLAT-PLATE.

Exercise 3.22a: FLAT-PLATE Part

Create the FLAT-PLATE Part on the Top Plane. The FLAT-PLATE is machined from .090, [2.3] 6061 Alloy flat stock. The default units are inches.

Utilize the Top Plane for the Sketch plane.

Locate the Origin at the Midpoint of the left vertical line.

The 8.690, [220.68mm] x 5.688, [144.48mm] FLAT PLATE contains a Linear Pattern of ∅.190, [4.83mm] Thru holes.

The Holes are equally spaced .500, [12.7mm] apart.

DETAIL A
SCALE 1 : 1

Determine the maximum number of holes contained in the FLAT-PLATE.

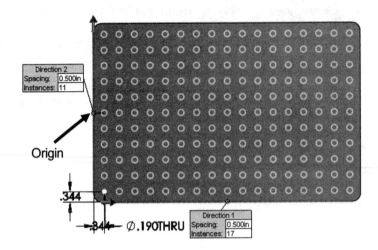

Maximum # of holes_____.

- Utilize a Linear Pattern in two Directions to create the holes.

- Utilize the Geometric Pattern Option.

Exercise 3.22b: IM15-MOUNT Part

- Create the IM15-MOUNT part on the Right plane.

- Center the part on the Origin. Utilize the features in the FeatureManager.

- The IM15-MOUNT Part is machined from 0.060, [1.5mm] 6061 Alloy flat stock. The default units are inches.

Exercise 3.22c: ANGLE BRACKET Part

• Create the ANGLE BRACKET part.

• The Extruded Base (Boss-Extrude1) feature is sketched with an L-Shaped profile on the Right Plane. The ANGLE BRACKET Part is machined from 0.060, [1.5mm] 6061 Alloy flat stock. The default units are inches.

Exercise 3.22d: Reservoir Assembly

The Reservoir stores compressed air. Air is pumped through a Schrader Valve into the Reservoir.

A Quick Connect Straight Fitting is utilized to supply air to the Pneumatic Test Module Assembly. Quick Connect Fittings allow air tubing to be assembled and disassembled without removing the fitting.

Copy the Pneumatic Components folder to your hard drive.

Open the part Reservoir from the Pneumatics Components folder. The Reservoir default units are in millimeters (MMGS).

Schrader Valve

Quick Connect
Straight Fitting

Reservoir and Fittings
Courtesy of SMC Corporation of America and
Gears Educational Systems

Engineers and designers work in metric and english units. Always verify your units for parts and other engineering data. In pneumatic systems, common units for volume, pressure and temperature are defined in the table below.

Magnitude	Metric Unit (m)	English (e)
Mass	kg	pound
	g	ounce
Length	m	foot
	m	yard
	mm	inch
Temperature	°C	°F
Area, Section	m²	sq.ft
	cm²	sq.inch
Volume	m³	cu.yard
	cm³	cu.inch
	dm³	cu.ft.
Volume Flow	m³n / min	scfm
	dm³n /min (ℓ/min)	scfm
Force	N	pound force (ℓbf.)
Pressure	bar	ℓbf./sq.inch (psi)

Common Metric and English Units

The ISO unit of pressure is the Pa (Pascal). $1Pa = 1N/m$.

Exercise 3.22e: AIR RESERVOIR SUPPORT AND PLATE Assembly

Create the AIR RESERVOIR SUPPORT AND PLATE assembly. Note: There is more than one solution for the mate types illustrated below.

The FLAT-PLATE is the first component in the AIR RESERVOIR SUPPORT AND PLATE assembly. Insert the FLAT-PLATE. The FLAT-PLATE is fixed to the Origin.

AIR RESERVOIR SUPPORT AND PLATE Assembly
Courtesy of SMC Corporation of America

- Insert the ANGLE BRACKET.

- Mate the ANGLE BRACKET to the FLAT-PLATE. The bottom flat face of the ANGLE BRACKET is coincident to the top face of the FLAT-PLATE.

- The center hole of the ANGLE BRACKET is concentric to the upper left hole of the FLAT-PLATE.

- The first hole of the ANGLE bracket is concentric with the hole in the 8th row, 1st column of the FLAT-PLATE.

- Insert the IM15-MOUNT.

- Mate the IM15-MOUNT. The IM15-MOUNT flat back face is coincident to the flat inside front face of the ANGLE BRACKET.

- The bottom right hole of the IM15-MOUNT is concentric with the right hole of the ANGLE BRACKET.

- The bottom edge of the IM15-MOUNT is parallel to the bottom edge of the ANGLE BRACKET.

- Insert the Reservoir Assembly.

- Mate the Reservoir Assembly. The conical face of the Reservoir is concentric to the IM15-MOUNT center hole.

- The left end cap of the Reservoir Assembly is coincident to the front face of the IM15-MOUNT.

- The Hex Nut flat face is parallel to the top face of the FLAT-PLATE.

- Insert the second ANGLE BRACKET.

- Mate the ANGLE BRACKET to the FLAT-PLATE. The bottom flat face of the ANGLE BRACKET is coincident to the top face of the FLAT-PLATE.

- The center hole of the ANGLE BRACKET is concentric with the hole in the 11th row, 13th column of the FLAT-PLATE.

- The first hole of the ANGLE bracket is concentric with the hole in the 8th row, 13th column of the FLAT-PLATE.

- Insert the second IM15-MOUNT.

- Mate the IM15-MOUNT to the outside face of the ANGLE BRACKET. The bottom right hole of the IM15-MOUNT is concentric with the right hole of the ANGLE BRACKET.

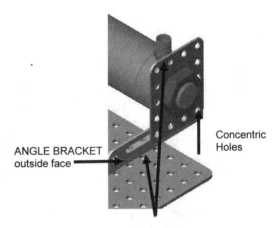

- The top edge of the IM15-MOUNT is parallel to the top edge of the ANGLE BRACKET.

- Save the assembly. Insert the required SCREWS. The AIR RESERVOIR SUPPORT AND PLATE assembly is complete.

Chapter 4

Fundamentals of Drawing

ITEM NO.	PART NUMBER	DESCRIPTION	MATERIAL	QTY.
1	GIDS-PC-10001	LINEAR ACTUATOR		1
2	GIDS-SC-10017	AXLE ROD	Plain Carbon Steel	1
3	GIDS-SC-10001-9	9 HOLES	2014 Alloy	2
4	GIDS-SC-10012-3-16	SHAFT-COLLAR	Plain Carbon Steel	2

Below are the desired outcomes and usage competencies based on the completion of Chapter 4.

Desired Outcomes:	Usage Competencies:
• CUSTOM-A Sheet Format. • A-ANSI-MM Drawing Template.	• Ability to create a Custom Sheet Format, Drawing Template, Company logo and Title block.
• FLATBAR Configurations. • FLATBAR Part Drawing. • LINKAGE Assembly Drawing. • FLATBAR-SHAFTCOLLAR Assembly.	• Understand Standard, Isometric, Detail, Section and Exploded views. • Knowledge of the View Palette. • Ability to incorporate a Bill of Materials with Custom Properties.
	• Proficiency to create and edit drawing dimensions and annotations. • Aptitude to create a Design Table.

Notes:

Chapter 4 - Fundamentals of Drawing

Chapter Objective

Create a FLATBAR drawing with a customized Sheet Format and a Drawing Template containing a Company logo and Title block.

Obtain an understanding to display the following views with the ability to insert, add, and edit dimensions and annotations:

- Standard: Top, Front and Right.

- Isometric, Detail, Section and Exploded.

Create a LINKAGE assembly drawing with a Bill of Materials. Obtain knowledge to develop and incorporate a Bill of Materials with Custom Properties. Create a FLATBAR-SHAFTCOLLAR assembly.

On the completion of this chapter, you will be able to:

- Create a customized Sheet Format.

- Generate a custom Drawing Template.

- Produce a Bill of Materials with Custom Properties.

- Develop various drawing views.

- Reposition views on a drawing.

- Move dimensions in the same view.

- Apply Edit Sheet Format mode and Edit Sheet mode.

- Modify the dimension scheme.

- Create a Parametric drawing note.

- Link notes in the Title block to SOLIDWORKS properties.

- Generate an Exploded view.

- Create and edit a Design Table.

- Insert a Center of Mass Point.

Chapter Overview

Generate the LINKAGE assembly drawing with two sheets and the FLATBAR part drawing using configurations from a design table.

The LINKAGE assembly drawing contains two sheets:

- Sheet1 contains the LINKAGE assembly in an Exploded view with a Bill of Materials.

- Sheet2 contains the AirCylinder assembly with a Section view, Detail view and a Scale view.

The FLATBAR drawing utilizes a custom Drawing Template and a custom Sheet Format. The FLATBAR drawing contains two sheets:

- Sheet1 contains a Front, Top and Isometric view with dimensions and a linked Parametric note.

- Sheet2 contains the 3HOLE configuration of the FLATBAR. Configurations are created with a Design Table.

Create the FLATBAR-SHAFTCOLLAR assembly. Utilize a
Design Table to create four new configurations of the
assembly.

There are two major design modes used to develop a drawing:

- Edit Sheet Format and Edit Sheet.

The Edit Sheet Format mode provides the ability to:

- Change the Title block size and text headings.

- Incorporate a Company logo.

- Define the Zone Tag Editor.

- Add Custom Properties, text and more.

The Edit Sheet mode provides the ability to:

- Add or modify views.

- Add or modify dimensions.

- Add or modify notes and more.

Drawing Template and Sheet Format

The foundation of a SOLIDWORKS drawing is the
Drawing Template. Drawing size, drawing standards,
company information, manufacturing and/or assembly
requirements, units and other properties are defined in the
Drawing Template.

The Sheet Format is incorporated into the Drawing
Template. The Sheet Format contains the border, Title
block information, Revision block information, Company
name and or Logo information, Custom Properties, and
SOLIDWORKS Properties.

Custom Properties and SOLIDWORKS Properties are shared values between documents.
Utilize an A-size Drawing Template with Sheet format for the FLATBAR drawing and
LINKAGE assembly drawing.

View the provided videos on Drawing Fundamentals to enhance your experience
with the chapter.

During the initial SOLIDWORKS installation, you are requested to select either the ISO or ANSI drafting standard. ISO is typically a European drafting standard and uses First Angle Projection. This book is written using the ANSI (US) overall drafting standard and Third Angle Projection for drawings.

Views from the part or assembly are inserted into the SOLIDWORKS drawing.

Create Sheet Formats for different parts types. Example: sheet metal parts, plastic parts, and high precision machined parts.

Create Sheet Formats for each category of parts that are manufactured with unique sets of title block notes.

Note: The Third Angle Projection scheme is illustrated in this chapter.

Third Angle
Projection icon

Third Angle Projection

For non-ANSI dimension standards, the dimensioning techniques are the same, even if the displayed arrows and text size are different. For printers supporting millimeter paper sizes, select A4 (ANSI) Landscape (297mm × 210mm).

The default Drawing Templates contain predefined Title block Notes linked to Custom Properties and SOLIDWORKS Properties.

Activity: Create a New Drawing

Create a New drawing. Close all parts and drawings.
1)   Click **Windows**, **Close All** from the Menu bar.

2)   Click **New** 🗋 from the Menu bar.

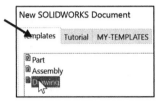

3)   Double-click **Drawing** from the Templates tab.

4)   Select **A (ANSI) Landscape**. If needed uncheck the Only show standard formats box.

5)   Click **OK** from the Sheet Format/Size box.

6)   Click **Cancel** ✖ from the Model View PropertyManager. The Draw FeatureManager is displayed.

🔆 A new drawing invokes the Model View PropertyManager if the Start Command When Creating New Drawing option is checked.

The A (ANSI) Landscape paper is displayed in a new Graphics window. The sheet border defines the drawing size, 11″ × 8.5″ or (279.4mm × 215.9mm).

🔆 To view the Sheet properties, right-click Properties in the drawing sheet. Expand the drop-down menu. View the Sheet Properties dialog box. Click OK to return to the drawing sheet.

💡 Draw1 is the default drawing name. Sheet1 is the default first Sheet name. For an active drawing document, the View Layout, Annotation, Sketch, Evaluate and SOLIDWORKS Add-Ins, and Sheet Format tabs are displayed in the CommandManager.

💡 Utilize the CommandManager tabs or individual toolbars to access the needed tools in this chapter.

The Automatic Border tool provides the ability to control every aspect of a sheet format's border, including zone layout and border size once you are in the Edit Sheet Format mode.

Set the Sheet Properties.

7)   Right-click in the **Graphics window**.

8)   Click **Properties**. If needed expand the drop-down menu to view the Properties command. The Sheet Properties are displayed. Enter Sheet Scale **1:1**.

9)   Check the **Third angle** box for Type of projection.

10)   Click **OK** from the Sheet Properties dialog box.

Activity: Drawing-Document Properties

Set the drawing document properties.

11)   Click **Options** ⚙ from the Main menu.

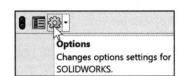

12)   Click the **Document Properties** tab from the dialog box.

13)   Select **ANSI** for Overall drafting standard from the drop-down menu.

14)   Click **Units**. Click **MMGS** (millimeter, gram, second) for Unit system.

15)   Select **.12** for Length units Decimal places.

16)   Select **None** for Angular units Decimal places.

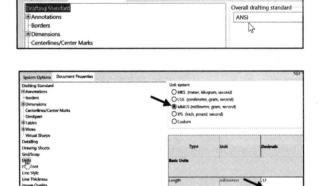

💡 Available Document Properties are document dependent.

Companies develop drawing format standards and use specific text height for Metric and English drawings. Numerous engineering drawings use the following format:

- *Font*: Century Gothic - All capitals.

- *Text height*: 3mm for drawings up to B Size, 17in. × 22in.

- *Text height*: 5mm for drawings larger than B Size, 17in × 22in.

- *Arrowheads*: Solid filled with a 1:3 ratio - width to height.

Set the dimension font.

17) Click **Annotations** folder as illustrated.

18) Click the **Font** button. The Choose Font dialog box is displayed.

Set the dimension text height.

19) Click the **Units** box from the Choose Font dialog box.

20) Enter **3.0**mm for Height.

21) Click **OK** from the Choose Font dialog box.

Set the arrow size.

22) Click the **Dimensions** folder as illustrated.

23) Enter **1**mm for arrow Height. Enter **3**mm for arrow Width.

24) Enter **6**mm for arrow Length.

25) Click **OK** from the Document Properties dialog box.

There are three dimension style type buttons: Outside, Inside, and Smart. Smart is the default option.

Check the Dual dimensions display box to display dual dimensions for your model or drawing.

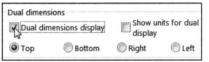

Utilize the Search feature in the System Options dialog box to quickly locate information for System Options or Document Properties.

Title Block

The Title block contains text fields linked to System Properties and Custom Properties. System Properties are determined from the SOLIDWORKS documents. Custom Property values are assigned to named variables.

The Automatic Border command provides the ability to select columns and then select annotation notes that represent column labels for the sheet zones. Click rows and then select annotation notes that represent row labels for the sheet zones.

Save time. Utilize System Properties and define Custom Properties in your Sheet Formats.

System Properties Linked to fields in default Sheet Formats:	Custom Properties of drawings linked to fields in default Sheet Formats:		Custom Properties of parts and assemblies linked to fields in default Sheet Formats:
SW-File Name (in DWG. NO. field):	CompanyName:	EngineeringApproval:	Description (in TITLE field):
SW-Sheet Scale:	CheckedBy:	EngAppDate:	Weight:
SW-Current Sheet:	CheckedDate:	ManufacturingApproval:	Material:
SW-Total Sheets:	DrawnBy:	MfgAppDate:	Finish:
	DrawnDate:	QAApproval:	Revision:
	EngineeringApproval:	QAAppDate:	

The Title block is located in the lower right hand corner of Sheet1. The Drawing contains two modes:

1. Edit Sheet Format.

2. Edit Sheet.

Insert views and dimensions in the Edit Sheet mode. Modify the Sheet Format text, lines or title block information in the Edit Sheet Format mode.

The CompanyName Custom Property is located in the title block above the TITLE box. There is no value defined for CompanyName. A small text box indicates an empty field.

Define a value for the Custom Property CompanyName. Example: D&M ENGINEERING.

Activity: Create a Title Box

Activate the Edit Sheet Format Mode.
26) Right-click in **Sheet1**. Do not click in a drawing view. Click **Edit Sheet Format**. The Title block lines turn blue.

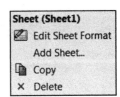

View the right side of the Title block.

27) Click the **Zoom to Area** tool from the Heads-up View toolbar.

28) **Zoom in** on the Title block.

29) Click the **Zoom to Area** tool to deactivate.

Define CompanyName Custom Property.
30) Position the **mouse pointer** in the middle of the box above the TITLE box as illustrated.

31) Click **File**, **Properties** from the Menu bar. The Summary Information dialog box is displayed.

32) Click the **Custom** tab.

33) Click inside the **Property Name** box.

34) Click the **drop down arrow** in the Property Name box.

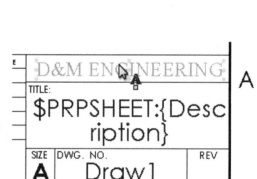

35) Select **CompanyName** from the Property menu.

36) Enter **D&M ENGINEERING** (or your company name) in the Value/Text Expression box.

37) Click inside the **Evaluated Value** box. The CompanyName is displayed in the Evaluated Value box.

38) Click **OK** from the dialog box.

39) Move your **mouse pointer** in the center of the block as illustrated. The Custom Property, $PRP: "COMPANYNAME," is displayed in the Title block.

Modify the font size.
40) Double-click the **D&M ENGINEERING** text. The Formatting dialog box is displayed.

41) Click the **drop down arrows** to set the Text Font and Height from the Formatting toolbar.

42) Click the **Style buttons** and **Justification buttons** to modify the selected text.

43) Close the Formatting dialog box.

44) Click **OK** from the Note PropertyManager.

Click a position outside the selected text box to save and exit the text.

The Tolerance block is located in the Title block. The Tolerance block provides information to the manufacturer on the minimum and maximum variation for each dimension on the drawing. If a specific tolerance or note is provided on the drawing, the specific tolerance or note will override the information in the Tolerance block.

General tolerance values are based on the design requirements and the manufacturing process.

 Create Sheet Formats for different part types; examples: sheet metal parts, plastic parts and high precision machined parts. Create Sheet Formats for each category of parts that are manufactured with unique sets of Title block notes.

Modify the Tolerance block in the Sheet Format for ASME Y14.5 machined millimeter parts. Delete unnecessary text. The FRACTIONAL text refers to inches. The BEND text refers to sheet metal parts. The Three Decimal Place text is not required for this millimeter part in the chapter.

Modify the Tolerance Note.

45) Double-click the text **INTERPRET GEOMETRIC TOLERANCING PER:**

46) Enter **ASME Y14.5**.

47) Click **OK** ✔ from the Note PropertyManager.

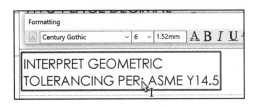

48) Double-click inside the **Tolerance block** text. The Formatting dialog box and the Note PropertyManager is displayed.

49) Delete the text **INCHES**.

50) Enter **MILLIMETERS**.

51) Delete the line **FRACTIONAL ±**.

52) Delete the text **BEND ±**.

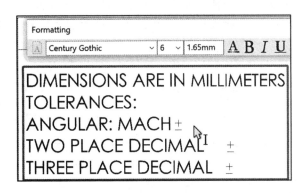

53) Click a **position** at the end of the ANGULAR: MACH ± line.

54) Enter **0**.

55) Click the **Add Symbol** button from the Text Format box. The Symbols dialog box is displayed.

56) Select **Degree** ° from the Symbols dialog box.

57) Enter **30'** for minutes of a degree.

Modify the TWO and THREE PLACE DECIMAL LINES.
58) Delete the **TWO** and **THREE PLACE DECIMAL lines**.

59) Enter **ONE PLACE DECIMAL ± 0.5**.

60) Enter **TWO PLACE DECIMAL ± 0.15**.

61) Click **OK** ✔ from the Note PropertyManager.

Fit the drawing to the Graphics window.
62) Press the **f** key.

Save Draw1.
63) Click **Save** . Accept the default name. Draw1 is the first default drawing file name.

DIMENSIONS ARE IN MILLIMETERS
TOLERANCES:
ANGULAR: MACH± 0°30'
ONE PLACE DECIMAL ±0.5
TWO PLACE DECIMAL ±.15

Various symbols are available through the Symbol dialog box. The ± symbol is located in the Modify Symbols list. The ± symbol is sometimes displayed as <MOD-PM>. The degree symbol ° is sometimes displayed as <MOD-DEG>.

Interpretation of tolerances is as follows:

- The angular dimension 110° is machined between 109.5° and 110.5°.

- The dimension 2.5 is machined between 2.0 and 3.0.

- The dimension 2.05 is machined between 1.90 and 2.20.

Company Logo

A Company logo is normally located in the Title block of the drawing. You can create your own Company logo or copy and paste an existing picture.

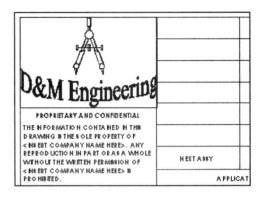

The Logo.jpeg file is provided. Copy the **LOGO** folder to your hard drive. Insert the Company logo in the Edit Sheet Format mode.

If you have your own Logo, use it for the drawing and skip the process of copying the logo below.

Activity: Insert a Company Logo

Insert a Company Logo.

64) Copy the **LOGO** folder to your hard drive. Note: If you have your own Logo, use it for the drawing.

65) Click **Insert**, **Picture** from the Menu bar. The Open dialog box is displayed.

66) Double-click the **Logo.jpg**. The Sketch Picture PropertyManager is displayed. Uncheck the **Lock aspect ratio** box.

67) Drag the picture handles to size the **picture** to the left side of the Title block. Note: Text was added to the picture.

68) Click **OK** ✔ from the Sketch Picture PropertyManager.

Text can be added to create a custom logo. You can insert a picture or an object.

View the provided videos on Drawing Fundamentals to enhance your experience in the chapter.

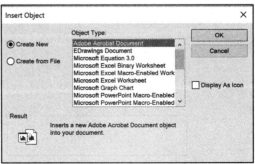

Return to the Edit Sheet mode.

69) Right-click in the **Graphics window**.

70) Click **Edit Sheet**. The Title block is displayed in black.

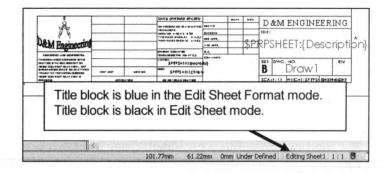

Title block is blue in the Edit Sheet Format mode.
Title block is black in Edit Sheet mode.

Fit the Sheet Format to the Graphics window.

71) Press the **f** key.

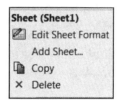

Draw1 displays Editing Sheet1 in the Status bar. The Title block is displayed in black when in Edit Sheet mode.

Save Sheet Format and Save As Drawing Template

Save the drawing document in the Graphics window in two forms: Sheet Format and Drawing Template. Save the Sheet Format as a custom Sheet Format named CUSTOM-A. Use the CUSTOM-A Sheet Format for the drawings in this chapter. The Sheet Format file extension is .slddrt.

The Drawing Template can be displayed with or without the Sheet Format. Combine the Sheet Format with the Drawing Template to create a custom Drawing Template named A-ANSI-MM. Utilize the Save As option to save a Drawing Template. The Drawing Template file extension is .drwdot.

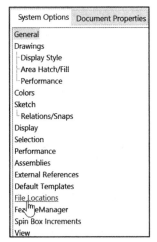

Always select the Save as type option first, then select the Save in folder to avoid saving in default SOLIDWORKS installation directories.

The System Options, File Locations, Document Templates option is only valid for the current session of SOLIDWORKS in some network locations. Set the File Locations option in order to view the SW-TUTORIAL-2017/MY-TEMPLATE tab in the New Document dialog box.

Activity: Save Sheet Format and Save As Drawing Template

Save the Sheet Format.

72) Click **File**, **Save Sheet Format** from the Menu bar. The Save Sheet Format dialog box is displayed.

The default Sheet Format folder is C:\ProgramData\SOLIDWORKS\SOLIDWORKS 2017\templates on a new installation (non-network). Do not select this folder. The file extension for Sheet Format is .slddrt.

73) Select **SW-TUTORIAL-2017\MY-TEMPLATES** for the Save in folder. If needed, create the MY-TEMPLATES sub-folder under SW-TUTORIAL-2017.

74) Enter **CUSTOM-A** for File name.

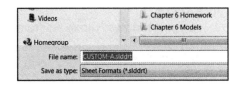

75) Click **Save** from the Save Sheet Format dialog box.

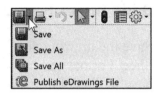

Save the Drawing Template.
76) Click **Save As** from the Menu bar.

77) Click **Drawing Templates (*.drwdot)** from the Save as type box.

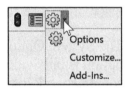

78) Select **SW-TUTORIAL-2017\MY-TEMPLATES** for the Save in folder.

79) Enter **A-ANSI-MM** for File name.

80) Click **Save**.

The A-ANSI-MM.drwdot drawing template is displayed in the Graphics window. Create and add the MY-TEMPLATES folder, under the SW-TUTORIAL-2017 folder to the File Locations Document Template System Option.

Set System Options - File Locations. Only perform this procedure if you are working on a non-network, private system.

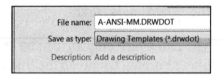

81) Click **Options** ⚙ from the Main menu.

82) Click **File Locations** under the System Options tab.

83) Click **Add**.

84) Select the **MY-TEMPLATES** folder. If needed create the folder under the **SW-TUTORIAL-2017** folder.

85) Click **OK** from the Browse for Folder menu.

86) Click **OK** to exit System Options.

87) Click **Yes**.

Close all files.
88) Click **Windows**, **Close All** from the Menu bar.

Create a New drawing.

89)   Click **New** ⬜ from the Menu bar.

90)   Click the **MY-TEMPLATES** tab.

91)   Double-click the **A-ANSI-MM** Drawing Template.

92)   If required, click **Cancel** ✖ from the Model View
PropertyManager. Draw2 is displayed in the Graphics window.

🔆 The Draw2-Sheet1 drawing is displayed in the Graphics
window. You have successfully created a new drawing
Template with a Custom sheet format.

Close all files.
93)   Click **Windows**, **Close All** from the Menu bar.

🔆 Combine customized
Drawing Templates and Sheet
Formats to match your
company's drawing standards.
Save the empty Drawing
Template and Sheet Format
separately to reuse
information.

🔍 Additional details on
Drawing Templates, Sheet
Format and Custom Properties
are available in
SOLIDWORKS Help Topics.
Keywords: Documents
(templates, properties); Sheet
Formats (new, new drawings,
note text); Properties (drawing
sheets); Customize Drawing
Sheet Formats.

Review Drawing Templates

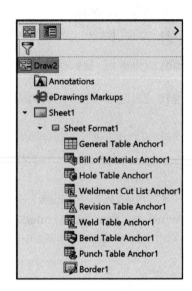

The Custom Drawing Template was created from the default Drawing Template. You modified Sheet Properties and Document Properties to control the Sheet size, Scale, Annotations and Dimensions.

The Sheet Format contained a Title block and Custom Property information. You inserted a Company Logo and modified the Title block.

The Save Sheet Format option was utilized to save the CUSTOM-A.slddrt Sheet Format. The Save As option was utilized to save the A-ANSI-MM.drwdot template.

The Sheet Format and Drawing Template were saved in the MY-TEMPLATES folder.

FLATBAR Drawing

A drawing contains part views, geometric dimensioning and tolerances, notes and other related design information. When a part is modified, the drawing automatically updates. When a dimension in the drawing is modified, the part is automatically updated.

Create the FLATBAR drawing from the FLATBAR part. Display the Front, Top, Right and Isometric views. Utilize the Model View tool from the View Layout toolbar.

Insert dimensions from the part. Utilize the Insert Model Items tool from the Annotation toolbar. Insert and modify dimensions and notes.

Insert a Parametric note that links the dimension text to the part depth. Utilize a user defined Part Number. Define the part material with the Material Editor. Add Custom Properties for Material and Number.

Activity: FLATBAR Drawing. Open the FLATBAR Part

Open the FLATBAR part. The FLATBAR part was created in Chapter 2.

94)   Click **Open** from the Menu bar.

95)   Select the **SW-TUTORIAL-2017** folder.

96)   Double-click **FLATBAR**. The FLATBAR FeatureManager is displayed.

Create a New drawing.

97)   Click **New** ⬜ from the Menu bar.

98)   Click the **MY-TEMPLATES** tab.

99)   Double-click **A-ANSI-MM**. Note: if you did not create the MY-TEMPLATES tab, create a drawing document, A-(ANSI) Landscape, Third Angle projection using the MMGS unit system. Add all needed Custom Properties.

The Model View PropertyManager is displayed if the Start command when creating new drawing box is checked. If the Model View PropertyManager is not displayed, click the Model View tool from the View Layout toolbar.

The FLATBAR 🕭 FLATBAR part icon is displayed in the Open documents box. Drawing view names are based on the part view orientation. The Front view is the first view inserted into the drawing. The Top view and Right view are projected from the Front view.

Insert the Front, Top and Right view.

100)   Click **Next** ➡ from the Model View PropertyManager.

101)   Check the **Create multiple views** box.

102)   Click *****Front**, *****Top** and *****Right** view from the Standard views box.

De-activate the Isometric view.
103)   Click the *****Isometric** icon from the Standard views box.

104)   Click **OK** ✔ from the Model View PropertyManager. View the three views on the drawing.

A part cannot be inserted into a drawing when the *Edit Sheet Format* mode is selected. You are required to be in the *Edit Sheet* mode.

Insert an Isometric view using the View Palette.

105) Click the **View Palette** tab on the right side of the Graphics window.

106) Select **FLATBAR** from the View Palette drop-down menu as illustrated. View the available views.

107) Click and drag the **Isometric view** in the top right corner as illustrated.

108) Click **OK** ✔ from the Drawing View PropertyManager.

*Isometric

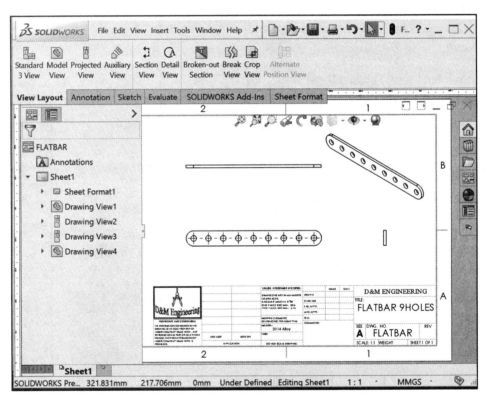

Click the View Palette tab in the Task Pane. Click the drop-down arrow to view any active documents or click the Browse button to locate a document. Click and drag the desired view/views into the active drawing sheet.

Modify the Sheet Scale.

109) Right-click Sheet1 in the FLATBAR FeatureManager as illustrated.

110) Click **Properties**. The Sheet Properties dialog box is displayed.

111) Enter **1:1** for Sheet Scale.

112) Click Close ⊠ from the Sheet Properties dialog box.

If needed, hide the Origins.

113) Click **View**, **Hide/Show,** un-check **Origins** from the Menu bar.

Save the drawing.

114) Click **Save As** from the Menu bar.

115) Enter **FLATBAR** in the SW-TUTORIAL-2017 folder.

116) Click **Save**.

117) Click **Save** 💾.

Text in the Title block is linked to the Filename and Description created in the part. The DWG. NO. text box utilizes the Property, $PRP:"SW-File Name" passed from the FLATBAR part to the FLATBAR drawing.

The Title text box utilizes the Property, $PRPSHEET: "Description."

The filename FLATBAR is displayed in the DWG. NO. box. The Description FLATBAR 9 HOLE is displayed in the Title box.

The FLATBAR drawing contains three Principle views (Standard views): Front, Top, Right and Isometric view.

Insert drawing views as follows:

- Utilize the Model View tool.

  o Drag a part into the drawing to create three Standard views.

  o Predefine views in a custom Drawing Template.

  o Drag a hyperlink through Internet Explorer.

- Drag an active part view from the View Palette. The View Palette is located in the Task Pane. With an open part, drag the selected view into the active drawing sheet.

The View Palette populates when you:

- Click Make Drawing from Part/Assembly.

- Browse to a document from the View Palette.

- Select from a list of open documents in the View Palette.

Move Views and Properties of the Sheet

Move Views on Sheet1 to create space for additional Drawing View placement.

The mouse pointer provides feedback in both the Drawing Sheet and Drawing View modes.

The mouse pointer displays the Drawing Sheet icon when the Sheet properties and commands are executed.

The mouse pointer displays the Drawing View icon when the View properties and commands are executed.

View the mouse pointer icon for feedback to select Sheet, View, and Component and Edge properties in the Drawing.

Use the Pack and Go option to save an assembly or drawing with references. The Pack and Go tool saves either to a folder or creates a zip file to e-mail. View SOLIDWORKS help for additional information.

Sheet Properties

- Sheet Properties display properties of the selected sheet.

  Right-click in the sheet boundary to view the available commands.

View Properties

- View Properties display properties of the selected view.

  Right-click inside the view boundary. Modify the View Properties in the Display Style box or the View Toolbar.

Component Properties

- Component Properties display properties of the selected

  component. Right-click on the face of the component. View the available options.

Edge Properties

- Edge Properties display properties of the selected

  geometry. Right-click on an edge inside the view boundary. View the available options.

Reposition the views on the drawing. Provide approximately 25mm - 50mm between each view for dimension placement.

Activity: FLATBAR Drawing-Position Views

Position the views.

118) Click inside the view boundary of **Drawing View1** (Front). The mouse pointer displays the Drawing View icon.

119) Position the **mouse pointer** on the edge of the view boundary until the Drawing View icon is displayed.

120) Drag **Drawing View1** in an upward vertical direction. The Top and Right views move aligned to Drawing View1 (Front).

121) Press **Shift + Z** key to Zoom in on Sheet1.

122) Click the **Right view** boundary.

123) Position the **mouse pointer** on the edge of the view until the Drawing Move View icon is displayed.

124) Drag the **Right view** in a right to left direction towards the Front view.

💡 Tangent edges are displayed for educational purposes.

Move the Top view in a downward vertical direction.

125) Click the **Top view**, "Drawing View3" boundary.

126) Drag the **Top view** in a downward direction towards Drawing View1.

Fit Sheet1 to the Graphics window.

127) Press the **f** key.

Detail Drawing

The design intent of this project is to work with dimensions inserted from parts and to incorporate them into the drawings. Explore methods to move, hide and recreate dimensions to adhere to a drawing standard.

There are other solutions to the dimensioning schemes illustrated in this project. Detail drawings require dimensions, annotations, tolerance, materials, Engineering Change Orders, authorization, etc. to release the part to manufacturing and other notes prior to production.

Review a hypothetical "worst case" drawing situation. You just inserted dimensions from a part into a drawing. The dimensions, extension lines and arrows are not in the correct locations. How can you address the position of these details? Answer: Dimension to an ASME Y14.5 standard.

No.	Situation:
1	Extension line crosses dimension line. Dimensions not evenly spaced.
2	Largest dimension placed closest to profile.
3	Leader lines overlapping.
4	Extension line crossing arrowhead.
5	Arrow gap too large.
6	Dimension pointing to feature in another view. Missing dimension – inserted into Detail view (not shown).
7	Dimension text over centerline, too close to profile.
8	Dimension from other view – leader line too long.
9	Dimension inside section lines.
10	No visible gap.
11	Arrows overlapping text.
12	Incorrect decimal display with whole number (millimeter), no specified tolerance.

Worst Case Drawing Situation

The ASME Y14.5 standard defines an engineering drawing standard.

Review the twelve changes made to the drawing to meet the standard.

Dimensions are displayed in MILLIMETERS.

No.	Preferred Application of the Dimensions:
1	Extension lines do not cross unless situation is unavoidable. Stagger dimension text.
2	Largest dimension placed farthest from profile. Dimensions are evenly spaced and grouped.
3	Arrowheads do not overlap.
4	Break extension lines that cross close to arrowhead.
5	Flip arrows to the inside.
6	Move dimensions to the view that displays the outline of the feature. Ensure that all dimensions are accounted for.
7	Move text off of reference geometry (centerline).
8	Drag dimensions into their correct view boundary. Create reference dimensions if required. Slant extension lines to clearly illustrate feature.
9	Locate dimensions outside off section lines.
10	Create a visible gap between extension lines and profile lines.
11	Arrows do not overlap the text.
12	Whole numbers displayed with no zero and no decimal point (millimeter).

Apply these dimension practices to the FLATBAR and other drawings in this project.

A Detailed drawing is used to manufacture a part. A mistake on a drawing can cost your company substantial loss in revenue. The mistake could result in a customer liability lawsuit.

Dimension and annotate your parts clearly to avoid common problems and mistakes.

Dimensions and Annotations

Dimensions and annotations are inserted from the part. The annotations are not in the correct location. Additional dimensions and annotations are required.

Dimensions and annotations are inserted by selecting individual features, views or the entire sheet. Select the entire sheet. Insert Model Items command from the Annotations toolbar.

Activity: FLATBAR Drawing-Dimensions and Annotations

Insert dimensions.

128) Click **Sheet1** in the center of the drawing. The mouse pointer displays the Sheet 🗔 icon.

129) Click the **Annotation** tab from the CommandManager.

130) Click the **Model Items** 🖈 tool from the Annotation toolbar. The Model Items PropertyManager is displayed. The Import items into all views option is checked.

131) Select **Entire model** from the Source box.

132) Click **OK** ✔ from the Model Items PropertyManager. Dimensions are inserted into the drawing.

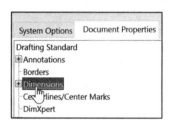

Remove trailing zeroes.

133) Click **Options** ⚙ from the Main menu.

134) Click the **Document Properties** tab from the dialog box.

135) Click the **Dimensions** folder.

136) Select **Remove** for the Trailing zeroes drop-down menu.

137) Click **OK** from the Document Properties - Dimensions dialog box.

💡 Dimensions are inserted into the drawing. The dimensions MAY NOT BE in the correct location with respect to the feature lines per the ANSI Y-14.5 standard. Move them later in the chapter and address extension line gaps (5mm).

The dimensions and text in the next section have been enlarged
for visibility. Drawing dimension location is dependent on
Feature dimension creation and *Selected drawing views*.

Move dimensions within the same view. Use the mouse pointer to
drag dimensions and leader lines to a new location. Leader lines
reference the size of the profile. A gap must exist between the
profile lines and the leader lines. Shorten the leader lines to
maintain a drawing standard. Use the blue Arrow buttons to flip
the dimension arrows.

Plan ahead for general drawing notes. Notes provide relative part
or assembly information. Example: Material type, material finish,
special manufacturing procedure or considerations, preferred
supplier, etc.

Below are a few helpful guidelines to create general drawing notes:

- Use capital letters.

- Use left text justification.

- Font size should be the same as the dimension text.

Create parametric notes by selecting dimensions in the drawing. Example: Specify the
material thickness of the FLATBAR as a note in the drawing. If the thickness is
modified, the corresponding note is also modified.

Hide superfluous feature dimensions. Do not delete feature dimensions. Recall hidden
dimension with the View, Show Annotations command. Move redundant, dependent
views outside the sheet boundary.

Move the linear dimensions in Drawing View1, (Front).
138) Click the vertical dimension text **101.6**. The dimension text turns blue.

139) Drag the **dimension text** downward.

140) Click the horizontal dimension **12.7**.

141) Drag the **text** approximately 10mms from the profile. The smallest linear dimensions are
closest to the profile.

142) Click the radial dimension **R6.35**.

143) Drag the **text** diagonally
off the profile if required.

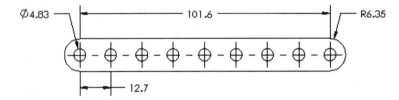

Modify dimension text.

144) Click the diameter dimension **4.83**. The Dimension
PropertyManager is displayed.

145) Click inside the **Dimension Text** box.

146) Enter **9X** before <MOD-DIAM>. Enter **EQ SP** after <DIM>.

147) Click **OK** ✔ from the Dimension PropertyManager.

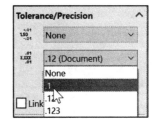

Inserted dimensions can be moved from one drawing view
to another. Hold the Shift key down. Click and drag the
dimension text from one view into the other view boundary.
Release the Shift key.

Modify the precision of the material thickness.

148) Click the **depth dimension** text in the Top view.

149) Select **.1** from the Unit Precision drop-down menu.

150) Click **OK** ✔ from the Dimension PropertyManager. The
text displays the dimension.

Insert a Parametric note.

151) Click the **Annotation** tab from the CommandManager.

152) Click the **Note** 𝖠 tool from the Annotation toolbar. The Note 🢡 icon is displayed.

153) Click a **position** above Front view. Enter **MATERIAL THICKNESS**. Click the depth
dimension text in the Top view. The variable name for the dimension is displayed in the text
box. Note: Your material thickness may vary if you modified the FLATBAR model.

154) Enter **MM**.

155) Click **OK** ✔ from the
Note PropertyManager.

Hide superfluous dimensions.
156) Right-click the **dimension in** the Top view. Note: Your Material Thickness may vary if you modified the FLATBAR model.

157) Click **Hide**.

Hide the Right view.
158) Right-click the **Right view** boundary.

159) Click **Hide**. Note: If required, expand the drop-down menu. The Right view is not displayed in the Graphics window.

160) Click **OK** ✔ from the Drawing View PropertyManager.

Fit the model to the drawing and address all needed extension line gaps.
161) Press the **f** key.

Save the drawing.
162) Click **Save** 🖫.

Locate the Top view off of Sheet1.
163) Click and drag the **Top view boundary** off of the Sheet1 boundary as illustrated.

Views and notes outside the sheet boundary do not print. The Parametric note is controlled through the FLATBAR Boss-Extrude1 feature depth. Modify the depth to update the note.

🔅 Click the dimension Palette rollover button 🔲 to display the dimension palette. Use the dimension palette in the Graphics window to save mouse travel to the Dimension PropertyManager. Click on a dimension in a drawing view, and modify it directly from the dimension palette.

🔅 To show a hidden dimension, click **View, Hide/Show, Annotations** from the Menu bar.

Open the FLATBAR part.
164) Right-click inside the **Front view** boundary.

165) Click **Open Part**. The FLATBAR part is displayed.

Modify the Boss-Extrude1 depth dimension.
166) Click **Boss-Extrude1** from the FeatureManager.

167) Click .**090**in, [2.29] in the Graphics window.

168) Enter **2.5mm** as illustrated. Note: You need to enter mm.

169) **Rebuild** the model.

Save the model.
170) Click **Save** 💾.

Return to the drawing.
171) Click **Window, FLATBAR - Sheet1** from the Menu bar. The Parametric note is updated to reflect the dimension change in the part.

172) **Return** to the FLATBAR part and **undo** the dimension change from 2.5mm to 2.3mm.

173) **Return** to the drawing. View the update.

The FLATBAR drawing references the FLATBAR part. Do not delete the part or move the part location. Work between multiple documents:

- Press Ctrl-Tab to toggle between open SOLIDWORKS documents.

- Right-click inside the Drawing view boundary. Select Open Part.

- Right-click the part icon in the FeatureManager. Select Open Drawing.

🔆 Commands are accessed through the toolbars and drop-down menus. Commands are also accessed with a right-click in the Graphics window and FeatureManager.

A majority of FLATBAR drawing dimensions are inserted from
the FLATBAR part. An overall dimension is required to
dimension the slot shape profile. Add a dimension in the
drawing.

Add a dimension to Drawing View1.

174) Click the **Smart Dimension** tool from the Annotation toolbar.
The Autodimension tab is selected by default.

175) Click the **Smart dimensioning** box.

176) Click the **top horizontal line** of the FLATBAR.

177) Click the **bottom horizontal line** of the FLATBAR.

178) Click a **position** to the right of the Front view as illustrated.

Modify the Radius text. R will be a stated reference dimension.
179) Click the **R6.36** dimension text.

180) Delete **R<DIM>** in the Dimension Text box.

181) Click **Yes** to confirm dimension override.

182) Enter **2X R** for Dimension text. Do not enter the radius value.

183) Click **OK** from the Dimension PropertyManager.

184) Insert all needed **extension line gaps (5mm)** as illustrated.

Save the FLATBAR drawing.
185) Click **Save**.

Part Number and Document Properties

Engineers manage the parts they create and modify. Each part requires a Part Number
and Part Name. A part number is a numeric representation of the part. Each part has a
unique number. Each drawing has a unique number. Drawings incorporate numerous part
numbers or assembly numbers.

There are software applications that incorporate unique part numbers to create and perform Bill of Materials, Manufacturing procedures, Cost analysis and Inventory control/Just in Time, JIT.

You are required to procure the part and drawing numbers from the documentation control manager. Utilize the following prefix codes to categorize created parts and drawings. The part name, part number and drawing numbers are as follows:

Category:	Prefix:	Part Name:	Part Number:	Drawing Number:
Machined Parts	56-	FLATEPLATE	GIDS-SC-10001-9	56-10222
		AXLE	GIDS-SC-10017	56-10223
		SHAFT-COLLAR	GIDS-SC-10012-3-16	56-10224
Purchased Parts	99-	AIRCYLINDER	99-FBM8x1.25	999-101-8
Assemblies	10-	LINKAGE ASM	GIDS-SC-1000	10-10123

Link notes in the Title block to SOLIDWORKS Properties. Properties are variables shared between documents and applications.

The machined parts are manufactured from Aluminum. Specify the Material Property in the part. Link the Material Property to the drawing title block. Create a part number that is utilized in the Bill of Materials. Create additional notes in the title block to complete the drawing.

Activity: FLATBAR Drawing-Part Number and Document Properties

Return to the FLATBAR part. Apply Material.
186) Right-click in the **Front view** boundary.

187) Click **Open Part**.

188) Right-click **Material** in the FLATBAR FeatureManager.

189) Click **Edit Material**. The Material dialog box is displayed.

190) Expand the Aluminum Alloys folder.

191) Select **2014 Alloy**. View the material properties.

192) Click the **Apply** button.

193) Click **Close**. The 2014 Alloy is displayed in the FeatureManager.

Save the FLATBAR.
194) Click **Save** .

Define the part number property for the BOM.
195) Click the FLATBAR **ConfigurationManager** tab.

196) Right-click **Default**.

197) Click **Properties**. The Configuration Properties PropertyManager is displayed.

198) Click **User Specified Name** from the drop-down box under Document Name.

199) Enter **GIDS-SC-10001-9** in the Part number text box.

Define a material property.
200) Click the **Custom Properties** button.

201) Click inside the **Property Name** box.

202) Click the **down arrow**. Select **Material** from the Property Name list.

203) Click inside the **Value/Text Expression** box.

204) Click the **down arrow**. Select **Material**.

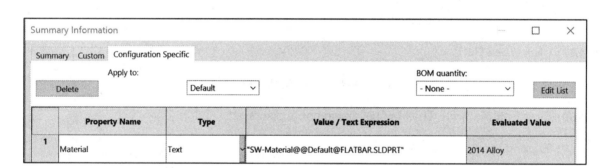

Define the Number Property.
205) Click inside the **second Property Name** box.

206) Click the **down arrow**.

207) Select **Number** from the Name list.

208) Click inside the **Value/Text Expression** box.

209) Enter **56-10222** for Drawing Number.

210) Click **OK** from the Summary Information dialog box.

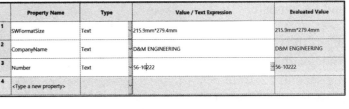

211) Click **OK** ✔ from the Configuration Properties PropertyManager.

Return to the FeatureManager.

212) Click the FLATBAR **FeatureManager** tab.

Save the FLATBAR part.

213) Click **Save** 💾.

Return to the drawing.

214) Click **Windows**, **FLATBAR - Sheet1** from the Main menu.

INTERPRET GEOMETRIC
TOLERANCING PER: ASME Y14.5

MATERIAL
2014 Alloy

The Material Property is inserted into the Title block.

Activity: FLATBAR Drawing-Linked Note

Create a Linked Note. First set the Drawing Number.

215) Click **File**, **Properties** from the Main menu. Click the **Custom** tab.

216) Click inside the **Property Name** box.

217) Click the **down arrow**. Select **Number** from the Property Name list.

218) Click inside the **Value/Text Expression** box.

219) Click the **down arrow**.

220) Enter **56-10222**.

221) Click **OK** from the Summary Information dialog box.

	Property Name	Type	Value / Text Expression	Evaluated Value
1	SWFormatSize	Text	215.9mm*279.4mm	215.9mm*279.4mm
2	CompanyName	Text	D&M ENGINEERING	D&M ENGINEERING
3	Number	Text	56-10222	56-10222
4	<Type a new property>			

222) **Right-click** in Sheet1.

223) Click **Edit Sheet Format**.

224) **Zoom in** on the lower right corner of the drawing.

225) Double-click on the DWG. NO. text **FLATBAR**. The Note PropertyManager is displayed.

226) Delete **FLATBAR**. Note: The Formatting dialog is still active.

227) Click **Link to Property** from the Text Format box.

228) Select **Current** document.

229) Select **Number** from the Link to Property drop-down menu.

230) Click **OK** from the Link to Property box.

231) Click **OK** ✔ from the Note PropertyManager.

Return to the drawing sheet.
232) Right-click a **position** in the Graphics window.

233) Click **Edit Sheet**.

234) If needed, **remove all Tangent Edges** from the Top and Isometric view.

235) Address **all extension line gaps (5mm) and any additional needed information** as illustrated below.

Save the FLATBAR drawing.

236) Click **Save** 💾.

As an exercise, insert the Third Angle projection icon located in the LOGO folder.

Add drawing Custom properties: DrawnBy and Drawndate.

Insert the reference dimension symbol for the second 12.7mm dimension as illustrated.

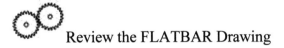 Additional details on Drawing Views, New Drawing, Details, Dimensions, Dimensions and Annotations are available in SOLIDWORKS Help.

Keywords: Drawing Views (overview); Drawing Views (model); Move (drawing views); Dimensions (circles, extension lines, inserting into drawings, move, parentheses); Annotations Hole Callout; Centerline; Center Mark; Properties and Sheet format.

Review the FLATBAR Drawing

You created the FLATBAR drawing with the A-ANSI-MM Drawing Template. The FLATBAR drawing utilized the FLATBAR part with the Model View tool and the View Palette tool.

The Model View PropertyManager provided the ability to insert new views of a document. You selected the Front, Top and Right view. You applied the View Palette to insert an Isometric view.

You moved the views by dragging the blue view boundary. You inserted part dimensions and annotations into the drawing with the Insert Model Items tool. Dimensions were moved to new positions. Leader lines and dimension text were repositioned. Annotations were edited to reflect the dimension standard.

You created a Parametric note that referenced part dimensions in the drawing text. Material was assigned in the FLATBAR part. The Material Custom Property and Number Custom Property were assigned in the FLATBAR part and referenced in the drawing Title block.

Know inch/mm decimal display. The ASME Y14.5 standard states:

- For millimeter dimensions < 1, display the leading zero. Remove trailing zeros.

- For inch dimensions < 1, delete the leading zero. The dimension is displayed with the same number of decimal places as its tolerance.

Note: The FLATBAR drawing linked Title block notes to Custom Properties in the drawing and in the part. The additional drawings in this project utilize drawing numbers linked to the model file name. The Title of the drawing utilizes a Note.

LINKAGE Assembly Drawing - Sheet1

The LINKAGE assembly drawing Sheet 1 utilizes the LINKAGE assembly. Add an Exploded view and a Bill of Materials to the drawing.

Create an Exploded view in the LINKAGE assembly. The Bill of Materials reflects the components of the LINKAGE assembly. Create a drawing with a Bill of Materials. Perform the following steps:

- Create a new drawing with the custom A-ANSI-MM size Drawing Template with the CUSTOM-A sheet format.

- Create and display the Exploded view of the LINKAGE assembly.

- Insert the Exploded view of the assembly into the drawing.

- Insert a Bill of Materials.

- Label each component with Balloon text.

Activity: LINKAGE Assembly Drawing-Sheet1

Close all parts and drawings.
237) Click **Windows**, **Close All** from the Menu bar.

Create a New drawing.

238) Click **New** ⬜ from the Menu bar.

239) Double-click **A-ANSI-MM** from the MY-TEMPLATES tab. The Model View PropertyManager is displayed. Note: if you did not create the MY-TEMPLATES tab, create a drawing document, A-(ANSI) Landscape, Third Angle projection using the MMGS unit system. Add all needed Custom Properties.

Open the LINKAGE assembly.
240) Click the **Browse** button.

241) Select **Assembly** for file type in the SW-TUTORIAL-2017 folder.

242) Double-click **LINKAGE**. Single view is selected by default.

243) If needed, click **Isometric view** from the Standard views box.

244) Select **Shaded With Edges** from the Display Style box.

245) Check the **Use custom scale** box.

246) Select **User Defined** from the drop down menu.

247) Enter **2:3** for Scale.

248) Click a **position** in the middle of Sheet1 as illustrated.

249) Click **OK** ✅ from the Drawing View1 PropertyManager.

Deactivate the Origins if needed.
250) Click **View**, **Hide/Show**, un-check **Origin** from the Menu bar.

Save the LINKAGE assembly drawing.

251) Click **Save** 💾. Accept the default file name.

252) Click **Save**.

Display modes for a Drawing view are similar to a part document. The 3D Drawing View tool provides the ability to manipulate the model view in 3D, to select a difficult face, edge, or point.

Wireframe and Shaded Display modes provide the best graphic performance. Mechanical details require Hidden Lines Visible display and Hidden Lines Removed display. Select Shaded/Hidden Lines Removed to display Auxiliary Views to avoid confusion.

Tangent Edges Visible provides clarity for the start of a Fillet edge. Tangent Edges Removed provides the best graphic performance.

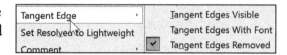

Right-click in the view boundary to access the Tangent Edge options.

Utilize the Lightweight Drawing option to improve performance for large assemblies.

Wireframe

Hidden Lines Visible

Hidden Lines Removed

Shaded

Tangent Edges Visible

Tangent Edges With Font

Tangent Edges Removed

To address Tangent lines views:

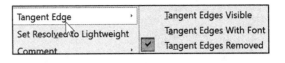

- Right-click in a Drawing view.

- Click Tangent Edge.

- Click a Tangent Edge view option.

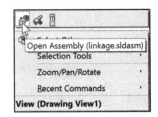

Return to the LINKAGE assembly. Set Configuration Properties.
253) Right-click inside the **Isometric view** boundary.

254) Click **Open Assembly**. The LINKAGE assembly is displayed.

255) Click the **ConfigurationManager** tab.

256) Right-click **Default [LINKAGE]**. Click **Properties**. The Configuration Properties PropertyManager is displayed.

257) Select **User Specified Name** from the Part number displayed when used in Bill of Materials.

258) Enter **GIDS-SC-1000** in the Part number text box. Click **OK** ✔ from the Configuration Properties PropertyManager.

Return to the FeatureManager.
259) Click the LINKAGE **FeatureManager** tab.

Save the model.
260) Click **Save** .

Exploded View

The Exploded View illustrates how to assemble the components in an assembly. Create an Exploded View with four steps. Click and drag components in the Graphics window. The Manipulator icon indicates the direction to explode. Select an alternate component edge for the Explode direction. Drag the component in the Graphics window or enter an exact value in the Explode distance box.

Manipulate the top-level components in the assembly. Access the Explode view option as follows:

- Right-click the configuration name in the ConfigurationManager.

- Select the Exploded View tool in the Assembly toolbar.

- Select Insert, Exploded View from the Menu bar.

Activity: LINKAGE Assembly Drawing-Exploded View

Insert an Exploded view.

261) Click the **ConfigurationManager** 🔲 tab.

262) Right-click **Default [GIDS-SC-1000]**.

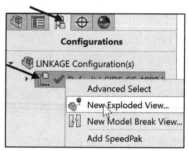

263) Click **New Exploded view** . The Explode PropertyManager is displayed.

264) Click the **Regular step (translate and rotate)** icon.

Create Explode Step 1. Use the distance box option.
265) Click the back **SHAFT-COLLAR** as illustrated.

266) Enter **50**mm in the Explode distance box.

267) Click **Apply**. The SHAFT-COLLAR moves 50mm to the back of the model. If required, click the **Reverse direction** button.

268) Click **Done**. Explode Step1 is created.

Create Explode Step 2. Use the Manipulator icon.
269) Click the front **SHAFT-COLLAR** in the Graphics window as illustrated.

270) Drag the **Manipulator icon** to the front of the assembly approximately 50mm.

271) Click **inside** the Graphics window. Explode Step2 is created.

Create Explode Step 3.
272) Click the **back FLATBAR** in the Graphics window as illustrated.

273) Drag the **Manipulator icon** to the back of the assembly. Explode Step3 is created.

Create Explode Step 4.
274) Click the **front FLATBAR** in the Graphics window.

275) Drag the **Manipulator icon** to the front of the assembly. Explode Step4 is created.

276) Click **inside** the Graphics window.

277) **Expand** each Explode Step to review.

278) Click **OK** ✔ from the Explode PropertyManager.

Save the LINKAGE part in the Exploded State.
279) Click **Save** 💾.

🔆 Create exploded view steps that rotate a component with or without linear translation. Use the rotation and translation handles of the triad. Include rotation and translation in the same explode step. You can also edit the explode step translation distance and rotation angle values in the PropertyManager.

Activity: LINKAGE Assembly Drawing-Animation

Animate the Exploded view.
280) **Expand** the Default [GIDS-SC-1000] folder.

281) Right-click **ExplView1** in the ConfigurationManager.

282) Click **Animate collapse** to play the animation. View the Animation.

Return the Exploded view in its collapsed state.
283) **Close** 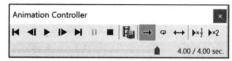 the Animation Controller dialog box.

Return to the Assembly FeatureManager.
284) Click the LINKAGE **FeatureManager** tab.

Save the assembly.
285) Click **Save** .

Open the LINKAGE drawing.
286) Click **Window, LINKAGE - SHEET1** from the Menu bar.

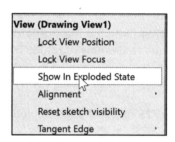

Display the Exploded view in the drawing.
287) Right-click inside the **Isometric view**.

288) Click **Show in Exploded State**. Note: You can also click **Properties,** Check the **Show in Exploded State** box and then click **OK** from the Drawing Views Properties box.

289) Click **OK** from the Drawing View1 PropertyManager. View the exploded state in the drawing on Sheet1.

Rebuild the Model.
290) Click **Rebuild** .

Bill of Materials

A Bill of Materials (BOM) is a table inserted into a drawing to keep a record of the parts used in an assembly. The default BOM template contains the Item Number, Quantity, Part No. and Description. The default Item number is determined by the order in which the component is inserted into the assembly. Quantity is the number of instances of a part or assembly.

Part No. is determined by the following: file name, default and the User Defined option, Part number used by the Bill of Materials. Description is determined by the description entered when the document is saved.

Activity: LINKAGE Assembly Drawing-Bill of Materials

Create a Bill of Materials.
291) Click inside the **Isometric view** boundary.

292) Click the **Annotation** tab from the CommandManager.

293) Click the **Bill of Materials** tool from the Consolidated Tables toolbar. The Bill of Materials PropertyManager is displayed.

294) Select **bom-material** for Table Template.

295) Select **Top-level only** for BOM Type.

296) Click **OK** ✔ from the Bill of Materials PropertyManager.

297) Double-click a position in the **upper left corner** of the Sheet1.

298) Click a **position** in Sheet1.

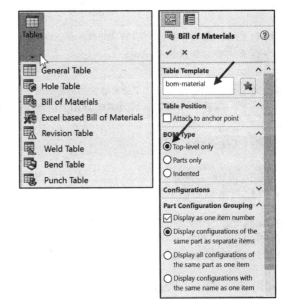

ITEM NO.	PART NUMBER	DESCRIPTION	MATERIAL	QTY.
1	Flexible	LINEAR ACTUATOR		1
2	AXLE	AXLE ROD		1
3	FLATBAR	9HOLES	2014 Alloy	2
4	SHAFT-COLLAR	SHAFT-COLLAR		2

The Bill of Materials requires some editing. The AXLE and SHAFT-COLLAR PART NUMBER values are not defined. The current part file name determines the PART NUMBER value.

The current part description determines the
DESCRIPTION values. Redefine the PART NUMBER for
the Bill of Materials. Note: You will also scale the
LINKAGE assembly.

Modify the AXLE Part number.
299) Right-click the **AXLE** part in the LINKAGE drawing.

300) Click **Open Part**. The AXLE FeatureManager is displayed.

301) Click the AXLE **ConfigurationManager** tab.

302) Right-click **Default [AXLE]** in the ConfigurationManager.

303) Click **Properties**. Select **User Specified Name** from the
Configuration Properties dialog box.

304) Enter **GIDS-SC-10017** for the Part Number to be utilized
in the Bill of Materials.

305) Click **OK** ✔ from the Configuration Properties
PropertyManager. **Return** to the FeatureManager.

306) Click **Save** 🖫.

Return to the LINKAGE drawing. Save the drawing.
307) Click **Window**, **LINKAGE - Sheet1** from the Menu bar.

Modify the SHAFT-COLLAR PART NUMBER.
308) Right-click the front **SHAFT-COLLAR** part in the LINKAGE drawing
as illustrated.

309) Click **Open Part**. The SHAFT-COLLAR FeatureManager is
displayed. Click the SHAFT-COLLAR **ConfigurationManager** 🔠
tab.

310) Right-click **Default [SHAFT-COLLAR]** from the
ConfigurationManager.

311) Click **Properties**. Select the **User Specified Name** from the
Configuration Properties box.

312) Enter **GIDS-SC-10012-3-16** for the Part Number in the Bill of
Materials. Click **OK** ✔ from the Configuration Properties
PropertyManager.

313) **Return** to the FeatureManager. Click **Save** 🖫.

💡 Double-click the values in the BOM table (Keep Link) to directly edit the Custom
Property of the Part/Assembly.

Return to the LINKAGE assembly drawing.
314) Click **Window, LINKAGE - Sheet1** from the Menu bar.

315) Rebuild the drawing and update the BOM.

Modify the LINKAGE assembly scale.
316) Click inside the **Isometric view** boundary.

317) Enter **1:2** for Scale.

318) Click **OK** ✅ from the Drawing View1 PropertyManager.

Save the drawing.
319) Click **Save** 💾.

ITEM NO.	PART NUMBER	DESCRIPTION	MATERIAL	QTY.
1	GIDS-PC-10001	LINEAR ACTUATOR		1
2	GIDS-SC-10017	AXLE ROD		1
3	GIDS-SC-10001-9	9HOLES	2014 Alloy	2
4	GIDS-SC-10012-3-16	SHAFT-COLLAR		2

Note: As an exercise, complete the Bill of Materials. Add Material to each component. Label each component with a unique item number. The item number is placed inside a circle. The circle is called Balloon text. List each item in a Bill of Materials table. Utilize Auto Balloon to apply Balloon text to all BOM components.

The Circle Split Line option contains the Item Number and Quantity. Item number is determined by the order listed in the assembly FeatureManager. Quantity lists the number of instances in the assembly.

Activity: LINKAGE Assembly Drawing-Automatic Balloons

Insert the Automatic Balloons.
320) Click inside the **Isometric view** boundary of the LINKAGE.

321) Click the **Auto Balloons** tool from the Annotation toolbar. The Auto Balloon PropertyManager is displayed. Accept the defaults. Note: The Insert Magnet line option inserts one or more magnetic lines when Pattern type is not Circular.

322) Click **OK** ✅ from the Auto Balloon PropertyManager.

Reposition the Balloon text.
323) Click and drag each **Balloon** to the desired position.

324) Click and drag the **Balloon arrowhead** to reposition the arrow on a component edge.

325) Click **OK** ✔ from the Balloon PropertyManager.

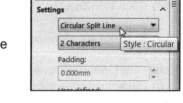

Display Item Number/Quantity.
326) Ctrl-Select the **four Balloon text** in the Graphics window. The Balloon PropertyManager is displayed.

327) Select **Circular Split Line** for Style.

328) Click **OK** ✔ from the Balloon PropertyManager.

Save the LINKAGE assembly drawing.
329) Click **Save** 💾.

🔆 Select the BOM table in the drawing and Right-click Properties to modify entries and display table parameters.

LINKAGE Assembly Drawing - Sheet2

A drawing consists of one or more sheets. Utilize the Model View tool in the View Layout toolbar to insert the AirCylinder assembly. The LINKAGE drawing Sheet2 displays the Front view and Top view of the AirCylinder assembly.

Insert a Section View to display the internal features of the AirCylinder. Insert a Detail View to display an enlarged area of the AirCylinder.

Activity: LINKAGE Assembly Drawing-Sheet2

Add Sheet2.
330) Right-click in the Graphics window.

331) Click **Add Sheet**. Sheet2 is displayed.

🔆 You can also add a sheet by clicking the Add Sheet icon in the lower left corner of the Graphics window.

332) Right-click **Sheet2** in the Drawing FeatureManager.

333) Click **Properties**.

Select the CUSTOM-A Sheet Format.
334) Click **Browse** from the Sheet Properties box.

335) Select the **SW-TUTORIAL-2017\MY-TEMPLATES** folder.

336) Double-click **CUSTOM-A**. Click **Apply Changes** from the Sheet Properties box. Sheet 2 of 2 is displayed in the Graphics window. CUSTOM-A was created at the beginning of the chapter. If you did not create CUSTOM A, accept the default sheet format and fill in all of the needed icons and Custom Properties.

Insert the AirCylinder assembly.
337) Click the **View Layout** tab from the CommandManager.

338) Click the **Model View** tool from the View Layout toolbar. The Model View PropertyManager is displayed.

339) Click the **Browse** button.

340) Double-click the **AirCylinder** assembly from the SW-TUTORIAL-2017 folder.

341) Check the **Create multiple views** box. Create a Top and Front view drawing.

342) Click **Top view** as illustrated in the Standard views box.

343) Click **OK** from the Model View PropertyManager.

Save Sheet2.
344) Click **Save** .

💡 Drawing sheets are ordered as they are created. The names are displayed in the FeatureManager design tree and as Excel-style tabs at the bottom of the Graphics window. Activate a sheet by right-clicking in FeatureManager design tree and clicking Activate or click the tab name.

Enter Title Name and Modify font size.
345) **Right-click** in the Graphics window.

346) Click **Edit Sheet Format**.

347) **Double-click** on the Title:

348) Enter **LINEAR ACTUATOR**. Resize the text to the Title block. Enter **5**mm for text height.

349) Click inside the **Graphics window**.

350) **Right-click** in the Graphics window.

351) Click **Edit Sheet**.

Section views display the interior features. Define a cutting plane with a sketched line in a view perpendicular to the Section view. Create a full Section view by sketching a section line in the Top view. Detailed views enlarge an area of an existing view. Specify location, shape and scale. Create a Detail view from a Section view at a 2:1 scale.

Activity: LINKAGE Assembly Drawing-Sheet2 Section View

Add a Section View to the drawing.
352) Click inside the **Drawing View3** boundary.

353) Click the **Section View** ⤵ tool from the View Layout toolbar. The Section View PropertyManager is displayed.

354) Click the **Section** tab from the PropertyManager.

355) Click the **Horizontal** Cutting Line button. Check the **Auto-start section view** box.

356) Click the **midpoint** of the model as illustrated.

Position Section View A-A and Modify the Drawing Scale.
357) Click **OK** from the Section View dialog box. Click a **location** above the Top view. The section arrows point upward.

358) If needed, check the **Flip direction** box.

359) Click **OK** ✔ from the Section View PropertyManager.

360) Modify the Drawing Scale to 1:2.

SECTION A-A

Fit the views to the drawing.
361) Press the **f** key.

Activity: LINKAGE Assembly Drawing-Sheet2 Detail view

Add a Detail view to the drawing.
362) Click inside the **Section View** boundary. The Section View A-A PropertyManager is displayed.

363) Zoom in to enlarge the view.

SECTION A-A

364) Click the **Detail View** tool from the View Layout toolbar. The Circle Sketch tool is selected.

365) Click the **center** of the air fitting on the left side in the Section View as illustrated.

366) Sketch a **Circle** to encompass the air fitting. If required, enter **B** for Detail View Name in the Label text box.

Position Detail View B.
367) Press the **f** key.

368) Click a **location** on Sheet2 to the right of the SECTION View.

369) Enter **2:1** for Scale.

370) Click **OK** from the Detail View B PropertyManager.

Select a view boundary before creating Projected Views, Section Views or Detail Views.

Move views if required.
371) Click and drag the **view boundary** to allow for approximately 1 inch, [25mm] spacing between views.

Save the LINKAGE assembly drawing.
372) Click **Save** 💾.

Close all parts and assemblies.
373) Click **Window**, **Close All** from the Menu bar.

Additional details on Exploded View, Notes, Properties, Bill of Materials, Balloons, Section View and Detail View are available in SOLIDWORKS Help. Keywords: Exploded, Notes, Properties (configurations), Bill of Materials, Balloons, Auto Balloon, Section and Detail.

Review the LINKAGE Assembly Drawing

The LINKAGE Assembly drawing consisted of two sheets. Sheet1 contained an Exploded view. The Exploded view was created in the LINKAGE assembly.

The Bill of Materials listed the Item Number, Part Number, Description, Material and Quantity of components in the assembly. Balloons were inserted to label top level components in the LINKAGE assembly. You developed Custom Properties in the part and utilized the Properties in the drawing and Bill of Materials.

Sheet2 contained the Front view, Top view, Section view and Detail view of the AirCylinder assembly.

Design Tables

A Design Table is a spreadsheet used to create multiple configurations in a part or assembly. The Design Table controls the dimensions and parameters in the part. Utilize the Design Table to modify the overall length and number of holes in each FLATBAR.

Create three configurations of the FLATBAR: 3HOLE, 5HOLE and 7HOLE

Utilize the Design Table to control the Part Number and Description in the Bill of Materials. Insert the custom parameter $PRP@DESCRIPTION into the Design Table. Insert the system parameter $PARTNUMBER into the Design Table.

Activity: FLATBAR Part-Design Table

Open the FLATBAR part.

374) Click **Open** 📂 from the Menu bar.

375) Double-click the **FLATBAR** part from the SW-TUTORIAL-2017 folder. The FLATBAR FeatureManager is displayed.

Insert a Design Table.
376) Click **Insert**, **Tables**, **Design Table** from the Menu bar. The Auto-create option is selected. Accept the default settings.

377) Click **OK** ✅ from the Design Table PropertyManager.

Select the input dimension.
378) Hold the **Ctrl key** down.

379) Click the **D1@Sketch1, D2@Sketch1, D1@Boss-Extude1, D1@Sketch2, D3@LPattern1** and **D1@LPattern1** from the Dimensions box.

380) Release the **Ctrl key**.

381) Click **OK** from the Dimensions dialog box.

The illustrated dimension variable names in the Dimensions dialog box will be different if sketches or features were deleted when creating the FLATBAR part.

The input dimension names and default values are automatically entered into the Design Table. The Design Table displays the Primary Units of the Part. Example: Inches. The value Default is entered in Cell A3.

The values for the FLATBAR are entered in Cells B3 through G9. The FLATBAR length is controlled in Column B. The Number of Holes is controlled in Column G.

Enter the three configuration names.
382) Click **Cell A4**.

383) Enter **3HOLE**.

384) Click **Cell A5**.

385) Enter **5HOLE**.

386) Click **Cell A6**.

387) Enter **7HOLE**.

388) Click Cell **D3**.

389) If needed, enter **0.09** to round off the Thickness value.

Enter the dimension values for the 3HOLE configuration.
390) Click **Cell B4**. Enter **1**.

391) Click **Cell G4**. Enter **3**.

	A	B	C	D	E	F	G	H
1	Design Table for: FLATBAR							
2		D1@Sketch1	D2@Sketch1	D1@Boss-Extrud	D1@Sketch2	D3@LPattern1	D1@LPattern1	
3	Default	4	0.25	0.090551181	0.19	0.5	9	
4	3HOLE	1					3	
5	5HOLE							
6	7HOLE							
7								
8								

Enter the dimension values for the 5HOLE
configuration.

392) Click **Cell B5**.

393) Enter **2**.

394) Click **Cell G5**.

395) Enter **5**.

Enter the dimension values for the 7HOLE
configuration.

396) Click **Cell B6**.

397) Enter **3**.

398) Click **Cell G6**.

399) Enter **7**.

Build the three configurations.

400) Click a **position** outside the EXCEL
Design Table in the Graphics window.

401) Click **OK** to generate the configurations.
The Design Table icon is displayed in the
FLATBAR FeatureManager.

Display the configurations.

402) Double-click **3HOLE**.

403) Double-click **5HOLE**.

404) Double-click **7HOLE**.

405) Double-click **Default**.

Save the model.

406) Click **Save** .

407) Edit the Design Table.

408) Right-click **Design Table** in the ConfigurationManager.

409) Click **Edit Table**. The Add Rows and Columns dialog
box is displayed.

410) Click **Cancel** from the Add Rows and Columns dialog
box.

Columns C through G are filled with the default FLATBAR values.

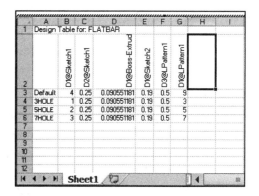

Enter parameters for DESCRIPTION and PARTNUMBER. Custom Properties begin with the prefix "$PRP@". SOLIDWORKS Properties begin with the prefix "$".

Enter DESCRIPTION custom Property.
411) Double-click **Cell H2**.

412) Enter **$PRP@DESCRIPTION**.

413) Click **Cell H3**. Enter **9HOLES**.

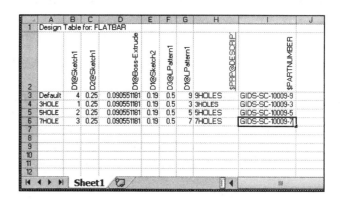

414) Click **Cell H4**. Enter **3HOLES**.

415) Click **Cell H5**. Enter **5HOLES**.

416) Click **Cell H6**. Enter **7HOLES**.

Enter the PARTNUMBER Property.
417) Double-click **Cell I2**.

418) Enter **$PARTNUMBER**.

419) Click **Cell I3**.

420) Enter **GIDS-SC-10009-9**.

421) Click **Cell I4**.

422) Enter **GIDS-SC-10009-3**.

423) Click **Cell I5**.

424) Enter **GIDS-SC-10009-5**.

425) Click **Cell I6**.

426) Enter **GIDS-SC-10009-7**.

427) Click a **position** in the Graphics window to update the Design Table. View the updated ConfigurationManager.

Activity: FLATBAR Drawing - Sheet2

Select configurations in the drawing. The Properties option in the Drawing view displays a list of configuration names.

Open the FLATBAR drawing.

428) Click **Open** 📂 from the Menu bar.

429) Double-click the **FLATBAR drawing** from the SW-TUTORIAL-2017 folder. The FLATBAR drawing is displayed. The dimensions tied to the Design table are displayed in a different color. The dimension color is controlled from the System Options, Colors section.

Copy the Front view.
430) Click inside the FLATBAR **Front view** boundary.

431) Press **Ctrl C**. **Right-click** in the Graphics window.

432) Click **Add Sheet**. Sheet2 is displayed. Right-click **Properties**.

433) Click **Browse** from the Sheet Properties dialog box.

434) Double-click **CUSTOM-A** Sheet Format from the SW-TUTORIAL-2017/MY-TEMPLATES folder. Click **OK** from the Sheet Properties box. CUSTOM-A was created at the beginning of the chapter. If you did not create CUSTOM A, accept the default sheet format and fill in all of the needed icons and Custom Properties.

Paste the Front view from Sheet1.
435) Click a **position** inside the Sheet2 boundary.

436) Press **Ctrl V**. The Front view is displayed.

Display the 3HOLE FLATBAR configuration on Sheet2.
437) Right-click inside the **Front view** boundary.

438) Click **Properties**.

439) Select **3HOLE** from the Use named configuration list.

440) Click **OK** from the Drawing View Properties dialog box. The 3HOLE FLATBAR configuration is displayed.

441) Right-click inside the **Drawing View** boundary.

442) Click **Open Part**.

443) View the **model configuration**. 3 HOLE is selected by the drawing.

Return to the FLATBAR Drawing Sheet2.
444) Click **Window**, **FLATBAR - Sheet2** from the Menu bar.

445) Click on the **9X** dimension text in the Graphics window. The Dimension PropertyManager is displayed. Note: You can also use the Pop-up menu in this procedure.

446) Replace the 9X dimension text with **3X** in the Dimension Text box as illustrated.

447) Click **OK** ✔ from the Dimension PropertyManager.

448) **Align** all dimension text as illustrated below.

449) Address **all extension line gaps and any other needed information**.

Save the FLATBAR Sheet2 drawing.

450) Click **Save** 💾.

The 5HOLE and 7HOLE configurations are explored as an exercise. Combine the FLATBAR configurations with the SHAFT-COLLAR part to create three different assemblies. Select configuration in the assembly. The Properties in the FeatureManager option displays a list of configuration names.

The FLATBAR-SHAFTCOLLAR assembly contains a FLATBAR fixed to the assembly Origin and a SHAFTCOLLAR mated to the FLATBAR left hole. The default configuration utilizes the FLATBAR-9HOLE part.

Design Tables exist in the assembly. Utilize a Design Table to control part configurations 3HOLE, 5HOLE and 7HOLE. Utilize the Design Table to Control Suppress/Resolve state of a component in an assembly. Insert the parameter $STATE into the Design Table.

Activity: FLATBAR-SHAFTCOLLAR Assembly

Return to the Default FLATBAR configuration.
451) Right-click in the **3HOLE FLATBAR** view boundary.

452) Click **Open Part**.

453) Click the **ConfigurationManager** tab.

454) Double-click the **Default** configuration.

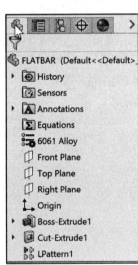

455) Click the **FeatureManager** tab. The FLATBAR (Default) FeatureManager is displayed.

Save the model.
456) Click **Save**.

Create the FLATBAR-SHAFTCOLLAR assembly.
457) Click **New** from the Menu bar.

458) Double-click **Assembly** from the Templates tab. The Begin Assembly PropertyManager is displayed. FLATBAR is an active document. FLATBAR is displayed in the Open documents box.

459) Click **FLATBAR** from the Open documents box.

460) Click **OK** from the Begin Assembly PropertyManager. The FLATBAR is fixed to the Origin.

Save the FLATBAR-SHAFTCOLLAR assembly.

461) Click **Save** 💾.

462) Enter **FLATBAR-SHAFTCOLLAR** for Assembly name. Click **Save**.

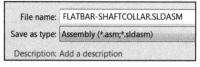

Insert the SHAFTCOLLAR part.

463) Click the **Insert Components** 📎 tool from the Assembly toolbar. The Insert Component PropertyManager is displayed.

464) Click **BROWSE**.

465) Double-click the **SHAFT-COLLAR** part.

466) Click a **position** to the front left of the FLATBAR as illustrated in the Graphics window.

Fit the model to the Graphics window. Save the model.
467) Press the **f** key.

468) Click **Save** 💾.

Mate the SHAFTCOLLAR. Insert a Concentric mate.
469) Click the **left inside hole face** of the FLATBAR.

470) Hold the **Ctrl** key down.

471) Click the outside **cylindrical face** of the SHAFT-COLLAR.

472) Release the **Ctrl** key. The Mate pop-up menu is displayed. Click **Concentric** from the Mate pop-up menu.

Insert a Coincident mate.
473) Click the **back flat face** of the SHAFT-COLLAR.

474) **Rotate** to view the front face of the FLATBAR.

475) Hold the **Ctrl** key down.

476) Click the **front face** of the FLATBAR.

477) Release the **Ctrl** key.

478) Click **Coincident** from the Mate pop-up menu.

Insert and mate the second SHAFT-COLLAR to the right hole.

479) Click the **Insert Components** tool from the Assembly toolbar. The Insert Component PropertyManager is displayed.

480) Click the **Browse** button.

481) Double-click the **SHAFT-COLLAR** part.

482) Click a **position** to the front right of the FLATBAR as illustrated.

Mate the second SHAFTCOLLAR. Insert a Concentric mate.

483) Click the **right hole face** of the FLATBAR.

484) Hold the **Ctrl** key down.

485) Click the **outside cylindrical face** of the SHAFT-COLLAR.

486) Release the **Ctrl** key.

487) Click **Concentric** from the Mate pop-up menu.

Insert a Coincident mate.

488) Click the **back flat face** of the SHAFT-COLLAR.

489) **Rotate** to view the front face of the FLATBAR.

490) Hold the **Ctrl** key down. Click the **front face** of the FLATBAR.

491) Release the **Ctrl** key. Click **Coincident** from the Mate pop-up menu.

Save the FLATBAR-SHAFTCOLLAR assembly.

492) Click **Save** .

The FLATBAR-SHAFTCOLLAR FeatureManager displays the Default configuration of the FLATBAR in parentheses, FLATBAR<1> (Default).

The instance number <1> indicates the first instance of the FLATBAR. Note: Your instance number will be different if you delete the FLATBAR and then reinsert into the assembly. The exact instance number is required for the Design Table.

Create a Design Table that contains three new configurations. Each configuration utilizes a different FLATBAR configuration. Control the Suppress/Resolve State of the second SHAFT-COLLAR.

Insert a Design Table.
493) Click **Insert**, **Tables**, **Design Table** from the Menu bar. The Auto-create option is selected by default.

494) Click **OK** ✔ from the Design Table PropertyManager.

Enter the Design Table values.
495) Default is displayed in Cell A3. Click **Cell A4**.

496) Enter **NO SHAFT-COLLAR**.

497) Double-click **CELL B2**.

498) Enter **\$STATE@SHAFT-COLLAR<2>**.

499) Click **Cell B3**.

500) Enter **R** for Resolved.

501) Click **Cell B4**.

502) Enter **S** for Suppressed.

503) Click a **position** outside the Design Table in the Graphics window.

504) Click **OK** to display the NO SHAFT-COLLAR configuration.

Display the configurations.
505) If needed, click the **ConfigurationManager** tab.

506) Double-click the **NO SHAFT-COLLAR** configuration. The second SHAFT-COLLAR is suppressed in the Graphics window.

507) Double-click the **Default** configuration. The second SHAFT-COLLAR is resolved. Both SHAFT-COLLARs are displayed in the Graphics window.

Tangent edges are displayed for educational purposes.

Insert FLATBAR configurations.
508) Right-click **Design Table**.

509) Click **Edit Table**.

510) Click **Cancel** from the Add Rows and Columns dialog box.

Enter Configuration names.
511) Click **Cell A5**. Enter **3HOLE FLATBAR**.

512) Click **Cell A6**. Enter **5HOLE FLATBAR**.

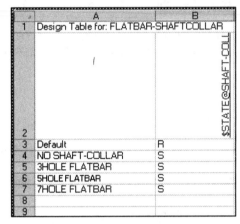

513) Click **Cell A7**. Enter **7HOLE FLATBAR**.

Enter STATE values.
514) Click **Cell B5**. Enter **S** for Suppress.

515) Click Cell **B6**. Enter **S**.

516) Click **Cell B7**. Enter **S**.

Enter Design Table values.
517) Double-click **Cell C2**.

518) Enter **$CONFIGURATION@FLATBAR<1>**.

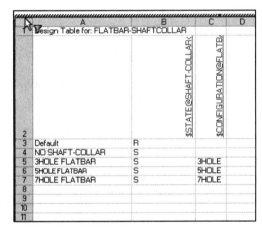

519) Click **Cell C5**.

520) Enter **3HOLE**.

521) Click **Cell C6**.

522) Enter **5HOLE**.

523) Click **Cell C7**.

524) Enter **7HOLE**.

525) Click a **position** in the Graphics window to exit.

526) Click **OK** to create the three configurations.

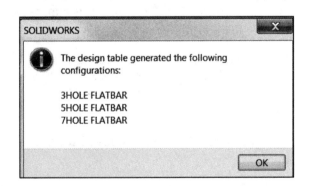

Display the configurations.
527) Double-click the **3HOLE FLATBAR** configuration.

528) Double-click the **5HOLE FLATBAR** configuration.

529) Double-click the **7HOLE FLATBAR** configuration.

530) Double-click the **Default** configuration.

531) Click the **Assembly FeatureManager** tab.

Display an Isometric view. Save the assembly.
532) Display an **Isometric view** ⬛.

533) Click **Save** 🖫.

Close all documents.
534) Click **Windows**, **Close All** from the Menu bar.

Always return to the default configuration in the assembly. Control the individual configuration through properties of a view in a drawing and properties of a component in the assembly.

🔍 Additional details on Design Tables and Configurations are available in SOLIDWORKS Help.

Insert a Center of Mass Point

Add a center of mass (COM) point to parts, assemblies or drawings. COM points added in component documents also appear in the assembly document. In a drawing document of parts or assemblies that contain a COM point, you can display and reference the COM point.

Add a COM to a part or assembly by clicking **Center of Mass** (Reference Geometry toolbar) or **Insert, Reference Geometry, Center of Mass** ⊕ or checking the **Create Center of Mass feature** box in the Mass Properties dialog box.

The center of mass of the model is displayed in the Graphics window and in the FeatureManager design tree just below the origin.

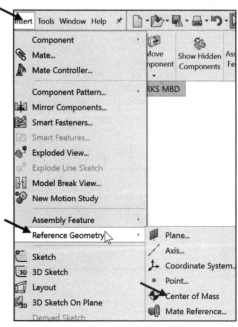

The position of the **COM** point
updates when the model's center of mass
changes. The COM point can be
suppressed and unsuppressed for
configurations.

You can measure distances and add
reference dimensions between the COM
point and entities such as vertices, edges,
and faces.

Add a center of mass (COM) point to a
drawing view. The center of mass is a
selectable entity in drawings, and you can
reference it to create dimensions.

In a drawing document, click **Insert,
Model Items**. The Model Items
PropertyManager is displayed. Under
Reference Geometry, click the **Center of
Mass** icon. Enter any needed additional
information. Click **OK** from the Model
Items PropertyManager. View the results
in the drawing.

The part or assembly **needs to have
a COM before** you can view the COM in
the drawing. To view the center of mass
in a drawing, click **View, Hide/Show,
Center of mass**.

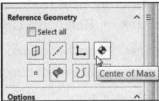

Chapter Summary

You created two drawings: the FLATBAR drawing and the LINKAGE assembly drawing. The drawings contained Standard views, Detail view, Section view and an Isometric view.

The drawings utilized a Custom Sheet Format and a Custom Drawing Template. The Sheet Format contained the Company logo and Title block information.

The FLATBAR drawing consisted of two Sheets: Sheet1 and Sheet2. You obtained an understanding of displaying views with the ability to insert, add, and modify dimensions. You used two major design modes in the drawings: Edit Sheet Format and Edit Sheet.

The LINKAGE assembly drawing contained two sheets. Sheet1 contained an Exploded view and a Bill of Materials. The Properties for the Bill of Materials were developed in each part and assembly. Sheet2 utilized a Detail view and a Section view of the AirCylinder assembly.

You created three configurations of the FLATBAR part with a Design Table. The Design Table controlled parameters and dimensions of the FLATBAR part. You utilized these three configurations in the FLATBAR-SHAFTCOLLAR assembly.

Drawings are an integral part of the design process. Part, assemblies and drawings all work together. From your initial design concepts, you created parts and drawings that fulfilled the design requirements of your customer.

🔆 View the provided videos on Drawing Fundamentals in this book to enhance your experience with the chapter.

🔆 To show a hidden dimension, click **View**, **Hide/Show**, **Annotations** from the Menu bar.

Questions

1. Describe a Bill of Materials and its contents.

2. Name the two major design modes used to develop a drawing in SOLIDWORKS.

3. True or False. Units, Dimensioning Standards, Arrow size, Font size are modified in the Options, Document Properties section.

4. How do you save a Sheet Format?

5. Identify seven components that are commonly found in a title block.

6. Describe the procedure to insert an Isometric view to the drawing.

7. In SOLIDWORKS, a drawing file name ends with a _____ suffix. A part file name ends with a _____ suffix.

8. True or False. In SOLIDWORKS, if a part is modified, the drawing is updated with a Rebuild command.

9. True or False. In SOLIDWORKS, when a dimension in the drawing is modified, the part is updated with a Rebuild command.

10. Name three guidelines to create General Notes on a drawing.

11. True or False. Most engineering drawings use the following font: Times New Roman - all small letters.

12. What are Leader lines? Provide an example.

13. Describe the key differences between a Detail view and a Section view on a drawing.

14. Identify the procedure to create an Exploded view.

15. Describe the purpose of a Design Table in a part and in an assembly.

16. Review the Design Intent section in the Introduction. Identify how you incorporated design intent into the drawing.

17. Identify how you incorporate design intent into configurations with a Design Table.

Exercises

Exercise 4.1: FLATBAR - 3 HOLE Drawing

Note: Dimensions are enlarged for clarity. Utilize inch, millimeter, or dual dimensioning.

- Create the A (ANSI) Landscape IPS Third Angle Projection FLATBAR - 3HOLE drawing. First create the part from the drawing. Then create the drawing. Use the default A (ANSI) Landscape Sheet Format/Size.

- Insert a Shaded Isometric view. No Tangent Edges displayed.

- Insert a Front and Top view. Insert dimensions. Address all needed extension line gaps. Insert 3X - EQ. SP.

- Insert the Company name, logo and Third Angle Projection icon.

- Add a Parametric Linked Note for MATERIAL THICKNESS.

- Hide the Thickness dimension in the Top view. Insert needed Centerlines. Insert the correct drawing views display modes.

- Insert Custom Properties for Material (2014 Alloy), DRAWNBY, DRAWNDATE, COMPANYNAME, etc.

Exercise 4.2: CYLINDER Drawing

Create the A (ANSI) Landscape IPS - Third Angle CYLINDER drawing.

- First create the part from the drawing. Then create the drawing. Use the default A (ANSI) Landscape Sheet Format/Size.

- Insert the Front and Right view as illustrated. Insert dimensions. Address all needed extension line gaps. Think about the proper view for your dimensions.

- Insert the Company name, logo and Third Angle projection icon. The Third Angle Projection icon is available in the homework folder.

- Insert needed Centerlines and Center Marks. Insert the correct drawing views display modes.

- Insert Custom Properties: Material, Description, DrawnBy, DrawnDate, CompanyName, etc.

- Material is AISI 1020.

- Utilize the Mass Properties tool from the Evaluate toolbar. Calculate the volume and mass of the CYLINDER part.

- Set decimal places to 4 under the Options button in the Mass Properties dialog box.

Exercise 4.3: PRESSURE PLATE Drawing

Create the A (ANSI) Landscape IPS - Third Angle PRESSURE PLATE drawing.

- First create the part from the drawing. Then create the drawing. Use the default A (ANSI) Landscape Sheet Format/Size.

- Insert the Front and Right view as illustrated. Insert dimensions. Address all needed extension line gaps. Insert the correct drawing views display modes. Think about the proper view for your dimensions.

- Insert Company name, logo, and Third Angle projection icon. The Third Angle Projection icon is available in the homework folder.

- Insert needed Centerlines and Center Marks.

- Insert Custom Properties: Material, Description, DrawnBy, DrawnDate, CompanyName, etc.

- Material is 1060 Alloy.

Exercise 4.4: LINKS Assembly Drawing

- Create the LINK assembly. Utilize three different
  FLATBAR configurations and a SHAFT-COLLAR.
  The parts are located in the chapter folder.

- Create the LINK assembly drawing as illustrated. Use
  the default A (ANSI) Landscape Sheet Format/Size.

- Insert Company name, logo and Third Angle
  projection icon. The icon is available in the homework
  folder. Remove all Tangent Edges.

- Insert Custom Properties: Description, DrawnBy,
  DrawnDate, CompanyName, etc.

- Insert a Bill of
  Materials as
  illustrated with
  Balloons.

ITEM NO.	PART NUMBER	DESCRIPTION	MATERIAL	QTY.
1	GIDS-SC-10009-7	7 HOLES	2014 Alloy	1
2	GIDS-SC-10009-5	5 HOLES	2014 Alloy	1
3	GIDS-SC-10009-3	3 HOLES	2014 Alloy	1
4	GIDS-SC-10012-3-16	SHAFT-COLLAR	1060 Alloy	1

Exercise 4.5: PLATE-1 Drawing

Create the PLATE-1 drawing.

- First create the part from the drawing. Then create the drawing. Utilize the default A (ANSI) Landscape Sheet Format/Size.

- Insert the Front and Top views as illustrated. Insert dimensions.

- Address all needed extension line gaps. Insert the correct drawing views display modes. Think about the proper view for your dimensions.

- Insert Company name, logo, and Third Angle projection icon. The Third Angle projection icon is available in the homework folder.

- Insert needed Centerlines and Center Marks.

- Insert Custom Properties: Material, Description, DrawnBy, DrawnDate, CompanyName, etc.

- Material is 1060 Alloy.

Exercise 4.6: FLAT-PLATE Drawing

Create the FLAT-PLATE drawing.

- Create the part from the drawing. Then create the drawing.

- Utilize the default A (ANSI) Landscape Sheet Format/Size.

- Insert the Front, Top, Right and Isometric view as illustrated. Insert dimensions. Address all needed extension line gaps. Insert the correct drawing views display modes. Think about the proper view for your dimensions.

- Insert Company name, logo and Third Angle projection icon. The icon is available in the homework folder. Insert needed Centerlines and Center Marks.

- Insert Custom Properties: Material, Description, DrawnBy, DrawnDate, CompanyName, Hole Annotation, etc.

- Material is 1060 Alloy. Remove all Tangent Edges.

Exercise 4.7: LINKAGE-2 Drawing

- Create the LINKAGE-2 assembly drawing. Utilize the default A (ANSI) Landscape Sheet Format/Size.

- Insert an Isometric view, shaded view of the LINKAGE-2 Assembly created in the Chapter 2 exercises.

- Define the PART NO. Property and the DESCRIPTION Property for the AXLE, FLATBAR- 9HOLE, FLATBAR - 3HOLE and SHAFT COLLAR.

- Save the LINKAGE-2 assembly to update the properties. Return to the LINKAGE-2 Drawing. Insert a Bill of Materials with Auto Balloons as illustrated.

- Insert the Company and Third Angle Projection icon. Insert Custom Properties for DRAWNBY, DRAWNDATE and COMPANYNAME.

☀ Use the Pack and Go option to save an assembly or drawing with references. The Pack and Go tool saves either to a folder or creates a zip file to e-mail. View SOLIDWORKS help for additional information.

Exercise 4.8: Vertical Section view
Create a vertical section view. Modify the drawing view scale.

1. **Copy** the Chapter 4 Homework folder to your hard drive.

2. Open **Section View** from the Chapter 4 Homework\Section folder.

3. Click inside the **Drawing View1** view boundary. The Drawing View1 PropertyManager is displayed.

Display the origin on Sheet1.

4. Click **View ➢ Hide/Show ➢ Origins** from the Menu bar.

5. Click the **Section View** ⇄ drawing tool. The Section View PropertyManager is displayed.

6. Click the **Section** tab.

7. Click the **Vertical** Cutting Line button.

8. Click the **origin** as illustrated. Note: You can select the midpoint vs. the origin.

Place the Section view.

9. Click a **position** to the right of Drawing View1. The Section arrows point to the right. If required, click Flip direction.

10. Check **Auto hatching** from the Section View box.

11. Check the **Shaded With Edges** option from the Display Style box.

12. Click **OK** ✔ from the Section View A-A PropertyManager. Section View A-A is created and is displayed in the Drawing FeatureManager.

13. Click inside the **Drawing View1** view boundary. The Drawing View1 PropertyManager is displayed.

14. Modify the Scale to **1.5:1**.

15. Click **OK** ✔ from the Drawing View1 PropertyManager. Both drawing views are modified (parent and child).

SECTION A-A

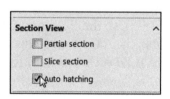

Exercise 4.9: Aligned Section view
Create an Aligned Section view.

1. **Copy** the Chapter 4 Homework folder to your hard drive.

2. Open **Aligned Section** from the Chapter 4 Homework\Aligned Section folder.

3. Click inside the **Drawing View1** view boundary. The Drawing View1 PropertyManager is displayed.

4. Click the **Section View** ⇆ drawing tool. The Section View PropertyManager is displayed.

5. Click the **Half Section** tab.

6. Click the **Leftside Down** Half Section button.

7. Select the **center** of the drawing view as illustrated. The Section View dialog box is displayed.

8. Click the **LENSCAP** in the Graphics window as illustrated. The LENSCAP component is displayed in the Excluded components box.

9. Check the **Auto hatching** box.

10. Click **OK** from the Section View dialog box.

Place the Section View.

11. Click a **position** above Drawing View1.

12. Click **OK** ✔ from the Section View A-A PropertyManager.

13. Modify the **scale** to **1:4**.

14. **Rebuild** 🔵 the drawing.

15. **Move** the drawing views to fit the Sheet. View the drawing FeatureManager.

16. **Close** the drawing.

SECTION A-A
SCALE 1 : 4

💡 Use Section View Assist, previously called the Section View User Interface, to add offsets to existing section views. To edit existing section views with Section View Assist: Right-click the section view or its cutting line and click **Edit Cutting Line**.

Exercise 4.10: Auxiliary view
Create an Auxiliary view from an existing Front view.

1. **Copy** the Chapter 4 Homework folder to your hard drive.

2. Open **Auxiliary view** from the Chapter 4 Homework\Auxiliary folder.

3. Click the **angled edge** in Drawing View1 as illustrated.

4. Click the **Auxiliary View** 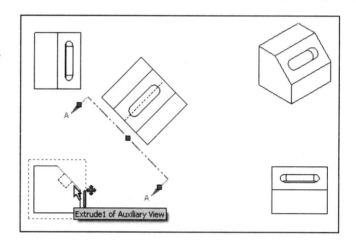 drawing tool.

5. Click a **position** up and to the right.

6. Drag the **A-A arrow** as illustrated.

7. Drag the **text** off the view.

8. Click **OK** ✔ from the Auxiliary View PropertyManager.

9. **Close** the drawing.

Exercise 4.11: CAM Drawing

- Create the CAM drawing. Utilize the default A (ANSI) Landscape Sheet Format/Size.

- Units: IPS. First create the part from the provided information. Then create the drawing.

- Insert a Front, Top, Right and Isometric view.

- Insert all needed drawing view dimensions, annotations, local and general notes, title block information, gaps, etc.

- Material is 1060 Alloy. Remove all Tangent Edges.

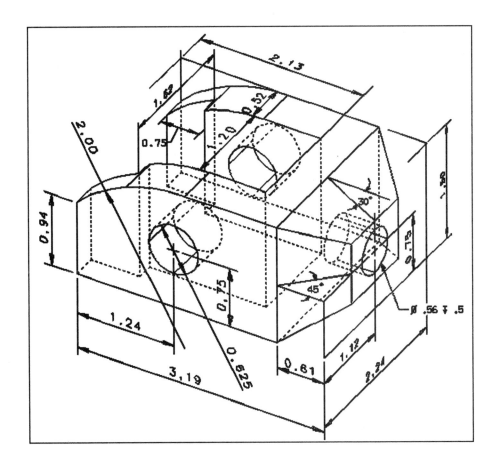

Notes:

Chapter 5
Advanced Features

Below are the desired outcomes and usage competencies based on the completion of Chapter 5.

Desired Outcomes:	Usage Competencies:

• Six parts for the PNEUMATIC-TEST-MODULE assembly:
    o WEIGHT
 	
    o HOOK
 	
    o WHEEL
 	
    o HEX-ADAPTER
 	
    o AXLE-3000
 	
    o SHAFTCOLLAR-500
	• Apply the following Advanced modeling features: Plane, Lofted Base, Extruded Cut, Swept Base, Dome, Thread, Extruded Boss/Base, Revolved Cut, Extruded Cut, Circular Pattern, Axis, Instant3D, Hole Wizard, Advanced Hole, Split Line and Thread Wizard.
	
	• Reuse geometry.
	
	• Modify existing parts to create new parts with the Save as copy command.

Notes:

Chapter 5 - Advanced Features

Chapter Objective

Obtain the ability to reuse geometry by modifying existing parts and to create new parts. Knowledge of the following SOLIDWORKS features: *Plane, Lofted Base, Extruded Cut, Swept Base, Dome, Thread, Extruded Boss/Base, Revolved Cut, Extruded Cut, Circular Pattern, Axis, Instant3D, Hole Wizard, Advanced Hole, Split Line and Thread Wizard.*

Create six individual parts:

- WEIGHT

- HOOK

- WHEEL

- HEX-ADAPTER

- AXLE-3000

- SHAFTCOLLAR-500

Develop a working understanding with multiple documents in an assembly. Build on sound assembly modeling techniques that utilize symmetry, component patterns, and mirrored components.

Create five assemblies:

- 3HOLE-SHAFTCOLLAR assembly

- 5HOLE-SHAFTCOLLAR assembly

- WHEEL-FLATBAR assembly

- WHEEL-AND-AXLE assembly

- PNEUMATIC-TEST-MODULE assembly

On the completion of this chapter, you will be able to:

- Create new parts and copy parts with the Save As command to reuse similar geometry.

- Utilize Construction geometry in a sketch.

- Apply the following SOLIDWORKS features:

  o Extruded Boss/Base

  o Extruded Cut

  o Dome

  o Plane

  o Lofted Boss/Base

  o Swept Boss/Base

  o Thread

  o Revolved Cut

  o Hole Wizard

  o Axis

  o Circular Pattern

  o Instant3D

  o Advanced Hole

  o Split Line

Chapter Overview

Six additional parts are required for the final
PNEUMATIC-TEST-MODULE assembly. Each
part explores various modeling techniques.

Create three new parts in this chapter:

- WEIGHT

- HOOK

- WHEEL

The WEIGHT and HOOK parts were applied in
the Chapter 3 Homework exercises. View the
Chapter 3 Homework folder for the parts if needed.

Utilize the Save As command and modify existing parts that were created in the previous chapters to create three additional parts for the PNEUMATIC-TEST-MODULE assembly.

- HEX-ADAPTER

- AXLE-3000

- SHAFTCOLLAR-500

The HEX-ADAPTER part utilizes modified geometry from the HEX-STANDOFF part.

The AXLE-3000 part utilizes modified geometry from the AXLE part.

The SHAFTCOLLAR-500 part utilizes modified geometry from the SHAFT-COLLAR part.

Press the **g** key to activate the Magnifying glass tool. Use the Magnifying glass tool to inspect a model and make selections without changing the overall view of your model in the Graphics window.

Redeem the code on the inside cover of the book. Download the models and videos to your hard drive. View the provided videos to enhance the user experience.

Videos
Name
SOLIDWORKS_Basics_Videos 3 of 3.zip
SOLIDWORKS_Basics_Videos 2 of 3.zip
SOLIDWORKS_Basics_Videos 1 of 3.zip

WEIGHT Part

The WEIGHT part is a machined part. Utilize
the Lofted feature. Create a Loft by blending
two or more profiles. Each profile is sketched
on a separate plane.

Create Plane1. Offset Plane1 from the Top
Plane.

Sketch a rectangle for the first profile on the
Top Plane.

Sketch a square for the second profile on
Plane1.

Select the corner of each profile to create the
Lofted feature.

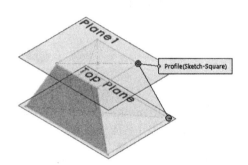

Utilize the Instant3D tool to create an Extruded
Cut feature to create a Though All hole
centered on the top face of the Loft feature.

🔆 Reference geometry defines the shape or
form of a surface or a solid. Reference geometry
includes planes, axes, coordinate systems, and
points.

🔆 When using the Instant3D tool, you lose
the ability to select an End Conditions to
maintain design intent.

All parts in this chapter utilize a custom part template. Create the custom part template from the default part template. Save the Custom Part template in the SW-TUTORIAL-2017\MY-TEMPLATE folder. If needed, create the SW-TUTORIAL-2017\MY-TEMPLATE folder.

Activity: Create the WEIGHT Part

Create a New part template.

1)   Click **New** ☐ from the Menu bar.

2)   Double-click **Part** from the Templates tab. The Part FeatureManager is displayed.

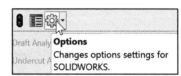

Set the Dimensioning standard.

3)   Click **Options** ⚙ from the Main menu.

4)   Click the **Document Properties** tab from the dialog box.

5)   Select **ANSI** from the Overall drafting standard drop-down menu.

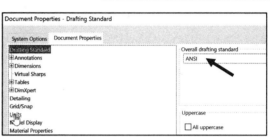

Set document unit.

6)   Click **Units**.

7)   Select **IPS**, **[MMGS]** for Unit system. Select **.123**, **[.12]** for linear units Decimal places.

8)   Select **None** for Angular units Decimal places.

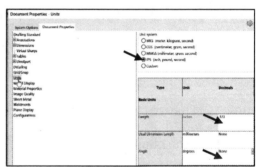

Set Leader arrow direction.

9)   Click **Dimensions**. Check the **Smart** box as illustrated.

10)   Click **OK** from the Document Properties - Detailing - Dimensions dialog box.

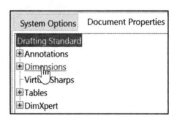

Save the Part template.

11)   Click **Save As** from the drop-down Menu bar.

12)   Select **Part Templates (*.prtdot)** for Save as type. Select **SW-TUTORIAL-2017\MY-TEMPLATES** for Save in folder.

13)   Enter **PART-ANSI-IN**, [PART-ANSI-MM] for File name. Click **Save**.

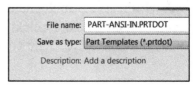

Close the Part template.

14)   Click **File**, **Close** from the Menu bar.

Create a New part.

15)   Click **New** ⬜ from the Menu bar.

16)   Click the **SW-TUTORIAL-2017\MY-TEMPLATES** tab.

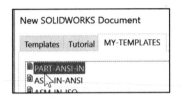

17)   Double-click **PART-ANSI-IN**, [PART-ANSI-MM]. The Part
FeatureManager is displayed.

Save the part.

18)   Click **Save As** from the drop-down Menu bar.

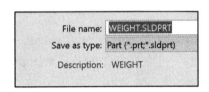

19)   Select the **SW-TUTORIAL-2017** folder.

20)   Enter **WEIGHT** for File name.

21)   Enter **WEIGHT** for Description.

22)   Click **Save**.

Insert Plane1.

23)   Right-click **Top Plane** from the FeatureManager.

24)   Click **Show**. The Top Plane is displayed in the Graphics
window. Note: In a new installation, Planes and Origins
may be displayed by default.

25)   Hold the **Ctrl** key down.

26)   Click the **boundary** of the Top Plane as illustrated.

27)   Drag the **mouse pointer** upward.

28)   Release the **mouse pointer**.

29)   Release the **Ctrl** key. The Plane PropertyManager
is displayed. Top Plane is displayed in the First
Reference box.

🔅 To display the Origin, click **View**, **Hide/Show**,
Origins from the Menu bar menu.

🔅 Utilize the Search feature in the Systems
Options dialog box to quickly locate information for
System Options or Document Properties.

30)   Enter .**500**in, [**12.70**] for Distance.

31)   Click **OK** ✔ from the Plane PropertyManager.

Plane1 is displayed in the Graphics window and is listed in the FeatureManager. Plane1 is offset from the Top Plane.

A Lofted feature requires two sketches. The first sketch, Sketch1, is a rectangle sketched on the Top Plane centered about the

Origin ⌞. The second sketch, Sketch2, is a square sketched on Plane1 centered about the Origin.

Create Sketch1 in the Top Plane.
32)   Right-click **Top Plane** from the FeatureManager.

33)   Click **Sketch** ⊞ from the Context toolbar. The Sketch toolbar is displayed.

34)   Click **Center Rectangle** ⌷ from the Consolidated Sketch tool. The Center Rectangle icon is displayed.

35)   Click the **Origin** ⌞.

36)   Click a **position** to the top right as illustrated.

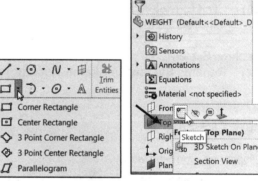

🔆 The Center Rectangle tool provides the ability to sketch a rectangle located at a center point, in this case the Origin. This eliminates the need for centerlines to the Origin with a Midpoint geometric relation.

Add dimensions.

37)   Click the **Smart Dimension** Sketch tool.

38)   Click the **top horizontal** line.

39)   Click a **position** above the line.

40)   Enter **1.000**in, [25.40].

41)   Click the **Green Check mark** ✔.

42)   Click the **right vertical** line.

43)   Click a **position** to the right.

44)   Enter **.750**in, [19.05].

45)   Click the **Green Check mark** ✔.

Close Sketch1.
46)   Click **Exit Sketch** from the Sketch toolbar. The sketch is fully defined and is displayed in black.

Rename Sketch1.
47)   Rename **Sketch1** to **Sketch-Rectangle**.

Save the part.
48)   Click **Save** 💾.

Display an Isometric view.
49)   Click **Isometric view** 🟦 from the Heads-up View toolbar.

Create Sketch2 on Plane1. Plane1 is your Sketch plane.
50)   Right-click **Plane1** from the FeatureManager. Plane1 is your Sketch plane.

51)   Click **Sketch** 🗔 from the Context toolbar. The Sketch toolbar is displayed.

52)   Click the **Center Rectangle** ▫️ Consolidated Sketch tool. The Center Rectangle icon is displayed.

53)   Click the **Origin** ⌞.

54) Click a **position** as illustrated.

55) Right-click **Select** to de-select the Center Rectangle tool.

Add an Equal relation between the left vertical line and the top horizontal line.

56) Click the **left vertical line** of the rectangle.

57) Hold the **Ctrl** key down.

58) Click the **top horizontal line** of the rectangle.

59) Release the **Ctrl** key.

60) Right-click **Make Equal** = from the Context toolbar.

61) Click **OK** ✔ from the Properties PropertyManager.

Add a dimension.

62) Click the **Smart Dimension** ⟨ Sketch tool.

63) Click the **top horizontal** line.

64) Click a **position** above the line.

65) Enter .**500**in, [**12.70**].

66) Click the **Green Check mark** ✔ .

Close Sketch2. Display an Isometric view.

67) Click **Exit Sketch** from the Sketch toolbar. Sketch2 is fully defined and is displayed in black.

68) Click **Isometric view** 📦 from the Heads-up View toolbar. View the results in the Graphics window.

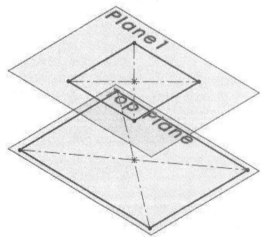

💡 If you did not select the Origin, insert a Coincident relation between the rectangle and the Origin to fully define Sketch2.

💡 Think design intent. When do you use the various End Conditions and Geometric sketch relations? What are you trying to do with the design? How does the component fit into an assembly?

Rename Sketch2.
69)   Rename **Sketch2** to **Sketch-Square**.

Save the WEIGHT part.
70)   Click **Save** 💾.

💡 Lofted features are comprised of multiple sketches. Name sketches for clarity.

Activity: WEIGHT Part-Lofted Feature

Insert a Lofted feature.
71)   Click the **Features** tab from the CommandManager.

72)   Click the **Lofted Boss/Base** ⬇ Feature tool. The Loft PropertyManager is displayed.

73)   Clear the **Profiles** box.

74)   Click the **back right corner** of Sketch-Rectangle as illustrated.

75)   Click the **back right corner** of Sketch-Square. Sketch-Rectangle and Sketch-Square are displayed in the Profiles box.

76)   Click **OK** ✔ from the Loft PropertyManager. Loft1 is displayed in the FeatureManager.

77)   **Hide** all planes.

💡 To display the Selection Filter toolbar, right-click in the Graphics window, and click the **Selection Filters** icon. The Selection Filter is displayed.

💡 To clear a Filter icon 🔽, click **Clear All Filters** from the Selection Filter toolbar.

78)   **Expand** Loft1 in the FeatureManager. Sketch-Rectangle and Sketch-Square are the two sketches that contain the Loft feature.

79)   **Zoom in** on the Loft1 feature.

Activity: WEIGHT Part-Instant3D - Extruded Cut Feature

Insert a New sketch for the Extruded Cut feature.

80)   Right-click the **top square face** of the Loft1 feature for the Sketch plane.

81)   Click **Sketch** ⬚ from the Context toolbar. The Sketch toolbar is displayed.

82)   Click the **Circle** ⬭ Sketch tool. The circle icon is displayed.

83)   Click the **center** ⬆ as illustrated.

84)   Click a **position** to the right as illustrated.

Add a dimension.

85)   Click the **Smart Dimension** ⟡ Sketch tool.

86)   Click the **circumference** of the circle.

87)   Click a **position** in the Graphics window above the circle to locate the dimension.

88)   Enter **.150**in, **[3.81]** in the Modify box.

Insert an Extruded feature using the Instant3D tool.

89)   **Exit** the Sketch. By default, Instant3D is active.

90)   Click the **diameter** of the circle, Sketch3, as illustrated.

91)   Click the **Arrowhead** and drag it below the model.

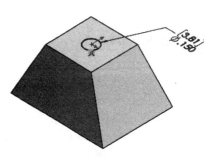

92)   Click a **position** on the Instant3D ruler. The Extrude feature is displayed in the FeatureManager.

Display Wireframe style.

93)   Click **Wireframe** ⬡ from the Heads-up View toolbar. View the Extrude feature.

Rename the Extrude feature.

94)   Rename the **Extrude** feature to **Hole-for-Hook** as illustrated.

Display an Isometric view. Display Shaded With Edges. Save the WEIGHT part.

95)   Click **Isometric view** from the Heads-up View toolbar.

96)   Click **Shaded With Edges** from the Heads-up View toolbar.

97)   Click **Save** . The WEIGHT part is complete.

 Review the WEIGHT Part

The WEIGHT part was created with the Loft feature. The Loft feature required two planes: Top Plane and Plane1. Profiles were sketched on each plane. Profiles were selected to create the Loft feature.

An Extruded Cut feature was created using the Instant3D tool to create a Through All center hole in the WEIGHT.

HOOK Part

The HOOK part fastens to the WEIGHT. The HOOK is created with a Swept Base feature. The Swept Base feature adds material by moving a profile along a path.

The Swept Base feature requires two sketches (path and profile) or a sketch path and a circular profile diameter. If the sketch profile is a circle, enter the circular profile diameter in the Swept PropertyManager.

For non-circular sketch profiles, create the sketch on a perpendicular plane to the path and use the pierce relation to locate the profile on the path.

Create the HOOK part with a Swept Base feature.

The Swept Base feature uses:

- A path sketched on the Right Plane.

- A circular profile diameter.

Utilize the Dome feature ⬭ tool to create a spherical feature on a circular face.

Utilize the Thread feature 🔩 tool to create a right-hand #8-36 thread for the HOOK. The Thread tool can add or remove material.

🔆 Reference geometry defines the shape or form of a surface or a solid. Reference geometry includes planes, axes, coordinate systems and points.

Activity: Create the HOOK Part

Create the New part.

98) Click **New** 🗋 from the Menu bar.

99) Select the **SW-TUTORIAL-2017\MY-TUTORIAL** tab.

100) Double-click **PART-ANSI-IN**, [PART-ANSI-MM].

Save the part.

101) Click **Save** 💾.

102) Select the **SW-TUTORIAL-2017** folder.

103) Enter **HOOK** for File name.

104) Enter **HOOK** for Description.

105) Click **Save**. The HOOK FeatureManager is displayed.

If the sketch profile is a circle, enter the diameter in the Swept PropertyManager. For non-circular sketch profiles, create the sketch on a perpendicular plane to the path and use the pierce relation to locate the profile on the path.

Sketch1 is the Sweep Path sketched on the Right Plane.

Sketch the Sweep Path.
106) Right-click **Right Plane** from the FeatureManager.

107) Click **Sketch** from the Context toolbar.

108) Click the **Line** Sketch tool. The Insert Line
PropertyManager is displayed.

109) Sketch a **vertical line** from the Origin as illustrated.   Origin

Add a dimension.
110) Click the **Smart Dimension** Sketch tool.

111) Click the **vertical line**.

112) Click a **position** to the right.

113) Enter **.250**in, [**6.35**].

114) Click the **Green Check mark** .

Fit the model to the Graphics window.
115) Press the **f** key.

Create the Centerpoint arc.
116) Click the **Centerpoint Arc** Sketch tool from
the Consolidated Sketch toolbar. The
Centerpoint Arc icon is displayed.

117) Click the **arc center point** vertically aligned to
the Origin.

118) Click the **arc start point** as
illustrated.

Arc start
point

119) Move (do not drag) the **mouse pointer** clockwise approximately 260°.

120) Click a point **horizontally aligned** to the arc start point.

121) Click the **3 Point Arc** ⌒ Sketch tool from the Consolidated Sketch toolbar. The Arc PropertyManager is displayed.

122) Click the **vertical line** endpoint.

123) Click the **center point arc** endpoint.

124) Drag and pull the center of the **3 Point Arc downwards**.

125) Click the center of the **center point arc line** as illustrated.

126) Click **OK** ✔ from the Arc PropertyManager.

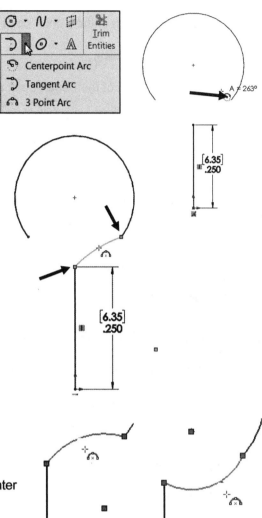

☀ It is important to draw the correct shape with the 3 Point Arc tool as illustrated.

Add a Vertical relation between the Origin and the center point of the arc.

127) Click the **Origin** ⌊.

128) Hold the **Ctrl** key down.

129) Click the **center point** of the Center point arc.

130) Release the **Ctrl** key.

131) Click **Vertical** | from the Add Relations box.

Correct shape   **Incorrect shape**

Add a Horizontal relation.
132) Click the **start point** of the Center point arc.

133) Hold the **Ctrl** key down.

134) Click the **end point** of the Center point arc.

135) Release the **Ctrl** key.

136) Click **Horizontal** ── from the Add Relations box.

Add a Tangent relation.
137) Click the **vertical line**.

138) Hold the **Ctrl** key down.

139) Click the **3 Point Arc**.

140) Release the **Ctrl** key.

141) Click **Tangent** ⟳ from the Add Relations box.

Add a second Tangent relation.

142) Click the **3 Point Arc**.

143) Hold the **Ctrl** key down.

144) Click the **Center point** arc.

145) Release the **Ctrl** key.

146) Click **Tangent** ⟳ from the Add Relations box.

Add dimensions.
147) Click the **Smart Dimension** ⟋ Sketch tool.

148) Click the **3 Point Arc**.

149) Click a **position** to the left.

150) Enter .500in, [**12.70**].

151) Click the **Green Check mark** ✔.

Dimension the overall length of the sketch.
152) Click the **top of the arc**.

153) Click the **Origin** L.

154) Click a **position** to the right of the profile. Accept the default dimension.

155) Click the **Green Check mark** ✔.

156) Click the **Leaders** tab in the Dimension PropertyManager.

If needed, modify the Arc condition.
157) Click the First arc condition: **Max**.

158) Click **OK** ✔ from the Dimension PropertyManager.

Modify the overall length.
159) Double-click the default **dimension**.

160) Enter **1.000**in, **[25.40]**.

161) Click the **Green Check mark** ✔.

Fit the model to the Graphics window.
162) Press the **f** key.

163) Move the **dimensions** to the correct location.

By default, the Dimension tool utilizes the center point of an arc or circle. Select the circle profile during dimensioning. Utilize the Leaders tab in the Dimension PropertyManager to modify the arc condition to Minimum or Maximum.

Close the sketch.
164) Click **Exit Sketch** from the Sketch toolbar.

Rename Sketch1.
165) Rename **Sketch1** to **Sketch-Path**.

Save the HOOK.
166) Click **Save** 💾.

Center point   Minimum Arc Conditions   Maximum

Activity: HOOK Part-Swept Base Feature

Insert the Swept feature.

167) Click the **Swept Boss/Base** 🦴 Features tool. The Sweep PropertyManager is displayed.

168) Select **Circular Profile**.

169) Click **Sketch-Path** from the fly-out FeatureManager. Sketch-Profile is displayed in the Profile box.

170) Enter **0.150**in diameter.

171) Click **OK** ✔ from the Sweep PropertyManager. Sweep1 is displayed in the FeatureManager.

Save the HOOK part.

172) Click **Save** 💾.

Activity: HOOK Part-Dome Feature

Insert a Dome feature.

173) Rotate the model with the middle mouse button.

174) Click the **flat face** of the Sweep1 feature in the Graphics window as illustrated.

175) Click the **Dome** 🔵 Features tool (Insert, Features, Dome). The Dome PropertyManager is displayed. Face<1> is displayed in the Parameters box.

176) Enter **.050**in, **[1.27]** for Distance.

177) Click **OK** ✔ from the Dome PropertyManager. Dome1 is displayed in the FeatureManager.

The HOOK requires a simplified right-hand #8-36 thread from the bottom of the Sweep1 feature. Utilize the Thread feature. The Thread feature provides the ability to create helical threads on cylindrical faces using profile sketches. Store custom thread profiles as library features.

Define the start thread location, specify an offset, set end conditions, specify the type, size, diameter, pitch and rotation angle, and choose options such as right-hand or left-hand thread.

Activity: HOOK Part-Thread Feature

Create a right-hand #8-36 thread from the bottom of the Sweep1 feature.

178) Click **Thread** from the Features toolbar. The Thread PropertyManager is displayed.

179) Click the **bottom circular** face of Sweep1. Edge <1> is displayed in the Edge of cylinder box.

180) Click inside the **Optional start location** box.

181) Click the **bottom face**. Face<1> is displayed.

Select End Condition.
182) Select **Up To Selection** for End Condition.

183) Click inside the **End Condition** box.

184) Click the **ending edge** as illustrated. Edge<2> is displayed in the End Condition box.

Set Thread Specification.
185) Click **Inch Die** from the drop down menu.

Set Thread Size.
186) Click **#8-36** for size from the drop down menu. View the Override diameter and Override pitch number.

Set the Thread method.
187) Click the **Cut thread** box.

Create a Right-hand thread.
188) Click **Right-hand thread** as illustrated.

189) Click the **Trim with start face** box.

190) Click **OK** ✔ from the Thread PropertyManager. Thread1 is displayed in the FeatureManager.

Apply Material and rebuild the model.
191) Right-click the **Material** folder in the FeatureManager.

192) Apply **Plain Carbon Steel.**

193) **Rebuild** ● the model.

Display an Isometric view. Save the model.
194) Click **Isometric view** ◉ from the Heads-up View toolbar.

195) Click **Save** 💾. The HOOK part is finished.

🔆 When you create a new part or assembly, the three default Planes (Front, Right and Top) are aligned with specific views. The Plane you select for the Base sketch determines the orientation of the part.

Review the HOOK Part

The HOOK part was created with a Swept, Dome, and Thread feature. A Swept Base feature added material by moving a profile along a path. The Swept Base feature requires two sketches (path and profile) or a sketch path and a circular profile diameter.

If the sketch profile is circular, enter the diameter in the Swept PropertyManager. For non-circular sketch profiles, create the sketch on a perpendicular plane to the path and use the pierce relation to locate the profile on the path.

The Dome feature created a spherical face on the end of the Swept Base feature.

The Thread feature provides the ability to create helical threads on cylindrical faces using profile sketches. Store custom thread profiles as library features.

🔍 Additional details on Swept, Dome, and Thread features are available in SOLIDWORKS Help.

💡 It's considered best practice to fully define all sketches in the model. However, there are times when this is not practical, generally when using the spline tool to create a complex freeform shape.

WHEEL Part

The WHEEL part is a machined part.

Create the WHEEL part with the Extruded Boss/Base feature tool. Utilize the Mid Plane option to center the WHEEL on the Front Plane.

Utilize the Revolved Cut feature tool to remove material from the WHEEL and to create a groove for a belt.

The WHEEL contains a complex pattern of holes. Apply the Extruded Cut feature tool.

Simplify the geometry by dividing the four holes into two Extruded Cut features.

The first Extruded Cut feature contains two small circles sketched on two bolt circles. The bolt circles utilize Construction geometry.

Utilize the Hole Wizard feature when creating non Through All complex geometry holes.

The second Extruded Cut feature utilizes two small circles sketched on two bolt circles. The bolt circles utilize Construction geometry.

Utilize the Circular Pattern Feature tool. The two Extruded Cut features are contained in the Circular Pattern. Revolve the Extruded Cut features about the Temporary Axis located at the center of the Hexagon.

Create a Reference Axis. The Reference Axis is utilized in the WHEEL-AXLE assembly.

 Construction geometry is used only to assist in creating the sketch entities and geometry that are ultimately incorporated into the part. Construction geometry is ignored when the sketch is used to create a feature. Construction geometry uses the same line style as centerlines.

 You can utilize the Hole Wizard feature tool instead of the Cut-Extrude feature tool, or use the Instant3D tool to create a Through All hole for any part. See SOLIDWORKS Help for additional information.

Slots are available in the Hole Wizard. Create regular slots as well and counterbore and countersink slots. You also have options for position and orientation of the slot. If you have hardware already mated in place, the mates will not be broken if you switch from a hole to a slot.

Activity: WHEEL Part

Create the New part.

196) Click **New** ⬚ from the Menu bar.

197) Click the **SW-TUTORIAL-2017\MY-TEMPLATES** tab.

198) Double-click **PART-ANSI-IN**, [PART-ANSI-MM].

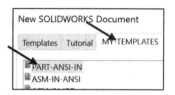

Save the part.

199) Click **Save** 💾.

200) Select the **SW-TUTORIAL-2017** folder.

201) Enter **WHEEL** for File name.

202) Enter **WHEEL** for Description.

203) Click **Save**. The WHEEL FeatureManager is displayed.

Insert the sketch for the Extruded Base feature.
204) Right-click **Front Plane** from the FeatureManager.

205) Click **Sketch** 📝 from the Context toolbar. The Sketch toolbar is displayed.

206) Click the **Circle** ⊙ Sketch tool. The Circle PropertyManager is displayed.

207) Click the **Origin** ↳ as illustrated.

208) Click a **position** to the right of the Origin.

Insert a polygon.
209) Click the **Polygon** ⬡ Sketch tool. The Polygon PropertyManager is displayed.

210) Click the **Origin** ↳.

211) Drag and click the **mouse pointer** horizontally to the right of the Origin to create the hexagon as illustrated.

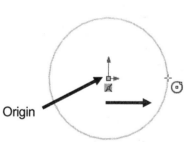

Origin

212) Click **OK** ✔ from the Polygon PropertyManager.

De-select the Polygon Sketch tool.
213) Right-click **Select**.

Add a Horizontal relation.

214) Click the **Origin** .

215) Hold the **Ctrl** key down.

216) Click the **right point** of the hexagon.

217) Release the **Ctrl** key.

218) Click **Horizontal** ▬ from the Properties PropertyManager.

219) Click **OK** ✅ from the Properties PropertyManager.

Add dimensions.

220) Click the **Smart Dimension** ✧ Sketch tool. Click the **circumference** of the large circle.

221) Click a **position** above the circle. Enter **3.000**in, [**76.20**].

222) Click the **Green Check mark** ✅.

223) Click the **circumference** of the inscribed circle for the Hexagon.

224) Click a **position** above the Hexagon.

225) Enter **.438**in, [**11.13**].

226) Click the **Green Check mark** ✅.

Activity: WHEEL Part-Extruded Boss/Base Feature

Insert an Extruded Boss/Base feature.

227) Click **Extruded Boss/Base** 📄 from the Features toolbar. The Boss-Extrude PropertyManager is displayed.

228) Select **Mid Plane** for End Condition in Direction 1.

229) Enter **.250**in, [**6.35**] for Depth.

230) Click **OK** ✅ from the Boss-Extrude PropertyManager. Boss-Extrude1 is displayed in the FeatureManager.

Fit the model to the Graphics window.
231) Press the **f** key.

Display Hidden Lines Removed. Save the WHEEL part.
232) Display **Hidden Lines Removed**.

233) Click **Save** .

Activity: WHEEL Part-Revolved Cut Feature

Insert a new sketch for the Revolved Cut feature.
234) Right-click **Right Plane** from the FeatureManager.

235) Click **Sketch** from the Context toolbar. The Sketch toolbar is displayed.

236) Click **Right view** from the
Heads-up View toolbar.

Sketch the axis of revolution.

237) Click the **Centerline** Sketch tool
from the Consolidated Sketch toolbar.
The Insert Line PropertyManager is
displayed.

238) Click the **Origin** . Click a **position**
horizontally to the right of the Origin
as illustrated.

De-select the sketch tool.
239) Right-click **Select**.

240) Zoom in on the top edge.

Sketch the profile.

241) Click the **Line** Sketch tool.

242) Sketch the **first vertical line** as illustrated.

243) Click the **Tangent Arc** Sketch tool. The Arc
PropertyManager is displayed.

244) Click the **end point** of the vertical line.

245) Sketch a **180° arc** as illustrated.

De-select the sketch tool.
246) Right-click **Select** in the Graphics window.

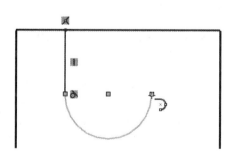

247) Click the **Line** ✎ Sketch tool.

248) Sketch the **second vertical line** as illustrated. The end point of the line is Coincident with the top horizontal edge of Extrude1.

249) Sketch a **horizontal line** collinear with the top edge to close the profile.

Add a Vertical relation.
250) Right-click **Select** in the Graphics window.

251) Click the **Origin** ⌐ from the FeatureManager.

252) Hold the **Ctrl** key down. Click the **center point** of the arc.

253) Release the **Ctrl** key.

Center point
of the arc

254) Click **Vertical** ┃ from the Add Relations box.

Add an Equal relation.
255) Click the **left vertical** line. Hold the **Ctrl** key down.

256) Click the **right vertical** line.

257) Release the **Ctrl** key. Click **Equal** from the Add Relations box.

Add dimensions.
258) Click the **Smart Dimension** ✐ Sketch tool.

259) Click the **arc**.

260) Click a position to the **left** of the profile.

261) Enter .063in, **[1.6]**.

[1.60]
R.063

262) Click the **Green Check mark** ✔ .

263) Click the **right vertical** line.

264) Click a position to the **right** of the profile.

[1.98]
.078

265) Enter .078in, **[1.98]**.

266) Click the **Green Check mark** ✔ .
The sketch should be fully defined.

[1.60]
R.063

If needed, add a Collinear relation.

267) Click the **horizontal line**. Hold the **Ctrl** key down.

268) Click the **horizontal silhouette edge** as illustrated. *Note the feedback icon*.

269) Release the **Ctrl** key.

270) Click **Collinear** from the Add Relations box.

Fit the model to the Graphics window.

271) Press the **f** key.

De-select the sketch tool.

272) Right-click **Select** in the Graphics window.

Activity: WHEEL Part-Revolved Cut Feature

Insert a Revolved Cut feature.

273) Select the Axis of Revolution. Click the **centerline** in the Graphics window as illustrated.

274) Click **Revolved Cut** from the Features toolbar. The Cut-Revolve PropertyManager is displayed. The Cut-Revolve PropertyManager displays 360 degrees for Direction 1 Angle.

275) Click **OK** from the Cut-Revolve PropertyManager. Cut-Revolve1 is displayed in the FeatureManager.

Save the WHEEL part.

276) Click **Save** .

Four bolt circles, spaced 0.5in, [12.7] apart, locate the 8 - ∅.190, [4.83] holes. Simplify the situation. Utilize two Extruded Cut features on each bolt circle.

Position the first Extruded Cut feature hole on the first bolt circle and third bolt circle.

Position the second Extruded Cut feature hole on the second bolt circle and fourth bolt circle.

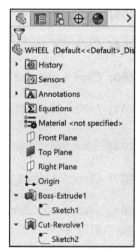

Activity: WHEEL Part- First Extruded Cut Feature

Display the Top Plane.

277) Right-click **Top Plane** from the FeatureManager.

278) Click **Show** 👁 from the Context toolbar.

Display a Front view - Hidden Lines Visible.

279) Click **Front view** 📦 from the Heads-up View toolbar.

280) Click **Hidden Lines Visible** 📦 from the Heads-up View toolbar.

Insert a new sketch for the first Extruded Cut feature.

281) Right-click the **Boss-Extrude1 front face** as illustrated.

282) Click **Sketch** 📝 from the Context toolbar. The Sketch toolbar is displayed.

Create the first construction bolt circle.

283) Click the **Circle** ⊙ Sketch tool. The Circle PropertyManager is displayed.

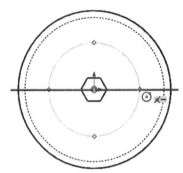

284) Click the **Origin** ↥.

285) Click a **position** to the right of the hexagon as illustrated.

286) Check the **For construction** box.

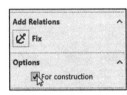

Create the second construction bolt circle.

287) Click the **Origin** ↥.

288) Click a **position** to the right of the first construction bolt circle as illustrated.

289) Check the **For construction** box. The two bolt circles are displayed with Construction style lines.

💡 Construction geometry is used only to assist in creating the sketch entities and geometry that are ultimately incorporated into the part. Construction geometry is ignored when the sketch is used to create a feature. Construction geometry uses the same line style as centerlines.

De-select the circle Sketch tool.

290) Right-click **Select**.

Insert a centerline.

291) Click the **Centerline** Sketch tool. The Insert Line PropertyManager is displayed.

292) Sketch a **45° centerline** (approximately) from the Origin to the second bolt circle as illustrated.

Sketch the two circle profiles.

293) Click the **Circle** Sketch tool. The Circle PropertyManager is displayed.

294) Sketch a **circle** at the intersection of the centerline and the first bolt circle.

295) Sketch a **circle** at the intersection of the centerline and the second bolt circle.

De-select the Circle Sketch tool.
296) Right-click **Select** in the Graphics window.

Note: An Intersection relation is created between three entities: the center point of the small circle, the centerline, and the bolt circle.

Add an Equal relation.
297) Click the **first circle**.

298) Hold the **Ctrl** key down.

299) Click the **second circle**.

300) Release the **Ctrl** key.

301) Right-click **Make Equal** = from the Context toolbar.

Add dimensions.
302) Click the **Smart Dimension** Sketch tool.

303) Click the **first construction** circle.

304) Click a **position** above the profile.

305) Enter **1.000**in, [25.4].

306) Click the **Green Check mark** .

307) Click the **second construction** circle.

308) Click a **position** above the profile.

309) Enter **2.000**in, [**50.80**].

310) Click the **Green Check mark** ✔.

311) Click the **second small** circle.

312) Click a **position** above the profile.

313) Enter **.190**in, [**4.83**].

314) Click the **Green Check mark** ✔.

315) Click **Top Plane** from the fly-out FeatureManager.

316) Click the **45° centerline**.

317) Click a **position** between the two lines.

318) Enter **45**deg for angle.

319) Click the **Green Check mark** ✔.

Note: If the sketch is not fully defined, you may need to add an Intersection relation between the center point of the small circle, the centerline, and the bolt circle.

Insert an Extruded Cut feature.
320) Click **Extruded Cut** 🔲 from the Features toolbar. The Cut-Extrude PropertyManager is displayed.

321) Select **Through All** for the End Condition in Direction 1.

322) Click **OK** ✔ from the Cut-Extrude PropertyManager. Cut-Extrude1 is displayed in the FeatureManager.

Activity: WHEEL Part- Second Extruded Cut Feature

Insert a new sketch for the second Extruded Cut feature.
323) Right-click the **Boss-Extrude1** front face.

324) Click **Sketch** 🗓 from the Context toolbar.

Sketch two additional Construction line bolt circles, 1.500in, [38.1] and 2.500in, [63.5]. Create the first Construction bolt circle.

325) Click the **Circle** ⌖ Sketch tool. The Circle PropertyManager is displayed.

326) Click the **Origin** ↳.

327) Click a **position** between the two small circles.

328) Check the **For construction** box.

Create the second additional construction bolt circle.

329) Click the **Origin** ↳.

330) Click a **position** to the right of the large construction bolt circle as illustrated.

331) Check the **For construction** box from the Circle PropertyManager. The two bolt circles are displayed with the two construction lines.

Insert a centerline.

332) Click the **Centerline** ✎ Sketch tool. The Insert Line PropertyManager is displayed.

333) Sketch a **22.5° centerline** to the right from the Origin to the second bolt circle as illustrated.

334) Select **.1** from the Unit Precision box.

Display Hidden Lines Removed.

335) Click **Hidden Lines Removed** ⬚ from the Heads-up View toolbar.

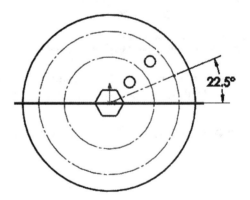

Sketch the two circle profiles.

336) Click the **Circle** ⊙ Sketch tool. The Circle
PropertyManager is displayed.

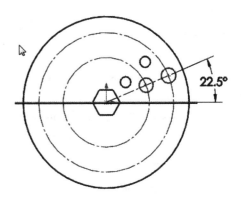

337) Sketch a **circle** at the intersection of the centerline
and the first bolt circle.

338) Sketch a **circle** at the intersection of the centerline
and the second bolt circle.

De-select the Circle Sketch tool.
339) Right-click **Select**.

Add an Equal relation.
340) Click the **first circle**.

341) Hold the **Ctrl** key down.

342) Click the **second circle**.

343) Release the **Ctrl** key.

344) Right-click **Make Equal** ═ from the shortcut
toolbar.

Add dimensions.
345) Click the **Smart Dimension** ✎ Sketch tool. The
Smart Dimension icon is displayed.

346) Click the **first construction** circle.

347) Click a **position** above the profile.

348) Enter **1.500**in, **[38.1]**.

349) Click the **second construction** circle.

350) Click a **position** above the profile.

351) Enter **2.500**in, **[63.5]**.

352) Click the **small circle** as illustrated.

353) Click a **position** above the profile.

354) Enter **.190**in, **[4.83]**. The sketch should be fully defined.

Insert an Extruded Cut feature.

355) Click **Extruded Cut** 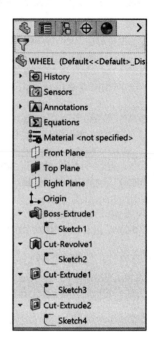 from the Features toolbar. The Cut-Extrude PropertyManager is displayed.

356) Select **Through All** for End Condition in Direction 1.

357) Click **OK** ✔ from the Cut-Extrude PropertyManager. Cut-Extrude2 is displayed in the FeatureManager.

Save the model.

358) Click **Save** 💾.

View the Temporary Axes.

359) Click **View**, **Hide/Show**, check **Temporary Axes** from the Menu bar.

💡 This book is designed to expose the new SOLIDWORKS user to many different tools, techniques and procedures. It may not always use the most direct tool or process.

Activity: WHEEL Part-Circular Pattern Feature

Insert a Circular Pattern.

360) Click **Isometric view** 📦 from the Heads-up View toolbar.

361) Click **Circular Pattern** from the Consolidated Features toolbar. The Circular Pattern PropertyManager is displayed. Click **inside** the Pattern Axis box.

362) Click the **Temporary Axis** in the Graphics window at the center of the Hexagon. Axis<1> is displayed in the Pattern Axis box.

363) Click the **Equal spacing** box.

364) Enter **360**deg for Angle.

365) Enter **8** for Number of Instances.

366) Click inside the **Features to Pattern** box.

367) Click **Cut-Extrude1** and **Cut-Extrude2** from the fly-out FeatureManager. Cut-Extrude1 and Cut-Extrude2 are displayed in the Features to Pattern box.

368) Check the **Geometry pattern** box.

369) Click **OK** ✔ from the Circular Pattern PropertyManager. CirPattern1 is displayed in the FeatureManager.

Save the WHEEL part.

370) Click **Save** 💾.

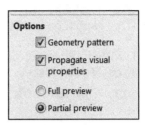

Utilize a Reference Axis to locate the WHEEL in the PNEUMATIC-TEST-MODULE assembly. The Reference Axis is located in the FeatureManager and Graphics window. The Reference Axis is a construction axis defined between two planes.

Insert a two Plane Reference axis.

371) Click the **Axis** ∕ tool from the Reference Geometry Consolidated Features toolbar. The Axis PropertyManager is displayed.

372) Click **Top Plane** from the fly-out FeatureManager.

373) Click **Right Plane** from the fly-out FeatureManager. The selected planes are displayed in the Selections box.

374) Click **Two Planes**.

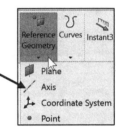

375) Click **OK** ✔ from the Axis PropertyManager. Axis1 is displayed in the FeatureManager.

Axis1 is positioned through the Hex Cut centered at

the Origin ⌞.

376) Click and drag the **Axis1 handles** outward to extend the length on both sides as illustrated.

Display an Isometric view - Shaded With Edges. Clear Temporary Axes. Hide all Planes.

377) Click **Isometric view** .

378) Click **View, Hide/Show,** un-check **Temporary Axes** from the Menu bar.

379) **Hide** all Planes. Click **Shaded With Edges** from the Heads-up View toolbar.

Save the WHEEL part.

380) Click **Save** .

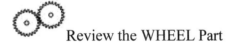 Sketched lines, arcs or circles are modified from profile geometry to construction geometry. Select the geometry in the sketch. Check the For construction box option.

 Review the WHEEL Part

The WHEEL part was created with the Extruded Boss/Base feature. You sketched a circular sketch on the Front Plane and extruded the sketch with the Mid Plane option.

A Revolved Cut feature removed material from the WHEEL and created the groove. The Revolved Cut feature utilized an arc sketched on the Right Plane. A sketched centerline was required to create the Revolved Cut feature.

The WHEEL contained a complex pattern of holes. The first Extruded Cut feature contained two small circles sketched on two bolt circles. The bolt circles utilized construction geometry. Geometric relationships and dimensions were used in the sketch. The second Extruded Cut feature utilized two small circles sketched on two bolt circles.

The two Extruded Cut features were contained in one Circular Pattern and revolved about the Temporary Axis. The Reference Axis was created with two perpendicular planes. Utilize the Reference Axis, Axis1 in the WHEEL-AXLE assembly.

Modify a Part

Conserve design time and cost. Modify existing parts and
assemblies to create new parts and assemblies. Utilize the
Save as copy tool to avoid updating the existing assemblies
with new file names.

The HEX-STANDOFF part was created in a previous
chapter. The HEX-ADAPTER is required to fasten the
WHEEL to the AXLE. Start with the HEX-STANDOFF part.

Utilize the Save As command and enter the HEX-ADAPTER for the
new file name. Check the Save as copy and continue check box. The
HEX-ADAPTER is the new part name. Open the HEX-ADAPTER.

Modify the dimensions of the Extruded Base feature.

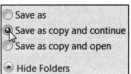

Utilize Edit Definition to modify the Hole Wizard Tap Hole to a
Standard Hole. Insert an Extruded Boss/Base feature to create the
head of the HEX-ADAPTER.

Insert an Extruded Cut feature. Sketch a circle on the Right Plane. Extrude the circle in
Direction1 and Direction2 with the Through All End Condition option. Note: You can
use the Hole Wizard feature with a 3D Sketch. Feature order determines the internal
geometry of the Hole. If the Hole feature is created before the Extrude2-Head feature, the
Through All End Condition will extend through the Boss-Extrude1 feature.

If the Hole feature is created after the Extrude2-Head feature, the Through All End
Condition will extend through the Boss-Extrude1 feature and the Extrude2-Head feature.

Modify feature order by dragging feature names in the FeatureManager. Utilize the Save
As command to create the AXLE3000 part from the AXLE part.

Utilize the Save As command to create the SHAFTCOLLAR-500 part from the
SHAFT-COLLAR part. Save the HEX-STANDOFF as the HEX-ADAPTER part.

Activity: HEX-ADAPTER Part

Create the HEX-ADAPTER.

381) Click **Open** 📂 from the Menu bar.

382) Double-click **HEX-STANDOFF**. The HEX-STANDOFF FeatureManager is displayed.

383) Click **Save As** from the drop-down Menu bar.

384) Select the **SW-TUTORIAL-2017** folder.

385) Enter **HEX-ADAPTER** for File name.

386) Enter **HEX-ADAPTER 10-24** for Description.

387) Check the **Save as copy and continue** box.

388) Click **Save**.

389) Click **File**, **Close** from the Menu bar.

Open the HEX-ADAPTER.

390) Click **Open** 🖰 from the Menu bar.

391) Double-click **HEX-ADAPTER** from the SW-TUTORIAL-2017 folder. The HEX-ADAPTER FeatureManager is displayed.

Modify the Boss-Extrude1 dimensions.

392) Double-click **Boss-Extrude1** from the FeatureManager.

393) Double-click **.735**in, [**18.67**].

394) Enter **.700**in, [**17.78**] for depth.

395) Double-click **.313**in, [**7.95**].

396) Enter **.438**in, [**11.13**] for diameter.

Modify the #10-24 Tapped Hole1 feature.

397) Right-click **#10-24 Tapped Hole1** from the FeatureManager.

398) Click **Edit Feature** 🖰 from the Context toolbar. The Hole Specification PropertyManager is displayed.

🔆 The Hole Specification PropertyManager is part of the Hole Wizard tool located in the Features toolbar.

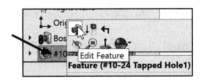

The Type tab is selected by default.

399) Select the **Hole** tab from the Hole Specification box.

400) Select **ANSI Inch** for Standard.

401) Select **Tap Drills** for Type.

402) Select **#10-24** for Size.

403) Select **Through All** for End Condition.

404) Click **OK** ✔ from the Hole Specification PropertyManager. The Tap Hole is modified.

Insert a sketch for the Extruded Boss feature.
405) Press the **Up Arrow key** approximately four times.

406) Right-click the **bottom hexagonal face** of the Boss-Extrude1 feature as illustrated.

407) Click **Sketch** ▦ from the Context toolbar.

408) Click **Bottom view** ▦ from the Heads-up View toolbar.

409) Click the **Circle** ⊙ Sketch tool. The Circle PropertyManager is displayed.

410) Click the **Origin** ↳ as illustrated.

411) Click a **position** in the Graphics window to the right of the Origin.

Add a dimension.
412) Click the **Smart Dimension** ⤢ Sketch tool.

413) Click the **circumference** of the circle.

414) Click a **position** above the circle to locate the dimension.

415) Enter **.625**in, **[15.88]** in the Modify dialog box.

Fit the model to the Graphics window.
416) Press the **f** key.

$$[15.88]$$
$$\varnothing\,.625$$

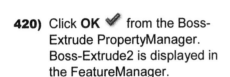

Activity: HEX-ADAPTER Part-Extruded Boss/Base Feature

Extrude the sketch to create the Extruded Boss/Base feature.

417) Click **Isometric view** from the Heads-up View toolbar.

418) Click **Extruded Boss/Base** from the Features toolbar. The Boss-Extrude PropertyManager is displayed.

419) Enter **.200**in, [6.35] for Depth. The Direction arrow points downward. Flip the **Direction arrow** if required.

420) Click **OK** from the Boss-Extrude PropertyManager. Boss-Extrude2 is displayed in the FeatureManager.

Rename Boss-Extrude2. Save the model.

421) Rename **Boss-Extrude2** to **Extrude2-Head**.

422) Click **Save**.

Rename a feature or sketch for clarity. Slowly click the feature or sketch name twice and enter the new name when the old one is highlighted.

Activity: HEX-ADAPTER Part-Extruded Cut Feature

Insert a new sketch for the Extruded Cut on the Right Plane.

423) Right-click **Right Plane** from the FeatureManager.

424) Click **Sketch** from the Context toolbar.

425) Click **Right view** from the Heads-up View toolbar. Note the location of the Origin.

426) Click **Hidden Lines Visible**.

427) Click the **Circle** Sketch tool. The Circle PropertyManager is displayed.

428) Sketch a **circle** below the Origin. The center point is vertically aligned to the Origin.

429) If required, add a Vertical relation between the center point of the circle and the Origin.

Origin

Add dimensions.

430) Click the **Smart Dimension** Sketch tool.

431) Click the **middle horizontal** edge.

432) Click the **center point** of the circle.

433) Click a **position** to the right of the profile.

434) Enter **.100**in, **[2.54]**.

435) Click the **Green Check mark** ✔ .

436) Click the **circumference** of the circle.

437) Click a **position** below the profile.

438) Enter **.120**in, **[3.95]**.

439) Click the **Green Check mark** ✔ .

Insert an Extruded Cut feature.

440) Click **Extruded Cut** ⬛ from the Features toolbar. The Cut-Extrude PropertyManager is displayed.

441) Select **Through All - Both** for End Condition in Direction 1.

442) Click **OK** ✔ from the Cut-Extrude PropertyManager.

Display an Isometric view. Rename the feature.

443) Click **Isometric view** 🔲 .

444) Rename the feature to **Extrude3-SetScrew**.

Save the HEX-ADAPTER part.

445) Click **Save** 💾 .

The Through All End Condition is required to penetrate both the Boss-Extrude1 and Extrude2 features. Reorder features in the FeatureManager. Position the Extrude2 feature before the Tap Drill for # 10-24 Tap 1 feature in the FeatureManager.

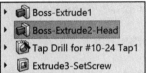

Reorder the Features.
446) Click and drag **Extrude2-Head** from the FeatureManager upward as illustrated.

447) Click a **position** below Boss-Extrude1. The Through All End Condition option for the Tap Drill for # 10-24 Tap 1 feature creates a hole through both Boss-Extrude1 and Boss-Extrude2.

Display a Section view.
448) Click **Front Plane** from the FeatureManager.

449) Click **Section view** 📖 from the Heads-up View toolbar in the Graphics window. The Section View PropertyManager is displayed. View the results.

450) Click **OK** ✔ from the Section View PropertyManager.

Display the full view.
451) Click **Section view** 📖 from the Heads-up View toolbar in the Graphics window.

452) Click **Shaded With Edges** 🔲 from the Heads-up View toolbar.

Save the HEX-ADAPTER.
453) Click **Save** 💾. Note the location of the Origin in the model.

Close all documents.
454) Click **Windows, Close All** from the Menu bar.

🔅 Utilize the Save As command and work on the copied version of the document before making any changes to the original. Keep the original document intact.

Origin

🔅 Tangent edges and Origins are displayed for educational purposes in this book.

Review the HEX-ADAPTER Part

The HEX-ADAPTER part was created by utilizing the Save As and the Save as copy command with the HEX-STANDOFF part. The Boss-Extrude1 feature dimensions were modified. Edit Definition was utilized to modify the Hole type from the Hole Wizard feature.

An Extruded Boss feature added material. An Extruded Cut feature, sketched on the Right Plane with the Through All End Condition for both Direction1 and Direction2, created a hole through the Extruded Boss feature. Reordering features in the FeatureManager modified the Hole. Utilizing existing geometry saved time with the Save as copy command. The original part and its references to other assemblies are not affected with the Save as copy command.

You require additional work before completing the PNEUMATIC-TEST-MODULE assembly. The AXLE and SHAFT-COLLAR were created in Chapter 2. Utilize the Save as copy command to save the parts.

Additional details on Save (Save As copy), Reorder (features), Section View PropertyManager are available in SOLIDWORKS Help.

Utilize Design Table configurations for the AXLE part and SHAFT-COLLAR part developed in the previous chapter.

The AXLE-3000 part and SHAFT-COLLAR-500 part utilize the Save As option in the next section. Utilize the Save As components or the configurations developed with Design Tables to create the WHEEL-AXLE assembly.

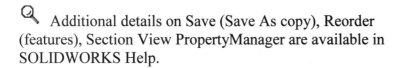

Activity: AXLE-3000 Part

Create the AXLE-3000 part from the AXLE part.

455) Click **Open** from the Menu bar.

456) Double-click **AXLE** from the SW-TUTORIAL-2017 folder. The AXLE FeatureManager is displayed.

457) Click **Save As** from the drop-down Menu bar.

458) Select the **SW-TUTORIAL-2017** folder.

459) Enter **AXLE-3000** for File name.

460) Enter **AXLE-3000** for Description.

461) Check the **Save as copy and continue** check box. Note: You can use the Save as copy and open command. This will open the new copy.

462) Click **Save**.

Close the AXLE part.
463) Click **File**, **Close** from the Menu bar.

Open AXLE-3000 part.

464) Click **Open** 📂 from the Menu bar.

465) Double-click **AXLE-3000** from the SW-TUTORIAL-2017 folder. The AXLE-3000 FeatureManager is displayed.

Modify the depth dimension.
466) Double-click the **cylindrical face** in the Graphics window. Dimensions are displayed.

467) Click **1.375**in, [**34.93**].

468) Enter **3.000**in, [**76.20**].

Fit the model to the Graphics window.
469) Press the **f** key.

Save the AXLE-3000 part.
470) Click **Save** 💾.

471) Click **inside** the Graphics window.

Activity: SHAFTCOLLAR-500 Part

Create the SHAFTCOLLAR-500 part.
472) Click **Open** 📂 from the Menu bar.

473) Double-click **SHAFT-COLLAR** from the SW-TUTORIAL-2017 folder.

474) Click **Save As** from the Menu bar.

475) Enter **SHAFT-COLLAR-500** for File name.

476) Enter **SHAFT-COLLAR-500** for Description.

477) Click the **Save as copy and open** check box.

478) Click **Save**. Both models are open at this time.

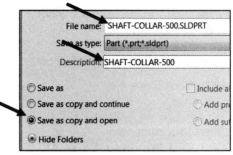

Modify the diameter dimensions of the SHAFT-COLLAR-500 Part.

479) Right-click **Annotations** in the FeatureManager.

480) Check the **Show Feature Dimensions** box.

481) Press the **f** key to fit the model to the graphics area.

482) Click **.438**in, [**11.11**].

483) Enter **.750**in, [**19.05**] for outside diameter.

484) Click **.190**in, [**4.83**].

485) Enter **.500**in, [**12.70**] for inside diameter. View the results.

486) Right-click **Annotations** in the FeatureManager.

487) Un-check the **Show Feature Dimensions** box.

488) **Rebuild** the model.

Fit the model to the Graphics window.
489) Press the **f** key.

Save the SHAFT-COLLAR-500 part.

490) Click **Save** 📼.

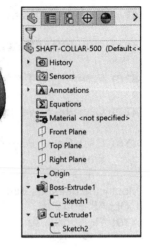

Close all documents.
491) Click **Windows**, **Close All** from the Menu bar.

🔆 Press the **s** key in the Graphics window. A Context Pop-up features toolbar is displayed. The features toolbar displays the last few feature tools applied.

🔆 Select the types of Annotations that you want to display and set text scale and other Annotations options. In the FeatureManager design tree, right-click the **Annotations** folder, and click **details**. View the options from the Annotation Properties dialog box.

🔆 Rename a feature or sketch for clarity. Slowly click the feature or sketch name twice and enter the new name when the old one is highlighted.

🔆 Add relations, then dimensions. This will keep the user from having too many unnecessary dimensions. This helps to show the design intent of the model. Dimension what geometry you intend to modify or adjust.

Chapter Summary

In this chapter, you created six parts. The WEIGHT part utilized the Plane feature, Lofted Base feature and the Extruded Cut (Instant3D tool) feature. The HOOK part utilized the Swept Base feature, Dome feature, and Thread feature. The WHEEL part utilized the Extruded Base feature, Revolved Cut feature, Extruded Cut feature, Circular Pattern feature and Axis feature.

The second three parts utilized existing parts created in an early chapter. The HEX-ADAPTER part, AXLE-3000 part and the SHAFTCOLLAR-500 part utilized existing part geometry along with the Hole Wizard feature.

Conserve design time and cost. Modify existing parts and assemblies to create new parts and assemblies. Utilize the Save As/Save as command to save the file in another file format.

Utilize the Save as copy and continue command to save the document to a new file name without replacing the active document. Utilize the Save as copy and open command to save the document to a new file name that becomes the active document. The original document remains open. References to the original document are not automatically assigned to the copy.

You applied the following Sketch tools in this chapter: Circle, Line, Centerline, Tangent Arc, Polygon, Smart Dimension, Center Rectangle, Centerpoint Arc, 3 Point Arc and Convert Entities.

This book is designed to expose the new SOLIDWORKS user to many different tools, techniques and procedures. It may not always use the most direct tool or process.

Questions

1. What is the minimum number of profiles and planes required for a Loft feature?

2. A Swept Boss/Base feature requires a _____ and a _____.

3. Describe the differences between a Loft feature and a Swept feature.

4. Identify the three default reference planes in an assembly.

5. True or False. A Revolved-Cut feature requires an axis of revolution.

6. True or False. A Circular Pattern Feature does not require a seed feature to pattern.

7. Describe the difference between a Swept Boss/Base feature and a Swept Cut feature.

8. Identify the type of Geometric relations that can be added to a sketch.

9. What function does the Save as option perform when saving a part under a new name?

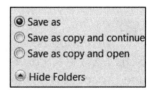

10. True or False. Never reuse geometry from one part to create another part.

Exercises

Exercise 5.1: Advanced Part

Build the illustrated model. Calculate the volume of the part and locate the Center of mass with the provided information.

Three holes are displayed with an Ø1.00in.

Set the document properties for the model.

💡 Tangent edges and Origin are displayed for educational purposes.

Origin

Given:
A = Ø1.00
All Thru Holes
Material: Brass
Density = .307 lb/in^3
Units: IPS
Precision = 2

Exercise 5.2: Advanced Part

Build the illustrated model. Calculate the overall mass of the part and locate the Center of mass with the provided information. Insert a Revolved Base feature and Extruded Cut feature to build this part.

Note: Select the Front Plane as the Sketch plane. Apply the Centerline Sketch tool for the Revolve1 feature. Insert the required geometric relations and dimensions. Sketch1 is the profile for the Revolve1 feature.

Origin

Given:
A = Ø12
Material: Cast Alloy
Steel
Density = .0073 g/mm^3
Units: MMGS
Precision = 2

Exercise 5.3: Advanced Part

Build the illustrated model. Calculate the overall mass of the part and locate the Center of mass with the provided information. Insert the required geometric relations and dimensions. Precision = 2.

Insert two features: Extruded Base and Revolved Boss.

Origin

Given:
A = 60, B = 40, C = 8
Material: Cast Alloy Steel
Density = .0073 g/mm^3
Units: MMGS

Exercise 5.4: Advanced Part

Build the illustrated model. Calculate the overall mass of the part and locate the Center of mass with the provided information.

Think about the various features that create the model. Insert the required geometric relations and dimensions.

Apply symmetry. Create the left half of the model first, and then apply the Mirror feature. Precision = 2. All Thru Holes.

38 DIA
57 DIA SF
1 DEEP
2 HOLES

Tangent Edges and Origin are displayed for educational purposes.

Origin

Given:
A = 76, B = 127
Material: 2014 Alloy
Density: .0028 g/mm^3
Units: MMGS
ALL ROUNDS
EQUAL 6MM

Exercise 5.5: Advanced Part

Build the illustrated model.
Calculate the overall mass of
the part and locate the Center
of mass with the provided
information. Precision = 2.
All Thru Holes.

Think about the various
features that create the part.

Apply reference
construction planes to build
the circular features. Insert
the required geometric
relations and dimensions.

Origin

Exercise 5.6: Advanced Part

Build the illustrated model. Calculate the
volume of the part and locate the Center of
mass with the provided information.
Precision = 2. All Thru Holes.

Think about the various features that create this
model. Insert the required geometric relations
and dimensions.

Origin

Given:
A = Ø3.00, B = 1.00
Material: 6061 Alloy
Density: .097 lb/in^3
Units: IPS
Decimal places = 2

Exercise 5.7: Advanced Part

Build the illustrated model.

Calculate the overall mass and locate the Center of mass of the illustrated model.

Think about the steps that you would take to build the illustrated part.

Identify the location of the part Origin.

Review the provided dimensions and annotations in the part illustration.

Precision = 2. All Thru Holes.

☀ Tangent edges and Origin are displayed for educational purposes.

Use Symmetry. When possible and if it makes sense, model objects symmetrically about the origin.

Given:
A = 2.00, B = Ø.35
Material: 1060 Alloy
Density: 0.097 lb/in^3
Units: IPS
Decimal places = 2

Origin

Exercise 5.8: Traditional Ice cream cone

Create a traditional Ice Cream Cone as illustrated.

Create an ANSI - IPS model.

Think about the design features that create this model. Why does the cone use ribs?

Ribs are used for structural integrity.

View the sample FeatureManager. Your FeatureManager can (should) be different. This is just one way to create this part.

Create your own ice cream cone design.

Below are a few sample models from my Freshman Engineering class.

Below are a few sample models from my Freshman Engineering (Cont:).

Exercise 5.9: Gem®
Paper clip

Create a simple paper
clip. Create an ANSI -
IPS model.

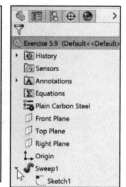

Apply material to the
model. Precision = 2.

What is your Base Sketch?

The paper clip model uses (lines and arcs) as the path.

Exercise 5.10: Spring

Create a variable pitch spring (ANSI - IPS) with 6 coils; two active as illustrated.

Sketch a circle, Coincident to the Origin on the Top plane with a .235in dimension.

Create the Helix/Spiral feature.

Create a Region parameters table.

Enter the following information as illustrated. Coils 1, 2, 5, 6 & 7 are the closed ends of the spring. The pitch needs to be slightly larger than the wire.

Enter .021in for the Pitch.

Enter .080in for the free state of the two active coils.

Enter Start angle of 0deg.

Create the Swept Boss feature.

Enter .015in for Depth (Circular Profile).

Add material to the model.

View the results.

Exercise 5.11: Bottle

Create the container as illustrated.

Create an ANSI - IPS model.

Apply material to the model.

What is your Base Sketch?

What is your Base Feature?

What are the dimensions?

View the sample FeatureManager. Your
FeatureManager can (should) be different.
This is just one way to create this part.
Estimate any needed dimension.

	P	Rev	H	Dia
1	0.1875in	0	0in	1.3in
2	0.1875in	0.25	0.0468	1.5in
3	0.1875in	2.25	0.4218	1.5in
4	0.1875in	2.5	0.4687	1.3in
5				

Exercise 5.12: Explicit Equation Driven Curve tool

Create an Explicit Equation Driven Curve on the Front plane. Revolve the curve. Calculate the volume of the solid.

Create a New part. Use the default ANSI, IPS Part template.

Create a 2D Sketch on the Front Plane.

Activate the Equation Driven Curve Sketch fx tool from the Consolidated drop-down menu.

Enter the Equation y_x as illustrated.

Enter the parameters x_1, x_2 that define the lower and upper bounds of the equation as illustrated. View the curve in the Graphics window.

Size the curve in the Graphics window. The Sketch is under defined.

Insert three lines to close the profile as illustrated. Fully define your sketch. Enter dimensions and any needed geometric relation.

Create the Revolved feature. View the results in the Graphics window. Revolve1 is displayed. Utilize the Section tool parallel with the Right plane to view how each cross section is a circle.

Apply Brass for material.

Precision = 2.

Density = 0.31 pounds per cubic inch

Mass = 16.10 pounds

Volume = 52.43 cubic inches

Surface area = 103.20 square inches

Calculate the volume of the part using the Mass Properties tool. View the results.

💡 You can create parametric (in addition to explicit) equation-driven curves in both 2D and 3D sketches.

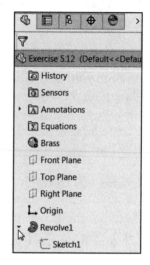

💡 Use regular mathematical notation and order of operations to write an equation. x_1 and x_2 are for the beginning and end of the curve. Use the transform options at the bottom of the PropertyManager to move the entire curve in x-, y- or rotation. To specify $x = f(y)$ instead of $y = f(x)$, use a 90 degree transform.

Exercise 5.13: Curve Through XYZ Points tool

The Curve Through XYZ Points 𝒰 feature provides the ability to either type in (using the Curve File dialog box) or click Browse and import a text file with x-, y-, z-, coordinates for points on a curve.

A text file can be generated by any program which creates columns of numbers. The Curve 𝒰 feature reacts like a default spline that is fully defined.

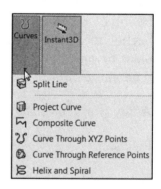

Create a curve using the Curve Through XYZ Points tool. Import the x-, y-, z- data.

Verify that the first and last points in the curve file are the same for a closed profile.

Create a new part.

Click the Curve Through XYZ Points 𝒰 tool from the Features CommandManager. The Curve File dialog box is displayed.

Import the curve data. Click
Browse from the Curve File
dialog box.

Browse to the downloaded
folder location: Chapter 5
Homework folder.

Set file type to Text Files.

Double-click cam2.text. View
the data in the Curve File dialog box.

View the sketch in the Graphics window.

Review the data points in the dialog box.

Click OK from the Curve File dialog box.

Fix the Curve to the Graphics window. Curve1 is displayed
in the FeatureManager. You created a curve using the Curve
Through XYZ Points tool with imported x-, y-, z- data from
a cam program.

This curve can now be used to create a sketch (closed
profile). In this case a cam.

Close the existing model.

Exercise 5.14: Advanced Part

Build the illustrated model below.

Calculate the overall mass of the model. Units - IPS. Decimal places: 2. Material: AISI 304.

Think about the steps that you would take to build the illustrated part.

Insert the required geometric relations and dimensions.

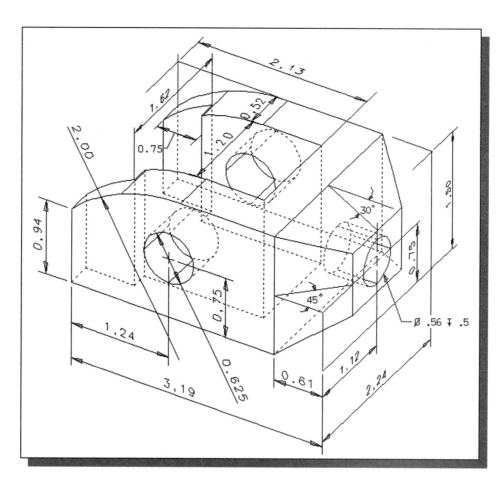

Exercise 5.15: Advanced Hole

Apply the Advanced Hole tool to create and modify a Counterbore hole with three elements position at the origin.

1. Open **Advanced Hole** from the Chapter 5 Homework folder.

2. Click the **Advanced Hole** 🔲 feature tool. The Advanced Hole PropertyManager is displayed. View your options. The default hole type is Counterbore.

3. Click the **Type** tab.

4. Click inside the **Near And Far side Faces** dialog box.

5. Click the **top face** of the model in the Graphic window. Face<1> is displayed in the dialog box. Add a Near Side element with Element specification.

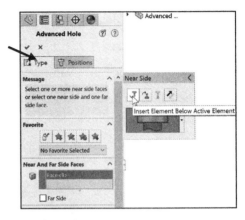

6. Click the **Insert Element Below Active Element** ⬇ icon.

7. Select the Far side for the Advanced hole. Click the **Far Side** box.

8. Click the **bottom face** of the model. Face<2> is displayed in the dialog box.

9. Set the first Element Specification. Click the **Top Element Specification** for Near Side as illustrated.

10. Select **ANSI Inch** for Standard.

11. Select **Socket Head Cap Screw** for Element Type.

12. Select ¼ for Size.

Create and modify the second Near Side Element.

13. **Expand** the second Near Side Element drop-down menu as illustrated.

14. Click the **Straight** icon as illustrated.

Set the second Element Specification.
15. Select **ANSI Inch** for Standard.

16. Select **Screw Clearances** for Type.

17. Select ¼ for Size.

18. Select **Blind** for End Condition.

19. Enter **1.0in** for Depth. View the updated model in the Graphics area.

The Far Side element is currently set to Counterbore. Modify the Counterbore to a Straight tapped thread element.

20. **Expand** the Far Side Element drop-down menu as illustrated.

21. Click the **Straight Tapped Thread** icon as illustrated.

Set the Far Side Element Specification.
22. Select **ANSI Inch** for Standard.

23. Select **Tapped hole** for Type.

24. Select **¼-20** for Size.

25. Select **Up To Next Element** for End Condition.
The Far Side Element updates to the middle Near
Side Element due to the selected End Condition.

Position the hole in the center of the block.
26. Click the **Positions** tab.

27. Click the **top face** at the origin.

28. Click **OK** from the Hole Position
PropertyManager.

29. **View** the results in the Graphics area.

30. **Close** the model.

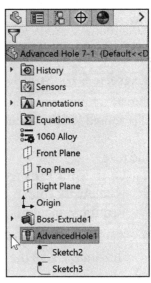

Split Line Curve tool

The Split Line Curve tool projects an entity (sketch, solid, surface, face, plane, or surface spline) to surfaces, or curved or planar faces. It divides a selected face into multiple separate faces. You can split curves on multiple bodies with a single command. You can create the following split lines:

- **Silhouette**. Creates a split line on a cylindrical part.

- **Projection**. Project a sketch on a surface. You can pattern split line features that were created using projected curves. You can create split lines using sketched text. This is useful for creating items such as decals or applying a force or pressure when using SOLIDWORKS Simulation.

- **Intersection**. Splits faces with an intersecting solid, surface, face, plane, or surface spline.

When you create a split line with an open profile sketch, the sketch must span at least two edges of the model.

Exercise 5.16: Split Line

Create a Split Line feature to apply a distributed load to a selected face. The Split Line feature in this case does not add depth to the part.

1. Open **Split Line** from the Chapter 5 Homework folder. The Split Line FeatureManager is displayed.

2. Create a **rectangular sketch** as illustrated. Use the sketch for the Split Line feature.

Create the Split Line feature.

3. Click **Insert ➤ Curve ➤ Curve Split Line**. The Split Line PropertyManger is displayed. The current Sketch is displayed. Projection is selected by default.

4. Click the **top face** of Boss-Extrude1. Face 1 is displayed in the Faces to Split box.

5. Click **OK** ✔ from the Split Line PropertyManager. Split Line1 is created and is displayed.

6. **Save** the part.

Start a SOLIDWORKS Simulation study and utilize the Split Line feature as your selected face for the applied force on the model.

7. Click **SOLIDWORKS Add-Ins tab** ➢ **SOLIDWORKS Simulation**. The Simulation tab is displayed.

Create a new Static Study.

8. Click the **Simulation** tab.

9. Click **New Study** from the Study drop-down menu. Static is selected by default. Accept the default study name.

10. Click **OK** ✔ from the Study PropertyManager.

Fix the model at one end and apply a
distributed load using the Split Line
feature.

11. Right-click the **Fixtures** folder.

12. Click **Fixed Geometry**. The Fixture
    PropertyManger is displayed.

13. Click the **left face of Boss-Extrude1**
    as illustrated. The left face is fixed.

14. Click **OK** ✔ from the Fixture
    PropertyManager. Fixed-1 is displayed.

Apply an External load (force) to the model using
the Split Line feature.

15. Right-click the **External Load** folder.

16. Click **Force**. The Force PropertyManager is
    displayed. In this example, the area of the
    applied force is the Split Line feature.

17. Click the **Split Line1** feature on the model in
    the Graphics window.

18. Enter **100lbf** for force.

19. Click **OK** ✔ from the Force
    PropertyManager. Force-1 is created and is
    displayed.

20. Apply **Alloy Steel** to the part.

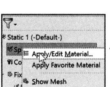

21. **Mesh and Run** the model. View the results.

22. **Close** the part. The Split Line feature divides
    a selected face into multiple separate faces.

🔆 When you create a split line with an open
profile sketch, the sketch must span at least two
edges of the model.

Thread Feature

The Thread Feature provides the
ability to create threads for standard and
non-standard threads for shafts and holes.
For prototypes and digital simulation use
the Thread feature. Select the start thread
location, specify an offset, set end
conditions, specify the type, size,
diameter, pitch and rotation angle and
choose options such as right-hand or left-
hand thread.

The Thread feature uses the Thread
PropertyManager. The Thread
PropertyManager provides the following
selections:

- ***Thread Location***. The Thread
  Location box provides the ability to
  select the following options:

  - **Edge of Cylinder**. Select a
    circular edge.

  - **Optional Start Location**. Provides the ability to select a
    Vertex, Edge, Plane or Planar Surface.

  - **Offset**. The offset value must be positive. You can also
    enter an equation by starting with = (equal sign).

  - **Offset Distance**. Distance of the Offset.

  - **Start Angle**. Defines the starting location of the helix.
    The start angle must be positive. You can also enter an
    equation by starting with = (equal sign).

- *End Condition*. The End Condition box provides the ability to select the following options:

  - **Blind**. Specify a value for Depth. Terminates the thread at the desired distance from the starting location, taking into account any input for offset.

  - **Revolutions**. Terminates the helix at the desired number of revolutions from the starting location, taking into account any input for offset. The value must be positive and greater than 0.00. You can also enter an equation by starting with = (equal sign).

  - **Up to Selection**. Select a vertex (sketch, model, or reference points), edge (sketch, model or reference axis), plane, or planar surface. A plane, planar face, or edge must be parallel to the circular edge (i.e. perpendicular to the thread axis). A vertex or point acts as the point through which a plane is created that is perpendicular to the cylindrical axis.

    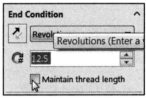

  - **Maintain thread length**. Keeps the thread at a constant length from the start surface. It only displays if the Start Surface Offset is selected and End Condition is set to Blind or Revolutions.

- *Specification*. The Specification box provides the ability to select the following options:

  - **Type**. Displays library part files initially found in C:\ProgramData\SolidWorks\SOLIDWORKS YYYY\Thread Profiles. **Inch Die, Inch Tap, Metric Die and SP4xx Bottle**.

  - **Size**. Displays each of the configurations found in the library part file selected from the Type list.

  - **Override diameter**. Displays diameter of the cylindrical face and will be the diameter of the helix.

  - **Override Pitch**. Enter a value or start with = to create an equation. The value in the dimension input field is determined from the selected configuration's profile sketch and the length of a vertical construction line drawn from the origin of the model.

  - **Thread method**. Select one of the following:

    - **Cut thread**.

    - **Extruded thread**.

  - **Mirror Profile**. Select one of the following:

    - **Mirror horizontally**.

- **Mirror vertically**.

- **Locate Profile**. Select a new point on the thread profile sketch from the graphics area to attach to the helical path. You can select any vertex created by the entities and sketch points in the profile sketch. The button is disabled when no circular edge has been selected.

- *Thread Options*. The Thread Options box provides the ability to select the following options:

  - **Right-hand thread**. Creates a right hand thread.

  - **Left-hand thread**. Creates a left hand thread.

  - **Multiple Start**. Set the number of starts to define the number of times the thread is created in an evenly-spaced circular pattern around the hole or shaft. The image shows a four-start thread with a different color per thread.

  - **Trim with start face**. Provides the ability to align threads to start faces.

  - **Trim with end face**. Provides the ability to align threads to end face.

In SOLIDWORKS 2017 you can align threads to end faces. A Cut thread is extended and cut to match the end face. An Extrude thread is cut to match the end face.

- *Preview Options*. The Preview Options box provides the ability to select the following options:

  - **Shaded preview**. Displays a fully tessellated preview of the thread.

  - **Wireframe preview**. Displays a wireframe preview of the thread.

  - **Partial preview**. Adjusts the number of wires displayed in the wireframe.

Exercise 5.17: Thread Wizard

Apply the Thread Wizard to create a thread feature.
1. Open **Thread Wizard** from the Chapter 5 homework folder.

Apply the Thread Feature.
2. Click **Thread** from the Hole Wizard drop-down menu.

3. Click **OK** if needed.

4. Click the **front circular edge** as illustrated. Edge1 is displayed in the Thread Location box.

5. Select **Up To Selection** for End Condition. Click inside the **End Condition** box.

6. Click the **front circular face** as illustrated. Face<1> is displayed.

7. Select **Inch Die** for Specification Type.

8. Select **#8-36** for Size.

9. Select **Cut thread** for Thread method.

10. Select **Right-hand thread** for Thread options.

11. Select **Trim with start face**.

12. Select **Trim with end face**.

13. Select **Shaded preview**.

14. Click **OK** ✔ from the Thread PropertyManager. Thread1 is created and is displayed.

15. **Zoom in** on the thread section. View the Trim with start face option.

16. **Close** the part.

☀ You can align threads to end faces. A Cut thread is extended and cut to match the end face. An Extrude thread is cut to match the end face. In the PropertyManager, under Thread Options, select Trim with start face and Trim with end face.

For additional assembly homework exercises, see Chapter 10 on CSWA - Assembly Creation and Modification.

Notes:

Chapter 6

PNEUMATIC-TEST-MODULE and Final ROBOT Assembly

Below are the desired outcomes and usage competencies based on the completion of Chapter 6.

Desired Outcomes:	Usage Competencies:
<ul><li>Create five sub-assemblies:<ul><li>WHEEL-AND-AXLE.</li><li>WHEEL-FLATBAR.</li><li>3HOLE-SHAFTCOLLAR.</li><li>5HOLE-SHAFTCOLLAR.</li><li>PNEUMATIC-TEST-MODULE.</li></ul></li><li>Create the final ROBOT assembly.</li></ul>	<ul><li>Reuse geometry.</li><li>Apply Standard Mate types.</li><li>Modify existing assemblies to create new assemblies.</li><li>Utilize the following Assembly tools: Mate, Linear Component Pattern, Feature Driven Component Pattern, Mirror Components, Replace Components and Performance Evaluation.</li><li>Work with multiple documents in an assembly.</li></ul>

Notes:

Chapter 6 - PNEUMATIC-TEST-MODULE and ROBOT Assembly

Chapter Objective

Develop a working understanding with multiple documents in an assembly. Build on sound assembly modeling techniques that utilize symmetry, component patterns and mirrored components.

Create five sub-assemblies and the final ROBOT assembly:

- 3HOLE-SHAFTCOLLAR sub-assembly.

- 5HOLE-SHAFTCOLLAR sub-assembly.

- WHEEL-FLATBAR sub-assembly.

- WHEEL-AND-AXLE sub-assembly.

- PNEUMATIC-TEST-MODULE sub-assembly.

- ROBOT final assembly.

On the completion of this chapter, you will be able to:

- Utilize various Assembly techniques.

- Suppress and hide components.

- Create new assemblies and copy assemblies to reuse similar parts.

- Use the following Assembly tools:

  o Insert Component.

  o Standard Mates: Concentric, Coincident and Parallel.

  o Linear Component Pattern.

  o Feature Driven Component Pattern.

  o Circular Component Pattern.

  o Mirror Components.

  o Replace Components.

  o Performance Evaluation.

Chapter Overview

Create the 3HOLE-
SHAFTCOLLAR sub-assembly.

Utilize the 3HOLE-
SHAFTCOLLAR sub-assembly
to create the 5HOLE-
SHAFTCOLLAR sub-
assembly.

The WHEEL-FLATBAR sub-
assembly contains the
following items:

- 3HOLE-SHAFTCOLLAR
  assembly.

- 5HOLE-SHAFTCOLLAR
  assembly.

- WHEEL part.

Mate to the first component added
to the assembly. If you mate to the
first component or base component
of the assembly and decide to
change its orientation later, all the
components will move with it.

Remove Tangent edges.
Click Display from the Options
dialog box, check the Removed
box as illustrated.

Determine the static and
dynamic behavior of mates in
each sub-assembly before
creating the top level assembly.

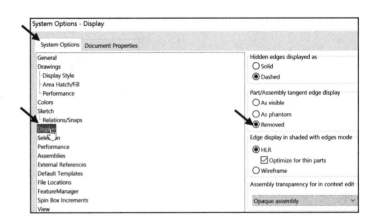

The WHEEL-AND-AXLE assembly contains the following items:

- WHEEL-FLATBAR assembly.

- AXLE-3000 part.

- SHAFTCOLLAR-500 part.

- HEX-ADAPTER part.

Combine the created new assemblies and parts to develop the PNEUMATIC-TEST-MODULE assembly.

Create the final ROBOT assembly. Insert the Robot-platform assembly, PNEUMATIC-TEST-MODULE assembly, basic_integration assembly and the HEX-STANDOFF components.

All assemblies and components for the final ROBOT assembly are located in the Chapter 6 Models folder. Copy the folder to your hard drive.

Tangent edges and Origins are displayed for educational purposes.

Utilize the Pack and Go option to save an assembly or drawing with references and toolbox components. The Pack and Go tool saves either to a folder or creates a zip file to e-mail. View SOLIDWORKS help for additional information.

Assembly Techniques

Assembly modeling requires practice and time. Below are a few helpful techniques to address Standard Mates. These techniques are utilized throughout the development of all assemblies.

Mating Techniques:
• Plan your assembly and sub-assemblies in an assembly layout diagram. Group components together to form smaller sub-assemblies.
• Utilize symmetry in an assembly. Utilize Mirror Component and Component Pattern to create multiple instances (copies) of components. Reuse similar components with Save as copy and configurations.
• Use the Zoom and Rotate commands to select the geometry in the Mate process. Zoom to select the correct face.
• Apply various colors to features and components to improve display.
• Activate Temporary Axes and Show Planes when required for Mates, otherwise Hide All Types from the View menu.
• Select Reference planes from the FeatureManager for complex components. Expand the FeatureManager to view the correct plane.
• Remove display complexity. Hide components when visibility is not required.
• Suppress components when Mates are not required. Group fasteners at the bottom of the FeatureManager. Suppress fasteners and their assembly patterns to save rebuild time and file size.
• Utilize Section views to select internal geometry.
• Use the Move Component and Rotate Component commands before Mating. Position the component in the correct orientation.
• Create additional flexibility in a Mate. Distance Mates are modified in configurations and animations. Rename Mates in the FeatureManager.
• Verify the position of the components. Use Top, Front, Right and Section views.

PNEUMATIC TEST MODULE Layout

The PNEUMATIC TEST MODULE assembly is comprised of four major sub-assemblies:

- LINKAGE assembly.

- RESERVOIR assembly.

- FRONT-SUPPORT assembly.

- WHEEL-AND-AXLE assembly.

There are over one hundred components in the PNEUMATIC TEST MODULE assembly. Complex assemblies require planning. The Assembly Layout diagram provides organization for a complex assembly by listing sub-assemblies and parts.

Chapter 2 LINKAGE Assembly

Chapter 3 AIR RESERVOIR Assembly

Chapter 3 FRONT SUPPORT Assembly

Chapter 5 WHEEL-AND-AXLE Assembly

Review the Assembly Layout diagram for the PNEUMATIC TEST MODULE assembly.

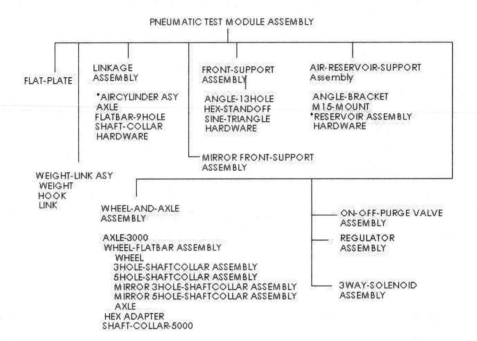

Physical space on the FLAT-PLATE is at a premium. Determine the requirements for hardware and placement after the mechanical components are assembled to the FLAT-PLATE part.

The FLAT-PLATE was created in the Chapter 3 exercises. The FLAT-PLATE is available in the Chapter 6 Models folder.

The LINKAGE assembly, FRONT-SUPPORT assembly and the AIR-RESERVOIR SUPPORT assembly were created in Chapter 2 and 3. The ON-OFF-PURGE VALVE assembly, REGULATOR assembly and the 3WAY SOLENOID VALVE assembly require additional hardware and are addressed in the chapter exercises.

This book is designed to expose the new SOLIDWORKS user to many different tools, techniques and procedures. It may not always use the most direct tool or process.

The WHEEL-FLATBAR assembly consists of the following:

- WHEEL part.

- 3HOLE-SHAFTCOLLAR assembly.

- 5HOLE-SHAFTCOLLAR assembly.

FLATBAR Sub-assembly

There are two similar sub-assemblies contained in the
WHEEL-FLATBAR assembly:

- 3HOLE-SHAFTCOLLAR assembly.

- 5HOLE-SHAFTCOLLAR assembly.

Create the 3HOLE-SHAFTCOLLAR assembly. Utilize parts
and mating techniques developed in Chapter 2 & 3.

Utilize the Save As command and create the 5HOLE-SHAFTCOLLAR assembly.

Combine the 3HOLE-SHAFTCOLLAR assembly, 5HOLE-SHAFTCOLLAR assembly
and the WHEEL part to create the WHEEL-FLATBAR assembly.

The FLATBAR-3HOLE and FLATBAR 5HOLE parts were created in the
Chapter 3 exercises. If needed, copy the models from the Chapter 6 Models folder.

Activity: 3HOLE-SHAFTCOLLAR Assembly

Create the 3HOLE-SHAFTCOLLAR assembly.

1)   Click **New** from the Menu bar.

2)   Double-click **Assembly** from the Templates tab. The Begin Assembly
PropertyManager is displayed.

3)   Click the **Browse** button.

4)   Browse to the **SW-TUTORIAL-2017\Chapter 6 Models** folder.

5)   Double-click **FLATBAR-3HOLE**. The FLATBAR-3HOLE part is located
in the Chapter 6 Models folder. If you want to create this part, follow
the below procedure; otherwise, skip the next few steps and go directly
to step 33.

6)   Click **Open** from the Menu bar.

7)   Double-click **FLATBAR** from the SW-
           TUTORIAL-2017 folder.

8)   Click **Save As** from the drop-down Menu bar.

9)   Select the **SW-TUTORIAL-2017** folder.

10)   Enter **FLATBAR-3HOLE** for File name.

11)   Enter **FLATBAR-3HOLE** for Description.

12)   Check the **Save as copy and continue** box.

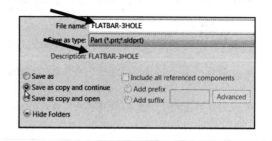

Save and close the FLATBAR model.
13)   Click **Save**.

14)   **Close** the FLATBAR model.

Open the FLATBAR-3HOLE model.
15)   Click **Open** 🗁 from the Menu bar.

16)   Double-click **FLATBAR-3HOLE** from the
           SW-TUTORIAL-2017 folder.

17)   Right-click **LPATTERN1** from the
           FeatureManager.

18)   Click **Edit Feature** from the Context toolbar.
           The LPattern1 PropertyManager is displayed.

19)   Enter **3** in the Number of Instances.

20)   Click **OK** ✔ from the LPattern1
           PropertyManager. Note: If needed, delete the
           Design Table in the CommandManager.

21)   Click **Boss-Extrude1** from the FeatureManager.
         View the dimensions in the Graphics window.

22)   Click the **4.000**in, [**101.60**] dimension.

23)   Enter **1.000**in, [**25.4**]. Click **Yes**.

24)   Click **Cut-Extrude1** from the FeatureManager.
         View the dimensions in the Graphics window.

25)   Click the **9X** dimension text in the Graphics window.
         The Dimension PropertyManager is displayed. Click
         Yes.

26)   Delete the **9X** text in the Dimension Text box.

27)   Enter **3X** in the Dimension Text box.

28)   Click **OK** ✔ from the Dimension PropertyManager.

Save the model.

29)   Click **Save** 🖫.

Create a new assembly.

30)   Click **New** ⬜ from the Main menu.

31)   Double-click **Assembly** from the Templates tab. The
         Begin Assembly PropertyManager is displayed.

32)   Double-click **FLATBAR-3HOLE.**

33)   Click **OK** ✔ from the Begin Assembly
         PropertyManager. The FLATBAR-3HOLE is fixed to
         the Origin.

Save the assembly.

34)   Click **Save As** from the drop-down Menu bar.

💡 Tangent edges and Origin are displayed for
educational purposes.

35) Enter **3HOLE-SHAFTCOLLAR** for File name.

36) Enter **3HOLE-SHAFTCOLLAR** for Description.

37) Click **Save**.

Save the 3HOLE-SHAFTCOLLAR assembly.

38) Click **Save** 💾.

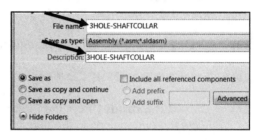

Utilize a Concentric/Coincident 📷 SmartMate between the SHAFT-COLLAR and the FLATBAR-3HOLE.

Open the **SHAFT-COLLAR** part.

39) Click **Open** 📂 from the Menu bar.

40) Double-click **SHAFT-COLLAR** from the SW-TUTORIAL-2017 folder. SHAFT-COLLAR is the current document name.

41) Press the **Left Arrow** key approximately 5 times to rotate the SHAFT-COLLAR to view the back circular edge.

42) Click **Window**, **Tile Horizontally** from the Menu bar.

43) Drag the **back circular edge** of the SHAFT-COLLAR to the left circular hole edge of the FLATBAR-3HOLE in the Assembly Graphics window as illustrated. The mouse pointer displays the Concentric/Coincident 📷 icon.

44) **Release** the mouse button. Note: Select the back circular edge of the SHAFT-COLLAR, not the face.

Save the 3HOLE-SHAFTCOLLAR assembly.

45) **Close** ✖ the SHAFT-COLLAR window.

46) **Maximize** ⬜ the 3HOLE-SHAFTCOLLAR assembly.

Fit the model to the Graphics window. **Save the assembly.**

47) Press the **f** key.

48) Click **Save** 💾.

Create the 5HOLE-SHAFTCOLLAR assembly. Utilize the Save As command with the Save as copy and continue option. Recover from Mate errors.

Save the 3HOLE-SHAFTCOLLAR assembly as the 5HOLE-SHAFTCOLLAR assembly.

49) Click **Save As** from the drop-down Menu bar.

50) Check the **Save as copy and continue** box.

51) Enter **5HOLE-SHAFTCOLLAR** for File name.

52) Enter **5HOLE-SHAFTCOLLAR** for Description.

53) Click **Save**.

Close the model.
54) Click **File**, **Close** from the Menu bar.

55) Click **Save All**.

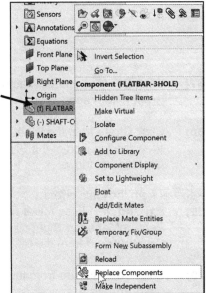

Open the **5HOLE-SHAFTCOLLAR** assembly.

56) Click **Open** 📂 from the Menu bar.

57) Select **Assembly** for file type.

58) Double-click **5HOLE-SHAFTCOLLAR**. The 5HOLE-SHAFTCOLLAR FeatureManager is displayed.

59) Right-click **FLATBAR-3HOLE** from the FeatureManager.

60) **Expand** the Pop-up menu if needed.

61) Click **Replace Components**. The Replace PropertyManager is displayed.

62) Click the **Browse** button.

63) Double-click **FLATBAR-5HOLE**. Note: The FLATBAR-5HOLE part is located in the Chapter 6 Models folder. Use the parts from your hard drive.

64) Check the **Re-attach mates** box.

65) Click **OK** ✔ from the Replace PropertyManager. The Mate Entities PropertyManager and the What's Wrong dialog box is displayed. There are two red Mate error marks displayed in the Mate Entities box.

66)   The What's Wrong dialog box is displayed. Recover from the Mate errors. Click **Close** from the What's Wrong dialog box.

67)   Click **OK** ✔ from the Mated Entities PropertyManager.

68)   Click **Close** from the What's Wrong dialog box. View the location of the SHAFT-COLLAR in the Graphics window.

Recover from the Mate errors.

69)   **Expand** the Mates folder from the FeatureManager. Right-click the first mate, **Concentric #** from the Mates folder.

70)   Click **Edit Feature** from the Context toolbar. The Mate PropertyManager is displayed.

71)   Right-click the **Mate Face error** in the Mate Selections box as illustrated.

72)   Click **Delete**.

73)   Click the **inside face** of the left hole of the FLATBAR as illustrated. Concentric is selected by default. Click **OK** ✔ from the Mate PropertyManager.

74)   Right-click the second mate, **Coincident #** from the Mates folder.

75)   Click **Edit Feature** from the Context toolbar. The Mate PropertyManager is displayed.

76) Right-click the **Mate Face error** in the Mate Selections box as illustrated.

77) Click **Delete** as illustrated.

78) Click the **front face** of the FLATBAR as illustrated. The selected faces are displayed in the Mate Selections box. Coincident is selected by default.

79) Click **OK** ✔ from the Mate PropertyManager.

80) Click **Rebuild** 🔴.

81) **Expand** the Mate folder from the FeatureManager. View the created mates.

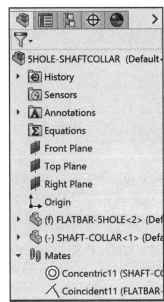

🔆 The Mate Entities box will list red X's if the faces, edges or planes are not valid. Expand the Mate Entities and select new references in the Graphics window to redefine the mates.

The FLATBAR-3HOLE is replaced with the FLATBAR-5HOLE part. The Mates are updated.

Fit the model to the Graphics window.
82) Press the **f** key.

Display an Isometric view. Save the 5HOLE-SHAFTCOLLAR assembly.
83) Click **Isometric view** ⬛.

84) Click **Save** 💾.

🔆 Incorporate symmetry into the assembly. Divide large assemblies into smaller sub-assemblies.

WHEEL-FLATBAR Assembly

The WHEEL-FLATBAR assembly consists of the following components:

- 3HOLE-SHAFTCOLLAR assembly.

- 5HOLE-SHAFTCOLLAR assembly.

- WHEEL part.

Create the WHEEL-FLATBAR assembly. Mate the 3HOLE-SHAFTCOLLAR assembly 67.5 degrees counterclockwise from the Top Plane.

The 3HOLE-SHAFTCOLLAR assembly is concentric with holes on the second and fourth bolt circle.

Mate the 5HOLE-SHAFTCOLLAR assembly 22.5 degrees clockwise from the Top Plane.

The 5HOLE-SHAFTCOLLAR assembly is concentric with holes on the second and fourth bolt circle.

Utilize the Quick mate procedure on Standard mates, Cam mate, Profile Center mate, Slot mate, Symmetric mate and Width mate. To activate the Quick Mates functionality, click Tools, Customize. On the toolbars tab, under Context toolbar settings, select Show quick mates. Quick Mates is selected by default.

Use the Quick mate procedure for reference geometry (such as planes, axes, and points) along with model geometry (such as faces, edges and vertices).

Remove the fixed state. Right-click the component name in the FeatureManager. Click **Float**. The component is free to move.

Activity: WHEEL-FLATBAR Assembly

Create the WHEEL-FLATBAR assembly.

85)   Click **New** 🗋 from the Menu bar.

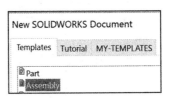

86)   Double-click **Assembly** from the Templates tab. The Begin Assembly PropertyManager is displayed.

Insert the WHEEL.

87)   Click the **Browse** button.

88)   Browse to the **SW-TUTORIAL-2017** folder.

89)   Double-click **WHEEL**.

90)   Click **OK** ✅ from the Begin Assembly PropertyManager. The WHEEL part is fixed to the assembly Origin.

If needed, deactivate the Origins.

91)   Click **View**, **Hide/Show**, uncheck **Origins** from the Menu bar menu.

Save the assembly.

92)   Click **Save As** from the drop-down Menu bar.

93)   Select the **SW-TUTORIAL-2017** folder.

94)   Enter **WHEEL-FLATBAR** for File name.

95)   Enter **WHEEL-FLATBAR** for Description.

96)   Click **Save**.

Display the Top Plane in the Front view.

97)   Click **Front view** from the Heads-up View toolbar. View the WHEEL part.

Locate the first set of holes from the Right plane (-Y-axis). Left Hole1 and Left Hole2 are positioned on the second and forth bolt circle, 22.5° from the Right plane. Select Left Hole1. The x, y, z coordinates, -.287, -.693, .125 are displayed.

$\text{Tan}^{-1}(-.287/.693) = 22.5°$

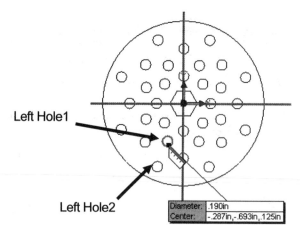

As an exercise, utilize the Measure tool to determine the center-to-center distance between the Left Hole1 and Left Hole2. The center-to-center distance is .500in.

Insert two Concentric mates between Left Hole1 and Left Hole2 and the 3HOLE-SHAFTCOLLAR assembly holes. The FLATBAR-3HOLE center-to-center distance is also .500in.

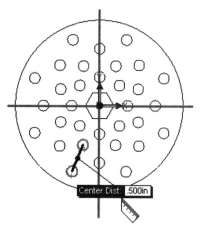

To determine tolerance issues, utilize two Concentric mates between components with mating cylindrical geometry. If the mating components center-to-center distance is not exact, a Mate error is displayed on the second Concentric mate.

Insert a Coincident mate between the back face of the 3HOLE-SHAFTCOLLAR assembly and the front face of the WHEEL.

Right Hole1 and Right Hole2 are 22.5° from the Top Plane.

Insert two Concentric mates between Right Hole1 and Right Hole2 and the 5HOLE-SHAFTCOLLAR assembly holes.

Insert a Coincident mate between the back face of the 5HOLE-SHAFTCOLLAR assembly and the front face of the WHEEL.

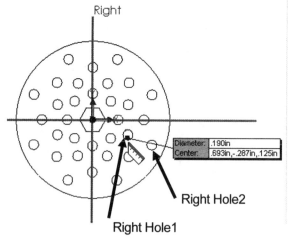

Activity: WHEEL-FLATBAR Assembly-Insert 3HOLE-SHAFTCOLLAR Assembly

---

Insert the 3HOLE-SHAFTCOLLAR assembly.

98)   Click **Isometric view** from the Heads-up View toolbar.

99)   Click **Insert Components** from the Assembly toolbar. The Insert Components PropertyManager is displayed.

100)   Click the **Browse** button.

101)   Browse to the **SW-TUTORIAL-2017** folder.

102)   Double-click the **3HOLE-SHAFTCOLLAR** assembly.

103)   Click a **position** to the left of the WHEEL as illustrated.

Move and rotate the 3HOLE-SHAFTCOLLAR component.
104)   Click the front face of the **3HOLE-SHAFTCOLLAR**.

105)   Right-click **Move with Triad**.

106)   Hold the **left mouse button** down on the X-axis (red).

107)   Drag the **component** to the left. View the ruler.

108)   Hold the **right mouse button** down on the Z-axis (blue).

109)   Drag the **component** and rotate it about the Z-axis. View the ruler.

110)   **Position** the component until the SHAFT-COLLAR part is approximately in front of the WHEEL Left Hole1.

111)   Release the **right mouse** button.

112)   Click a **position** in the Graphics window to deselect the face.

Insert a Concentric mate.

113) Click the **back top inside cylindrical face** of the SHAFT-COLLAR.

114) **Rotate** the model to view the WHEEL.

115) Hold the **Ctrl** key down.

116) Click the **WHEEL Left Hole1** cylindrical face as illustrated.

117) Release the **Ctrl** key. The Mate pop-up menu is displayed.

118) Click **Concentric** from the Mate pop-up menu.

Insert the second Concentric mate.

119) Click the back middle inside cylindrical face of the FLATBAR.

120) **Rotate** the model to view the WHEEL.

121) Hold the **Ctrl** key down.

122) Click the **WHEEL Left Hole2** inside cylindrical face as illustrated.

123) Release the **Ctrl** key. The Mate pop-up menu is displayed.

124) Click **Concentric** from the Mate pop-up menu.

Insert a Coincident mate.

125) Click the **FLATBAR-3HOLE back** face.

126) **Rotate** the model to view the WHEEL.

127) Hold the **Ctrl** key down.

128) Click the front face of the **WHEEL**.

129) Release the **Ctrl** key. The Mate pop-up menu is displayed.

130) Click **Coincident** from the Mate pop-up menu.

Display a Front view.

131) Click **Front view** .

Save the WHEEL-FLATBAR.

132) Click **Save** .

Activity: WHEEL-FLATBAR Assembly-Insert 5HOLE-SHAFTCOLLAR Assembly

Insert the 5HOLE-SHAFTCOLLAR assembly.

133) Click **Insert Components** from the Assembly toolbar. The Insert Components PropertyManager is displayed.

134) Click the **Browse** button. Double-click the **5HOLE-SHAFTCOLLAR** assembly from the SW-TUTORIAL-2017 folder.

135) Click a **position** to the right of the WHEEL.

Move the 5HOLE-SHAFTCOLLAR component.

136) Click the **5HOLE-SHAFTCOLLAR** front face.

137) Right-click **Move with Triad**.

138) Hold the **left mouse button** down on the X-axis (red).

139) Drag the **component** to the right. View the results.

140) Click **Isometric view** .

141) Click **inside** the Graphics window.

Mate the 5HOLE-SHAFTCOLLAR assembly. Insert a Concentric mate.

142) Click the **back inside cylindrical face** of the first hole on the FLATBAR-5HOLE assembly.

143) **Rotate** the model to view the WHEEL.

144) Hold the **Ctrl** key down.

145) Click the **WHEEL Right Hole1** cylindrical face.

146) Release the **Ctrl** key. The Mate pop-up menu is displayed.

147) Click **Concentric** from the Mate pop-up menu.

Insert a Concentric mate.

148) **Move** the 5HOLE-SHAFTCOLLAR to view the back side.

149) Click the **back inside cylindrical** face of the second hole on the FLATBAR-5HOLE assembly.

150) **Rotate** the model to view the WHEEL.

151) Hold the **Ctrl** key down.

152) Click the **WHEEL Right Hole2** cylindrical face.

153) Release the **Ctrl** key. The Mate pop-up menu is displayed.

154) Click **Concentric** from the Mate pop-up menu.

Right Hole2

Right Hole1

Right Hole2

Right Hole1

Insert a Coincident mate.

155) Click the **back face** of the FLATBAR-5HOLE.

156) **Rotate** the model to view the WHEEL.

157) Hold the **Ctrl** key down.

158) Click the **front face** of the WHEEL.

159) Release the **Ctrl** key. The Mate pop-up menu is displayed.

160) Click **Coincident** from the Mate pop-up menu.

Measure the angle between the 3HOLE-SHAFTCOLLAR assembly and the 5HOLE-SHAFTCOLLAR assembly.

161) Click **Front view** .

162) Click the **Measure** tool from the Evaluate tab in the CommandManager. The Measure dialog box is displayed.

163) Select the **two inside edges** of the FLATBAR assemblies. View the results.

164) If required, click the **Show XYZ Measurements button**. The items are perpendicular.

The Measure tool provides the ability to display dual units. Click the **Units/Precision** icon from the Measure dialog box. Set the desired units.

Utilize the Measure tool to measure distances and add reference dimensions between the COM point and entities such as vertices, edges, and faces.

165) **Close** the Measure dialog box.

Apply the Performance Evaluation tool. The Performance Evaluation tool displays statistics and checks the health of the current assembly.

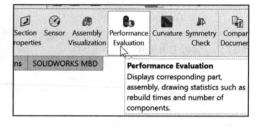

166) Click the **Performance Evaluation** tool in the Evaluate toolbar. The Performance Evaluation dialog box is displayed. Review the Status and description for the assembly.

167) Click **OK** from the Performance Evaluation dialog box.

Fit the model to the Graphics window. Display an Isometric view.

168) Press the **f** key.

169) Click **Isometric view** from the Heads-up View toolbar.

Save the WHEEL-FLATBAR assembly.

170) Click **Save**.

To remove the fixed state, Right-click the component name in the FeatureManager. Click **Float**. The component is free to move.

Mate to the first component added to the assembly. If you mate to the first component or base component of the assembly and decide to change its orientation later, all the components will move with it.

WHEEL-AND-AXLE Assembly

The WHEEL-AND-AXLE assembly contains the
following items:

- WHEEL-FLATBAR assembly.

- AXLE-3000 part.

- SHAFTCOLLAR-500 part.

- HEX-ADAPTER part.

Create the WHEEL-AND-AXLE assembly. The
AXLE-3000 part is the first component in the
assembly. A part or assembly inserted into a new
assembly is called a component. The WHEEL-
FLATBAR assembly rotates about the AXLE part.

Combine the created new assemblies and parts to develop the PNEUMATIC-TEST-
MODULE assembly.

Activity: WHEEL-AND-AXLE Assembly

Create the WHEEL-AND-AXLE assembly.

171) Click **New** from the Menu bar.

172) Double-click **Assembly** from the Templates tab. The
Begin Assembly PropertyManager is displayed.

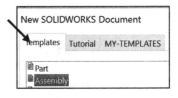

Insert the AXLE-3000 part.

173) Click the **Browse** button.

174) Browse to the **SW-TUTORIAL-2017** folder.

175) Double-click **AXLE-3000**. Note: AXLE-3000 is
located in the Chapter 6 Models folder if you did not
create it in Chapter 5.

176) Click **OK** from the Begin Assembly
PropertyManager. The AXLE-3000 part is fixed to the
assembly Origin.

Save the assembly.

177)   Click **Save As** from the drop-down Menu bar.

178)   Enter **WHEEL-AND-AXLE** for File name in the SW-TUTORIAL-2017 folder.

179)   Enter **WHEEL-AND-AXLE** for Description.

180)   Click **Save**.

Insert a Coincident mate between the Axis of the AXLE-3000 and the Axis of the WHEEL. Insert a Coincident mate between the Front Plane of the AXLE-3000 and the Front Plane of the WHEEL. The WHEEL-FLATBAR assembly rotates about the AXLE-3000 axis.

Display the Temporary Axes.

181)   Click **View**, **Hide/Show**, check **Temporary Axes** from the Menu bar.

Insert the WHEEL-FLATBAR assembly.

182)   Click **Insert Components** 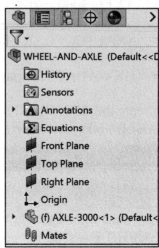 from the Assembly toolbar. The Insert Components PropertyManager is displayed.

183)   Click the **Browse** button.

184)   Double-click the **WHEEL-FLATBAR** assembly from the SW-TUTORIAL-2017 folder.

185)   Click a **position** to the right of AXLE-3000.

View the Reference WHEEL Axis.

186)   Click **View**, **Hide/Show**, check **Axes** from the Menu bar.

187)   If needed, click **View**, **Hide/Show**, un-check **Origins** from the Menu bar.

🔆 Reference geometry defines the shape or form of a surface or a solid. Reference geometry includes planes, axes, coordinate systems, and points.

🔆 This book is designed to expose the new SOLIDWORKS user to many different tools, techniques and procedures. It may not always use the most direct tool or process.

Insert a Coincident mate.

188) Click the **Mate** 🖉 tool from the Assembly toolbar. The Mate PropertyManager is displayed.

189) Pin the Mate PropertyManager. Click the **Keep Visible** ⊣ icon from the Mate PropertyManager.

190) Click **Axis1** in the Graphics window.

191) Click the **AXLE-3000 Temporary Axis**. Coincident is selected by default.

192) Click **OK** ✔ from the Coincident PropertyManager.

Insert a Coincident mate.

193) **Expand** WHEEL-AND-AXLE from the fly-out FeatureManager.

194) **Expand** AXLE-3000 from the fly-out FeatureManager.

195) Click **Front Plane** of AXLE-3000<1>.

196) **Expand** WHEEL from the fly-out FeatureManager.

197) Click **Front Plane** of the WHEEL. Coincident is selected by default.

198) Click **OK** ✔ from the Mate PropertyManager.

199) Un-Pin the Mate PropertyManager. Click the **Keep Visible** 📌 icon from the Mate PropertyManager.

200) Click **OK** ✔ from the Mate PropertyManager.

Rotate the WHEEL-FLATBAR assembly about AXLE-3000.

201) Click and drag the **WHEEL** around AXLE-3000.

Save the WHEEL-AND-AXLE assembly.

202) Click **Save** 💾.

This book is designed to expose the new SOLIDWORKS user to many different tools, techniques and procedures. It may not always use the most direct tool or process.

Activity: WHEEL-AND-AXLE Assembly-Insert the HEX-ADAPTER Part

Insert the HEX-ADAPTER part.

203) Click the **Insert Components** 📂 tool from the Assembly toolbar. The Insert Component PropertyManager is displayed.

204) Click the **Browse** button.

205) Browse to the **SW-TUTORIAL-2017** folder.

206) Double-click **HEX-ADAPTER**.

207) Click a **position** to the left of the WHEEL as illustrated. The HEX-ADAPTER is displayed in the FeatureManager.

208) **Expand** the Mates folder.

209) **View** the created mates for the assembly. View the inserted components: AXLE-3000, WHEEL-FLATBAR and HEX-ADAPTER.

Insert a Concentric mate. Mate the HEX-ADAPTER.

210) Click the **Mate** 🔗 tool from the Assembly toolbar. The Mate PropertyManager is displayed.

211) Click the **HEX-ADAPTER** cylindrical face as illustrated.

212) Click the **AXLE-3000** cylindrical face as illustrated. Concentric is selected by default. The selected faces are displayed in the Mate Selections box.

213) Click **Aligned** ⛶ from the Concentric1 PropertyManager to flip the HEX-ADAPTER, if required.

214) Click **OK** ✔ from the Concentric PropertyManager.

Insert a Coincident mate.

215) Click the **front face** of the WHEEL.

216) **Rotate** the assembly to view the flat back circular face of the HEX-ADAPTER as illustrated.

217) Hold the **Ctrl** key down.

218) Click the **flat back circular face** of the HEX-ADAPTER.

219) Release the **Ctrl** key. The Mate pop-up menu is displayed.

220) Click **Coincident** from the Mate pop-up menu.

Insert a Parallel mate.

221) **Rotate** the WHEEL-AND-AXLE assembly to view the back bottom edge of the HEX-ADAPTER.

222) **Zoom in** on the back bottom edge of the HEX-ADAPTER.

223) Click the **back bottom edge** of the WHEEL. Do not select the midpoint.

224) Hold the **Ctrl** key down.

225) Click the **top edge** of the HEX-ADAPTER. Do not select the midpoint.

226) Release the **Ctrl** key. The Mate pop-up menu is displayed.

227) Click **Parallel** ＼ from the Mate pop-up menu.

Fit the model to the Graphics window.
228) Press the **f** key.

Display an Isometric view.
229) Click **Isometric view** ▣.

View the created mates.
230) **Expand** the Mates folder.

Save the WHEEL-AND-AXLE assembly.
231) Click **Save** ▤.

Activity: WHEEL-AND-AXLE Assembly-Insert SHAFTCOLLAR-500 Part

---

Insert the SHAFTCOLLAR-500 part.

232) Click the **Insert Components** tool from the Assembly toolbar. The Insert Component PropertyManager is displayed.

233) Click the **Browse** button.

234) Browse to the **SW-TUTORIAL-2017** folder.

235) Double-click **SHAFTCOLLAR-500**.

236) Click a **position** behind the WHEEL-AND-AXLE assembly.

Insert a Concentric mate.

237) Click **View**, **Hide/Show**, un-check **Temporary Axes** from the Menu bar.

238) Click **View**, **Hide/Show**, un-check **Axes** from the Menu bar.

239) Hold the **Ctrl** key down.

240) Click the **inside cylindrical face** of the SHAFTCOLLAR-500 part.

241) Click the **cylindrical face** of the AXLE-3000 part.

242) Release the **Ctrl** key. The Mate pop-up menu is displayed.

243) Click **Concentric** from the Mate pop-up menu.

Insert a Coincident mate.

244) Click the **front face** of the SHAFTCOLLAR-500 part.

245) **Rotate** the WHEEL to view the back face.

246) Hold the **Ctrl** key down.

247) Click the **back face** of the WHEEL.

248) Release the **Ctrl** key. The Mate pop-up menu is displayed.

249) Click **Coincident** from the Mate pop-up menu.

Display an Isometric view.

250) Click **Isometric view** .

View the created Mates.

251) **Expand** the Mates folder. View the created mates.

Save the WHEEL-AND-AXLE assembly.

252) Click **Save** .

Close all files.

253) Click **Windows**, **Close All** from the Menu bar.

Determine the static and dynamic behavior of mates in each sub-assembly before creating the top-level assembly.

Review the WHEEL-AND-AXLE Assembly

You combined the WHEEL-FLATBAR sub assembly, the AXLE-3000 part, the HEX-ADAPTER part and the SHAFTCOLLAR-500 part to create the WHEEL-AND-AXLE assembly.

The WHEEL-FLATBAR sub-assembly rotated about the AXLE-3000 part. The WHEEL-FLATBAR assembly combined the 3HOLE-SHAFTCOLLAR assembly and the 5HOLE-SHAFTCOLLAR assembly. The 5HOLE-SHAFTCOLLAR assembly was created from the 3HOLE-SHAFTCOLLAR assembly by replacing the FLATBAR component and recovering from two Mate errors. Additional components are added to the WHEEL-AND-AXLE assembly in the chapter exercises.

PNEUMATIC-TEST-MODULE Assembly

Create the PNEUMATIC-TEST-MODULE assembly. The first component is the FLAT-PLATE. The FLAT-PLATE is fixed to the Origin. The FLAT-PLATE part was created in the Chapter 3 exercises.

Modify the LINKAGE assembly. Insert the HEX-STANDOFF part. Insert the LINKAGE assembly into the PNEUMATIC-TEST-MODULE assembly.

Insert the AIR-RESERVOIR-SUPPORT assembly. Utilize the Linear Component Pattern and Feature Driven Component Pattern tools. Insert the FRONT-SUPPORT assembly. Utilize the Mirror Components tool to create a mirrored version of the FRONT-SUPPORT assembly.

Insert the WHEEL-AND-AXLE assembly. Utilize Component Properties and create a Flexible State. Utilize the ConfigurationManager to select the Flexible configuration for the AirCylinder assembly.

Work between multiple part and sub-assembly documents to create the final assembly.

Activity: PNEUMATIC-TEST-MODULE Assembly

Create the PNEUMATIC-TEST-MODULE assembly.

254)   Click **New** 🗋 from the Menu bar.

255)   Double-click **Assembly** from the Templates tab. The Begin Assembly PropertyManager is displayed.

Insert the FLAT-PLATE part.

256)   Click the **Browse** button.

257)   Browse to the **SW-TUTORIAL-2017\Chapter 6 Models** folder.

258)   Double-click **FLAT-PLATE**. Note: FLAT-PLATE is located in the Chapter 6 Models folder.

259)   Click **OK** ✅ from the Begin Assembly PropertyManager. FLAT-PLATE is fixed to the Origin.

Save the assembly.

260)   Browse to the **SW-TUTORIAL-2017** folder.

261)   Click **Save As** from the drop-down Menu bar.

262)   Enter **PNEUMATIC-TEST-MODULE** for File name.

263)   Enter **PNEUMATIC-TEST-MODULE** for Description.

264)   Click **Save**.

Activity: Modify the LINKAGE Assembly

Modify the LINKAGE assembly created in Chapter 2. Note: The LINKAGE assembly is located in the Chapter 6 Models folder\LINKAGE Assembly folder.

265)   Click **Open** 📂 from the Menu bar.

266)   Double-click **LINKAGE** from the Chapter 6 Models folder\LINKAGE Assembly folder. The LINKAGE assembly is displayed.

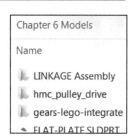

Chapter 6 Models

Name

⬛ LINKAGE Assembly

⬛ hmc_pulley_drive

⬛ gears-lego-integrate

⬛ FLAT-PLATE.SLDPRT

Insert the HEX-STANDOFF part into the LINKAGE assembly.

267)   Click the **Insert Components** tool from the
Assembly toolbar. The Insert Component
PropertyManager is displayed.

268)   Click the **Browse** button.

269)   Browse to the **SW-TUTORIAL-2017** folder.

270)   Double-click **HEX-STANDOFF**.

271)   Click a **position** to the front of the half
Slot Cut as illustrated.

View the Temporary Axes.
272)   Click **View**, **Hide/Show**, check
Temporary Axes from the Menu bar.

273)   Click **View**, **Hide/Show**, check **Axes**
from the Menu bar.

Insert a Coincident mate.
274)   **Zoom-in** to view the Temporary Axis of
the HEX-STANDOFF part.

275)   Click the **HEX-STANDOFF** tapped hole
Temporary Axis as illustrated.

276)   **Zoom-in** to view the half Slot Cut Axis1 as
illustrated.

277)   Hold the **Ctrl** key down.

278)   Click the **half Slot Cut Axis1**.

279)   Release the **Ctrl** key. The Mate pop-up menu
is displayed.

280)   Click **Coincident** from the Mate pop-up menu.

Reference geometry defines the shape or
form of a surface or a solid. Reference geometry
includes planes, axes, coordinate systems, and
points.

Insert a Coincident mate.
281) Click the **HEX-STANDOFF** top face.

282) **Rotate** to view the BRACKET bottom face.

283) Hold the **Ctrl** key down.

284) Click the **BRACKET bottom face**.

285) Release the **Ctrl** key. The Mate pop-up menu is displayed.

286) Click **Coincident** from the Mate pop-up menu.

Insert a Parallel mate.
287) **Rotate** to view the model as illustrated.

288) Click the **HEX-STANDOFF** front face.

289) Hold the **Ctrl** key down.

290) Click the **BRACKET front face**.

291) Release the **Ctrl** key. The Mate pop-up menu is displayed.

292) Click **Parallel** ⟍ from the Mate pop-up menu.

Fit the model to the Graphics window.
293) Press the **f** key.

Display an Isometric view. Save the model.
294) Click **Isometric view** .

295) Click **Save** .

View the created Mates.
296) **Expand** the Mates folder. View the created mates.

Insert the second HEX-STANDOFF.

297)   Click the **Insert Components** 🗐 tool from the Assembly toolbar. The Insert Component PropertyManager is displayed.

298)   Click the **Browse** button.

299)   Browse to the **SW-TUTORIAL-2017** folder.

300)   Double-click **HEX-STANDOFF**.

301)   Click a **position** to the back right of the back half Slot Cut as illustrated.

Insert a Concentric mate.

302)   **Rotate** the model to view the second HEX-STANDOFF. **Zoom-in** on the Temporary Axis.

303)   Click the **second HEX-STANDOFF** Tapped Hole Temporary Axis.

304)   **Rotate** to view the back half Slot Cut Axis1.

305)   Hold the **Ctrl** key down.

306)   Click the **back half Slot Cut Axis1**.

307)   Release the **Ctrl** key. The Mate pop-up menu is displayed.

308)   Click **Coincident** from the Mate pop-up menu.

Insert a Coincident mate.

309)   Click the **second HEX-STANDOFF top** face.

310)   **Rotate** to view the BRACKET bottom face.

311)   Hold the **Ctrl** key down.

312)   Click the **BRACKET bottom face**.

313)   Release the **Ctrl** key. The Mate pop-up menu is displayed.

314)   Click **Coincident** from the Mate pop-up menu.

Insert a Parallel mate.

315) Click the **second HEX-STANDOFF** face as illustrated.

316) Hold the **Ctrl** key down.

317) Click the **BRACKET back right** face.

318) Release the **Ctrl** key. The Mate pop-up menu is displayed.

319) Click **Parallel** ⟍ from the Mate pop-up menu.

💡 Use Selection Filter toolbar to select the correct face, edge, Axis, etc.

Fit the model to the Graphics window. Display an Isometric view.

320) Press the **f** key.

321) Click **Isometric view** 🟦.

Save the assembly.

322) Click **Save** 💾.

Insert the second AXLE.

323) Click the **Insert Components** 🗗 tool from the Assembly toolbar.

324) Click the **Browse** button.

325) Browse to the **SW-TUTORIAL-2017** folder.

326) Double-click **AXLE**.

327) Click a **position** to the front bottom of the FLATBAR as illustrated.

Insert a Concentric mate.

328) Click the **second AXLE cylindrical face**.

329) Hold the **Ctrl** key down.

330) Click the **FLATBAR bottom hole** face as illustrated.

331) Release the **Ctrl** key. The Mate pop-up menu is displayed.

332) Click **Concentric** from the Mate pop-up menu.

Insert a Coincident mate.

333) Click the second **AXLE Front Plane** from the FeatureManager.

334) Hold the **Ctrl** key down.

335) Click the **LINKAGE assembly Front Plane** from the FeatureManager.

336) Release the **Ctrl** key. The Mate pop-up menu is displayed.

337) Click **Coincident** from the Mate pop-up menu.

Fit the model to the Graphics window.

338) Press the **f** key.

Display an Isometric view. Save the assembly.

339) Click **Isometric view** from the Heads-up View toolbar.

Save the LINKAGE assembly.

340) Click **Save**.

Insert the first SHAFT-COLLAR on the second AXIS.

341) Click the **Insert Components** Assembly tool.

342) Click the **Browse** button.

343) Browse to the **SW-TUTORIAL-2017** folder.

344) Double-click **SHAFT-COLLAR**.

345) Click a **position** to the back of the second AXLE as illustrated.

Enlarge the view.
346) Zoom-in on the **SHAFT-COLLAR** and the **AXLE** to enlarge the view.

Insert a Concentric mate.
347) Click the inside **hole face** of the SHAFT-COLLAR.

348) Hold the **Ctrl** key down.

349) Click the **long cylindrical face** of the AXLE.

350) Release the **Ctrl** key. The Mate pop-up menu is displayed.

351) Click **Concentric** from the Mate pop-up menu.

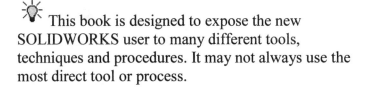 This book is designed to expose the new SOLIDWORKS user to many different tools, techniques and procedures. It may not always use the most direct tool or process.

Utilize the Quick mate procedure on Standard mates, Cam mate, Profile Center mate, Slot mate, Symmetric mate and Width mate. To activate the Quick Mates functionality, click Tools, Customize. On the toolbars tab, under Context toolbar settings, select Show quick mates. Quick Mates is selected by default.

The Quick mate procedure can be used for reference geometry (such as planes, axes, and points) along with model geometry (such as faces, edges and vertices).

Insert a Coincident mate.

352) Click the **front face** of the SHAFT-COLLAR as illustrated.

353) **Rotate** the assembly to view the back face of the FLATBAR.

354) Hold the **Ctrl** key down.

355) Click the **back face** of the FLATBAR.

356) Release the **Ctrl** key. The Mate pop-up menu is displayed.

357) Click **Coincident** from the Mate pop-up menu.

Display the Isometric view.

358) Click **Isometric view** .

Insert the second SHAFT-COLLAR.

359) Click the **Insert Components** Assembly tool. The Insert Component PropertyManager is displayed.

360) Click the **Browse** button.

361) Browse to the **SW-TUTORIAL-2017** folder.

362) Double-click **SHAFT-COLLAR**.

363) Click a **position** to the front of the AXLE.

Enlarge the view.

364) **Zoom in** on the second SHAFT-COLLAR and the AXLE.

Insert a Concentric mate.

365) Click the inside **hole face** of the second SHAFT-COLLAR. Note the icon face feedback symbol.

366) Hold the **Ctrl** key down.

367) Click the **long cylindrical face** of the AXLE.

368) Release the **Ctrl** key. The Mate pop-up menu is displayed.

369) Click **Concentric** from the Mate pop-up menu.

Insert a Coincident mate.

370) Press the **f** key to fit the model to the Graphics window.

371) **Zoom in** on the front face of the FLATBAR as illustrated.

372) Click the **front face** of the FLATBAR.

373) **Rotate** to view the back face of the second SHAFT-COLLAR.

374) Hold the **Ctrl** key down.

375) Click the **back face** of the second SHAFT-COLLAR.

376) Release the **Ctrl** key. The Mate pop-up menu is displayed.

377) Click **Coincident** from the Mate pop-up menu.

Display an Isometric view.

378) Click **Isometric view** .

Save the LINKAGE assembly.

379) **Rebuild** the model.

380) Click **View**, **Hide/Show**, un-check **Axis** from the Menu bar.

381) Click **View**, **Hide/Show**, un-check **Temporary Axis** from Menu bar.

382) Click **Save** . As an exercise, insert SCREWs between the AirCylinder assembly and the two HEX-STANDOFFs as illustrated.

SCREWs

Activity: PNEUMATIC-TEST-MODULE-Insert LINKAGE Assembly

Insert the LINKAGE assembly into the
PNEUMATIC-TEST-MODULE assembly.

383) Click **Window**, **Tile Horizontally** from
the Menu bar. The PNEUMATIC-TEST-
MODULE assembly should be open.

384) Rotate the two **FLATBARs**
approximately 45°.

385) Click and drag the **LINKAGE**
🔲 LINKAGE<1> assembly icon into the
PNEUMATIC-TEST-MODULE
assembly.

386) Click a **position** above the FLAT-
PLATE.

387) **Maximize** the PNEUMATIC-TEST-
MODULE Graphics window.

388) Click **View**, **Hide/Show**, un-
check **Origins** from the Menu
bar. If required, click View,
Hide/Show, un-check Planes
from the Menu bar.

Display a Trimetric view.

389) Click **Trimetric view** 🔲 from
the Heads-up View toolbar.

Insert a Concentric mate.

390) Click the **Front HEX-
STANDOFF Tapped** inside
hole face as illustrated.

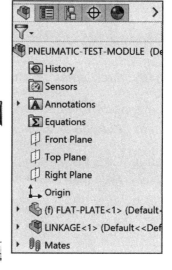

391) **Rotate** the model to view the FLAT-PLATE
hole as illustrated.

392) Hold the **Ctrl** key down.

393) Click the **FLAT-PLATE Hole** face in the 5th
row, 4th column as illustrated.

394) Release the **Ctrl** key. The Mate pop-up
menu is displayed.

395) Click **Concentric** from the Mate pop-up
menu.

Insert a Parallel mate between two Planes.

396) Click the **PNEUMATIC-TEST-MODULE Front Plane** from the FeatureManager.

397) Hold the **Ctrl** key down.

398) Click the **LINKAGE assembly Front Plane** from the FeatureManager.

399) Release the **Ctrl** key. The Mate pop-up menu is displayed.

400) Click **Parallel** from the Mate pop-up menu.

Insert a Coincident mate.

401) Click the **Front HEX-STANDOFF** bottom face.

402) Hold the **Ctrl** key down.

403) Click the **FLAT-PLATE top face**.

404) Release the **Ctrl** key. The Mate pop-up menu is displayed.

405) Click **Coincident** from the Mate pop-up menu.

Display an Isometric view.

406) Click **Isometric view** .

Save the PNEUMATIC-TEST-MODULE assembly.

407) Click **Save** .

The LINKAGE assembly is fully defined and located on the FLAT-PLATE part. Insert the AIR-RESERVOIR-SUPPORT assembly. The AIR-RESERVOIR-SUPPORT assembly was created in the Chapter 3 exercises. The AIR-RESERVOIR SUPPORT is located in Chapter 6 Models folder.

Activity: PNEUMATIC-TEST-MODULE Insert AIR-RESERVOIR-SUPPORT

Insert the AIR-RESERVOIR-SUPPORT assembly.

408) Click the **Insert Components** Assembly tool. The Insert Component
PropertyManager is displayed.

409) Click the **Browse** button.

410) Browse to the **SW-TUTORIAL-
2017\Chapter 6 Models** folder.

411) Double-click the **AIR-RESERVOIR-
SUPPORT** assembly. The AIR-
RESERVOIR SUPPORT assembly is
located in the Chapter 6 models
folder. Work from your local hard
drive.

412) Click a **position** above the FLAT-
PLATE as illustrated.

413) Click the **Rotate Component**
Assembly tool. The Rotate
Component PropertyManager is
displayed. The Rotate icon is
displayed in the Graphics
window.

414) Click and drag the **AIR-
RESERVOIR-SUPPORT** until
the tank is parallel with the
AirCylinder assembly as
illustrated.

415) Click **OK** from the Rotate
Component
PropertyManager.

Insert a Concentric mate.

416) Click the **FLAT-PLATE back left inside hole face** as illustrated.

417) Hold the **Ctrl** key down.

418) Click the **fourth ANGLE-BRACKET inside hole** face.

419) Release the **Ctrl** key. The Mate pop-up menu is displayed.

420) Click **Concentric** from the Mate pop-up menu.

Insert a Coincident mate.

421) Click the **ANGLE-BRACKET bottom** face.

422) **Rotate** the assembly to view the FLAT-PLATE top face. Hold the **Ctrl** key down.

423) Click the **FLAT-PLATE top** face.

424) Release the **Ctrl** key. The Mate pop-up menu is displayed.

425) Click **Coincident** from the Mate pop-up menu.

Insert a Parallel mate.

426) Click **Left view** from the Heads-up View toolbar.

427) Click the **ANGLE-BRACKET** narrow face.

428) Hold the **Ctrl** key down.

429) Click the **FLAT-PLATE narrow** face.

430) Release the **Ctrl** key. The Mate pop-up menu is displayed.

431) Click **Parallel** from the Mate pop-up menu. The second Parallel mate is created.

Display an Isometric view.

432) Click **Isometric view** from the Heads-up View toolbar.

Save the PNEUMATIC-TEST-MODULE assembly.

433) Click **Save** 💾.

Component Patterns in the Assembly

There are various methods to define a pattern in an assembly:

- Linear Component Pattern.

- Circular Component Pattern.

- Pattern Driven Component (Feature).

- Sketch Driven Component Pattern.

- Curve Driven Component Pattern.

- Chain Component Pattern.

- Mirror Components.

A Linear/Circular Component Pattern tool utilizes geometry in the assembly to arrange instances in a Linear or Circular pattern.

A Pattern Driven Component Pattern utilizes an existing feature pattern.

The SCREW part fastens the ANGLE-BRACKET part to the FLAT-PLATE part. Mate one SCREW to the first instance on the ANGLE-BRACKET Linear Pattern.

Utilize the Pattern Driven Component Pattern tool to create instances of the SCREW. Suppress the instances.

Utilize the Linear Component Pattern tool to copy the Pattern Driven Component Pattern of SCREWS to the second ANGLE-BRACKET part.

Drag the part by specific geometry to create a mate.

Activity: PNEUMATIC-TEST-MODULE-Component Pattern

Open the SCREW part.

434)   Click **Open** 🗋 from the Menu bar.

435)   Double-click **SCREW** from the Chapter 6 Models folder.

436)   Un-suppress the **Fillet1** and **Chamfer1** feature.

437)   Click **Window**, **Tile Horizontally** to display the SCREW and the PNEUMATIC-TEST-MODULE assembly.

Insert and mate the SCREW.
438)   Click the **bottom circular edge** of the SCREW.

439)   Drag the **SCREW** into the PNEUMATIC-TEST-MODULE assembly window. Note: Zoom in on the top circular edge of the ANGLE-BRACKET left hole.

440)   Release the mouse pointer on the **top circular edge** of the ANGLE-BRACKET left hole. The mouse pointer displays the Coincident/Concentric feedback symbol.

441)   **Return** to the PNEUMATIC-TEST-MODULE assembly window.

442)   Click **Left view** from the Heads-up View toolbar.

The SCREW part is positioned in the left hole with a Coincident/Concentric mate.

Create a Pattern Driven Component Pattern.

443)   Click the **Pattern Driven Component Pattern** tool from the Consolidate Assembly toolbar. The PropertyManager is displayed.

444)   Click the **SCREW** component in the Graphics window. SCREW<1> is displayed in the Components to Pattern box.

445)   Click inside the **Driving Feature or Component** box. **Expand** the AIR-RESERVOIR-SUPPORT assembly in the PNEUMATIC-TEST-MODULE fly-out FeatureManager.

446)   **Expand** ANGLE-BRACKET <1>.

447)   Click **LPattern1** in the fly-out FeatureManager. The SCREW is the seed feature.

448) Click **OK** ✅ from the PropertyManager. Six instances are displayed in the Graphics window. DerivedLPattern1 is displayed in the FeatureManager.

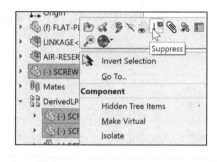

449) Click **SCREW<1>** from the FeatureManager.

450) Hold the **Ctrl** key down.

451) **Expand** DerivedLPattern1 from the FeatureManager.

452) Click the first two entries: **SCREW<2>** and **SCREW<3>**. Release the **Ctrl** key.

453) Right-click **Suppress**. The first three SCREWs are not displayed.

💡 The **Pattern Driven Component Pattern** PropertyManager contains an option to skip instances of a feature component in a pattern.

Activity: PNEUMATIC-TEST-MODULE-Linear Component Pattern

Create a Linear Component Pattern.

454) Click **Front view** 🔲 from the Heads-up View toolbar.

455) Click the **Linear Component Pattern** ⊞ tool from the Assembly toolbar. The Linear Pattern PropertyManager is displayed.

456) Click inside the **Pattern Direction** box for Direction 1.

457) Click the long front edge of the **FRONT-PLATE** as illustrated. Edge<1> is displayed in the Pattern Direction box. The direction arrow points to the right.

458) Enter **177.80**mm, [7in] for Spacing.

459) Enter **2** for Instances.

460) Click inside the **Components to Pattern** box.

461) Click **DerivedLPattern1** from the fly-out FeatureManager.

462) Click **OK** ✔ from the Linear Pattern PropertyManager.

463) Click **Top view** ⬜ from the Heads-up View toolbar. View the results.

The Linear Component Pattern feature is displayed in the second ANGLE-BRACKET part. LocalLPattern1 is displayed in the FeatureManager.

Display an Isometric view. Save the PNEUMATIC TEST MODULE assembly.

464) Click **Isometric view** .

465) **View** the FeatureManager and the created features in their states.

466) Click **Save** .

Hide the AIR-RESERVOIR-SUPPORT assembly.

467) Right-click **AIR-RESERVOIR-SUPPORT<1>** in the FeatureManager.

468) Click **Hide Components** . Utilize the Show components tool to display a component that has been hidden.

Hide the LINKAGE assembly.

469) Right-click **LINKAGE<1>** in the FeatureManager.

470) Click **Hide Components** .

Insert the FRONT-SUPPORT assembly into the PNEUMATIC-TEST-MODULE assembly. Mate the FRONT-SUPPORT assembly to the FLAT-PLATE part.

Utilize the Mirror Components tool to create a mirrored copy of the FRONT-SUPPORT assembly.

🔅 You can create new components by mirroring existing part or sub-assembly components. The new components can either be a copy or a mirror of the original components. A mirrored component is sometimes called a "right-hand" version of the original "left-hand" version.

🔅 Access the Mirror Components tool from the Consolidated Linear Component Pattern drop-down menu.

Activity: PNEUMATIC-TEST-MODULE-Insert FRONT-SUPPORT Assembly

---

Insert and mate the FRONT-SUPPORT assembly.

471) Click the **Insert Components** tool from the Assembly toolbar. The Insert Component PropertyManager is displayed.

472) Click the **Browse** button.

473) Double-click **FRONT-SUPPORT**.

Hide the SCREWs in the FRONT-SUPPORT.

474) Click a **position** above the FLAT-PLATE as illustrated.

475) Right-click **FRONT-SUPPORT** in the FeatureManager.

476) Click **Open Assembly**.

477) **Hide** the SCREW parts and HEX-NUTS if required in the assembly.

Save the model.

478) Click **Save** 💾.

Return to the PNEUMATIC-TEST-MODULE assembly.

479) Press **Ctrl Tab**.

480) Select the **PNEUMATIC-TEST-MODULE** document.

Save the model.

481) Click **Save** 💾.

482) Click **Yes** to the Message, "Save the document and referenced models now?"

The PNEUMATIC-TEST-MODULE is displayed. The SCREW and HEX-NUT components are hidden in the FRONT-SUPPORT assembly.

Insert a Concentric mate.

483) Click the **FLAT-PLATE hole face** in the 3rd row, right most column (17th column).

484) Hold the **Ctrl** key down.

485) Click the **HEX-STANDOFF Tapped Hole** as illustrated.

486) Release the **Ctrl** key. The Mate pop-up menu is displayed.

487) Click **Concentric** from the Mate pop-up menu. The mate is created.

Insert a Coincident mate.

488)   Click the bottom face of the **HEX-STANDOFF** part.

489)   **Rotate** the model to view the top face of the FLAT-PLATE.

490)   Hold the **Ctrl** key down.

491)   Click the top face of the **FLAT-PLATE**.

492)   Release the **Ctrl** key. The Mate pop-up menu is displayed.

493)   Click **Coincident** from the Mate pop-up menu.

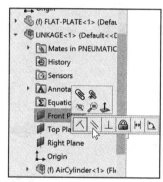

Insert a Parallel mate.

494)   Click the **FRONT-SUPPORT Front Plane** from the FeatureManager.

495)   **Show** the LINKAGE assembly.

496)   Hold the **Ctrl** key down.

497)   Click the **LINKAGE Front Plane** from the FeatureManager.

498)   Release the **Ctrl** key. The Mate pop-up menu is displayed.

499)   Click **Parallel** ⟍ from the Mate pop-up menu.

500)   **Hide** the LINKAGE assembly.

Save the PNEUMATIC-TEST-MODULE assembly.

501)   Click **Save** 📙.

Mirrored Components

Create new components by mirroring existing parts or sub-assemblies. New components are created as copied geometry or mirrored geometry.

A mirrored component is sometimes called a "right-hand" version of the original "left hand" version.

The copied or mirrored component changes when the original component is modified.

A mirrored component creates a new document. The default document prefix is mirror. A copied component does not create a new document.

Suppressed components in the original sub-assembly are not mirrored or copied. The SCREW parts in the FRONT-SUPPORT assembly are not copied.

Left Hand Version (Original)   Right Hand Version (Mirrored)

Instance Component

Mirrored Component

Instance Component

PNEUMATIC-TEST-MODULE

Activity: PNEUMATIC-TEST-MODULE Assembly: Mirrored Component

Insert a Mirrored Component.

502) Click the **Mirror Components** 🖳 tool from the Consolidated Assembly toolbar. The Mirror Components PropertyManager is displayed.

Step 1: The Selections box is displayed. Select face/plane to mirror about and the components to be mirrored.

503) **Expand** the PNEUMATIC-TEST-MODULE fly-out FeatureManager. Click the **FLAT-PLATE Front Plane**. The Front Plane is displayed in the Mirror plane box.

504) Click the **FRONT-SUPPORT** assembly from the fly-out FeatureManager.

505) Click **Next** ⊕. The FRONT-SUPPORT assembly is displayed in the Components to Mirror box.

Step 2: Verify the orientation of the components to be mirrored and adjust accordingly using the buttons below.

506) Click the **Create opposite hand version** button. View the results in the Graphics window.

507) Click **Next** ⊕. Accept the default settings.

Step 3: The mirrored components selected in step 2 need new geometries. This may be new files or new configurations in existing files. Specify the new configuration or file name using the options below.

508) Click **Next** ⊕. This is for any Import Features. Accept the default settings.

509) Click **OK** ✔ from the Mirror Components PropertyManager. Click Yes if needed. View the results in the Graphics window.

Select suppressed components and their mates to be mirrored in the Components to Mirror box.

The MirrorFRONT-SUPPORT, TRIANGLE, ANGLE-13HOLE, and SCREW components are mated.

Utilize the Fix option to mate the MirrorFRONT-SUPPORT to its current location in the PNEUMATIC-TEST-MODULE. No other mates are required.

Activity: PNEUMATIC-TEST-MODULE-Fix the MIRRORFRONT-SUPPORT

Fix the MirrorFRONT-SUPPORT.

510) Right-click **MirrorFRONT-SUPPORT** from the FeatureManager.

511) Click **Fix**. The MirrorFRONT assembly is fixed in the PNEUMATIC-TEST-MODULE assembly. The MirrorFRONT-SUPPORT does not move or rotate.

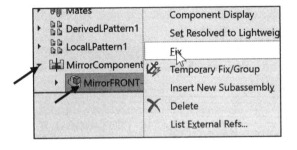

Display the LINKAGE assembly.

512) Right-click **LINKAGE** in the FeatureManager.

513) Click **Show Components**.

Save the PNEUMATIC-TEST-MODULE assembly.

514) Click **Save** ⬚.

Reuse geometry in the assembly. Utilize the Mirror Component tool to create a left and right version of parts and assemblies.

Component Properties

Component Properties control the flexibility of the sub-assembly when inserted into an assembly. Components do not translate or rotate after insertion into the assembly.

The FLATBAR parts in the LINKAGE assembly do not rotate after insertion into the PNEUMATIC TEST MODULE assembly. The LINKAGE assembly is in the Rigid State.

Insert the WHEEL-AND-AXLE assembly into the PNEUMATIC-TEST-MODULE assembly. Modify the Mate state of the LINKAGE assembly from the Rigid State to the Flexible State. The LINKAGE assembly is free to rotate.

Modify the Mate State of the AirCylinder assembly from the Rigid State to the Flexible State. The AirCylinder assembly is free to translate.

By default, when you create a sub-assembly, it is rigid. Within the parent assembly, the sub-assembly acts as a single unit and its components do not move relative to each other.

Activity: PNEUMATIC-TEST-MODULE Assembly-Insert WHEEL-AND-AXLE Assembly

Insert the WHEEL-AND-AXLE assembly.

515) Click the **Insert Components** tool from the Assembly toolbar. The Insert Component PropertyManager is displayed.

516) Click the **Browse** button.

517) Browse to the **WHEEL-AND-AXLE** assembly.

518) Click a **position** above the FLAT-PLATE part as illustrated.

Insert a Concentric mate.

519)   Click the **AXLE-3000 cylindrical** face.

520)   **Rotate** the model to view the inside TRIANGLE top hole face as illustrated.

521)   Hold the **Ctrl** key down.

522)   Click the inside **TRIANGLE top hole** face.

523)   Release the **Ctrl** key. The Mate pop-up menu is displayed.

524)   Click **Concentric** from the Mate pop-up menu.

Insert a Coincident mate.

525)   Click the **WHEEL-AND-AXLE Front Plane** from the FeatureManager.

526)   Hold the **Ctrl** key down.

527)   Click the **LINKAGE Front Plane** from the FeatureManager.

528)   Release the **Ctrl** key. The Mate pop-up menu is displayed.

529)   Click **Coincident** from the Mate pop-up menu.

A Concentric mate is required between the left hole of the FLATBAR-3HOLE and right AXLE of the LINKAGE assembly.

DO NOT INSERT A CONCENTRIC MATE AT THIS TIME.

A Concentric mate will result in Mate errors.

The WHEEL-AND-AXLE is free to rotate in the PNEUMATIC-TEST-MODULE assembly. The LINKAGE assembly interferes with the WHEEL-AND-AXLE. The LINKAGE assembly is not free to rotate or translate. Mate errors will occur.

Sub-assemblies within the LINKAGE assembly are in a Rigid Mate state when inserted into the PNEUMATIC-TEST-MODULE assembly. Remove the Rigid Mate state and insert a Concentric mate between the LINKAGE assembly and the WHEEL-AND-AXLE.

Activity: PNEUMATIC-TEST-MODULE Assembly-Remove Rigid state

Remove the Rigid State.

530) Right-click the **LINKAGE** assembly from the FeatureManager.

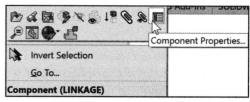

531) Click **Component Properties** from the Context toolbar. The Component Properties dialog box is displayed.

532) Check **Flexible** in the Solve as box.

533) Click **OK** from the Component Properties dialog box. Note the icon next to the LINKAGE assembly in the FeatureManager.

534) Right-click the **AirCylinder** assembly from the FeatureManager.

535) Click **Component Properties**. **Flexible** is selected in the Solve as box.

536) **Flexible** is selected in the Referenced configuration box.

537) Click **OK** from the Component Properties dialog box.

Hide the FRONT-SUPPORT assembly.

538) Right-click **FRONT-SUPPORT** from the FeatureManager.

539) Click **Hide Components**.

Move the LINKAGE assembly.

540) Click and drag the **front FLATBAR-9HOLE** downward. The FLATBAR-9HOLE rotates about the left AXLE.

541) Click a **position** below the WHEEL-AND-AXLE.

542) Click **inside** the Graphics window to deselect.

Insert a Concentric mate.

543) Click the second bottom **AXLE** face of the LINKAGE assembly.

544) Hold the **Ctrl** key down.

545) Click the inside face of the **bottom hole** of the FLATBAR-3HOLE as illustrated.

546) Release the **Ctrl** key. The Mate pop-up menu is displayed.

547) Click **Concentric** from the Mate pop-up menu.

Display an Isometric view. Save the PNEUMATIC-TEST-MODULE assembly.

548) Click **Isometric view** .

549) Click **Save** .

The AirCylinder assembly is inserted in a Rigid state by default. The AirCylinder contains three configurations:

- Default

- Extended

- Flexible

Open the AirCylinder assembly. Modify the configuration to Flexible.

Open the LINKAGE assembly. Modify the AirCylinder Component Properties from Default to Flexible.

Activity: PNEUMATIC-TEST-MODULE Assembly - Review AirCylinder Configurations

---

Review the AirCylinder configurations.

550) Right-click **LINKAGE** from the PNEUMATIC-TEST-MODULE FeatureManager.

551) Click **Open Subassembly** from the Context toolbar.

552) Right-click **AirCylinder** in the LINKAGE FeatureManager.

553) Click **Open Sub-assembly**.

554) Click the **Configuration Manager** 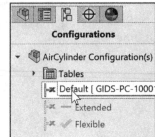 tab at the top of the AirCylinder FeatureManager. Three configurations are displayed: *Default*, *Extended* and *Flexible*. The current Default configuration sets the Piston Rod at 0mm.

Display the Extended Configuration.
555) Double-click **Extended**. The Piston Rod of the AirCylinder extends 25mm.

Display the Flexible Configuration.
556) Double-click **Flexible**.

557) Click the **Rod-Clevis** in the Graphics window.

558) Click and drag the **Piston Rod** from left to right.

559) Click a **position** near its original location. The AirCylinder remains in the Flexible configuration for the rest of this project.

Update the LINKAGE assembly.
560) Click **Window**, **LINKAGE** from the Menu bar. The current configuration of the AirCylinder part in the LINKAGE assembly is Default. Modify the configuration.

561) Right-click **AirCylinder** from the LINKAGE assembly FeatureManager.

562) Click **Component Properties**.

563) **Flexible** is selected in the Solve as section.

564) **Flexible** is selected in the Referenced configuration section.

565) Click **OK**. The AirCylinder displays the Flexible configuration next to its name in the FeatureManager.

Update the PNEUMATIC-TEST-MODULE.
566) Click **Window**, **PNEUMATIC-TEST-MODULE** assembly from the Menu bar.

Move the ROD-CLEVIS.
567) Click and drag the **ROD-CLEVIS** to the right. The WHEEL rotates in a counterclockwise direction.

568) Click and drag the **ROD-CLEVIS** to the left. The WHEEL rotates in a clockwise direction.

Display the AIR-RESERVOIR-SUPPORT assembly.
569) Right-click **AIR-RESERVOIR-SUPPORT** in the FeatureManager.

570) Click **Show Components**.

Display the second FRONT-SUPPORT assembly.
571) Right-click **FRONT-SUPPORT** in the FeatureManager.

572) Click **Show Components**.

573) **Display** the SCREWs in the FRONT-SUPPORT.

Display an Isometric view. Save the PNEUMATIC-TEST-MODULE.

574) Click **Isometric view** .

575) Click **Save** .

576) Click **Yes** to update referenced documents.

Close all documents.

577) Click **Windows**, **Close All** from the Menu bar.

Explore additional parts and assemblies at the end of this project. Add the WEIGHT, HOOK and FLATBAR parts.

A Rebuild icon may be displayed in the Assembly FeatureManager and a flexible rebuild icon at the sub-assembly level when the AirCylinder assembly is in the Flexible state.

Additional details on Show components, Hide components, Linear Component Pattern, Circular Component Pattern, Pattern Driven Component Pattern, Sketch Driven Component Patter, Curve Driven Component Pattern, Mirror Components, Configurations, and Configuration Manager are available in SOLIDWORKS Help. Select Help, SOLIDWORKS Help topics.

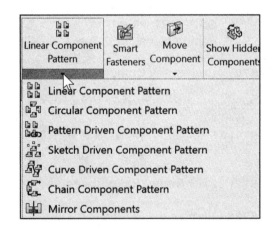

Review the PNEUMATIC-TEST-MODULE Assembly

The PNEUMATIC TEST MODULE assembly was created by combining five major mechanical sub-assemblies.

The PNEUMATIC TEST MODULE assembly utilized the FLAT-PLATE as the first component. The LINKAGE assembly, AIR-RESERVOIR-SUPPORT assembly, FRONT-SUPPORT assembly, MirrorFRONT-SUPPORT assembly and the WHEEL-AND-AXLE assembly were mated to the FLAT-PLATE part.

Work at the lowest assembly level. The LINKAGE assembly required two HEX-STANDOFF parts. The HEX-STANDOFF components were inserted into the LINKAGE assembly. The LINKAGE assembly was inserted into the PNEUMATIC-TEST-MODULE assembly.

The AIR-RESERVOIR-SUPPORT assembly was inserted into the PNEUMATIC-TEST-MODULE assembly. The SCREW component utilized a Feature Driven Component Pattern tool and the Linear Component Pattern tool to create multiple copies.

The FRONT-SUPPORT assembly was inserted into the PNEUMATIC-TEST-MODULE assembly. The Mirror Components tool created a mirrored version of the FRONT-SUPPORT assembly.

The WHEEL-AND-AXLE assembly was inserted into the PNEUMATIC-TEST-MODULE assembly. Component Properties created a Flexible state mate.

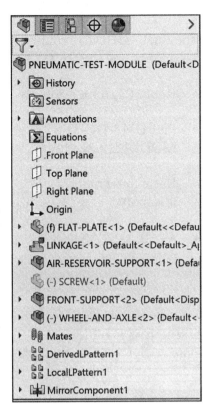

The LINKAGE assembly "AirCylinder" is in a Flexible state.

In the next section, create the final ROBOT assembly. Either use your created assemblies and components, or use the created assemblies and components provided in the Chapter 6 Models folder.

Final ROBOT Assembly

The final ROBOT assembly is comprised of three major sub-assemblies and the HEX-STANDOFF component:

- Robot Platform assembly.

- PNEUMATIC-TEST-MODULE assembly.

- Basic_integration assembly.

- 4 - HEX-STANDOFF components.

☀ The LINKAGE assembly is in a Flexible state.

☀ A Rebuild 🔄 icon may be displayed in the final ROBOT Assembly FeatureManager and a flexible rebuild 🔄 icon at the sub-assembly level when the AirCylinder assembly is in the Flexible state.

All assemblies and components for the final ROBOT assembly are provided in the Chapter 6 models folder.

☀ As an exercise apply PhotoView 360 to render the final ROBOT assembly.

Combine the created new assemblies and components to develop the final ROBOT assembly. In this next section, work from the Chapter 6 Models folder on your hard drive. Create the SW-TUTORIAL-2017\Chapter 6 Models folder.

Note: Step-by-step instructions are not provided in this section for the mates.

Activity: Create the ROBOT Assembly

Create the final ROBOT assembly.

578) Click **New** ▢ from the Menu bar.

579) Double-click **Assembly** from the Templates tab. The Begin Assembly PropertyManager is displayed.

Insert the Robot-platform assembly.
580) Click the **Browse** button.

581) Browse to the **SW-TUTORIAL-2017\Chapter 6 Models** folder on your hard drive. All files and folders should have been copied from the book.

582) Double-click **Robot-platform**. If needed click NO if a component is missing and the system wants you to find it. This will not change the final assembly.

583) Click **OK** ✔ from the Begin Assembly PropertyManager. The Robot-platform is fixed to the assembly Origin.

Save the Assembly.
584) Click **Save As** from the drop-down Menu bar.

585) Enter **ROBOT** for File name in the SW-TUTORIAL-2017\Chapter 6 Models folder.

586) Enter **Final ROBOT Assembly** for Description.

587) Click **Save**.

Insert the PNEUMATIC-TEST-MODULE assembly.

588) Click **Insert Components** 🗗 from the Assembly toolbar. The Insert Components PropertyManager is displayed.

589) Click the **Browse** button.

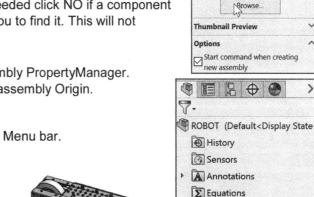

590) Browse to the **SW-TUTORIAL-2017\Chapter 6 Models** folder on your hard drive.

591) Double-click the **PNEUMATIC-TEST-MODULE** assembly.

592) Click a **position** above the Robot-platform.

☀ If an assembly or component is loaded in a Lightweight ⚙ state, right-click the **assembly name** or **component name** from the FeatureManager. Click **Set Lightweight to Resolved**.

Insert 4 HEX-STANDOFF components.

593) Click **Insert Components** 📷 from the Assembly toolbar. The Insert Components PropertyManager is displayed.

594) Click the **Browse** button.

595) Browse to the **SW-TUTORIAL-2017\Chapter 6 Models** folder on your hard drive.

596) Double-click the **HEX-STANDOFF** part.

597) **Pin** the Insert Components PropertyManager.

598) Click **four positions** as illustrated for the four HEX-STANDOFF components.

599) **Un-Pin** the Insert Components PropertyManager.

600) Click **OK** ✔ from the Insert Components PropertyManager.

Insert Coincident and Concentric mates between the four HEX-STANDOFF components and the PNEUMATIC-TEST-MODULE and the Robot-platform as illustrated. View the location of the HEX-STANDOFF components on the PNEUMATIC-TEST-MODULE assembly.

View the location of the HEX-STANDOFF components on the Robot-platform as illustrated.

601) **Expand** the Mates folder. View the created mates.

Insert the basic_integration assembly.

602) Click the **Browse** button.

603) Browse to the **SW-TUTORIAL-2017\Chapter 6 Models** folder.

604) Double-click the **basic_integration** assembly.

605) Click a position to the **left** of the assembly as illustrated.

Insert Coincident and Concentric mates between the two screws in the basic_integration assembly and the PNEUMATIC-TEST-MODULE assembly.

606) **Expand** the Mates folder. View the created mates.

Save the ROBOT assembly.

607) Click **Save** . You are finished with the final ROBOT assembly.

Chapter Summary

In this chapter, you created and worked with multiple documents in sub-assemblies and assemblies. You developed sound assembly modeling techniques that utilized Standard mates, fixed components, symmetry, component patterns and mirrored components.

The WHEEL-AND-AXLE assembly combined the WHEEL-FLATBAR assembly with the AXLE-3000 part, SHAFTCOLLAR-500 part and HEX-ADAPTER part.

The WHEEL-FLATBAR assembly combined the 3HOLE-SHAFTCOLLAR assembly and 5HOLE-SHAFTCOLLAR assembly.

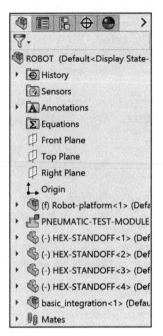

The PNEUMATIC-TEST-MODULE assembly combined four major mechanical sub-assemblies. The final ROBOT assembly was comprised of three major sub-assemblies and the HEX-STANDOFF component.

Organize your assemblies. For an exercise, create an assembly Layout Diagram of the final ROBOT assembly to determine the grouping of components and assemblies.

Utilize the Quick mate procedure on Standard mates, Cam mate, Profile Center mate, Slot mate, Symmetric mate and Width mate. To activate the Quick Mates functionality, click Tools, Customize. On the toolbars tab, under Context toolbar settings, select Show quick mates. Quick Mates is selected by default.

The Quick mate procedure can be used for reference geometry (such as planes, axes, and points) along with model geometry (such as faces, edges and vertices).

As an exercise apply PhotoView 360 to render the final ROBOT assembly.

Questions

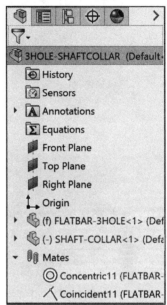

1. What function does the Save as copy and continue check box perform when saving a part under a new name?

2. True or False. Never reuse geometry from one part to create another part.

3. Describe five Assembly techniques utilized in this chapter.

4. True or False. A fixed (f) component cannot move and is locked to the Origin.

5. Describe the purpose of an Assembly Layout diagram.

6. Describe the difference between a Pattern Driven Component Pattern and a Linear Component Pattern.

7. Describe the difference between copied geometry and mirrored geometry utilizing the Mirror Components tool.

8. True or False. An assembly contains one or more configurations.

9. Identify how you can incorporate design intent into an assembly.

10. Review the Keyboard Short Cut keys in the Appendix. Identify the Short Cut keys you incorporated into this chapter. What is the g key used for?

Project assemblies below are created by students in my Freshman Engineering class.

Chapter 6 Homework

Name

- Welder Arm Assembly Project
- Shock Assembly Project
- Shaper Tool Head Assembly Project
- Radial Engine Assembly Project
- Quick Acting Clamp Assembly Project
- Pulley Assembly Project
- Pipe Vice Assembly Project
- Kant Twist Clamp Assembly Project
- Drill Guide Assembly Project
- Butterfly Valve Assembly Project
- Bench Vice Assembly Project

Exercises

Exercise 6.1: Butterfly Valve Assembly Project

Copy the components from the Chapter 6
Homework\Butterfly Valve Assembly Project folder.
View all components.

Create an ANSI IPS Butterfly Valve assembly document.
Insert all needed components and mates to assemble the
assembly. Simulate the proper movement per the provided
avi file located in the folder. You are the designer.
Address all tolerancing and dimension modifications. Use
Standard, Advanced and Mechanical Mates. Create and
insert any additional components if needed.

Create a C-ANSI Landscape - Third Angle Isometric Exploded
Drawing document with Explode lines of the assembly using
your knowledge of SOLIDWORKS. Insert a BOM with
Balloons. Insert all needed General notes and Custom Properties
in the Title Block.

Chapter 6 Homework

Name

- Welder Arm Assembly Project
- Shock Assembly Project
- Shaper Tool Head Assembly Project
- Radial Engine Assembly Project
- Quick Acting Clamp Assembly Project
- Pulley Assembly Project
- Pipe Vice Assembly Project
- Kant Twist Clamp Assembly Project
- Drill Guide Assembly Project
- Butterfly Valve Assembly Project
- Bench Vice Assembly Project

Exercise 6.2: Shock Assembly Project

Copy the components from the Chapter 6 Homework\Shock Assembly Project folder.

Create an ANSI IPS Shock assembly document. Insert all needed components and mates to assemble the assembly. Simulate the proper movement per the provided avi file located in the folder.

You are the designer. Address all tolerancing and dimension modifications if needed. Be creative. Use Standard, Advanced and Mechanical Mates. Create and insert any additional components if needed.

Create a C-ANSI Landscape - Third Angle Isometric Exploded Drawing document with Explode lines of the assembly using your knowledge of SOLIDWORKS. Insert a BOM with Balloons. Insert all needed General notes in the Title Block.

Chapter 6 Homework

Name

- Welder Arm Assembly Project
- Shock Assembly Project
- Shaper Tool Head Assembly Project
- Radial Engine Assembly Project
- Quick Acting Clamp Assembly Project
- Pulley Assembly Project
- Pipe Vice Assembly Project
- Kant Twist Clamp Assembly Project
- Drill Guide Assembly Project
- Butterfly Valve Assembly Project
- Bench Vice Assembly Project

Exercise 6.3: Quick Acting Clamp Assembly Project

Copy the components from the Chapter 6 Homework\Quick Acting Clamp Assembly Project folder. View all components.

Create an ANSI IPS Quick Acting Clamp assembly document. Insert all needed components and mates to assemble the assembly. Simulate the proper movement per the provided avi file located in the folder.

You are the designer. Address all tolerancing and dimension modifications if needed. Be creative. Use Standard, Advanced and Mechanical Mates. Create and insert any additional components if needed.

Chapter 6 Homework

Name

- Welder Arm Assembly Project
- Shock Assembly Project
- Shaper Tool Head Assembly Project
- Radial Engine Assembly Project
- Quick Acting Clamp Assembly Project
- Pulley Assembly Project
- Pipe Vice Assembly Project
- Kant Twist Clamp Assembly Project
- Drill Guide Assembly Project
- Butterfly Valve Assembly Project
- Bench Vice Assembly Project

Create a C-ANSI Landscape - Third Angle Isometric Exploded Drawing document with Explode lines of the assembly using your knowledge of SOLIDWORKS. Insert a BOM with Balloons. Insert all needed General notes in the Title Block.

Exercise 6.4: Drill Guide Assembly Project

Copy the components from the Chapter 6
Homework\Drill Guide Assembly Project folder.
View all components.

Create an ANSI IPS Drill Guide assembly document.
Insert all needed components and mates to assemble
the assembly. Simulate the proper movement per the
provided avi file located in the folder.

You are the designer. Address all tolerancing and
dimension modifications if needed. Be creative. Use
Standard, Advanced and Mechanical Mates. Create
and insert any additional components if needed.

Create a C-ANSI Landscape - Third Angle Isometric
Exploded Drawing document with Explode lines of
the assembly using your knowledge of
SOLIDWORKS. Insert a BOM with Balloons. Insert all needed
General notes in the Title Block.

Chapter 6 Homework

Name

- Welder Arm Assembly Project
- Shock Assembly Project
- Shaper Tool Head Assembly Project
- Radial Engine Assembly Project
- Quick Acting Clamp Assembly Project
- Pulley Assembly Project
- Pipe Vice Assembly Project
- Kant Twist Clamp Assembly Project
- Drill Guide Assembly Project
- Butterfly Valve Assembly Project
- Bench Vice Assembly Project

ITEM NO.	PART NUMBER	DESCRIPTION	MATERIAL	QTY.
1	WFI-1000-01	BASE	2014 ALLOY	1
2	WFI-1000-02	ROTATOR	PLAIN CARBON STEEL	2
3	WFI-1000-03	ROD GUIDE	CAST ALLOY STEEL	2
4	WFI-1000-04	SLIDE	2014 ALLOY	1
5	WFI-1000-05	COLLAR	2014 ALLOY	2
6	WFI-1000-06	BUSHING	ALUMINUM BRONZE	2
7	WFI-1000-07	RETAINING RING B27.1 - NA2-45	ALLOY STEEL	2
8	WFI-1000-08	DRILL ADAPTOR	PLAIN CARBON STEEL	1
9	WFI-1000-09	THUMB SCREW .25-20x0.51 TYPE B, FLAT POINT-C	2014 ALLOY	6

Exercise 6.5: Pulley Assembly Project

Copy the components from the Chapter 6 Homework\Pulley Assembly Project folder. View all components.

Create an ANSI Pulley assembly document. Insert all needed components and mates to assemble the assembly. Simulate the proper movement per the provided avi file located in the folder.

You are the designer. Address all tolerancing and dimension modifications if needed. Be creative. Use Standard, Advanced and Mechanical Mates.

Create and insert any additional components if needed.

Create a C-ANSI Landscape - Third Angle Isometric Exploded Drawing document with Explode lines of the assembly using your knowledge of SOLIDWORKS. Insert a BOM with Balloons. Insert all needed General notes in the Title Block.

Chapter 6 Homework

Name

- Welder Arm Assembly Project
- Shock Assembly Project
- Shaper Tool Head Assembly Project
- Radial Engine Assembly Project
- Quick Acting Clamp Assembly Project
- Pulley Assembly Project
- Pipe Vice Assembly Project
- Kant Twist Clamp Assembly Project
- Drill Guide Assembly Project
- Butterfly Valve Assembly Project
- Bench Vice Assembly Project

Exercise 6.6: Welder Arm Assembly Project

Copy the components from the Chapter 6 Homework\Welder Arm Assembly Project folder. View all components.

Create an ANSI Welder Arm assembly document. Insert all needed components and mates to assemble the assembly. Simulate the proper movement per the provided avi file located in the folder.

You are the designer. Address all tolerancing and dimension modifications if needed. Be creative. Use Standard, Advanced and Mechanical Mates. Create and insert any additional components if needed.

Chapter 6 Homework

Name

- Welder Arm Assembly Project
- Shock Assembly Project
- Shaper Tool Head Assembly Project
- Radial Engine Assembly Project
- Quick Acting Clamp Assembly Project
- Pulley Assembly Project
- Pipe Vice Assembly Project
- Kant Twist Clamp Assembly Project
- Drill Guide Assembly Project
- Butterfly Valve Assembly Project
- Bench Vice Assembly Project

Create a C-ANSI Landscape - Third Angle Isometric Exploded Drawing document with Explode lines of the assembly using your knowledge of SOLIDWORKS. Insert a BOM with Balloons. Insert all needed General notes in the Title Block.

**Exercise 6.7: Radial Engine Assembly
Project**

Copy the components from the Chapter 6
Homework\Radial Engine Assembly
Project folder. View all components.

Create an ANSI Radial Engine assembly
document. Insert all needed components
and mates to assemble the assembly.
Simulate the proper movement per the
provided avi file located in the folder.

You are the designer. Address all
tolerancing and
dimension modifications
if needed. Be creative.

Use Standard, Advanced
and Mechanical Mates.

Create and insert any
additional components if
needed.

Create a C-ANSI
Landscape - Third Angle
Isometric Exploded
Drawing document with
Explode lines of the
assembly using your
knowledge of
SOLIDWORKS.

Insert a BOM with
Balloons. Insert all
needed General notes in
the Title Block.

Exercise 6.8: Bench Vice Assembly Project

Copy the components from the Chapter 6 Homework\Bench Vice Assembly Project folder. View all components.

Create an ANSI IPS Bench Vice assembly document. Insert all needed components and mates to assemble the assembly. Simulate the proper movement per the provided avi file located in the folder.

You are the designer. Address all tolerancing and dimension modifications if needed. Use Standard, Advanced and Mechanical Mates.

Create and insert any additional components if needed.

Create a C-ANSI Landscape - Third Angle Isometric Exploded Drawing document with Explode lines of the assembly using your knowledge of SOLIDWORKS.

Insert a BOM with Balloons. Insert all needed General notes and Custom Properties in the Title Block.

Chapter 6 Homework

Name

- Welder Arm Assembly Project
- Shock Assembly Project
- Shaper Tool Head Assembly Project
- Radial Engine Assembly Project
- Quick Acting Clamp Assembly Project
- Pulley Assembly Project
- Pipe Vice Assembly Project
- Kant Twist Clamp Assembly Project
- Drill Guide Assembly Project
- Butterfly Valve Assembly Project
- Bench Vice Assembly Project

ITEM NO.	PART NUMBER	DESCRIPTION	MATERIAL	QTY.
1	WPI - 0001	Base	Alloy Steel	1
2	WPI - 0002	Base Plate	Alloy Steel	2
3	WPI - 0003	Vice Jaw	Alloy Steel	1
4	WPI - 0004	Clamping Plate	Alloy Steel	1
5	WPI - 0005	Jaw Screw	Alloy Steel	1
6	WPI - 0006	Screw Bar	Alloy Steel	1
7	WPI - 0007	Bar Globes	Alloy Steel	2
8	WPI-008	Hex Screw M6x1.0x14-14WN	Alloy Steel	4
9	WPI-0009	Bolt	Alloy Steell	1
10	WPI-00019	Blot1	Alloy Steel	2

Exercise 6.9: Kant Twist Clamp Assembly Project

Copy the components from the Chapter 6 Homework\Kant Twist Clamp Assembly Project folder. View all components.

Create an ANSI IPS Kant Twist Clamp assembly document. Insert all needed components and mates to assemble the assembly. Simulate the proper movement per the provided avi file located in the folder.

You are the designer. Address all tolerancing and dimension modifications if needed.

Use Standard, Advanced and Mechanical Mates. Create and insert any additional components if needed.

Create a C-ANSI Landscape - Third Angle Isometric Exploded Drawing document with Explode lines of the assembly using your knowledge of SOLIDWORKS.

Insert a BOM with Balloons. Insert all needed General notes and Custom Properties in the Title Block.

Notes:

CHAPTER 7 - CSWA INTRODUCTION AND DRAFTING COMPETENCIES

Introduction

DS SOLIDWORKS Corp. offers various types of certification. Each stage represents increasing levels of expertise in 3D CAD: Certified SOLIDWORKS Associate CSWA, Certified SOLIDWORKS Professional CSWP and Certified SOLIDWORKS Expert CSWE along with specialty fields.

The CSWA certification indicates a foundation in and apprentice knowledge of 3D CAD design and engineering practices and principles. The main requirement for obtaining the CSWA certification is to take and pass the two part on-line proctored exams. This first exam (part 1) is 90 minutes, minimum passing score is 80, with 6 questions. The second exam (part 2) is 90 minutes, minimum passing score is 80 with 8 questions.

The CSWA exam consists of 14 questions in the following five categories and subject areas:

- *Drafting Competencies*: (Three questions - multiple choice - 5 points each).

  - Questions on general drawing views: Projected, Section, Break, Crop, Detail, Alternate Position, etc.

> Drafting Competencies - To create drawing view 'B' it is necessary to select drawing view 'A' and insert which SolidWorks view type?

- *Basic Part Creation and Modification*: (Two questions - one multiple choice/one single answer - 15 points each).

  - Sketch Planes:

    - Front, Top, Right.

  - 2D Sketching:

> Basic Part (Hydraulic Cylinder Half) - Step 1
> Build this part in SolidWorks.
> (Save part after each question in a different file in case it must be reviewed)
>
> Unit system: MMGS (millimeter, gram, second)
> Decimal places: 2
> Part origin: Arbitrary
> All holes through all unless shown otherwise.
> Material: Aluminium 1060 Alloy

Screen shots from an exam

- Geometric Relations and Dimensioning.

- Extruded Boss/Base Feature.

- Extruded Cut feature.

- Modification of Basic part.

💡 In the *Basic Part Creation and Modification* category, there is a dimension modification question based on the first (multiple choice) question. You should be within 1% of the multiple choice answer before you go on to the modification single answer section.

- *Intermediate Part Creation and Modification;* (Two questions - one multiple choice/one single answer - 15 points each).

  - Sketch Planes:

    - Front, Top, Right.

  - 2D Sketching:

    - Geometric Relations and Dimensioning.

  - Extruded Boss/Base Feature.

  - Extruded Cut Feature.

  - Revolved Boss/Base Feature.

  - Mirror and Fillet Feature.

  - Circular and Linear Pattern Feature.

  - Plane Feature.

  - Modification of Intermediate Part:

    - Sketch, Feature, Pattern, etc.

  - Modification of Intermediate part.

💡 In the *Intermediate Part Creation and Modification* category, there are two dimension modification questions based on the first (multiple choice) question. You should be within 1% of the multiple choice answer before you go on to the modification single answer section.

Intermediate Part (Wheel) - Step 1
Build this part in SolidWorks.
(Save part after each question in a different file in case it must be reviewed)

Unit system: MMGS (millimeter, gram, second)
Decimal places: 2
Part origin: Arbitrary
All holes through all unless shown otherwise.
Material: Aluminium 1060 Alloy

A = 134.00
B = 890.00

Note: All geometry is symmetrical about the plane represented by the line labeled F"" in the M-M Section View.

What is the overall mass of the part (grams)?

Hint: If you don't find an option within 1% of your answer please re-check your model(s).

Screen shots from an exam

- *Advanced Part Creation and Modification; (Three questions - one multiple choice/two single answers – 15 points each).*

    - Sketch Planes:

        - Front, Top, Right, Face, Created Plane etc.

        - 2D Sketching or 3D Sketching.

    - Sketch Tools:

        - Offset Entities, Convert Entitles, etc.

    - Extruded Boss/Base Feature.

    - Extruded Cut Feature.

    - Revolved Boss/Base Feature.

    - Mirror and Fillet Feature.

    - Circular and Linear Pattern Feature.

    - Shell Feature.

    - Plane Feature.

    - More Difficult Geometry Modifications.

Advanced Part (Bracket) - Step 1
Build this part in SolidWorks.
(Save part after each question in a different file in case it must be reviewed).

Unit system: MMGS (millimeter, gram, second)
Decimal places: 2
Part origin: Arbitrary
All holes through all unless shown otherwise.
Material: AISI 1020 Steel
Density = 0.0079 g/mm^3

A = 64.00
B = 20.00
C = 26.50

What is the overall mass of the part (grams)?

Hint: If you don't find an option within 1% of your answer please re-check your model(s).

🔆 In the *Advanced Part Creation and Modification* category, there are two dimension modification questions based on the first (multiple choice) question. You should be within 1% of the multiple choice answer before you go on to the modification single answer section.

- *Assembly Creation and Modification; (Two different assemblies - four questions - two multiple choice/two single answers - 30 points each).*

    - Insert the first (fixed) component.

    - Insert all needed components.

    - Standard Mates.

    - Modification of key parameters in the assembly.

Screen shots from an exam

🔆 In the *Assembly Creation and Modification* category, expect to see five to seven components. There are two dimension modification questions based on the first (multiple choice) question. You should be within 1% of the multiple choice answer before you go on to the modification single answer section.

Download the needed components in a zip folder during the exam to create the assembly.

Do not use feature recognition when you open the downloaded components for the assembly. This is a timed exam. Additional model information is not needed in the exam.

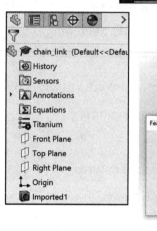

Illustrations may vary depending on your SOLIDWORKS version and system setup.

Use the view indicator to increase or decrease the active model in the view window.

Additional model views

View indicator

Screen shots from an exam

This first exam (part 1) is 90 minutes, minimum passing score is 80, with 6 questions. The second exam (part 2) is 90 minutes, minimum passing score is 80 with 8 questions.

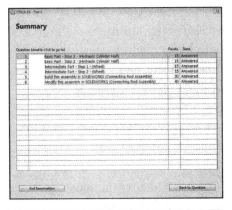

You are allowed to answer the questions in any order you prefer. Use the Summary Screen during the CSWA exam to view the list of all questions you have or have not answered.

During the exam, use the control keys at the bottom of the screen to:

- *Show the Previous Question.*

- *Reset the Question.*

- *Show the Summary Screen.*

- *Move to the Next Question.*

When you are finished, press the End Examination button. The tester will ask you if you want to end the test. Click Yes.

If there are any unanswered questions, the tester will provide a warning message as illustrated.

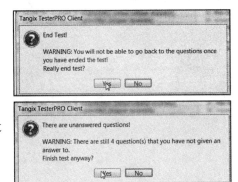

If you do not pass the certification exam, you will need to wait 30 days until you can retake each part of the exam.

Use the clock in the tester to view the amount of time that you used and the amount of time that is left in the exam.

Screen shots from the exam

During the exam, SOLIDWORKS provides the ability to click on a detail view below (as illustrated) to obtain additional details and dimensions during the exam.

☀ No Simulation questions are on the CSWA exam.

☀ No Sheetmetal questions are on the CSWA exam.

☀ FeatureManager names were changed through various revisions of SOLIDWORKS. Example: Extrude1 vs. Boss-Extrude1. These changes do not affect the models or answers in this book.

☀ No Surface questions are on the CSWA exam.

Objectives

Drafting Competencies is one of the five categories *(Drafting Competencies, Basic Part Creation and Modification, Intermediate Part Creation and Modification, Advance Part Creation and Modification and Assembly Creation and Modification)* on the CSWA exam.

There are three questions (total) on the CSWA exam in the *Drafting Competencies* category. Each question is worth five (5) points. Drafting Competency questions are addressed in part 2 of the CSWA exam.

The three questions are in a multiple choice single answer format. You are allowed to answer the questions in any order you prefer. Use the Summary Screen during the exam to view the list of all questions you have or have not answered.

Screen shot from the exam

In the *Drafting Competencies* category of the exam, you are **not required** to create or perform an analysis on a part, assembly, or drawing but you are required to have general drafting/drawing knowledge and understanding of various drawing view methods.

On the completion of the chapter, you will be able to:

- Identify the procedure to create a named drawing view:

    - Projected view, Section view, Break view, Crop view, Detail, Alternate Position view, etc.

In the *Basic Part Creation and Modification, Intermediate Part Creation and Modification, Advanced Part Creation and Modification and Assembly Creation and Modification* categories, you are required to read and interpret various types of drawing views and understand various types of drawing annotations.

All SOLIDWORKS models for the next few chapters (initial and final) are provided in the SOLIDWORKS CSWA Model Folder. Download the SOLIDWORKS CSWA Model Folder to your local hard drive.

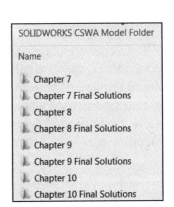

SOLIDWORKS CSWA Model Folder

Name

- Chapter 7
- Chapter 7 Final Solutions
- Chapter 8
- Chapter 8 Final Solutions
- Chapter 9
- Chapter 9 Final Solutions
- Chapter 10
- Chapter 10 Final Solutions

Procedure to Create a Named Drawing view

You need the ability to identify the procedure to create a named drawing view: *Standard 3 View, Model View, Projected View, Auxiliary View, Section View, Detail View, Broken-out Section, Break, Crop View and Alternate Position View.*

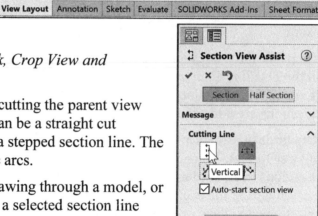

Create a Section view in a drawing by cutting the parent view with a section line. The Section view can be a straight cut section or an offset section defined by a stepped section line. The section line can also include concentric arcs.

Create an Aligned Section view in a drawing through a model, or portion of a model, that is aligned with a selected section line segment. The Aligned Section view is similar to a Section view, but the section line for an aligned section comprises two or more lines connected at an angle.

Create a Detail view in a drawing to show a portion of a view, usually at an enlarged scale. This detail may be of an Orthographic view, a Non-planar (isometric) view, Section view, Crop view, an Exploded Assembly view, or another Detail view.

☀ Crop any drawing view except a Detail view, a view from which a Detail view has been created, or an Exploded view. To create a Crop view, sketch a closed profile such as a circle or spline. The view outside the closed profile disappears as illustrated.

A-A

A-A

☀ Create a Detail view in a drawing to display a portion of a view, usually at an enlarged scale. This detail may be of an orthographic view, a non-planar (isometric) view, a Section view, a Crop view, an Exploded assembly view, or another Detail view.

Tutorial: Drawing Named Procedure 7-1

Identify the drawing name view and understand the procedure to create the name view.

1. **View** the illustrated drawing views. The top drawing view is a Break view. The Break view is created by adding a break line to a selected view.

🔆 Broken views make it possible to display the drawing view in a larger scale on a smaller size drawing sheet. Reference dimensions and model dimensions associated with the broken area reflect the actual model values.

🔆 In views with multiple breaks, the Break line style must be the same.

Tutorial: Drawing Named Procedure 7-2

Identify the drawing name view and understand the procedure to create the name view.

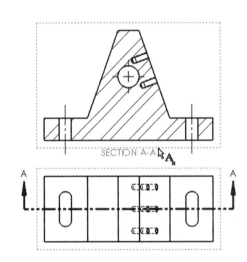

1. **View** the illustrated drawing views. The top drawing view is a Section view of the bottom view. The Section view is created by cutting the parent view with a cutting section line.

🔆 Create a Section view in a drawing by cutting the parent view with a section line. The section view can be a straight cut section or an offset section defined by a stepped section line. The section line can also include Concentric arcs.

Tutorial: Drawing Named Procedure 7-3

Identify the drawing name view and understand the procedure to create the name view.

1. **View** the illustrated drawing views. The view to the right is an Auxilary view of the Front view. Select a reference edge to create an Auxiliary view as illustrated.

🔆 An Auxiliary view is similar to a Projected view, but it is unfolded normal to a reference edge in an existing view.

Tutorial: Drawing Named Procedure 7-4

Identify the drawing name view and understand the procedure to create the name view.

1. **View** the illustrated drawing views. The right drawing view is an Aligned half Section view of the view to the left. The Section view is created by using two lines connected at an angle. Create an Aligned half Section view in a drawing through a model, or portion of a model, that is aligned with a selected section line segment.

The Aligned Section view is very similar to a Section View, with the exception that the section line for an aligned half section is comprised of two or more lines connected at an angle.

Tutorial: Drawing Named Procedure 7-5

Identify the drawing name view and understand the procedure to create the name view.

1. **View** the illustrated drawing views. The left drawing view is a Detail view of the Section view. The Detail view is created by sketching a circle with the Circle Sketch tool. Click and drag for the location.

SECTION A-A

The Detail view 🅖 tool provides the ability to add a Detail view to display a portion of a view, usually at an enlarged scale.

To create a profile other than a circle, sketch the profile before clicking the Detail view tool. Using a sketch entity tool, create a closed profile around the area to be detailed.

Tutorial: Drawing Named Procedure 7-6

Identify the drawing name view and understand the procedure to create the name view.

1. **View** the illustrated drawing views. The top drawing view is a Broken-out Section view of the bottom drawing view. The Broken-out Section View is part of an existing drawing view, not a separate view. Create the Broken-out Section view with a closed profile, usually by using the Spline Sketch tool. Material is removed to a specified depth to expose inner details.

Tutorial: Drawing Named Procedure 7-7

Identify the drawing name view and understand the procedure to create the name view.

1. **View** the illustrated drawing view. The top drawing view is a Crop view. The Crop view is created by a closed sketch profile such as a circle or spline as illustrated.

The Crop View provides the ability to crop an existing drawing view. You cannot use the Crop tool on a Detail view, a view from which a Detail view has been created, or an Exploded view.

Use the Crop tool to save steps. Example: instead of creating a Section View and then a Detail view, then hiding the unnecessary Section view, use the Crop tool to crop the Section view directly.

In the exam, you are allowed to answer the questions in any order. Use the Summary Screen during the exam to view the list of all questions you have or have not answered.

Tutorial: Drawing Named Procedure 7-8

Identify the drawing name view and understand the procedure to create the name view.

1. **View** the illustrated drawing view. The drawing view is an

    Alternate Position View. The Alternate Position view tool provides the ability to superimpose an existing drawing view precisely on another. The alternate position is displayed with phantom lines.

Use the Alternate Position view to display the range of motion of an assembly. You can dimension between the primary view and the Alternate Position view. You cannot use the Alternate Position view tool with Broken, Section, or Detail views.

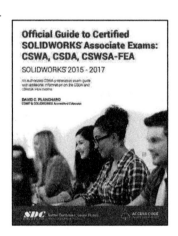

Summary

Drafting Competencies is one of the five categories on the CSWA exam. There are three questions on the CSWA exam in this category. Each question is worth five (5) points. The three questions are in a multiple choice single answer format.

Spend no more than 10 minutes on each question in this category. This is a timed exam. Manage your time.

Basic Part Creation and Modification and *Intermediate Part Creation and Modification* is the next chapter in this book. This chapter covers the knowledge to create and modify models for these categories from detailed dimensioned illustrations.

The complexity of the models along with the features progressively increases throughout the chapter to simulate the final types of model that could be provided on the exam.

The **Official Guide to Certified SOLIDWORKS Associate Exams**: CSWA, CSDA, CSWSA-FEA book is written to assist the SOLIDWORKS user to pass the associate level exams. Information is provided to aid the user to pass the Certified Associate - Mechanical Design exam, the SOLIDWORKS Certified Associate - Sustainable Design exam, and the SOLIDWORKS Certified Associate - Simulation (FEA) exam. The primary goal of this book is not only to help you pass the exams but also to ensure that you understand and comprehend the concepts and implementation details of the process.

Questions

1. Identify the illustrated Drawing view.

- A: Projected

- B: Alternative Position

- C: Extended

- D: Aligned Section

2. Identify the illustrated Drawing view.

- A: Crop

- B: Break

- C: Broken-out Section

- D: Aligned Section

3. Identify the illustrated Drawing view.

- A: Section

- B: Crop

- C: Broken-out Section

- D: Aligned

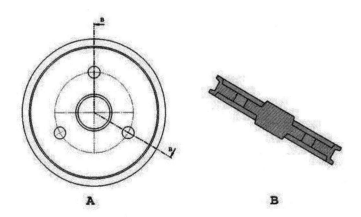

4. Identify the view procedure. To create the following view, you need to insert a:

- A: Rectangle Sketch tool

- B: Closed Profile: Spline

- C: Open Profile: Circle

- D: None of the above

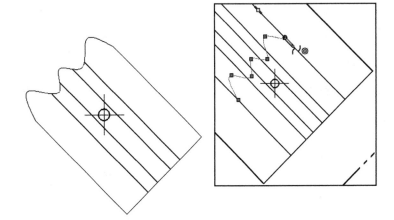

5. Identify the view procedure. To create the following view, you need to insert a:

- A: Open Spline

- B: Closed Spline

- C: 3 Point Arc

- D: None of the above

6. Identify the illustrated view type.

- A: Crop

- B: Section

- C: Projected

- D: Detail

7. To create View B from Drawing View A insert which View type?

- A: Crop

- B: Section

- C: Aligned Section

- D: Projected

A   B

8. To create View B it is necessary to sketch a closed spline on View A and insert which View type?

- A: Broken out Section
- B: Detail
- C: Section
- D: Projected

9. To create View B it is necessary to sketch a closed spline on View A and insert which View type?

- A: Horizontal Break
- B: Detail
- C: Section
- D: Broken out Section

Notes:

Chapter 8 - Basic Part and Intermediate Part Creation and Modification

Objectives

Basic Part Creation and Modification and Intermediate Part Creation and Modification are two of the five categories on the CSWA exam. This chapter covers the knowledge to create and modify models in these categories from detailed dimensioned illustrations.

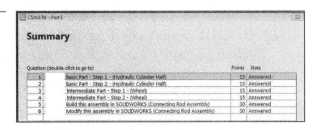

The main difference between the *Basic Part Creation and Modification* category and the *Intermediate Part Creation and Modification* or the *Advance Part Creation and Modification* category is the complexity of the sketches and the number of dimensions and geometric relations along with an increase in the number of features.

There are two questions on the CSWA exam (part 1) in the *Basic Part Creation and Modification* category and two questions in the *Intermediate Part Creation and Modification* category.

The first question is in a multiple choice single answer format. You should be within 1% of the multiple choice answer before you move on to the modification single answer section (fill in the blank format).

Each question is worth fifteen (15) points for a total of thirty (30) points. You are required to build a model with six or more features and to answer a question either on the overall mass, volume, or the location of the Center of mass for the created model relative to the default part Origin location. You are then requested to modify the part and answer a fill in the blank format question.

Screen shots from an exam

On the completion of the chapter, you will be able to:

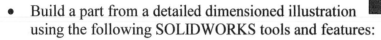

- Read and understand an Engineering document used in the CSWA exam:

  - Identify the Sketch plane, part Origin location, part dimensions, geometric relations and design intent of the sketch and feature.

- Build a part from a detailed dimensioned illustration using the following SOLIDWORKS tools and features:

  - 2D & 3D sketch tools, Extruded Boss/Base, Extruded Cut, Fillet, Mirror, Revolved Base, Chamfer, Reference geometry, Plane, Axis, Calculate the overall mass and volume of the created part and Locate the Center of mass for the created part relative to the Origin.

💡 The complexity of the models along with the features progressively increases throughout this chapter to simulate the final types of models that would be provided on the exam.

💡 FeatureManager names were changed through various revisions of SOLIDWORKS. Example: Extrude1 vs. Boss-Extrude1. These changes do not affect the models or answers in this book.

Read and Understand an Engineering Document

DETAIL A
SCALE 2 : 1

A 2D drawing view is displayed in the *Basic Part Creation and Modification, Intermediate Part Creation and Modification, Advance Part Creation and Modification, and Assembly Creation and Modification* categories of the CSWA exam to clarify dimensions and details.

The ability to interpret a 2D drawing view is required.

- Example 1: *8X Ø.19 EQ. SP.* Eight holes with a .19in. diameter are required that are equally (.55in.) spaced.

- Example 2: *R2.50 TYP.* Typical radius of 2.50. The dimension has a two decimal place precision.

- Example 3: ⍔. The Depth/Deep ⍔ symbol with a 1.50 dimension associated with the hole. The hole Ø.562 has a three decimal place precision.

- Example 4: *A+40*. A is provided to you on the CSWA exam. A + 40mm.

🔅 N is a Detail view of the M-M Section view.

- Example 5: *ØB*. Diameter of B. B is provided to you on the exam.

- Example 6: Ⓝ. Parallelism.

- Example 7: ⊗ The faces are coincident.

During the exam, each question will display an information table on the left side of the screen and drawing information on the right. Read the provided information and apply it to the drawing. Various values are provided on each question.

🔅 If you don't find your answer (within 1%) in the multiple choice single answer format section - recheck your solid model for precision and accuracy.

🔅 All SOLIDWORKS models for the next few chapters (initial and final) are provided in the SOLIDWORKS CSWA Model Folder. Download the SOLIDWORKS CSWA Model Folder to your local hard drive.

Modify the part in SolidWorks.

Unit system: MMGS (millimeter, gram, second)
Decimal places: 2
Part origin: Arbitrary
All holes through all unless shown otherwise.
Material: Aluminium 1060 Alloy
Density = 0.0027 g/mm^3

Modify the part using the following variable values:

A = 140.00
B = 50.00
C = 55 degrees

Note: Assume all unshown dimensions are the same as in the previous question.

What is the overall mass of the part (grams)?

Screen shot from an exam

Build a Basic Part from a Detailed illustration

Tutorial: Volume/Center of Mass 8-1

Build this model in SOLIDWORKS. Calculate the volume of the part and locate the Center of mass with the provided information.

1. **Create** a New part in SOLIDWORKS.

2. **Build** the illustrated dimensioned model. The model displays all edges on perpendicular planes. Think about the steps to build the model. Insert two features: Extruded Base (Boss-Extrude1) and Extruded Cut (Cut-Extrude1). The part Origin is located in the front left corner of the model. Think about your Base Sketch plane. Keep your Base Sketch simple.

3. **Set** the document properties for the model.

4. Create **Sketch1**. Select the Front Plane as the Sketch plane. Sketch1 is the Base sketch. Sketch1 is the profile for the Extruded Base (Boss-Extrude1) feature. Insert the required geometric relations and dimensions.

5. Create the **Extruded Base** feature. Boss-Extrude1 is the Base feature. Blind is the default End Condition in Direction 1. Depth = 2.25in. Identify the extrude direction to maintain the location of the Origin.

6. Create **Sketch2**. Select the Top right face as the Sketch plane for the second feature. Sketch a square. Sketch2 is the profile for the Extruded Cut feature. Insert the required geometric relations and dimensions.

7. Create the **Extruded Cut** feature. Select Through All for End Condition in Direction 1.

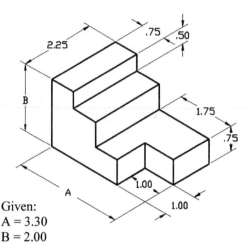

Given:
A = 3.30
B = 2.00
Material: 2014 Alloy
Density = .101 lb/in^3
Units: IPS
Decimal places = 2

Origin

8. **Assign** 2014 Alloy material to the part. Material is required to locate the Center of mass.

9. **Calculate** the volume. The volume = 8.28 cubic inches.

🔆 There are numerous ways to build the models in this chapter. A goal is to display different design intents and techniques.

Origin

Mass = 0.84 pounds

Volume = 8.28 cubic inches

Surface area = 29.88 square inches

Center of mass: (inches)
X = 1.14
Y = 0.75
Z = -1.18

10. **Locate** the Center of mass. The location of the Center of mass is derived from the part Origin.

- X: 1.14 inch

- Y: 0.75 inch

- Z: -1.18 inch

11. **Save** the part and name it Volume-Center of mass 8-1.

12. **Close** the model.

Origin

🔆 The principal axes and Center of mass are displayed graphically on the model in the Graphics window.

Tutorial: Volume/Center of Mass 8-2

Build this model. Calculate the volume of the part and locate the Center of mass with the provided information.

1. **Create** a New part in SOLIDWORKS.

2. **Build** the illustrated dimensioned model. The model displays all edges on perpendicular planes. Think about the steps that are required to build this model. Remember, there are numerous ways to create the models in this chapter.

Given:
A = 100
B = 40
Material: Brass
Density = .0085 g/mm^3
Units: MMGS

Origin

The CSWA exam is timed. Work efficiently.

View the provided Part FeatureManagers. Both FeatureManagers create the same illustrated model. In Option1, there are four sketches and four features (Extruded Base and three Extruded Cuts) that are used to build the model.

In Option2, there are three sketches and three features (Extruded Boss/Base) that are used to build the model. Which FeatureManager is better? In a timed exam, optimize your time and use the least amount of features through mirror, pattern, symmetry, etc.

Use Centerlines to create symmetrical sketch elements and revolved features, or as construction geometry.

Create the model using the Option2 Part FeatureManager.

3. **Set** the document properties for the model. Create **Sketch1**. Select the Top Plane as the Sketch plane. Sketch a rectangle. Insert the required dimensions.

4. Create the **Extruded Base** feature. Boss-Extrude1 is the Base feature. Blind is the default End Condition in Direction 1. Depth = 10mm.

5. Create **Sketch2**. Select the back face of Boss-Extrude1. Select **Normal To** view. Sketch2 is the profile for the second Extruded Boss/Base feature. Insert the required geometric relations and dimensions as illustrated.

6. Create the second Extruded Boss/Base feature (**Boss-Extrude2**). Blind is the default End Condition in Direction 1. Depth = 20mm. Note the direction of the extrude towards the front of the model.

7. Create **Sketch3**. Select the left face of Boss-Extrude1 as the Sketch plane. Sketch3 is the profile for the third Extrude feature. Insert the required geometric relations and dimensions.

8. Create the third Extruded Boss/Base feature (**Boss-Extrude3**). Blind is the default End Condition in Direction 1. Depth = 20mm.

9. **Assign** brass material to the part.

10. **Calculate** the volume of the model. The volume = 130,000.00 cubic millimeters.

11. **Locate** the Center of mass. The location of the Center of mass is derived from the part Origin.

    Mass = 1105.00 grams

    Volume = 130000.00 cubic millimeters

    Surface area = 23400.00 square millimeters

    Center of mass: (millimeters)
    - X: 43.46 millimeters
    - Y: 15.00 millimeters
    - Z: -37.69 millimeters

12. **Save** the part and name it Volume-Center of mass 8-2.

13. **Calculate** the volume of the model using the IPS unit system. The volume = 7.93 cubic inches.

Origin

14. **Locate** the Center of mass using the IPS unit system. The location of the Center of mass is derived from the part Origin.

    - X: 1.71 inches
    - Y: 0.59 inches
    - Z: -1.48 inches

    Mass = 2.44 pounds

    Volume = 7.93 cubic inches

    Surface area = 36.27 square inches

    Center of mass: (inches)
    X = 1.71
    Y = 0.59
    Z = -1.48

15. **Save** the part and name it Volume-Center of mass 8-2-IPS.

16. **Close** the model.

🔅 There are numerous ways to create the models in this chapter. A goal is to display different design intents and techniques.

🔅 All SOLIDWORKS models for the next few chapters (initial and final) are provided in the SOLIDWORKS CSWA Model Folder.

SOLIDWORKS CSWA Model Folder

Name

📁 Chapter 7
📁 Chapter 7 Final Solutions
📁 Chapter 8
📁 Chapter 8 Final Solutions
📁 Chapter 9
📁 Chapter 9 Final Solutions
📁 Chapter 10
📁 Chapter 10 Final Solutions

Tutorial: Mass-Volume 8-3

Build this model. Calculate the overall mass of the illustrated model with the provided information.

1. **Create** a New part in SOLIDWORKS.

2. **Build** the illustrated model. The model displays all edges on perpendicular planes. Think about the steps required to build the model. Apply the Mirror Sketch tool to the Base sketch. Insert an Extruded Base (Boss-Extrude1) and Extruded-Cut (Cut-Extrude1) feature.

Given:
A = 50, B = 50, C = 120
Material: 6061 Alloy
Density = .0027 g/mm^3
Units: MMGS

3. **Set** the document properties for the model.

☀ To activate the Mirror Sketch tool, click **Tools**, **Sketch Tools**, **Mirror** from the Menu bar menu. The Mirror PropertyManager is displayed.

4. Create **Sketch1**. Select the Front Plane as the Sketch plane. Apply the Mirror Sketch tool. Select the construction geometry to mirror about as illustrated. Select the Entities to mirror. Insert the required geometric relations and dimensions.

Origin

☀ Construction geometry is ignored when the sketch is used to create a feature. Construction geometry uses the same line style as centerlines.

☀ When you create a new part or assembly, the three default Planes (Front, Right and Top) are aligned with specific views.

5. Create the **Boss-Extrude1** feature. Boss-Extrude1 is the Base feature. Apply the Mid Plane End Condition in Direction 1 for symmetry. Depth = 50mm.

6. Create **Sketch2**. Select the right face for the Sketch plane. Sketch2 is the profile for the Extruded Cut feature. Insert the required geometric relations and dimensions. Apply construction geometry.

7. Create the **Extruded Cut** feature. Through All is the selected End Condition in Direction 1.

8. **Assign** 6061 Alloy material to the part.

9. **Calculate** the overall mass. The overall mass = 302.40 grams.

10. **Save** the part and name it Mass-Volume 8-3.

11. **Close** the model.

Tutorial: Mass-Volume 8-4

Build this model. Calculate the overall mass of the part and locate the Center of mass with the provided information.

1. **Create** a New part in SOLIDWORKS.

2. **Build** the illustrated model. All edges of the model are not located on Perpendicular planes. Think about the steps required to build the model. Insert two features: Extruded Base (Boss-Extrude1) and Extruded Cut (Cut-Extrude1).

3. **Set** the document properties for the model.

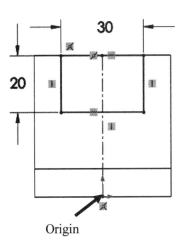

Origin

Mass = 302.40 grams

Volume = 112000.00 cubic millimeters

Surface area = 26200.00 square millimeters

Center of mass: (millimeters)
  X = 0.00
  Y = 19.20
  Z = 0.00

Given:
A = 3.00, B = 1.00
Material: 6061 Alloy
Density = .097 lb/in^3
Units: IPS
Decimal places = 2

Origin

4. Create **Sketch1**. Select the Right Plane as the Sketch plane. Apply construction geometry. Insert the required geometric relations and dimensions.

5. Create the **Extruded Base** feature. Boss-Extrude1 is the Base feature. Apply symmetry. Select Mid Plane as the End Condition in Direction 1. Depth = 3.00in.

6. Create **Sketch2**. Select the Right Plane as the Sketch plane. Select the Line Sketch tool. Insert the required geometric relations. Sketch2 is the profile for the Extruded Cut feature.

7. Create the **Extruded Cut (Cut-Extrude1)** feature. Apply symmetry. Select Mid Plane as the End Condition in Direction 1. Depth = 1.00in.

8. **Assign** 6061 Alloy material to the part.

9. **Calculate** overall mass. The overall mass = 0.87 pounds.

10. **Locate** the Center of mass. The location of the Center of mass is derived from the part Origin.

- X: 0.00 inches
- Y: 0.86 inches
- Z: 0.82 inches

Mass = 0.87 pounds

Volume = 8.88 cubic inches

Surface area = 28.91 square inches

Center of mass: (inches)
X = 0.00
Y = 0.86
Z = 0.82

In this category an exam question could read "Build this model. Locate the Center of mass with respect to the part Origin."

- A: X = 0.10 inches, Y = -0.86 inches, Z = -0.82 inches

- B: X = 0.00 inches, Y = 0.86 inches, Z = 0.82 inches

- C: X = 0.15 inches, Y = -0.96 inches, Z = -0.02 inches

- D: X = 1.00 inches, Y = -0.89 inches, Z = -1.82 inches

The correct answer is B.

11. **Save** the part and name it Mass-Volume 8-4.

12. **Close** the model.

As an exercise, modify the Mass-Volume 8-4 part using the MMGS unit system. Assign Nickel as the material. Calculate the overall mass. The overall mass of the part = 1236.20 grams. Save the part and name it Mass-Volume 8-4-MMGS.

Tutorial: Mass-Volume 8-5

Build this model. Calculate the overall mass of the part and locate the Center of mass with the provided information.

1. **Create** a New part in SOLIDWORKS.

2. **Build** the illustrated model. Insert five sketches and five features to build the model: Extruded Base, three Extruded Cut features and a Mirror feature.

💡 There are numerous ways to build the models in this chapter. A goal is to display different design intents and techniques.

3. **Set** the document properties for the model.

4. Create **Sketch1**. Select the Front Plane as the Sketch plane. Sketch a rectangle. Insert the required dimensions. The part Origin is located in the lower left corner of the sketch.

Given:
A = 100, B = 50, C = 60
Material: Alloy Steel
Density = .007 g/mm^3
Units: MMGS

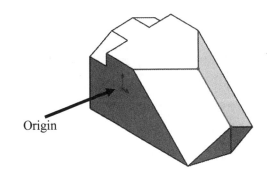

Origin

5. Create the **Extruded Base (Boss-Extrude1)** feature. Apply symmetry. Select the Mid Plane End Condition for Direction 1. Depth = 60mm.

6. Create **Sketch2**. Select the left face of Boss-Extrude1 as the Sketch plane. Insert the required geometric relations and dimensions.

7. Create the first **Extruded Cut** feature. Blind is the default End Condition in Direction 1. Depth = 15mm. Note the direction of the extrude feature.

8. Create **Sketch3**. Select the bottom face of Boss-Extrude1 for the Sketch plane. Insert the required geometric relations and dimension.

9. Create the second **Extruded Cut** feature. Blind is the default End Condition in Direction 1. Depth = 20mm.

10. Create **Sketch4**. Select Front Plane as the Sketch plane. Sketch a diagonal line. Sketch4 is the direction of extrusion for the third Extruded Cut feature. Insert the required dimension.

11. Create **Sketch5**. Select the top face of Boss-Extrude1 as the Sketch plane. Sketch5 is the sketch profile for the third Extruded Cut feature. Apply construction geometry. Insert the required geometric relations and dimensions.

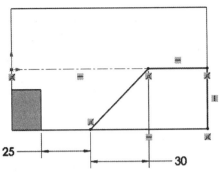

12. Create the third **Extruded Cut** feature. Select Through All for End Condition in Direction 1.

13. Select **Sketch4** in the Graphics window for Direction of Extrusion. Line1@Sketch4 is displayed in the Cut-Extrude PropertyManager.

14. Create the **Mirror** feature. Mirror the three Extruded Cut features about the Front Plane. Use the fly-out FeatureManager.

15. **Assign** Alloy Steel material to the part.

16. **Calculate** the overall mass. The overall mass = 1794.10 grams.

Mass = 1794.10 grams

Volume = 233000.00 cubic millimeters

Surface area = 23060.20 square millimeters

Center of mass: (millimeters)
     X = 41.17
     Y = 22.38
     Z = 0.00

17. **Locate** the Center of mass. The location of the Center of mass is derived from the part Origin.

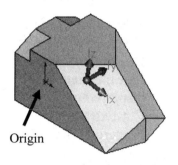

Mass = 1794.10 grams

Volume = 233000.00 cubic millimeters

Surface area = 23060.20 square millimeters

Center of mass: (millimeters)
   X = 41.17
   Y = 22.38
   Z = 0.00

- X = 41.17 millimeters

- Y = 22.38 millimeters

- Z = 0.00 millimeters

View the triad location of the Center of mass for the part.

18. **Save** the part and name it Mass-Volume 8-5.

19. **Close** the model.

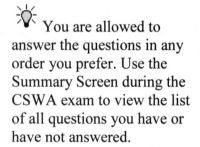

Set document precision from the Document Properties dialog box or from the Dimension PropertyManager. You can also address Callout value, Tolerance type, and Dimension Text symbols in the Dimension PropertyManager.

Origin

You are allowed to answer the questions in any order you prefer. Use the Summary Screen during the CSWA exam to view the list of all questions you have or have not answered.

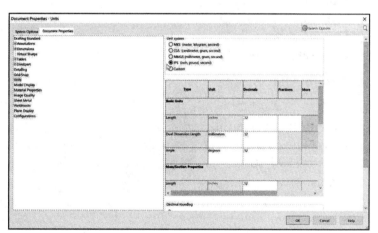

There are no Surfacing or Boundary feature questions on the CSWA exam at this time.

Build Additional Basic Parts

Tutorial: Mass-Volume 8-6

Build this model. Calculate the overall mass of the part and locate the Center of mass with the provided information.

1. **Create** a New part in SOLIDWORKS.

2. **Build** the illustrated model. Think about the required steps to build this part. Insert four features: Extruded Base, two Extruded Cuts, and a Fillet. All Thru Holes.

Given:
A = 4.00
B = R.50
Material: 6061 Alloy
Density = .0975 lb/in^3
Units: IPS
Decimal places = 2

💡 There are numerous ways to build the models in this chapter. A goal is to display different design intents and techniques.

3. **Set** the document properties for the model.

4. Create **Sketch1**. Select the Right Plane as the Sketch plane. The part Origin is located in the lower left corner of the sketch. Insert the required geometric relations and dimensions.

5. Create the **Extruded Base (Boss-Extrude1)** feature. Apply symmetry. Select the Mid Plane End Condition for Direction 1. Depth = 4.00in.

6. Create **Sketch2**. Select the top flat face of Boss-Extrude1 as the Sketch plane. Sketch a circle. The center of the circle is located at the part Origin. Insert the required dimension.

7. Create the first **Extruded Cut** feature. Select Through All for End Condition in Direction 1.

8. Create **Sketch3**. Select the front vertical face of Extrude1 as the Sketch plane. Sketch a circle. Insert the required geometric relations and dimensions.

9. Create the second **Extruded Cut** feature. Select Through All for End Condition in Direction 1.

10. Create the **Fillet** feature. Constant radius is selected by default. Fillet the top two edges as illustrated. Radius = .50in.

🔆 A Fillet feature removes material. Selecting the correct radius value is important to obtain the correct mass and volume answer in the exam.

11. **Assign** the defined material to the part.

12. **Calculate** the overall mass. The overall mass = 0.66 pounds.

13. **Locate** the Center of mass. The location of the Center of mass is derived from the part Origin.

Mass = 0.66 pounds

Volume = 6.76 cubic inches

Surface area = 36.99 square inches

Center of mass: (inches)
   X = 0.00
   Y = 0.90
   Z = -1.46

- X: 0.00 inches

- Y: 0.90 inches

- Z: -1.46 inches

In this category an exam question could read "Build this model. Locate the Center of mass relative to the part Origin."

- A: X = -2.63 inches, Y = 4.01 inches, Z = -0.04 inches

- B: X = 4.00 inches, Y = 1.90 inches, Z = -1.64 inches

- C: X = 0.00 inches, Y = 0.90 inches, Z = -1.46 inches

- D: X = -1.69 inches, Y = 1.00 inches, Z = 0.10 inches

The correct answer is C. Note: Tangent edges and Origin is displayed for educational purposes.

14. **Save** the part and name it Mass-Volume 8-6.

15. **Close** the model.

As an exercise, calculate the overall mass of the part using the MMGS unit system, and assign 2014 Alloy material to the part.

The overall mass of the part = 310.17 grams.

Save the part and name it Mass-Volume 8-6-MMGS.

Mass = 310.17 grams

Volume = 110774.26 cubic millimeters

Surface area = 23865.83 square millimeters

Center of mass: (millimeters)
   X = 0.00
   Y = 22.83
   Z = -37.11

Tutorial: Mass-Volume 8-7

Build this model. Calculate the overall mass of the part and locate the Center of mass with the provided information.

1. **Create** a New part in SOLIDWORKS.

2. **Build** the illustrated model. Insert two features: Extruded Base (Boss-Extrude1) and Revolved Boss.

3. **Set** the document properties for the model.

Tangent edges and the Origin are displayed for educational purposes.

4. Create **Sketch1**. Select the Top Plane as the Sketch plane. Apply construction geometry. Apply the Tangent Arc and Line Sketch tool. Insert the required geometric relations and dimensions.

5. Create the **Extruded Base** feature. Blind is the default End Condition. Depth = 8mm.

6. Create **Sketch2**. Select the Front Plane as the Sketch plane. Apply construction geometry for the Revolved Boss feature. Insert the required geometric relations and dimension.

Given:
A = 60, B = 40, C = 8
Material: Cast Alloy Steel
Density = .0073 g/mm^3
Units: MMGS

Origin

Origin

7. Create the **Revolved Boss** feature. The default angle is 360deg. Select the centerline for Axis of Revolution.

8. **Assign** the defined material to the part.

9. **Calculate** the overall mass. The overall mass = 229.46 grams.

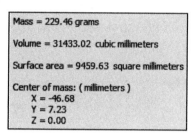

Mass = 229.46 grams

Volume = 31433.02 cubic millimeters

Surface area = 9459.63 square millimeters

Center of mass: (millimeters)
    X = -46.68
    Y = 7.23
    Z = 0.00

10. **Locate** the Center of mass. The location of the Center of mass is derived from the part Origin.

- X = -46.68 millimeters

- Y = 7.23 millimeters

- Z = 0.00 millimeters

In this category an exam question could read "Build this model. What is the overall mass of the part?"

- A: 229.46 grams

- B: 249.50 grams

- C: 240.33 grams

- D: 120.34 grams

The correct answer is A.

11. **Save** the part and name it Mass-Volume 8-7.

12. **Close** the model.

Origin

Tangent edges and Origin is displayed for educational purposes.

When you create a new part or assembly, the three default Planes (Front, Right and Top) are aligned with specific views. The Plane you select for the Base sketch determines the orientation of the part.

Tutorial: Basic/Intermediate Part 8-1

Build this model. Calculate the overall mass of the part and locate the Center of mass with the provided information.

Given:
A = 52, B = 58
ALL-ROUNDS R 4MM
Material: 6061 Alloy
Density: .0027 g/mm^3
Units: MMGS

1. **Create** a New part in SOLIDWORKS.

2. **Build** the illustrated model. Think about the various features that create the part. Insert seven features and a plane to build this part: Extruded-Thin1, Boss-Extrude1, Cut-Extrude1, Cut-Extrude2 and three Fillets. Apply reference construction planes to build the circular features. All Thru Holes.

3. **Set** the document properties for the model.

4. Create **Sketch1**. Select the Front Plane as the Sketch plane. Apply construction geometry as the reference line for the 30deg angle. Insert the required geometric relations and dimensions. Note the location of the Origin.

5. Create the **Extrude-Thin1** feature. This is the Base feature. Apply symmetry. Select Mid Plane for End Condition in Direction 1 to maintain the location of the Origin. Depth = 52mm. Thickness = 12mm.

Origin

Use the Thin Feature option to control the extrude thickness, not the Depth.

6. Create **Plane1**. Plane1 is the Sketch plane for the Extruded Boss (Boss-Extrude1) feature. Select the midpoint and the top face as illustrated. Plane1 is located in the middle of the top and bottom faces. Select Parallel Plane at Point for option.

Plane1 uses the Depth dimension of 32mm.

7. Create **Sketch2**. Select Plane1 as the Sketch plane. Use the Normal To view tool. Sketch a circle to create the Extruded Boss feature. Insert the required geometric relations.

The Normal To view tool rotates and zooms the model to the view orientation normal to the selected plane, planar face, or feature.

8. Create the **Extruded Boss** feature. Apply Symmetry. Select Mid Plane for End Condition in Direction 1. Depth = 32mm.

9. Create **Sketch3**. Select the top circular face of Boss-Extrude1 as the Sketch plane. Sketch a circle. Insert the required geometric relation and dimension.

There are numerous ways to create the models in this chapter. A goal is to display different design intents and techniques.

10. Create the first **Extruded Cut** feature. Select Through All for End Condition in Direction 1.

11. Create **Sketch4**. Select the top face of Extrude-Thin1 as the Sketch plane. Apply construction geometry. Insert the required geometric relations and dimensions.

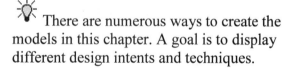

12. Create the second **Extruded Cut** feature. Select Through All for End Condition in Direction 1.

13. Create the **Fillet1** feature. Fillet the left and right edges of Extrude-Thin1 as illustrated. Radius = 12mm.

14. Create the **Fillet2** feature. Fillet the top and bottom edges of Extrude-Thin1 as illustrated. Radius = 4mm.

15. Create the **Fillet3** feature. Fillet the rest of the model, six edges as illustrated. Radius = 4mm.

16. **Assign** the defined material to the part.

17. **Calculate** the overall mass of the part. The overall mass = 300.65 grams.

18. **Locate** the Center of mass. The location of the Center of mass is derived from the part Origin.

- X: 34.26 millimeters

- Y: -29.38 millimeters

- Z: 0.00 millimeters

> Mass = 300.65 grams
>
> Volume = 111352.30 cubic millimeters
>
> Surface area = 23765.33 square millimeters
>
> Center of mass: (millimeters)
>   X = 34.26
>   Y = -29.38
>   Z = 0.00

19. **Save** the part and name it Part-Modeling 8-1.

20. **Close** the model.

As an exercise, modify the Fillet2 and Fillet3 radius from 4mm to 2mm. Modify the Fillet1 radius from 12m to 10mm. Modify the material from 6061 Alloy to ABS.

Modify the Sketch1 angle from 30deg to 45deg. Modify the Extrude depth from 32mm to 38mm. Recalculate the location of the Center of mass with respect to the part Origin.

- X = 27.62 millimeters

- Y = -40.44 millimeters

- Z = 0.00 millimeters

21. **Save** the part and name it Part-Modeling 8-1-Modify.

> Mass = 123.60 grams
>
> Volume = 121173.81 cubic millimeters
>
> Surface area = 25622.46 square millimeters
>
> Center of mass: (millimeters)
>   X = 27.62
>   Y = -40.44
>   Z = 0.00

In the exam, you are allowed to answer the questions in any order. Use the Summary Screen during the exam to view the list of all questions you have or have not answered.

Tutorial: Basic/Intermediate-Part 8-2

Build this model. Calculate the volume of the part and locate the Center of mass with the provided information.

1. **Create** a New part in SOLIDWORKS.

2. **Build** the illustrated model. Think about the various features that create this model. Insert five features and a plane to build this part: Extruded Base, two Extruded Bosses, Extruded Cut and a Rib. Insert a reference plane to create the Boss-Extrude2 feature. All Thru Holes.

Given:
A = Ø3.00, B = 1.00
Material: 6061 Alloy
Density: .097 lb/in^3
Units: IPS
Decimal places = 2

3. **Set** the document properties for the model.

4. Create **Sketch1**. Select the Top Plane as the Sketch plane. Sketch a rectangle. Apply two construction lines for an Intersection relation. Use the horizontal construction line as the Plane1 reference. Insert the required relations and dimensions.

5. Create the **Extruded Base** feature. Blind is the default End Condition in Direction 1. Depth = 1.00in. Note the extrude direction is downward.

Create planes to aid in the modeling for the exam. Use planes to sketch, to create a section view, for a neutral plane in a draft feature, and so on.

The created plane is displayed 5% larger than the geometry on which the plane is created, or 5% larger than the bounding box. This helps reduce selection problems when planes are created directly on faces or from orthogonal geometry.

6. Create **Plane1**. Plane1 is the Sketch plane for the Extruded Boss feature. Show Sketch1. Select the horizontal construction line in Sketch1 and the top face of Boss-Extrude1. Angle = 48deg.

💡 Click **View, Hide/Show, Sketches** from the Menu bar menu to displayed sketches in the Graphics window.

💡 The Normal To view tool rotates and zooms the model to the view orientation normal to the selected plane, planar face, or feature.

7. Create **Sketch2**. Select Plane1 as the Sketch plane. Create the Extruded Boss profile. Insert the required geometric relations and dimension. Note: Dimension to the front top edge of Boss-Extrude1 as illustrated.

8. Create the first **Extruded Boss** feature. Select the Up To Vertex End Condition in Direction 1. Select the back top right vertex point as illustrated.

9. Create **Sketch3**. Select the back angled face of Boss-Extrude2 as the Sketch plane. Sketch a circle. Insert the required geometric relations.

10. Create the third **Extruded Boss** feature. Blind is the default End Condition in Direction 1. Depth = 3.00in.

11. Create **Sketch4**. Select the front face of Boss-Extrude3 as the Sketch plane. Sketch a circle. Sketch4 is the profile for the Extruded Cut feature. Insert the required geometric relation and dimension.

The part Origin is displayed in blue.

12. Create the **Extruded Cut** feature. Select Through All for End Condition in Direction 1.

13. Create **Sketch5**. Select the Right Plane as the Sketch plane. Insert a Parallel relation to partially define Sketch5. Sketch5 is the profile for the Rib feature. Sketch5 does not need to be fully defined. Sketch5 locates the end conditions based on existing geometry.

14. Create the **Rib** feature. Thickness = 1.00in.

The Rib feature is a special type of extruded feature created from open or closed sketched contours. The Rib feature adds material of a specified thickness in a specified direction between the contour and an existing part. You can create a rib feature using single or multiple sketches.

15. **Assign** 6061 Alloy material to the part.

16. **Calculate** the volume. The volume = 30.65 cubic inches.

17. **Locate** the Center of mass. The location of the Center of mass is derived from the part Origin.

- X: 0.00 inches

- Y: 0.73 inches

- Z: -0.86 inches

Mass = 2.99 pounds

Volume = 30.65 cubic inches

Surface area = 100.96 square inches

Center of mass: (inches)
 X = 0.00
 Y = 0.73
 Z = -0.86

18. **Save** the part and name it Part-Modeling 8-2.

19. **Close** the model.

As an exercise, modify the Rib1 feature from 1.00in to 1.25in. Modify the Extrude depth from 3.00in to 3.25in. Modify the material from 6061 Alloy to Copper.

Origin

Modify the Plane1 angle from 48deg to 30deg. Recalculate the volume of the part. The new volume = 26.94 cubic inches.

Mass = 8.66 pounds

Volume = 26.94 cubic inches

Surface area = 98.18 square inches

Center of mass: (inches)
 X = 0.00
 Y = 0.58
 Z = -0.85

20. **Save** the part and name it Part-Modeling 8-2-Modify.

Summary

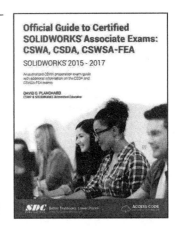

Basic Part Creation and Modification and Intermediate Part Creation and Modification are two of the five categories on the CSWA exam.

There are two questions on the CSWA exam (Part 1) in the *Basic Part Creation and Modification* category. One question is in a multiple choice single answer format and the other question (Modification of the model) is in the fill in the blank format. Each question is worth fifteen (15) points for a total of thirty (30) points.

The main difference between the *Basic Part Creation and Modification* category and the *Intermediate Part Creation and Modification* or the *Advance Part Creation and Modification* category is the complexity of the sketches and the number of dimensions and geometric relations along with an increase in the number of features.

At this time, there are no modeling questions on the exam that require you to use Sheet Metal, Lofted, Surfacing or Swept features.

The **Official Guide to Certified SOLIDWORKS Associate Exams**: CSWA, CSDA, CSWSA-FEA book is written to assist the SOLIDWORKS user to pass the associate level exams. Information is provided to aid the user to pass the Certified Associate - Mechanical Design exam, the SOLIDWORKS Certified Associate - Sustainable Design exam, and the SOLIDWORKS Certified Associate - Simulation (FEA) exam. The primary goal of this book is not only to help you pass the exams, but also to ensure that you understand and comprehend the concepts and implementation details of the process.

During the CSWA exam SOLIDWORKS provides various model views. Click on the additional views during the exam to better understand the part and provided information. Read each question carefully. Identify the dimensions, center of mass, units and location of the Origin. Apply needed material.

Screen shot from the exam

Questions

1. Build this model from the provided information using SOLIDWORKS. Set document properties. Identify the correct Sketch planes, apply the correct Sketch and Feature tools and apply material.

Calculate the overall mass of the part, volume, and locate the Center of mass with the provided illustrated information.

- Material: 6061 Alloy.

- Units: MMGS.

- All Thru Holes.

🔅 When you create a new part or assembly, the three default planes (Front, Right and Top) are aligned with specific views. The plane you select for the Base sketch determines the orientation of the part.

Origin

2. Build this model from the provided information using SOLIDWORKS. Set document properties. Apply material.

Calculate the overall mass of the part, volume, and locate the Center of mass with the provided information.

- Material: 6061 Alloy.

- Units: MMGS.

Origin

3. Build this model from the provided information using SOLIDWORKS. Set document properties. Apply material.

Calculate the overall mass of the part, volume, and locate the Center of mass with the provided information.

- Material: 6061.

- Units: IPS.

- View the provided drawing views for details.

VIEW A-A

4. Build this model from the provided information using SOLIDWORKS. Set document properties. Apply material.

Calculate the overall mass of the part, volume, and locate the Center of mass with the provided information.

- Material: 6061.

- Units: IPS.

- View the provided drawing views for details.

5. Build the illustrated model using SOLIDWORKS.

Calculate the overall mass and volume of the part with the provided information.

- Precision for linear dimensions = **2**.

- Material: **AISI 304**.

- Units: **MMGS**.

- All Holes ⊽**25**mm.

- All Rounds **5**mm.

- All Holes Ø**4**mm.

As a general rule, add fillets at the end of the modeling procedure.

Front views

Top and Auxiliary view

Calculate the mass:

A = **888.48grams**

B = 990.50grams

C = 788.48grams

D = 809.57grams

Back view

☀ If you don't find your answer (within 1%) in the multiple choice single answer format section, recheck your solid model for precision and accuracy. It could be as simple as missing a few fillets.

Calculate the volume:

A = 122259.43 cubic millimeters
B = 133359.47 cubic millimeters
C = 111059.43 cubic millimeters
D = 145059.49 cubic millimeters

Create a new coordinate system.

Center a new coordinate system with the provided illustration. The new coordinate system location is at the front right bottom point (vertex) of the model.

Enter the Center of Mass:

X = -15.59 millimeters

Y = 15.93 millimeters

Z = -2.65 millimeters

Modify the model:

- Modify all fillets (rounds) to 7mm.

- Modify the overall length to 140mm.

- Modify material to 1060 alloy.

Enter the mass:

309.75

Enter the volume:

114721.22

 If you don't find your answer (within 1%) in the multiple choice single answer format section, recheck your solid model for precision and accuracy. It could be as simple as missing a few fillets.

6. Build the illustrated model using SOLIDWORKS.

Calculate the overall mass and volume of the part with the provided information.

- Precision for linear dimensions = **2**.

- Material: **1060 Alloy**.

- Units: **MMGS**.

- TYP $\emptyset$12.

Front view

Top view

Calculate the mass:

A = 610.92 grams

B = 509.92 grams

C = 701.93 grams

D = 619.34 grams

Right view

Calculate the volume:

A = 188860.93 cubic millimeters
B = 206660.93 cubic millimeters
C = 198880.65 cubic millimeters
D = 230021.67 cubic millimeters

Modify the model:

- Modify material to Plain Carbon Steel.

- Modify TYP Hole diameter from TYP 12 to TPY 10.

Enter the mass:

1465.70

Enter the volume:

187910.60

Create a new coordinate system.

Center a new coordinate system with the provided illustration. The new coordinate system location is at the front left bottom point (vertex) of the model.

Enter the Center of Mass:

X = 31.39

Y = 16.55

Z = -48.63

7. Build the illustrated model using SOLIDWORKS.

Calculate the overall mass and volume of the part with the provided information.

- Precision for linear dimensions = **2**.

- Material: **Plain Carbon Steel**.

- Units: **MMGS**.

- The part is **symmetrical** about the Front Plane.

Top view

Front view

Calculate the mass:

A = 4311.5 grams

B = 4079.32 grams

C = 4234.30 grams

D = 5322.00 grams

Right view

Calculate the volume:

A = 522989.22 cubic millimeters
B = 555655.11 cubic millimeters
C = 591233.34 cubic millimeters
D = 655444.00 cubic millimeters

Create a new coordinate system.

Center a new coordinate system with the provided illustration. The new coordinate system location is at the back right bottom point (vertex) of the model.

Enter the Center of Mass:

X = -64.9

Y = 75.00

Z = 40.70

8. Build the provided model using SOLIDWORKS.

Calculate the overall mass and volume of the part. There are no illustrated dimensions.

Open Homework problem 8-8 from the Homework chapter exercises. Use the rollback bar to obtain features and dimensions. Think about the various ways that this model can be built.

- Precision for linear dimensions = **2**.

- Material: **1060 Alloy**.

- Units: **MMGS**.

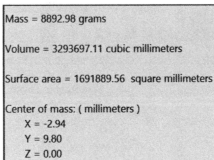

Mass = 8892.98 grams

Volume = 3293697.11 cubic millimeters

Surface area = 1691889.56 square millimeters

Center of mass: (millimeters)
    X = -2.94
    Y = 9.80
    Z = 0.00

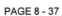

Sample screen shots from an older CSWA exam for a simple part. Click on the additional views to understand the part and to provide information. Read each question carefully. Understand the dimensions, center of mass and units. Apply needed materials.

Screen shots from an exam

💡 Zoom in on the part or view if needed.

Screen shots from an exam

D-D

Screen shots from an exam

Chapter 9 - CSWA Advanced Part Creation and Modification

Objectives

Advanced Part Creation and Modification is one of the five categories on the CSWA exam. The main difference between the *Advanced Part Creation and Modification* and the *Basic Part Creation and Modification* or the *Intermediate Part Creation and Modification* category is the complexity of the sketches and the number of dimensions and geometric relations along with an increased number of features.

There are three questions on the CSWA exam (part 2) in this category. The first question is in a multiple choice single answer format and the other two questions (Modification of the model) are in the fill in the blank format. Each question is worth fifteen (15) points for a total of forty five (45) points.

You are required to build a model with six or more features and to answer a question either on the overall mass, volume, or the location of the Center of mass for the created model relative to the default part Origin location. You are then requested to modify the model and answer fill in the blank format questions.

Screen shots from an exam

On the completion of the chapter, you will be able to:

- Specify Document Properties.

- Interpret Engineering terminology.

- Build an advanced part from a detailed dimensioned illustration using the following tools and features:

    - 2D & 3D Sketch tools, Extruded Boss/Base, Extruded Cut, Fillet, Mirror, Revolved Boss/Base, Linear & Circular Pattern, Chamfer and Revolved Cut.

- Locate the Center of mass relative to the part Origin.

- Create a coordinate system location.

- Locate the Center of mass relative to a created Coordinate system.

Build an Advanced Part from a Detailed Dimensioned Illustration

Tutorial: Advanced Part 9-1

An exam question in this category could read "Build this part. Calculate the overall mass and locate the Center of mass of the illustrated model."

1. **Create** a New part in SOLIDWORKS.

2. **Build** the illustrated model. Insert seven features: Extruded Base, two Extruded Bosses, two Extruded Cuts, a Chamfer and a Fillet.

Given:
A = 2.00, B = Ø.35
Material: 1060 Alloy
Density: 0.097 lb/in^3
Units: IPS
Decimal places = 2

Think about the steps that you would take to build the illustrated part. Identify the location of the part Origin. Start with the back base flange. Review the provided dimensions and annotations in the illustration.

Origin

💡 The main difference between the *Advanced Part Creation and Modification* and the *Basic Part Creation and Modification* or the *Intermediate Part Creation and Modification* category is the complexity of the sketches and the number of dimensions and geometric relations along with an increased number of features.

⌐ Origin
▸ 🔩 Boss-Extrude1
▸ 🔩 Boss-Extrude2
▸ 🔩 Boss-Extrude3
▸ ▣ Cut-Extrude1
▸ ▣ Cut-Extrude2
   🔵 Chamfer1
   🔵 Fillet1

💡 All SOLIDWORKS models for the next few chapters (initial and final) are provided in the SOLIDWORKS CSWA Model Folder. Download the SOLIDWORKS CSWA Model Folder to your local hard drive. Use them if needed.

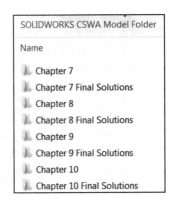

SOLIDWORKS CSWA Model Folder

Name

📁 Chapter 7
📁 Chapter 7 Final Solutions
📁 Chapter 8
📁 Chapter 8 Final Solutions
📁 Chapter 9
📁 Chapter 9 Final Solutions
📁 Chapter 10
📁 Chapter 10 Final Solutions

3. **Set** the document properties for the model.

4. Create **Sketch1**. Sketch1 is the Base sketch. Select the Front Plane as the Sketch plane. Apply construction geometry. Sketch a horizontal and vertical centerline. Sketch four circles. Insert an Equal relation. Insert a Symmetric relation about the vertical and horizontal centerlines. Sketch two top angled lines and a tangent arc. Apply the Mirror Sketch tool. Complete the sketch. Insert the required geometric relations and dimensions.

💡 In a Symmetric relation, the selected items remain equidistant from the centerline, on a line perpendicular to the centerline. Sketch entities to select: a centerline and two points, lines, arcs or ellipses.

R.50

2.00

Ø.35

2.00

In the exam, you are allowed to answer the questions in any order. Use the Summary Screen during the exam to view the list of all questions you have or have not answered.

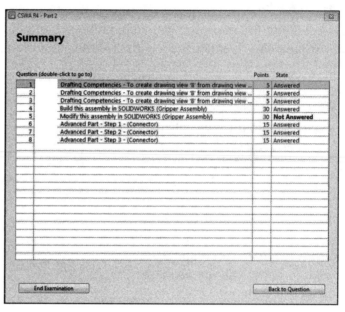

🔅 The Sketch Fillet tool rounds the selected corner at the intersection of two sketch entities, creating a tangent arc.

5. Create the **Extruded Base** feature. Boss-Extrude1 is the Base feature. Blind is the default End Condition in Direction 1. Depth = .40in.

6. Create **Sketch2**. Select the front face of Boss-Extrude1 as the Sketch plane. Sketch a circle. Insert the required geometric relation and dimension.

7. Create the first **Extruded Boss** feature. Blind is the default End Condition in Direction 1. The Extrude feature is the tube between the two flanges. Depth = 1.70in. Note: 1.70in = 2.60in - (.50in + .40in).

The complexity of the models along with the features progressively increases throughout this chapter to simulate the final types of parts that could be provided on the CSWA exam.

🔅 When you create a new part or assembly, the three default Planes (Front, Right and Top) are aligned with specific views. The Plane you select for the Base sketch determines the orientation of the part.

🔅 There are no Surfacing or Boundary feature questions on the CSWA exam at this time.

🔅 This book is designed to expose the new user to many tools, techniques and procedures. It may not always use the most direct tool or process.

8. Create **Sketch3**. Select the front circular face of Boss-Extrude2 as the Sketch plane. Sketch a horizontal and vertical centerline. Sketch the top two circles. Insert an Equal and Symmetric relation between the two circles. Mirror the top two circles about the horizontal centerline. Insert dimensions to locate the circles from the Origin. Apply either the 3 Point Arc or the Centerpoint Arc Sketch tool. The center point of the Tangent Arc is aligned with a Vertical relation to the Origin. Complete the sketch.

🔆 Use the Centerpoint Arc Sketch tool to create an arc from a centerpoint, a start point, and an end point.

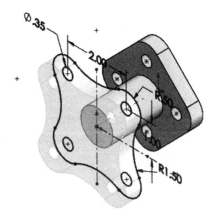

🔆 Apply the Tangent Arc Sketch tool to create an arc, tangent to a sketch entity.

The Arc PropertyManager controls the properties of a sketched Centerpoint Arc, Tangent Arc, and 3 Point Arc.

9. Create the second **Extruded Boss** feature. Blind is the default End Condition in Direction 1. Depth = .50in.

10. Create **Sketch4**. Select the front face of the Extrude feature as the Sketch plane. Sketch a circle. Insert the required geometric relation and dimension.

11. Create the first **Extruded Cut** feature. Select the Through All End Condition for Direction 1.

∅**1.50**

12. Create **Sketch5**. Select the front face of the Extrude feature as the Sketch plane. Sketch a circle. Insert the required geometric relation and dimension.

13. Create the second **Extruded Cut** feature. Blind is the default End Condition for Direction1. Depth = .10in.

14. Create the **Chamfer** feature. In order to have the outside circle 1.50in, select the inside edge of the sketched circle. Create an Angle distance chamfer. Distance = .10in. Angle = 45deg.

🔆 The Chamfer feature creates a beveled feature on selected edges, faces or a vertex.

15. Create the **Fillet** feature. Fillet the two edges as illustrated. Radius = .10in.

16. **Assign** 1060 Alloy material to the part. Material is required to calculate the overall mass of the part.

17. **Calculate** the overall mass. The overall mass = 0.59 pounds.

18. **Locate** the Center of mass. The location of the Center of mass is relative to the part Origin.

- X: 0.00

- Y: 0.00

- Z: 1.51

19. **Save** the part and name it Advanced Part 9-1.

20. **Close** the model.

Mass = 0.59 pounds

Volume = 6.01 cubic inches

Surface area = 46.61 square inches

Center of mass: (inches)
  X = 0.00
  Y = 0.00
  Z = 1.51

Tutorial: Advanced Part 9-2

An exam question in this category could read "Build this part in SOLIDWORKS. Calculate the overall mass and locate the Center of mass of the illustrated model."

Given:
A = 70, B = 76
Material: 6061 Alloy
Density: .0027 g/mm^3
Units: MMGS

1. **Create** a New part in SOLIDWORKS.

2. **Build** the illustrated dimensioned model. Insert eight features: Extruded Base, Extruded Cut, Circular Pattern, two Extruded Bosses, Extruded Cut, Chamfer and Fillet.

Think about the steps that you would take to build the illustrated part. Review the provided information. Start with the six hole flange.

🔅 Tangent Edges are displayed for educational purposes.

3. **Set** the document properties for the model.

4. Create **Sketch1**. Sketch1 is the Base sketch. Select the Front Plane as the Sketch plane. Sketch two circles. Insert the required geometric relations and dimensions.

5. Create the **Extruded Base** feature. Blind is the default End Condition in Direction 1. Depth = 10mm. Note the direction of the extrude feature to maintain the Origin location.

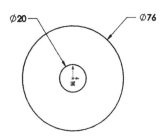

6. Create **Sketch2**. Select the front face of Boss-Extrude1 as the Sketch plane. Sketch2 is the profile for first Extruded Cut feature. The Extruded Cut feature is the seed feature for the Circular Pattern. Apply construction reference geometry. Insert the required geometric relations and dimensions.

7. Create the **Extruded Cut** feature. Cut-Extrude1 is the first bolt hole. Select Through All for End Condition in Direction 1.

8. Create the **Circular Pattern** feature. Default Angle = 360deg. Number of instances = 6. Select the center axis for the Pattern Axis box.

🔅 The Circular Pattern PropertyManager is displayed when you pattern one or more features about an axis.

9. Create **Sketch3**. Select the front face of the Extrude feature as the Sketch plane. Sketch two circles. Insert a Coradial relation on the inside circle. The two circles share the same center point and radius. Insert the required dimension.

10. Create the first **Extruded Boss (Boss-Extrude2)** feature. The Boss-Extrude2 feature is the connecting tube between the two flanges. Blind is the default End Condition in Direction 1. Depth = 48mm.

11. Create **Sketch4**. Select the front circular face of Extrude3 as the Sketch plane. Sketch a horizontal and vertical centerline from the Origin. Sketch the top and bottom circles symmetric about the horizontal centerline. Dimension the distance between the two circles and their diameter. Create the top center point arc with the center point Coincident to the top circle. The start point and the end point of the arc are horizontal. Sketch the two top angled lines symmetric about the vertical centerline. Apply symmetry. Mirror the two lines and the center point arc about the horizontal centerline. Insert the left and right tangent arcs with a center point Coincident with the Origin. Complete the sketch.

12. Create the second **Extruded Boss** (Boss-Extrude3) feature. Blind is the default End Condition in Direction 1. Depth = 12mm.

13. Create **Sketch5**. Select the front face of the Extrude feature as the Sketch plane. Sketch a circle. The part Origin is located in the center of the model. Insert the required dimension.

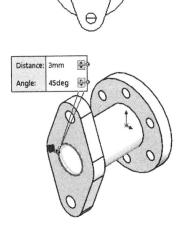

14. Create the second **Extruded Cut** feature. Blind is the default End Condition in Direction 1. Depth = 25mm.

15. Create the **Chamfer** feature. Chamfer1 is an Angle distance chamfer. Chamfer the inside edge of the Extrude feature as illustrated. Distance = 3mm. Angle = 45deg.

16. Create the **Fillet** feature. Fillet the two edges of Extrude1. Radius = 2mm.

17. **Assign** 6061 Alloy material to the part.

18. **Calculate** the overall mass of the part. The overall mass = 276.97 grams.

19. **Locate** the Center of mass. The location of the Center of mass is relative to the part Origin.

- X: 0.00 millimeters

- Y: 0.00 millimeters

- Z: 21.95 millimeters

20. **Save** the part and name it Advanced Part 9-2.

21. **Close** the model.

In the Advanced Part Modeling category, an exam question could read "Build this model. Locate the Center of mass with respect to the part Origin."

- A: X = 0.00 millimeters, Y = 0.00 millimeters, Z = 21.95 millimeters

- B: X = 21.95 millimeters, Y = 10.00 millimeters, Z = 0.00 millimeters

- C: X = 0.00 millimeters, Y = 0.00 millimeters, Z = -27.02 millimeters

- D: X = 1.00 millimeters, Y = -1.01 millimeters, Z = -0.04 millimeters

Mass = 276.97 grams

Volume = 102579.75 cubic millimeters

Surface area = 29703.14 square millimeters

Center of mass: (millimeters)
   X = 0.00
   Y = 0.00
   Z = 21.95

The correct answer is A.

Calculate the Center of Mass Relative to a Created Coordinate System Location

In the Simple Part Modeling chapter, you located the Center of mass relative to the default part Origin. In the Advanced Part Modeling category, you may need to locate the Center of mass relative to a created coordinate system location. The exam model may display a created coordinate system location. Example:

💡 The SOLIDWORKS software displays positive values for (X, Y, Z) coordinates for a reference coordinate system. The CSWA exam displays either a positive or negative sign in front of the (X, Y, Z) coordinates to indicate direction as illustrated (-X, +Y, -Z).

The following section reviews creating a Coordinate System location for a part.

Tutorial: Coordinate location 9-1

Use the Mass Properties tool to calculate the Center of mass for a part located at a new coordinate location through a point.

1. **Open** the Plate-3-Point part from the SOLIDWORKS CSWA Folder\Chapter 9 location. View the location of the part Origin.

2. **Locate** the Center of mass. The location of the Center of mass is relative to the part Origin.

- X = 28 millimeters

- Y = 11 millimeters

- Z = -3 millimeters

Create a new coordinate system location. Locate the new coordinate system location at the center of the center hole as illustrated.

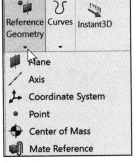

3. **Exit** the Mass Properties dialog box.

4. Right-click the **front face** of Base-Extrude.

5. Click **Sketch** from the Context toolbar.

6. Click the **edge** of the center hole as illustrated.

7. Click **Convert Entities** from the Sketch toolbar. The center point for the new coordinate location is displayed.

8. **Exit** the sketch. Sketch4 is displayed.

9. Click the **Coordinate System** tool from the Consolidated Reference Geometry toolbar. The Coordinate System PropertyManager is displayed.

10. Click the **center point** of the center hole in the Graphics window. Point2@Sketch4 is displayed in the Selections box as the Origin.

11. Click **OK** from the Coordinate System PropertyManager. Coordinate System1 is displayed.

12. **View** the new coordinate location at the center of the center hole.

View the Mass Properties of the part with the new coordinate location.

13. Click the **Mass Properties** tool from the Evaluate tab.

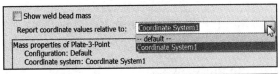

14. Select **Coordinate System1** from the Output box. The Center of mass relative to the new location is located at the following coordinates: X = 0 millimeters, Y = 0 millimeters, Z = -3 millimeters

15. **Reverse** the direction of the axes as illustrated. On the CSWA exam, the coordinate system axes could be represented by (+X, -Y, -Z).

16. **Close** the model.

🔆 To reverse the direction of an axis, click its **Reverse Axis Direction** button in the Coordinate System PropertyManager.

Tutorial: Coordinate location 9-2

Create a new coordinate system location. Locate the new coordinate system at the top back point as illustrated.

1. **Open** the Plate-X-Y-Z part from the SOLIDWORKS CSWA Folder\Chapter 9 location.

2. **View** the location of the part Origin.

3. Drag the **Rollback bar** under the Base-Extrude feature in the FeatureManager.

4. Click the **Coordinate System** tool from the Consolidated Reference Geometry toolbar. The Coordinate System PropertyManager is displayed.

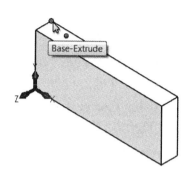

5. Click the **back left vertex** as illustrated. Address direction if needed.

6. Click the **top back horizontal** edge as illustrated. Do not select the midpoint. Address direction if needed.

7. Click the **back left vertical** edge as illustrated. Address direction if needed.

8. Click **OK** from the Coordinate System PropertyManager. Coordinate System1 is displayed in the FeatureManager and in the Graphics window.

9. Drag the **Rollback bar** to the bottom of the FeatureManager.

10. **Calculate** the Center of mass relative to the new coordinate system.

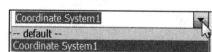

11. Select **Coordinate System1**. The Center of mass relative to the new location is located at the following coordinates:

X = -28 millimeters

Y = 11 millimeters

Z = 4 millimeters

12. **Close** the model.

Coordinate System1

🔆 Define a Coordinate system for a part or assembly. Apply a Coordinate system with the Measure and Mass Properties tool.

Tutorial: Advanced Part 9-3

An exam question in this category could read "Build this part in SOLIDWORKS. Calculate the overall mass and locate the Center of mass of the illustrated model."

1. **Create** a New part in SOLIDWORKS.

2. **Build** the illustrated dimensioned model. Insert thirteen features: Extrude-Thin1, Fillet, two Extruded Cuts, Circular Pattern, two Extruded Cuts, Mirror, Chamfer, Extruded Cut, Mirror, Extruded Cut and Mirror.

Given:
A = 110, B = 55,
C = 5 X 45Ø CHAMFER
Material: 5MM, 6061 Alloy
Density: .0027 g/mm^3
Units: MMGS
ALL HOLES 6MM

Think about the steps that you would take to build the illustrated part. Review the provided information. The depth of the left side is 50mm. The depth of the right side is 60mm.

🔆 There are numerous ways to build the models in this chapter. A goal is to display different design intents and techniques.

Origin

💡 If the inside radius = 5mm and the material thickness = 5mm, then the outside radius = 10mm.

Origin

3. **Set** the document properties for the model.

4. Create **Sketch1**. Sketch1 is the Base sketch. Select the Top Plane as the Sketch plane. Apply the Line and Sketch Fillet Sketch tools. Apply construction geometry. Insert the required geometric relations and dimensions.

5. Create the **Extrude-Thin1** feature. Extrude-Thin1 is the Base feature. Apply symmetry in Direction 1. Depth = 60mm. Thickness = 5mm. Check the Auto-fillet corners box. Radius = 5mm.

💡 The Auto-fillet corners option creates a round at each edge where lines meet at an angle.

6. Create the **Fillet** feature. Fillet1 is a full round fillet. Fillet the three illustrated faces: top, front and bottom.

7. Create **Sketch2**. Select the right face as the Sketch plane. Wake-up the center point. Sketch a circle. Insert the required relation and dimension.

8. Create the first **Extruded Cut** feature. Select Up To Next for the End Condition in Direction 1.

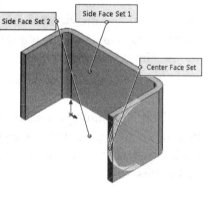

Side Face Set 2   Side Face Set 1

Center Face Set

💡 The Up To Next End Condition extends the feature from the sketch plane to the next surface that intercepts the entire profile. The intercepting surface must be on the same part.

Ø20

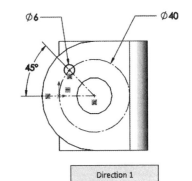

9. Create **Sketch3**. Select the right face as the Sketch plane. Create the profile for the second Extruded Cut feature. This is the seed feature for CirPattern1. Apply construction geometry to locate the center point of Sketch3. Insert the required relations and dimensions.

10. Create the second **Extruded Cut** feature. Select Up To Next for the End Condition in Direction 1.

11. Create the **Circular Pattern** feature. Number of Instances = 4. Default angle = 360deg.

12. Create **Sketch4**. Select the left outside face of Extrude-Thin1 as the Sketch plane. Apply the Line and Tangent Arc Sketch tool to create Sketch4. Insert the required geometric relations and dimensions.

13. Create the third **Extruded Cut** feature. Select Up To Next for End Condition in Direction 1. The Slot on the left side of Extrude-Thin1 is created.

14. Create **Sketch5**. Select the left outside face of Extrude-Thin1 as the Sketch plane. Sketch two circles. Insert the required geometric relations and dimensions.

15. Create the fourth **Extruded Cut** feature. Select Up To Next for End Condition in Direction 1.

There are numerous ways to create the models in this chapter. A goal is to display different design intents and techniques.

16. Create the first **Mirror** feature. Mirror the top two holes about the Top Plane.

17. Create the **Chamfer** feature. Create an Angle distance chamfer. Chamfer the selected edges as illustrated. Distance = 5mm. Angle = 45deg.

18. Create **Sketch6**. Select the front face of Extrude-Thin1 as the Sketch plane. Insert the required geometric relations and dimensions.

19. Create the fifth **Extruded Cut** feature. Select Through All for End Condition in Direction 1.

20. Create the second **Mirror** feature. Mirror Extrude5 about the Right Plane.

21. Create **Sketch7**. Select the front face of Extrude-Thin1 as the Sketch plane. Apply the 3 Point Arc Sketch tool. Apply the min First Arc Condition option. Insert the required geometric relations and dimensions.

22. Create the last **Extruded Cut** feature. Through All is the End Condition in Direction 1 and Direction 2.

23. Create the third **Mirror** feature. Mirror the Extrude feature about the Top Plane as illustrated.

24. **Assign** the material to the part.

25. **Calculate** the overall mass of the part. The overall mass = 132.45 grams.

26. **Locate** the Center of mass relative to the part Origin:

- X: 1.83 millimeters

- Y: -0.27 millimeters

- Z: -35.38 millimeters

Mass = 132.45 grams

Volume = 49055.56 cubic millimeters

Surface area = 24219.80 square millimeters

Center of mass: (millimeters)
    X = 1.83
    Y = -0.27
    Z = -35.38

27. **Save** the part and name it Advanced Part 9-3.

28. **Close** the model.

Tangent edges and Origin are displayed for educational purposes.

All questions on the exam are in a multiple choice single answer or fill in the blank format. In the Advanced Part Modeling category, an exam question could read "Build this model. Calculate the overall mass of the part with the provided information."

- A: 139.34 grams

- B: 155.19 grams

- C: 132.45 grams

- D: 143.91 grams

The correct answer is C.

🔆 Use the Options button in the Mass Properties dialog box to apply custom settings to units.

Tutorial: Advanced Part 9-3A

An exam question in this category could read "Build this part in SOLIDWORKS. Locate the Center of mass." Note the coordinate system location of the model as illustrated.

Where do you start? Build the model as you did in the Tutorial: Advanced Part 9-3. Create Coordinate System1 to locate the Center of mass.

1. **Open** Advanced Part 9-3 that you created in the previous exercise.

Create the illustrated coordinate system location.

2. Show **Sketch2** from the FeatureManager design tree.

3. Click the **center point** of Sketch2 in the Graphics window as illustrated.

🔆 Click on the additional views during the CSWA exam to better understand the part and provided information.

A = 110, B = 55, C = 5 X 45Ø CHAMFER
Material: 5MM, 6061 Alloy
Density: .0027 g/mm^3
Units: MMGS
ALL HOLES 6MM

Coordinate system: +X, +Y, +Z

4. Click the **Coordinate System** tool from the Consolidated Reference Geometry toolbar. The Coordinate System PropertyManager is displayed. Point2@Sketch2 is displayed in the Origin box.

5. Click **OK** from the Coordinate System PropertyManager. Coordinate System1 is displayed.

6. **Locate** the Center of mass based on the location of the illustrated coordinate system. Select Coordinate System1.

- X: -53.17 millimeters

- Y: -0.27 millimeters

- Z: -15.38 millimeters

Mass = 132.45 grams

Volume = 49055.56 cubic millimeters

Surface area = 24219.80 square millimeters

Center of mass: (millimeters)
X = -53.17
Y = -0.27
Z = -15.38

7. **Save** the part and name it Advanced Part 9-3A.

8. **Close** the model.

Tutorial: Advanced Part 9-3B

Build this part in SOLIDWORKS. Locate the Center of mass. View the location of the coordinate system. The coordinate system is located at the left front point of the model.

Build the illustrated model as you did in the Tutorial: Advanced Part 9-3. Create Coordinate System1 to locate the Center of mass for the model.

1. **Open** Advanced Part 9-3 that you created in the previous exercise.

Create the illustrated coordinate system.

2. Click the **vertex** as illustrated for the Origin location.

Given:
A = 110, B = 55,
C = 5 X 45Ø CHAMFER
Material: 5MM, 6061 Alloy
Density: .0027 g/mm^3
Units: MMGS
ALL HOLES 6MM

To reverse the direction of an axis, click the **Reverse Axis Direction** button in the Coordinate System PropertyManager.

3. Click the **Coordinate System** tool from the Consolidated Reference Geometry toolbar. The Coordinate System PropertyManager is displayed. Vertex<1> is displayed in the Origin box.

4. Click the **bottom horizontal edge** as illustrated. Edge<1> is displayed in the X Axis Direction box.

5. Click the **left back vertical edge** as illustrated. Edge<2> is displayed in the Y Axis Direction box.

6. Click **OK** from the Coordinate System PropertyManager. Coordinate System1 is displayed.

7. **Locate** the Center of mass based on the location of the illustrated coordinate system. Select Coordinate System1.

- X: -56.83 millimeters

- Y: -29.73 millimeters

- Z: -35.38 millimeters

Mass = 132.45 grams

Volume = 49055.56 cubic millimeters

Surface area = 24219.80 square millimeters

Center of mass: (millimeters)
   X = -56.83
   Y = -29.73
   Z = -35.38

8. **Save** the part and name it Advanced Part 9-3B.

9. **Close** the model.

In the Advanced Part Modeling category, an exam question could read "Build this model. Locate the Center of mass."

- A: X = -56.83 millimeters, Y = -29.73 millimeters, Z = -35.38 millimeters

- B: X = 1.80 millimeters, Y = -0.27 millimeters, Z = -35.54 millimeters

- C: X = -59.20 millimeters, Y = -0.27 millimeters, Z = -15.54 millimeters

- D: X= -1.80 millimeters, Y = 1.05 millimeters, Z = -0.14 millimeters

The correct answer is A.

Tutorial: Advanced Part 9-4

An exam question in this category could read "Build this part. Calculate the overall mass and locate the Center of mass of the illustrated model."

1. **Create** a new part in SOLIDWORKS.

2. **Build** the illustrated dimensioned model. Insert twelve features and a Reference plane: Extrude-Thin1, two Extruded Bosses, Extruded Cut, Extruded Boss, Extruded Cut, Plane1, Mirror and five Extruded Cuts.

Think about the steps that you would take to build the illustrated part. Create an Extrude-Thin1 feature as the Base feature.

3. **Set** the document properties for the model. Review the given information.

Given:
A = Ø19
Material: Gray Cast Iron
Density: .0072 g/mm^3
Units: MMGS
ALL HOLES THROUGH UNLESS
OTHERWISE NOTED

Origin

4. Create **Sketch1**. Sketch1 is the Base sketch. Select the Right Plane as the Sketch plane. Apply construction geometry. Insert the required geometric relations and dimensions. Sketch1 is the profile for Extrude-Thin1. Note the location of the Origin.

5. Create the **Extrude-Thin1** feature. Apply symmetry. Select Mid Plane as the End Condition in Direction 1. Depth = 64mm. Thickness = 19mm.

6. Create **Sketch2**. Select the top narrow face of Extrude-Thin1 as the Sketch plane. Sketch three lines: two vertical and one horizontal and a tangent arc. Insert the required geometric relations and dimensions.

7. Create the **Boss-Extrude1** feature. Blind is the default End Condition in Direction 1. Depth = 18mm.

8. Create **Sketch3**. Select the Right Plane as the Sketch plane. Sketch a rectangle. Insert the required geometric relations and dimensions. Note: 61mm = (19mm - 3mm) x 2 + 29mm.

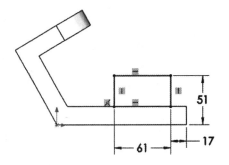

9. Create the **Boss-Extrude2** feature. Select Mid Plane for End Condition in Direction 1. Depth = 38mm. Note: 2 x R19.

10. Create **Sketch4**. Select the Right Plane as the Sketch plane. Sketch a vertical centerline from the top midpoint of the sketch. The centerline is required for Plane1. Plane1 is a Reference plane. Sketch a rectangle symmetric about the centerline. Insert the required relations and dimensions. Sketch4 is the profile for Extrude3.

11. Create the first **Extruded Cut** feature. Extrude in both directions. Select Through All for End Condition in Direction 1 and Direction 2.

12. Create **Sketch5**. Select the inside face of the Extrude feature for the Sketch plane. Sketch a circle from the top midpoint. Sketch a construction circle. Construction geometry is required for future features. Complete the sketch.

13. Create the **Extruded Boss** (Boss-Extrude3) feature. Blind is the default End Condition. Depth = 19mm.

14. Create **Sketch6**. Select the inside face for the Sketch plane. Show Sketch5. Select the construction circle in Sketch5. Apply the Convert Entities Sketch tool.

15. Create the second **Extruded Cut** feature. Select the Up To Next End Condition in Direction 1.

💡 There are numerous ways to create the models in this chapter. A goal is to display different design intents and techniques.

💡 Tangent edges and Origin are displayed for educational purposes.

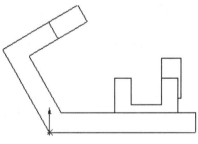

16. Create **Plane1**. Apply symmetry. Create Plane1 to mirror Cut-Extrude2 and Boss-Extrude3. Create a Parallel Plane at Point. Select the midpoint of Sketch4 and Face<1> as illustrated. Point1@Sketch4 and Face<1> is displayed in the Selections box.

17. Create the **Mirror** feature. Mirror Cut-Extrude2 and Boss-Extrude3 about Plane1.

The Mirror feature creates a copy of a feature (or multiple features) mirrored about a face or a plane. You can select the feature or you can select the faces that comprise the feature.

18. Create **Sketch7**. Select the top front angled face of Extrude-Thin1 as the Sketch plane. Apply the Centerline Sketch tool. Insert the required geometric relations and dimensions.

19. Create the third **Extruded Cut** feature. Select Through All for End Condition in Direction 1. Select the angle edge for the vector to extrude as illustrated.

Click on the additional views during the CSWA exam to better understand the part and provided information. Read each question carefully. Identify the dimensions, center of mass and units. Apply needed material.

20. Create **Sketch8**. Select the top front angled face of Extrude-Thin1 as the Sketch plane. Sketch a centerline. Sketch two vertical lines and a horizontal line. Select the top arc edge. Apply the Convert Entities Sketch tool. Apply the Trim Sketch tool to remove the unwanted arc geometry. Insert the required geometric relations and dimension.

21. Create the fourth **Extruded Cut** feature. Blind is the default End Condition in Direction 1. Depth = 6mm.

22. Create **Sketch9**. Create a Cbore with Sketch9 and Sketch10. Select the top front angled face of Extrude-Thin1 as illustrated for the Sketch plane. Extrude8 is the center hole in the Extrude-Thin1 feature. Sketch a circle. Insert the required geometric relations and dimension.

23. Create the fifth **Extrude Cut** feature. Blind is the default End Condition. Depth = 9mm. Note: This is the first feature for the Cbore.

24. Create **Sketch10**. Select the top front angled face of Extrude-Thin1 as the Sketch plane. Sketch a circle. Insert the required geometric relation and dimension. Note: A = Ø19.

25. Create the sixth **Extruded Cut** feature. Select the Up To Next End Condition in Direction 1. The Cbore is complete.

※ In the exam, you are allowed to answer the questions in any order. Use the Summary Screen during the exam to view the list of all questions you have or have not answered.

26. Create **Sketch11**. Select the front angle face of the Extrude feature for the Sketch plane. Sketch two circles. Insert the required geometric relations and dimensions.

27. Create the last **Extruded Cut** feature. Select the Up To Next End Condition in Direction 1.

🔆 The FilletXpert manages, organizes and reorders constant radius fillets.

🔆 The FilletXpert automatically calls the FeatureXpert when it has trouble placing a fillet on the specified geometry.

28. **Assign** the material to the part.

29. **Calculate** the overall mass of the part. The overall mass = 2536.59 grams.

30. **Locate** the Center of mass relative to the part Origin:

- X: 0.00 millimeters

- Y: 34.97 millimeters

- Z: -46.67 millimeters

31. **Save** the part and name it Advanced Part 9-4.

🔆 This book is designed to expose the new user to many tools, techniques and procedures. It may not always use the most direct tool or process.

Origin

Mass = 2536.59 grams

Volume = 352304.50 cubic millimeters

Surface area = 61252.90 square millimeters

Center of mass: (millimeters)
    X = 0.00
    Y = 34.97
    Z = -46.67

Tutorial: Advanced Part 9-4A

An exam question in this category could read "Build this part. Locate the Center of mass for the illustrated coordinate system."

Where do you start? Build the illustrated model as you did in the Tutorial: Advanced Part 9-3. Create Coordinate System1 to locate the Center of mass for the model.

1. **Open** Advanced Part 9-4 that you created in the previous exercise.

Create the illustrated Coordinate system.

2. Click the **Coordinate System** tool from the Consolidated Reference Geometry toolbar. The Coordinate System PropertyManager is displayed.

3. Click the **bottom midpoint** of Extrude-Thin1 as illustrated. Point<1> is displayed in the Origin box.

4. Click **OK** from the Coordinate System PropertyManager. Coordinate System1 is displayed.

5. **Locate** the Center of mass based on the location of the illustrated coordinate system. Select Coordinate System1.

- X: 0.00 millimeters

- Y: 34.97 millimeters

- Z: 93.33 millimeters

Mass = 2536.59 grams

Volume = 352304.50 cubic millimeters

Surface area = 61252.90 square millimeters

Center of mass: (millimeters)
    X = 0.00
    Y = 34.97
    Z = 93.33

6. **Save** the part and name it Advanced Part 9-4A.

7. **View** the Center of mass with the default coordinate system.

8. **Close** the model.

Summary

Advanced Part Creation and Modification is one of the five categories on the CSWA exam. The main difference between the *Advanced Part Creation and Modification* and the *Basic Part Creation and Modification* or the *Intermediate Part Creation and Modification* category is the complexity of the sketches and the number of dimensions and geometric relations along with an increased number of features.

CSWA R4 - Part 2

Summary

Question (double-click to go to)	Points	State
1. Drafting Competencies - To create drawing view 'B' from drawing view ...	5	Answered
2. Drafting Competencies - To create drawing view 'B' from drawing view ...	5	Answered
3. Drafting Competencies - To create drawing view 'B' from drawing view ...	5	Answered
4. Build this assembly in SOLIDWORKS (Gripper Assembly)	30	Answered
5. Modify this assembly in SOLIDWORKS (Gripper Assembly)	30	**Not Answered**
6. Advanced Part - Step 1 - (Connector)	15	Answered
7. Advanced Part - Step 2 - (Connector)	15	Answered
8. Advanced Part - Step 3 - (Connector)	15	Answered

There are three questions on the CSWA exam in this category. One question is in a multiple choice single answer format and the other two questions (Modification of the model) are in the fill in the blank format.

Each question is worth fifteen (15) points for a total of forty-five (45) points. You are required to build a model with six or more features and to answer a question either on the overall mass, volume, or the location of the Center of mass for the created model relative to the default part Origin location. You are then requested to modify the model and answer a fill in the blank format question.

Assembly Creation and Modification (Bottom-up) is the next chapter in this book. Up to this point, a Basic Part, Intermediate Part or an Advanced part was the focus. The *Assembly Creation and Modification* category addresses an assembly with numerous sub-components. All sub-components are provided to you in the exam.

The next chapter covers the general concepts and terminology used in the *Assembly Creation and Modification* category and then addresses the core elements. Knowledge of Standard mates is required in this category.

There are four questions. Multiple choice/single answer in the category. Each question is worth 30 points.

Click on the additional views during the CSWA exam to better understand the part and provided information. Read each question carefully. Identify the dimensions, center of mass and units. Apply needed material.

Questions

1. In Tutorial: Advanced Part 9-1 you created the illustrated part. Modify the Base flange thickness from .40in to .50in. Modify the Chamfer feature angle from 45deg to 33deg. Modify the Fillet feature radius from .10in to .125in. Modify the material from 1060 Alloy to Nickel.

Calculate the overall mass of the part, volume, and locate the Center of mass with the provided information.

Given:
A = 2.00, B = Ø.35
Material: 1060 Alloy
Density: 0.097 lb/in^3
Units: IPS
Decimal places = 2

2. In Tutorial: Advanced Part 9-2 you created the illustrated part. Modify the CirPattern1 feature. Modify the number of instances from 6 to 8. Modify the seed feature from an 8mm diameter to a 6mm diameter.

Calculate the overall mass, volume, and the location of the Center of mass relative to the part Origin.

Given:
A = 70, B = 76
Material: 6061 Alloy
Density: .0027 g/mm^3
Units: MMGS

3. Build the illustrated model in SOLIDWORKS. Set document properties, identify the correct Sketch planes, apply the correct Sketch and Feature tools, and apply material.

Calculate the overall mass of the part, volume and locate the Center of mass with the provided information.

- Material: 6061 Alloy

- Units: MMGS

4. Build the illustrated model in SOLIDWORKS. Calculate the overall mass of the part, volume and locate the Center of mass with the provided information. Where do you start? Build the model as you did in the above exercise. Create Coordinate System1 to locate the Center of mass for the model.

- Material: 6061 Alloy

- Units: MMGS

5. Build the illustrated model in SOLIDWORKS. Calculate the overall mass of the part, volume, and locate the Center of mass with the provided information.

- Material: 6061 Alloy

- Units: MMGS

Origin

6. Build the illustrated model in SOLIDWORKS. Calculate the overall mass of the part, volume and locate the Center of mass with the provided information. Where do you start? Build the illustrated model as you did in the above exercise. Create Coordinate System1 to locate the Center of mass for the model.

- Material: 6061 Alloy

- Units: MMGS

7. Build the provided model using SOLIDWORKS.

The model is provided in the SOILDWORKS CSWA Folder\Chapter 9.

Open Homework Part 9-7.

Utilize the rollback bar to view the sketches and features. Note: This is only one way to create the model.

Calculate the overall mass and volume of part with the provided information.

- Precision for linear dimensions = **2**.

- Material: **Case Stainless Steel**.

- Units: **MMGS**.

Mass properties of Homework Part 9-7
    Configuration: Default
    Coordinate system: -- default --

Density = 0.01 grams per cubic millimeter

Mass = 3442.00 grams

Volume = 447012.75 cubic millimeters

Surface area = 67768.84 square millimeters

Center of mass: (millimeters)
    X = 0.00
    Y = 50.00
    Z = 0.00

Sample screen shots from an older CSWA exam for an Advanced Modeling part. Click on the additional views to understand the part and provided information. Read each question carefully. Understand the dimensions, center of mass and units. Apply needed materials.

Screen shots from an exam

Zoom in on the part if needed.

Notes:

Chapter 10 - CSWA - Assembly Creation and Modification

Objectives

Assembly Creation and Modification is one of the five categories on the CSWA exam. In the last two chapters, a Basic, Intermediate or Advanced model was the focus. The Assembly Creation and Modification (Bottom-up) category addresses an assembly with numerous components.

This chapter covers the general concepts and terminology used in Assembly modeling and then addresses the core elements that are aligned to the CSWA exam. Knowledge to insert Standard mates and to create a new Coordinate system location is required in this category.

There are four questions on the CSWA exam (2 questions in part 1, 2 questions in part 2) in the Assembly Creation and Modification category: (2) different assemblies - (4) questions - (2) multiple choice/(2) single answer - 30 points each.

The first question is in a multiple choice single answer format. You should be within 1% of the multiple choice answer before you move on to the modification single answer section, (fill in the blank format).

You are required to download the needed components from a provided zip file and insert them correctly to create the assembly.

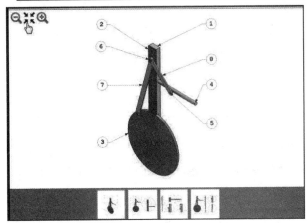

Screen shots from a CSWA exam

On the completion of the chapter, you will be able to:

- Specify Document Properties.

- Identify the first fixed component in an assembly.

- Create a Bottom-up assembly with the following Standard mates:

  - Coincident, Concentric, Perpendicular, Parallel, Tangent, Distance, Angle, and Aligned, Anti-Aligned options.

- Apply the Mirror Component tool.

- Locate the Center of mass relative to the assembly Origin.

- Create a Coordinate system location.

- Locate the Center of mass relative to a created Coordinate system.

☀ All SOLIDWORKS models (initial and final) are provided in the SOLIDWORKS CSWA Model Folder. Copy the needed folders to your local hard drive.

Assembly Modeling

There are two key Assembly Modeling techniques:

- Top-down, "In-Context" assembly modeling.

- Bottom-up assembly modeling.

In Top-down assembly modeling, one or more features of a part are defined by something in an assembly, such as a sketch or the geometry of another component. The design intent comes from the top, and moves down into the individual components, hence the name Top-down assembly modeling.

☀ Mate the first component with respect to the assembly reference planes.

Bottom-up assembly modeling is a traditional method that combines individual components. Based on design criteria, the components are developed independently. These are the three major steps in a Bottom-up design approach:

1. Create each part independent of any other component in the assembly.

2. Insert the parts into the assembly.

3. Mate the components in the assembly as they relate to the physical constraints of your design.

☀ To modify a component in an assembly using the bottom-up assembly approach, you must edit the individual part.

Build an Assembly from a Detailed Dimensioned illustration

An exam question in this category could read; Build this assembly in SOLIDWORKS. Locate the Center of mass of the model with respect to the illustrated coordinate system. Set decimal place to 2."

The assembly contains the following: (1) Clevis component, (3) Axle components, (2) 5 Hole Link components, (2) 3 Hole Link components, and (6) Collar components. All holes Ø.190 THRU unless otherwise noted. Angle A = 150deg. Angle B = 120deg. Unit system: IPS.

Note: The location of the illustrated coordinate system (+X, +Y, +Z).

In the exam, download the zip file of the components. Unzip the components. Do not use feature recognition when you open the downloaded components. This is a timed exam. You do not need the additional feature information.

- Clevis, (Item 1): Material: 6061 Alloy. The two (5) Hole Link components are positioned with equal Angle mates, (150deg) to the Clevis component.

- Axle, (Item 2): Material: AISI 304. The first Axle component is mated Concentric and Coincident to the Clevis. The second and third Axle components are mated Concentric and Coincident to the 5 Hole Link and the 3 Hole Link components respectively.

- 5 Hole Link, (Item 3): Material: 6061 Alloy. Material thickness = .100in. Radius = .250in. Five holes located 1in. on center. The 5 Hole Link components are positioned with equal Angle mates, (120deg) to the 3 Hole Link components.

- 3 Hole Link, (Item 4): Material: 6061 Alloy. Material thickness = .100in. Radius = .250in. Three holes located 1in. on center. The 3 Hole Link components are positioned with equal Angle mates, (120deg) to the 5 Hole Link components.

- Collar, (Item 5): Material: 6061 Alloy. The Collar components are mated Concentric and Coincident to the Axle and the 5 Hole Link and 3 Hole Link components respectively.

Think about the steps that you would take to build the illustrated assembly. Identify the first fixed component. Insert the required Standard mates.

Locate the Center of mass of the model with respect to the illustrated coordinate system. In this example, start with the Clevis component.

Do not use feature recognition when you open the downloaded components for the assembly in the CSWA exam. This is a timed exam. Manage your time. You do not need the additional feature information.

View the .pdf in the SOLIDWORKS CSWA Model Folder for a sample CSWA exam.

Screen shot from an exam

Tutorial: Assembly Model 10-1

Build the assembly in SOLIDWORKS.

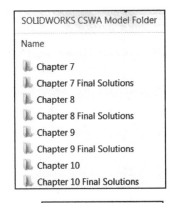

1. **Download** the needed components from the SOLIDWORKS CSWA Model Folder\Chapter 10\Assembly Model 10-1 folder.

2. **Create** a new IPS assembly in SOLIDWORKS.

3. Click **Cancel** ✖ from the Begin Assembly PropertyManager. Assem1 is the default document name. Assembly documents end with the extension .sldasm.

4. **Set** the document properties for the model.

5. **Insert** the Clevis part.

6. **Fix** the component to the assembly Origin. Click OK from the Insert Component PropertyManager. The Clevis is displayed in the Assembly FeatureManager and in the Graphics window.

🔅 The first component or subassembly should be fixed **(f)** to the origin, fully defined to the assembly document or mated to an axis about the assembly origin.

🔅 Only insert the required mates (timed exam) to obtain the needed Mass properties information.

7. **Insert** the Axle part above the Clevis component as illustrated.

8. **Insert** a Concentric mate between the inside cylindrical face of the Clevis and the outside cylindrical face of the Axle.

9. **Insert** a Coincident mate between the Right Plane of the Clevis and the Right Plane of the Axle.

10. **Insert** the 5 Hole Link part. Locate and rotate the component as illustrated.

11. **Insert** a Concentric mate between the outside cylindrical face of the Axle and the inside cylindrical face of the 5 Hole Link. Concentric2 is created.

12. **Insert** a Coincident mate between the right face of the Clevis and the left face of the 5 Hole Link. Coincident2 is created.

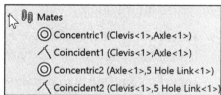

13. **Insert** an Angle mate between the bottom face of the 5 Hole Link and the back face of the Clevis. Angle = 30deg. The selected faces are displayed in the Mate Selections box. Angle1 is created. Flip direction if needed.

💡 Depending on the component orientation, select the Flip direction option and/or enter the supplement of the angle.

14. **Insert** the second Axle part. Locate the second Axle component near the end of the 5 Hole Link as illustrated.

15. **Insert** a Concentric mate between the inside cylindrical face of the 5 Hole Link and the outside cylindrical face of the Axle. Concentric3 is created.

16. **Insert** a Coincident mate between the Right Plane of the assembly and the Right Plane of the Axle. Coincident3 is created.

17. **Insert** the 3 Hole Link part. Locate and rotate the component as illustrated.

18. **Insert** a Concentric mate between the outside cylindrical face of the Axle and the inside cylindrical face of the 3 Hole Link. Concentric4 is created.

19. **Insert** a Coincident mate between the right face of the 5 Hole Link and the left face of the 3 Hole Link.

20. **Insert** an Angle mate between the bottom face of the 5 Hole Link and the bottom face of the 3 Hole Link. Angle = 60deg. Angle2 is created.

💡 Depending on the component orientation, select the Flip direction option and/or enter the supplement of the angle when needed.

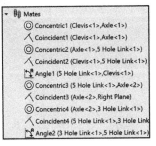

Apply the Measure tool to check the angle.

21. **Insert** the third Axle part.

22. **Insert** a Concentric mate between the inside cylindrical face of the 3 Hole Link and the outside cylindrical face of the Axle.

23. **Insert** a Coincident mate between the Right Plane of the assembly and the Right Plane of the Axle.

24. **Insert** the Collar part. Locate the Collar near the first Axle component.

25. **Insert** a Concentric mate between the inside cylindrical face of the Collar and the outside cylindrical face of the first Axle.

26. **Insert** a Coincident mate between the right face of the 5 Hole Link and the left face of the Collar.

27. **Insert** the second Collar part. Locate the Collar near the second Axle component.

28. **Insert** a Concentric mate between the inside circular face of the second Collar and the outside circular face of the second Axle.

29. **Insert** a Coincident mate between the right face of the 3 Hole Link and the left face of the second Collar.

30. **Insert** the third Collar part. Locate the Collar near the third Axle component.

31. **Insert** a Concentric mate between the inside cylindrical face of the Collar and the outside cylindrical face of the third Axle.

32. **Insert** a Coincident mate between the right face of the 3 Hole Link and the left face of the third Collar.

33. **Mirror** the components. Mirror the three Collars, 5 Hole Link and 3 Hole Link about the Right Plane. If using an older version of SOLIDWORKS, check the Recreate mates to new components box. Click Next in the Mirror Components PropertyManager. Check the Preview instanced components box.

Click **Insert**, **Mirror Components** from the Menu bar menu or click the **Mirror Components** tool from the Linear Component Pattern Consolidated toolbar.

If using an older release of SOLIDWORKS, no check mark in the Components to Mirror box indicates that the components are copied. The geometry of a copied component is unchanged from the original, only the orientation of the component is different.

If using an older release of SOLIDWORKS, a check mark in the Components to Mirror box indicates that the selected is mirrored. The geometry of the mirrored component changes to create a truly mirrored component.

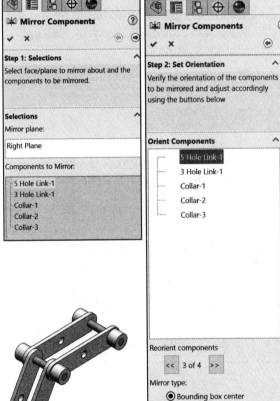

Create the coordinate system location for the assembly.

34. Select the front right **vertex** of the Clevis component as illustrated.

35. Click the **Coordinate System** tool from the Reference Geometry Consolidated toolbar. The Coordinate System PropertyManager is displayed.

36. Click the **right bottom edge** of the Clevis component.

37. Click the **front bottom edge** of the Clevis component as illustrated.

38. Address the **direction** for X, Y, Z as illustrated.

39. Click **OK** from the Coordinate System PropertyManager. Coordinate System1 is displayed.

40. **Locate** the Center of mass based on the location of the illustrated coordinate system. Select Coordinate System1.

- X: 1.79 inches

- Y: 0.25 inches

- Z: 2.61 inches

41. **Save** the part and name it Assembly Modeling 10-1.

42. **Close** the model.

Boss-Extrude1 of Clevis<1>

Mass properties of Assem1
   Configuration: Default
   Coordinate system: Coordinate System1

Mass = 0.14 pounds

Volume = 1.20 cubic inches

Surface area = 27.04 square inches

Center of mass: (inches)
   X = 1.79
   Y = 0.25
   Z = 2.61

There are numerous ways to create the models in this chapter. A goal in this text is to display different design intents and techniques.

If you don't find an option within 1% of your answer on the exam re-check your assembly.

Tutorial: Assembly Model 10-2

An exam question in this category could read, "Build this assembly in SOLIDWORKS. Locate the Center of mass of the model with the illustrated coordinate system. Set decimal place to 2. Unit system: MMGS."

The assembly contains the following: (2) U-Bracket components, (4) Pin components and (1) Square block component.

- U-Bracket, (Item 1): Material: AISI 304. Two U-Bracket components are combined together Concentric to opposite holes of the Square block component. The second U-Bracket component is positioned with an Angle mate to the right face of the first U-Bracket and a Parallel mate between the top face of the first U-Bracket and the top face of the Square block component. Angle A = 125deg.

- Square block, (Item 2): Material: AISI 304. The Pin components are mated Concentric and Coincident to the 4 holes in the Square block (no clearance). The depth of each hole = 10mm.

- Pin, (Item 3): Material: AISI 304. The Pin components are mated Concentric to the hole (no clearance). The end face of the Pin components are Coincident to the outer face of the U-Bracket components. The Pin component has a 5mm spacing between the Square block component and the two U-Bracket components.

Think about the steps that you would take to build the illustrated assembly. Identify the first fixed component. This is the Base component of the assembly. Insert the required Standard mates. Locate the Center of mass of the model with respect to the illustrated coordinate system. In this example, start with the U-Bracket part.

Create the assembly.

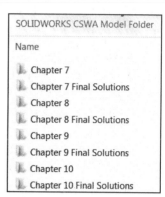

1. **Download** the needed components from the SOLIDWORKS CSWA Model Folder\Chapter 10\Assembly Model 10-2 folder.

2. **Create** a new assembly in SOLIDWORKS. The created models are displayed in the Open documents box.

3. Click **Cancel** ✖ from the Begin Assembly PropertyManager.

4. **Set** the document properties for the model.

5. **Insert** the first U-Bracket component into the assembly document.

6. **Fix** the component to the assembly Origin. Click OK from the PropertyManager. The U-Bracket is displayed in the Assembly FeatureManager and in the Graphics window.

7. **Insert** the Square block above the U-Bracket component as illustrated.

8. **Insert** the first Pin part. Locate the first Pin to the front of the Square block.

9. **Insert** the second Pin part. Locate the second Pin to the back of the Square block.

10. **Insert** the third Pin part. Locate the third Pin to the left side of the Square block. Rotate the Pin as illustrated.

11. **Insert** the fourth Pin part. Locate the fourth Pin to the right side of the Square block. Rotate the Pin as illustrated.

12. **Insert** a Concentric mate between the inside cylindrical face of the Square block and the outside cylindrical face of the first Pin. Concentric1 is created.

13. **Insert** a Coincident mate between the inside back circular face of the Square block and the flat back face of the first Pin. Coincident1 mate is created.

14. **Insert** a Concentric mate between the inside cylindrical face of the Square block and the outside cylindrical face of the second Pin. Concentric2 is created.

15. **Insert** a Coincident mate between the inside back circular face of the Square block and the front flat face of the second Pin. Coincident2 mate is created.

16. **Insert** a Concentric mate between the inside cylindrical face of the Square block and the outside cylindrical face of the third Pin. Concentric3 is created.

17. **Insert** a Coincident mate between the inside back circular face of the Square block and the right flat face of the third Pin. Coincident3 mate is created.

18. **Insert** a Concentric mate between the inside circular face of the Square block and the outside cylindrical face of the fourth Pin. Concentric4 is created.

19. **Insert** a Coincident mate between the inside back circular face of the Square block and the left flat face of the fourth Pin. Coincident4 mate is created.

Mates
◎ Concentric1 (Square block<1>,Pin<1>)
⋏ Coincident1 (Square block<1>,Pin<1>)
◎ Concentric2 (Square block<1>,Pin<2>)
⋏ Coincident2 (Square block<1>,Pin<2>)
◎ Concentric3 (Square block<1>,Pin<3>)
⋏ Coincident3 (Square block<1>,Pin<3>)
◎ Concentric4 (Square block<1>,Pin<4>)
⋏ Coincident4 (Square block<1>,Pin<4>)

20. **Insert** a Concentric mate between the inside right cylindrical face of the Cut-Extrude feature on the U-Bracket and the outside cylindrical face of the right Pin. Concentric5 is created.

21. **Insert** a Coincident mate between the Right Plane of the Square block and the Right Plane of the assembly. Coincident5 is created.

22. **Insert** the second U-Bracket part above the assembly. Position the U-Bracket as illustrated.

23. **Insert** a Concentric mate between the inside cylindrical face of the second U-Bracket component and the outside cylindrical face of the second Pin. The mate is created.

24. **Insert** a Coincident mate between the outside circular edge of the second U-Bracket and the back flat face of the second Pin. The mate is created.

There are numerous ways to mate the models in this chapter. A goal is to display different design intents and techniques.

25. **Insert** an Angle mate between the top flat face of the first U-Bracket component and the front narrow face of the second U-Bracket component as illustrated. Angle1 is created. An Angle mate is required to obtain the correct Center of mass.

26. **Insert** a Parallel mate between the top flat face of the first U-Bracket and the top flat face of the Square block component.

27. **Expand** the Mates folder and the components from the FeatureManager. View the created mates.

Create the coordinate location for the assembly.

28. Select the front **bottom left vertex** of the first U-Bracket component as illustrated.

29. Click the **Coordinate System** tool from the Reference Geometry Consolidated toolbar. The Coordinate System PropertyManager is displayed.

30. Click **OK** from the Coordinate System PropertyManager. Coordinate System1 is displayed.

31. **Locate** the Center of mass based on the location of the illustrated coordinate system. Select Coordinate System1.

- X: 31.54 millimeters

- Y: 85.76 millimeters

- Z: -45.00 millimeters

32. **Save** the part and name it Assembly Modeling 10-2.

33. **Close** the model.

⛅ If you don't find an option within 1% of your answer on the exam re-check your assembly.

⛅ Click on the additional views during the CSWA exam to better understand the assembly/component. Read each question carefully. Identify the dimensions, center of mass and units. Apply needed material.

Tutorial: Assembly Model 10-3

An exam question in this category could read, "Build this assembly in SOLIDWORKS. Locate the Center of mass using the illustrated coordinate system. Set decimal place to 2. Unit system: MMGS."

The assembly contains the following: (1) WheelPlate component, (2) Bracket100 components, (1) Axle40 component, (1) Wheel1 component and (4) Pin-4 components.

- WheelPlate, (Item 1): Material: AISI 304. The WheelPlate contains 4-Ø10 holes. The holes are aligned to the left Bracket100 and the right Bracket100 components. All holes are THRU ALL. The thickness of the WheelPlate = 10 mm.

- Bracket100, (Item 2): Material: AISI 304. The Bracket100 component contains 2-Ø10 holes and 1- Ø16 hole. All holes are through-all.

- Wheel1, (Item 3): Material AISI 304: The center hole of the Wheel1 component is Concentric with the Axle40 component. There is a 3mm gap between the inside faces of the Bracket100 components and the end faces of the Wheel hub.

- Axle40, (Item 4): Material AISI 304: The end faces of the Axle40 are Coincident with the outside faces of the Bracket100 components.

- Pin-4, (Item 5): Material AISI 304: The Pin-4 components are mated Concentric to the holes of the Bracket100 components (no clearance). The end faces are Coincident to the WheelPlate bottom face and the Bracket100 top face.

Think about the steps that you would take to build the illustrated assembly. Identify the first fixed component. This is the Base component of the assembly. Insert the required Standard mates.

Locate the Center of mass of the illustrated model with respect to the referenced coordinate system.

The referenced coordinate system is located at the bottom, right, midpoint of the Wheelplate. In this example, start with the WheelPlate part.

1. **Download** the needed components from the SOLIDWORKS CSWA Model Folder\Chapter 10\Assembly Model 10-3 folder.

2. **Create** a new assembly in SOLIDWORKS.

3. Click **Cancel** ✖ from the Begin Assembly PropertyManager.

4. **Set** the document properties for the assembly.

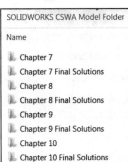

5. **Insert** the first component. Insert the WheelPlate. Fix the component to the assembly Origin. The WheelPlate is displayed in the Assembly FeatureManager and in the Graphics window. The WheelPlate component is fixed.

6. **Insert** the first Bracket100 part above the WheelPlate component as illustrated.

7. **Insert** a Concentric mate between the inside front left cylindrical face of the Bracket100 component and the inside front left cylindrical face of the WheelPlate. Concentric1 is created.

8. **Insert** a Concentric mate between the inside front right cylindrical face of the Bracket100 component and the inside front right cylindrical face of the WheelPlate. Concentric2 is created.

9. **Insert** a Coincident mate between the bottom flat face of the Bracket100 component and the top flat face of the WheelPlate component. Coincident1 is created.

10. **Insert** the Axle40 part above the first Bracket100 component as illustrated.

11. **Insert** a Concentric mate between the outside cylindrical face of the Axle40 component and the inside cylindrical face of the Bracket100 component. Concentric3 is created.

12. **Insert** a Coincident mate between the flat face of the Axle40 component and the front outside edge of the first Bracket100 component. Coincident2 is created.

To verify that the distance between holes of mating components is equal, utilize Concentric mates between pairs of cylindrical hole faces.

13. **Insert** the first Pin-4 part above the Bracket100 component.

14. **Insert** the second Pin-4 part above the Bracket100 component.

15. **Insert** a Concentric mate between the outside cylindrical face of the first Pin-4 component and the inside front left cylindrical face of the Bracket100 component. Concentric4 is created.

16. **Insert** a Coincident mate between the flat top face of the first Pin-4 component and the top face of the first Bracket100 component. Coincident3 is created.

17. **Insert** a Concentric mate between the outside cylindrical face of the second Pin-4 component and the inside front right cylindrical face of the Bracket100 component. Concentric5 is created.

18. **Insert** a Coincident mate between the flat top face of the second Pin-4 component and the top face of the first Bracket100 component. Coincident4 is created.

19. **Insert** the Wheel1 part as illustrated.

20. **Insert** a Concentric mate between the outside cylindrical face of Axle40 and the inside front cylindrical face of the Wheel1 component. Concentric6 is created.

21. **Insert** a Coincident mate between the Front Plane of Axle40 and the Front Plane of Wheel1. Coincident5 is created.

22. **Mirror** the components. Mirror the Bracket100 and the two Pin-4 components about the Front Plane.

Click **Insert, Mirror Components** from the Menu bar menu or click the **Mirror Components** tool from the Linear Component Pattern Consolidated toolbar.

🔆 If using an older version of SOLIDWORKS, click the Mirror Component tool from the Linear Component Pattern Consolidated toolbar to activate the Mirror Components PropertyManager.

Create the coordinate location for the assembly.

23. Click the **Coordinate System** tool from the Reference Geometry Consolidated toolbar. The Coordinate System PropertyManager is displayed.

24. **Select** the right bottom midpoint as the Origin location as illustrated.

25. **Select** the bottom right edge as the X axis direction reference as illustrated.

26. Click **OK** from the Coordinate System PropertyManager. Coordinate System1 is displayed.

27. **Locate** the Center of mass based on the location of the illustrated coordinate system. Select Coordinate System1.

- X: = 0.00 millimeters

- Y: = 37.14 millimeters

- Z: = -50.00 millimeters

🔆 If you don't find an option within 1% of your answer on the exam re-check your assembly.

28. **Save** the part and name it Assembly Modeling 10-3.

29. **Close** the model.

Summary

Assembly Creation and Modification is one of the five categories on the CSWA exam. In the last two chapters, a Basic, Intermediate or Advanced model was the focus. The Assembly Creation and Modification (Bottom-up) category addresses an assembly with numerous components.

There are four questions on the CSWA exam in the Assembly Creation and Modification category: (2) different assemblies - (4) questions - (2) multiple choice \ (2) single answers - 30 points each.

You are required to download the needed components from a provided zip file and insert them correctly to create the assembly as illustrated. You are then requested to modify the assembly and answer fill in the blank format questions.

The **Official Guide to Certified SOLIDWORKS Associate Exams**: **CSWA, CSDA, CSWSA-FEA** book is written to assist the SOLIDWORKS user to pass the associate level exams. Information is provided to aid the user to pass the Certified Associate - Mechanical Design exam, SOLIDWORKS Certified Associate - Sustainable Design exam, and SOLIDWORKS Certified Associate - Simulation (FEA) exam. The primary goal of this book is not only to help you pass the exams but also to ensure that you understand and comprehend the concepts and implementation details of the process.

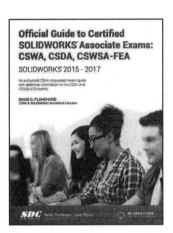

At this time, Advanced Mates and Mechanical Mates are not required for the CSWA exam.

Click on the additional views during the CSWA exam to better understand the assembly/component. Read each question carefully. Identify the dimensions, center of mass and units. Apply needed material.

Screen shots from a CSWA exam

Questions

1: Build this ANSI MMGS assembly from the provided information in SOLIDWORKS.

Calculate the overall mass and volume of the assembly.

Locate the Center of mass using the illustrated coordinate system.

The assembly contains the following: one Base100 component, one Yoke component, and one AdjustingPin component.

- Base100, (Item 1): Material 1060 Alloy. The distance between the front face of the Base100 component and the front face of the Yoke = 60mm.
- Yoke, (Item 2): Material 1060 Alloy. The Yoke fits inside the left and right square channels of the Base100 component (no clearance). The top face of the Yoke contains a Ø12mm through all hole.
- AdjustingPin, (Item 3): Material 1060 alloy. The bottom face of the AdjustingPin head is located 40mm from the top face of the Yoke component. The AdjustingPin component contains an Ø5mm Though All hole.

☀ The Coordinate system is located in the lower left corner of the Base100 component. The X axis points to the right.

2. Build the assembly from the provided information in SOLIDWORKS. Calculate the overall mass and volume of the assembly. Locate the Center of mass using the illustrated coordinate system. The assembly contains the following: three MachinedBracket components and two Pin-5 components. Apply the MMGS unit system.

Insert the Base component, float the component, then mate the first component with respect to the assembly reference planes.

- MachinedBracket, (Item 1): Material 6061 Alloy. The MachineBracket component contains two Ø10mm through all holes. Each MachinedBracket component is mated with two Angle mates. The Angle mate = 45deg. The top edge of the notch is located 20mm from the top edge of the MachinedBracket.
- Pin-5, (Item 2): Material Titanium. The Pin-5 component is 5mms in length and equal in diameter. The Pin-5 component is mated Concentric to the MachinedBracket (no clearance). The end faces of the Pin-5 component is Coincident with the outer faces of the MachinedBracket. There is a 1mm gap between the Machined Bracket components.

3. Build the assembly from the provided information in SOLIDWORKS. Calculate the overall mass and volume of the assembly. Locate the Center of mass using the illustrated coordinate system. The illustrated assembly contains the following components: three Machined-Bracket components and two Pin-6 components. Apply the MMGS unit system.

Insert the Base component, float the component, then mate the first component with respect to the assembly reference planes.

- Machined-Bracket, (Item 1): Material 6061 Alloy. The Machine-Bracket component contains two Ø10mm through all holes. Each Machined-Bracket component is mated with two Angle mates. The Angle mate = 45deg. The top edge of the notch is located 20mm from the top edge of the MachinedBracket.
- Pin-6, (Item 2): Material Titanium. The Pin-6 component is 5mms in length and equal in diameter. The Pin-5 component is mated Concentric to the Machined-Bracket (no clearance). The end faces of the Pin-6 component is Coincident with the outer faces of the Machined-Bracket. There is a 1mm gap between the Machined-Bracket components.

Sample screen shots from an older CSWA exam for an assembly. Click on the additional views to understand the assembly and provided information. Read each question carefully. Understand the dimensions, center of mass and units. Apply needed materials.

Zoom in on the part if needed.

Screen shots from an exam

Zoom in on the part if needed.

Screen shots from an exam

Notes:

Chapter 11

Additive Manufacturing - 3D Printing

Below are the desired outcomes and usage competencies based on the completion of Chapter 11.

Desired Outcomes:	Usage Competencies:
• Knowledge of Additive Manufacturing. • Identify key features of a low cost $500 - $2,000 3D printer. • Create an STL (STereoLithography) file. • 3D Print directly from SOLIDWORKS. • Select the proper Slicer engine and print parameters. • Create a successful print.	• Discuss the advantages and disadvantages of Additive Manufacturing. • Describe the differences between a Cartesian printer and Delta printer. • Explain 3D printer technology: STereoLithography (STL), Fused Filament Fabrication (FFF), Fused Deposition Model (FDM), and Digital Light Process (DLP). • Recognize common 3D printer terminology: Raft, Skirt, Brim, Support, Touching Buildplate, Heated vs. Non-Heated build area. • Choose the proper Slicer and print parameters. • Select the proper filament. • Understand part orientation during the print cycle. • Define general 3D printing tips. • Address fit tolerance for interlocking parts.

Notes:

Chapter 11 - Additive Manufacturing - 3D Printing

Chapter Objective

Provide a basic understanding between the differences of Additive vs. Subtractive Manufacturing. Comprehend 3D printer terminology along with a working knowledge of preparing, saving, and printing a 3D CAD model on a low cost ($500 - $2,000) printer.

On the completion of this chapter, you will be able to:

- Discuss Additive vs Subtractive Manufacturing.

- Determine the differences between a Cartesian printer and a Delta printer.

- Create a STereoLithography (STL) file in SOLIDWORKS.

- 3D print directly from SOLIDWORKS using an Add-In.

    o Save an STL file to G-code.

- Discuss printer hardware.

- Select the correct filament type:

    o PLA (Polylactic acid), ABS (Acrylonitrile butadiene styrene) or Nylon.

- Prepare the G-code.

    o Address model setup, print orientation, extruder temperature, and bed temperature.

- Comprehend the following 3D printer terminology:

    o (STereoLithography) file - STL.

    o Fused Filament Fabrication - FFF.

    o Fused Deposition Model - FDM.

    o Digital Light Process - DLP.

    o Dissolvable Support System - DDS.

    o Fast Layer Deposition - FLD.

    o Raft, Skirt and Brim.

    o Support and Touching Buildplate.

    o Slicer.

    o G-code.

- Address fit tolerance for interlocking parts.

- Define general 3D Printing tips.

Additive vs. Subtractive Manufacturing

In April, 2013, *The Economist* published an article on 3D printing. In the article they stated that this was the "beginning of a third industrial revolution, offering the potential to revolutionize how the world makes just about everything."

Avi Reichental, President and CEO, 3D Systems stated, "With 3D printing, complexity is free. The printer doesn't care if it makes the most rudimentary shape or the most complex shape, and that is completely turning design and manufacturing on its head as we know it."

Over the past five years, companies are now using 3D printing to evaluate more concepts in less time to improve decisions early in product development. As the design process moves forward, technical decisions are iteratively tested at every step to guide decisions big and small, to achieve improved performance, lower manufacturing costs, delivering higher quality and more successful product introductions. In pre-production, 3D printing is enabling faster first article production to support marketing and sales functions, and early adopter customers. And in final production processes, 3D printing is enabling higher productivity, increased flexibility, reduced warehouse and other logistics costs, economical customization, improved quality, reduced product weight, and greater efficiency in a growing number of industries.

Technology for 3D printing continues to advance in three key areas: **printers** and **printing methods**, **design software**, and **materials** used in printing.

Already, 3D printing is being used in the medical industry to help save lives and in some space exploration efforts. But how will 3D printing affect the average, middle-class person in the future? Low cost 3D printers are addressing this consumer market.

Additive manufacturing is the process of joining materials to create an object from a 3D model, usually adding layer over layer.

Subtractive manufacturing relies upon the removal of material to create something. The blacksmith hammered away at heated metal to create a product. Today, a Computer Numerical Control CNC machine cuts and drills and otherwise removes material from a larger initial block to create a product.

Additive manufacturing, sometimes known as *rapid prototyping*, can be slower than Subtractive manufacturing. Both take skill in creating the G-code and understanding the machine limitations.

A few advantages of Additive manufacturing:

- Lower cost (different entry levels) into the manufacturing environment.

- Lowers the barriers (space, power, safety, and training) to traditional subtractive manufacturing.

- Reduce part count in an assembly from traditional subtractive manufacturing (complex parts vs. assemblies).

- Build complex features, shapes, and objects.

- Reduce prototyping time.

- Faster development cycle.

- Quicker customer feedback.

- Faster product to market.

- Quicker product customization and configuration.

- Parallel verticals: develop and prototype at the same time.

- Open source slicing engines: (Slic3r, Skeinforge, Netfabb, KISSkice, Cura, etc.).

 A slicer takes a 3D model (most often in STereoLithography (STL) format and translates the model into individual layers. It then generates the machine code that the printer uses.

A slicer program allows the user to calibrate printer settings: filament type, part orientation, extruder speed, extruder temperature, bed temperature, cooling fan rate, raft, support, percent infill, infill pattern type, etc.

3D printers are controlled either through a small on-board control screen, an external memory device (USB, Sims card, etc.) or through a computer interface. User interface/control software allows a user to generate the needed machine code (G-code, .gcode) file from the computer to the 3D printer.

A few disadvantages of Additive manufacturing:

- Slow build rates. Many printers lay down material at a speed of one to five cubic inches per hour. Depending on the part needed, other manufacturing processes may be significantly faster.

- Requires post-processing. The surface finish and dimensional accuracy may be lower quality than other manufacturing methods.

- Poor mechanical properties. Layering and multiple interfaces can cause defects in the product.

- Frequent calibration is required. Without frequent calibration, prints may not be the correct dimensions, they may not stick to the build surface, and a variety of other not-so-wanted effects can occur.

- Limited component size/small build volume. In most cases, polymer products are about 1 cubic yard in size; metal parts may only be one cubic foot. While larger machines are available, they come at a cost.

Cartesian Printer vs. Delta Printer

Cartesian and Delta style 3D printers are the most common styles of desktop 3D printers currently available. What are the main differences? To understand their unique abilities one first needs to understand the basic technology of a Fused Deposition Model printer.

A Fused Filament Fabrication (FFF) printer takes a filament of a material (usually plastic) and extrudes it through a print-head-like nozzle. This material is then laid down in thin layers to form a 3D object on a platform, built from the bottom up.

Cartesian 3D printers are named after the dimensional coordinate system - the X, Y, and Z-axis - which is used to determine where and how to move in three dimensions.

Cartesian 3D printers typically have a print bed which moves only in the Z-axis. The extruder sits on the X-axis and Y-axis, where it can move in four directions on a gantry. This principle can be seen in action on popular models from Ultimaker, Sindoh, and MakerBot.

Controlling a linear Cartesian system is relatively simple, which is why most low cost 3D printers on the market today use this type of design. The Cartesian coordinate system has long been used for tools like plotters, CNC milling machines, and 2D printers.

Delta 3D printers also work within the Cartesian plane but use a very different approach to getting the print-nozzle where it needs to be.

Identifying characteristics start with the circular print bed. The extruder is suspended above the print bed by three arms in a triangular configuration, thus the name "Delta."

These arms move up and down independently to the print-nozzle keeping it precisely located throughout the print. Delta printers have the advantage in the ability to make taller objects due to the height of the printer and the tall arms.

Rather than using simple Cartesian geometry to calculate where the print-nozzle should go, Delta printers estimate the head position using trigonometric functions.

Create an STL file in SOLIDWORKS

STL (STereoLithography) is a file format native to the Stereolithography CAD software created by 3D Systems. STL has several after-the-fact backronyms such as "Standard Triangle Language" and "Standard Tessellation Language."

An STL file describes only the surface geometry of a three-dimensional object without any representation of color, texture, or other common CAD model attributes. The STL format specifies both ASCII and Binary representations.

Binary files are more common, since they are more compact. An STL file describes a raw unstructured triangulated (point cloud) surface by the unit normal and vertices (ordered by the right-hand rule) of the triangles using a three-dimensional Cartesian coordinate system.

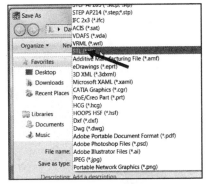

STL Save options allow you to control the number and size of the triangles by setting the various parameters in the CAD software.

To save a SOLIDWORKS model as a STL file, Click **File**, **Save As** from the Main menu or **Save As** from the Main menu toolbar. The Save As dialog is displayed. Select **STL(*.stl)** as the Save as type.

Click the **Options** button. The Export Options dialog box is displayed. View your options. For most parts, utilize the default setting.

Close the Export Options dialog box. Click **OK**. View the generate point cloud of the part. Click **Yes**. The STL file is now ready to be imported into your 3D printer software.

⚡ In SOLIDWORKS for a smoother STL file, change the Resolution to Custom. Change the deviation to 0.0005in (0.01mm). Change the angle to 5. Smaller deviations and angles produce a smoother file but increase the file size and print time.

3D Print Directly from SOLIDWORKS

With SOLIDWORKS you can print directly to 3D printers, similar to how you would print a document to your office printer. Although SOLIDWORKS can output .STL, a widely accepted format for 3D printing, the 3MF (3D Manufacturing Format), and AMF (Additive Manufacturing File) formats provide additional model information. Therefore, it requires no post-processing to define data such as the position of your model relative to the selected 3D printer, orientation, color, materials, etc.

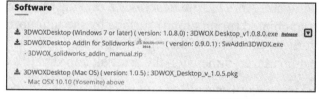

The Sindoh DP200, 3DWox printer provides the ability for users to print directly from SOLIDWORKS with an available Add-In for their printer. Visit http://3dprinter.sindoh.com/Downloads for additional information.

Through the 3D print application, users have access to dedicated command bars to address various print parameters, analysis, print direction optimization, and advanced printer settings.

During the print process, users can monitor the print time, needed filament, and estimated time to completion in the SOLIDWORKS graphics window.

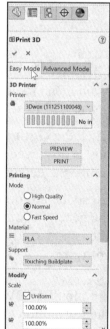

A camera feed can be monitored via an Android smart phone. The 3DWOXDesktop Add-in for SOLIDWORKS is available from http://3dprinter.sindoh.com/Downloads.

Print Material

As printed parts cool (PLA, ABS and Nylon), various areas of the object cool at different rates. Depending on the model being printed and the filament material, this effect can lead to warping, curling and or layer delamination.

There are many materials that are being explored for 3D printing; however, you will find that the two dominant plastics are ABS (Acrylonitrile butadiene styrene) and PLA (Polylactic acid). Both ABS and PLA are known as thermoplastics; that is, they become soft and moldable when heated and return to a solid when cooled.

This process can be repeated again and again. Their ability to melt and be processed again is what has made them so prevalent in society and is why most of the plastics you interact with on a daily basis are thermoplastics.

For a material to prove viable for 3D printing, it should pass four general criteria:

- Low cost and easily obtainable.

- Controllable extrusion.

- Second extrusion (two or more heads) and trace-binding during the 3D printing process.

- End use application.

☀ HIPS (High Impact Polystyrene) filament is a soluble support material used with dual head extruders.

ABS - Storage

ABS, PLA, and Nylon do best if, before use or when stored long term, they are sealed off from the atmosphere to prevent the absorption of moisture from the air. This does not mean your material will be ruined by a week of sitting on a bench in the shop, but long term exposure to a humid environment can have detrimental effects, both to the printing process and to the quality of finished parts.

Moisture laden ABS will tend to bubble and spurt from the tip of the extruder nozzle when printing, reducing the visual quality of the part, part accuracy, strength and introducing the risk of a stripping or clogging in the nozzle. ABS can be easily dried using a source of hot (preferably dry) air such as a food dehydrator.

ABS - Part Accuracy

For most, the single greatest hurdle for accurate parts in ABS is a curling upwards off the surface in direct contact with the 3D printer's print bed. A combination of heating the print surface and ensuring it is smooth, flat and clean helps to eliminate this issue. Additionally, some find various solutions can be useful when applied beforehand to the print surface; for example, a mixture of ABS dissolved in Acetone or a shot of hairspray on the build plate. Keep these solutions away from heat.

For fine features on parts involving sharp corners, such as gears, there may be a slight rounding of the corner. A fan, to provide a small amount of active cooling around the nozzle, can improve corners but one does also run the risk of introducing too much cooling and reducing adhesion between layers, eventually leading to cracks in the finished part.

PLA - Storage

PLA responds somewhat differently to moisture. In addition to bubbles or spurting at the nozzle, you may see discoloration and a reduction in 3D printed part properties. PLA (Polylactic acid) is a bioplastic derived from corn and is biodegradable and can react with water at high temperatures and undergo de-polymerization.

PLA can be dried using something as simple as a food dehydrator. It is important to note that this can alter the crystallinity ratio in the PLA and will lead to changes in extrusion temperature and other extrusion characteristics. For many 3D printers, moisture is not a major concern.

PLA - Part Accuracy

Compared to ABS and Nylon, PLA demonstrates much less part warping. For this reason it is possible to successfully print without a heated bed and use more commonly available "Blue" painter's tape as a print surface.

PLA undergoes more of a phase-change when heated and becomes much more liquid. If actively cooled, sharper details can be seen on printed corners without the risk of cracking or warping. The increased flow can also lead to stronger binding between layers, improving the strength of the printed part.

Nylon - Storage

Nylon is very hygroscopic, more so than PLA or ABS. Nylon can absorb more than 10% of its weight in water in less than 24 hours. Successful 3D printing with nylon requires dry filament. When you print with nylon that isn't dry, the water in the filament explodes causing air bubbles during printing that prevents good layer adhesion and greatly weakens the part. It also ruins the surface finish. To dry nylon, place it in an oven at 50 - 60C for 6-8 hours. After drying, store in an airtight container, preferably with desiccant.

Type 6, 6 Nylon requires a higher extruder temperature than ABS. Type 6, 6 Nylon melts at 255-265C (490-510F), type 6 nylon melts at 210-220C (410-428F) and polypropylene melts at 160-175C (320-347F).

Nylon - Part Accuracy

Compared to ABS and PLA, Nylon and ABS warp approximately the same. PLA demonstrates much less part warping. A heated plate (70 - 80C) is required for Nylon printing. It's best to apply a PVA (Polyvinyl acetate) Elmer's or Scotch based glue stick to the bed for adhesion in a cross-hatch pattern. Remember, less is more when using the glue stick on the plate.

☀ Nylon is a flexible, stronger and more durable alternative to PLA and ABS. With Nylon, do not use layer cooling fans and avoid drafty or cool rooms for best results.

☀ **Flex PLA** - Common flexible filaments are polyester-based (non-toxic) with a low melting point. Print temp: 120C. It is highly recommended to drastically lower your printing speed to around 20% from standard PLA. To take best advantage of the filament's properties, print it with 10% infill or less. Most flexible filament adheres well to acrylic; it does not adhere well to painter's tape and glass.

Build Plates

PLA in general has a lower shrinkage factor than ABS and Nylon. They are common materials which can warp, curl, delaminate and potentially destroy the print. The following equipment and procedures deal with these potential areas.

Non-Heated

People have experimented with different build surfaces such as steel, glass and various kinds of plastic. However, from experience, both ABS and PLA material seem to stick fairly well to any of the above build surfaces when used with a thin even layer of Polymide Kapton tape or a good quality blue painter's tape. It is not recommended to print ABS or Nylon with a non-heated build plate. Using a raft is always a good idea until you fully understand your system limitations.

☀ Some users apply a small amount of acetone to the build plate while rubbing an old print to the plate. This applies a base layer of material to improve adhesion.

Heated

A heated build plate or platform helps keep the lowest levels of a print warm as the higher layers are printed. This allows the overall print to cool more evenly. A heated build plate helps tremendously with most ABS prints and large PLA prints. You need a heated build plate for Nylon. Heated build plate temperatures should range between 90 - 95C for ABS, 60 - 65C for PLA and 70 - 80 for Nylon. Polymide Kapton tape works the best due to its temperature range capabilities for ABS and PLA. For Nylon, it is recommended to use a PVA (Elmer's or Scotch) based glue stick on the bed for adhesion in a cross-hatch pattern. Remember, less is more when applying the glue stick to the plate.

Ultimaker 3D printer with a heated build plate.

Polymide Kapton tape used in 3D printing.

💡 Some users apply a small amount of acetone to the build plate while rubbing an old print on the plate. This applies a base layer of material to improve adhesion.

Most PSUs (power supply units) supplied with non-heated build plate printers need to be upgraded to handle a heated plate upgrade.

Clean

Print materials stick better to a clean build plate. Clean your build plate after every build. Remove any build up material (hairspray, glue, old print residue, etc.). Replace needed tape (blue, Kapton, etc.).

Level

Level the build plate after every build. Do not print with a badly calibrated printer.

A level printing surface means every thin trace of support will be laid down at the intended height. A slope can cause some traces to be laid down too high from the print bed and prevent them from adhering.

Rule of thumb: For a low cost 3D printer, place the print surface (Z axis) approximately 0.1mm away from the nozzle at six points around the print bed.

Control Temperature

Eliminate all drafts (air conditioner, heater, windows) and control air flow that may cause a temperature gradient within the build area. Changes in temperature during a build cycle can cause curling, cracking and layer delamination, especially on long thin parts. Below are five fully enclosed 3D printers: A modified MakerBot Replicator 2, an Ultimaker 2 Go, a bq witbox, a Sindoh DP200 3DWox and an XYZ da Vinci.

☼ PLA in general is more forgiving to temperature fluctuations and moisture than ABS and Nylon during a build cycle.

Filament Storage

Below is a filament roll. The filament roll is packed with a package of desiccant. A desiccant is a hygroscopic substance that induces or sustains a state of dryness (desiccation) in its vicinity. Do not open filament packages before you need them. Moisture is your enemy. The filament will swell with moisture and can be an issue (size and temperature) in the extruder head during the print cycle.

☀ Darker colors in general (PLA and ABS) often require higher extruder temperatures. Extruding at higher temperatures may help prevent future delamination if you do not have a heated build plate or control build area.

Desiccant package

There are set defaults that come in many low cost printers. The default setting for the diameter of the filament in the Replicator G software is 1.85mm. If you are having build/extruder problems, use a pair of calipers to measure the diameter of the filament. Most calipers will have measurements down to .01mm. To measure your filament, take an average reading of at least three readings and re-set the default filament setting if needed.

Never focus too much on one single issue. These machines are complex, and trouble often arises from multiple reasons. A slipping filament may not only be caused by a bad gear drive, but also by an obstructed nozzle, a wrong feed value, a too low (or too high) temperature or a combination of all these.

The following images and models were created on the MakerBot Replicator 2 and the Sindoh DP200 3DWox 3D printer. Table 1 below displays a general comparison of the two machines.

Table 1: Sindoh DP200 vs. MakerBot Replicator 2

Manufacturer	Sindoh	MakerBot
Model	Sindoh DP200	Replicator 2
Print Technology	FFF	FDM
Printer Type	Cartesian	Cartesian
Extruder	Single Head	Single Head
Nozzle Diameter	0.4mm [0.015in]	0.4mm[0.015in]
Open Filament System	No	Yes
Print Material	PLA, ABS	PLA
Filament Diameter	1.75mm [0.069in]	1.75mm [0.069in]
Resolution	1mm (100-micron)	1mm (100-micron)
Build Plate	Heated Aluminum	Non-heated
Removable Print Platform	Yes	Yes
Self-Leveling	Yes	No
Self-Cleaning	Yes	No
Build Volume	8.3in L x 7.9in W x 7.7in H (210mm x 200mm x 195mm)	11.2in L x 6.0in W x 6.1in H (285mm x 152mm x 155mm)
Frame Design	Enclosed	Open
Supported File Types	STL, G-Code	STL, OBJ, Thing

Prepare the Model

There are many available open source software packages for preparing your model in an STL file format. To turn the .STL file into code for your printer, you'll need a slicing program. The MakerWare software (slicing program) for the MakerBot Replicator 2 Desktop and the Sindoh DP200 3DWox is displayed in this section.

The first action is to add/insert or load your STL file using the slicing program in the build area.

Depending on your printer "slicing program," you may or may not receive a message indicating your object is too large for the current build volume. If the object is too large, then you will need to scale it down or to redesign it into separate parts.

Use caution when scaling if you require fasteners or a minimum wall thickness.

You should center the part and have it lay flat on the build plate.

If you are printing more than one part, space them evenly on the plate or position them for a single build.

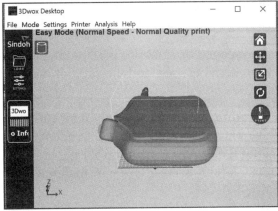

☀ In SOLIDWORKS, lay the parts out in an assembly. Save the assembly as a part. Save the part file as an STL file. Open the STL in the printer using your slicer.

Consideration should be used when printing an assembly. If the print takes 20 hours, and a failure happens after 19 hours, you just wasted a lot of time versus printing each part individually.

Example 1: Part Orientation

Part orientation is very important on build strength and the amount of raft and support material required for the build. Part orientations can also be related to warping, curling, and delamination.

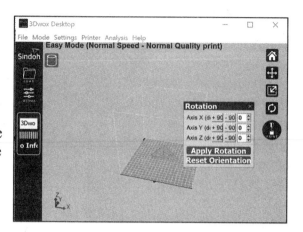

If maximizing strength is an issue, select the part orientation on the build plate so that the "grain" of the print is oriented to maximize the strength of the part.

First Orientation - Vertical

In the first orientation (vertical), due to the number of holes and slots, additional support material is required (with minimum raft material) to print the model.

First orientation - vertical

Removing this material in these geometrics can be very time consuming.

Second Orientation - Horizontal

In the second orientation (horizontal), additional raft material is used, and the support material is reduced.

The raft material can be easily removed with a pair of needle-nose pliers and no support material clean-up is required for the holes and slots. Note: In some cases, raft material is not needed.

Second orientation - horizontal

Example 2: Part Orientation

The lens part is orientated in a vertical position with the large face flat on the build plate. This reduces the required support material and ensures proper contact with the build plate.

The needed support material is created mainly internal to the part to print the CBORE feature. Note: There is some outside support material on the top section of the part.

Raft material

Internal support material for the CBORE

Outside support material for the
CBORE

3D Print Terminology

Stereolithography (SL or SLA)

Stereolithography (SL or SLA) is one of several methods used to create 3D printed objects. This is a liquid-based process that consists in the curing or solidification of a photosensitive polymer when an ultraviolet laser makes contact with the resin.

The process was patented as a means of rapid prototyping in 1986 by Charles Hull, co-founder of 3D Systems, Inc.

The process starts with a model in a CAD software and then it is translated to a STL (STereoLithography) file in which the pieces are "cut in slices" containing the information for each layer.

Fused Filament Fabrication (FFF)

Fused Filament Fabrication (FFF) is an additive manufacturing technology used for building three-dimensional products, prototypes or models. It is a rapid prototyping and manufacturing technique that adds layer after layer of molten plastic to create a model or product.

Typically, the FFF mechanism consists of a nozzle that emits material and deposits it onto a moving table. The FFF machine takes input from G-code and starts moving the nozzle and build plate to the needed coordinates. The material is heated in the nozzle to form liquid, which solidifies immediately when it is deposited onto the layer surface. The nozzle works layer-by-layer until the product is finished.

Fused Deposition Fabrication (FDM)

Fused Deposition Modeling (FDM) is an additive manufacturing technology that builds parts up layer-by-layer by heating and extruding thermoplastic filament. Ideal for building durable components with complex geometries in nearly any shape and size, FDM is the only 3D printing process that uses materials like ABS, PC-ISO polycarbonate, and ULTEM 9085. The actual term "Fused Deposition Modeling" and its abbreviation "FDM" are trademarked by Stratasys Ltd.

Digital Light Process (DLP)

Digital Light Processing (DLP) is a form of Stereolithography (SL, or SLA) that is used in Additive Manufacture or rapid prototyping. The main difference between DLP and SLA is the use of a projector light rather than a laser to cure photo-sensitive polymer resin. A DLP 3D printer projects the image of the object's cross section onto the surface of the resin. The exposed resin hardens while the machine's build platform descends, setting the stage for a new layer of fresh resin to be coated to the object and cured by light. Once a complete object is formed, additional post processing may be required such as removal of support material, chemical bath, and UV curing.

An example of a DLP 3D printer is the Formlabs Form1 printer as shown.

Raft, Skirt and Brim

A Raft is a horizontal latticework of filament located underneath the part. A Raft is used to help the part stick to the build plate (heated or non-heated).

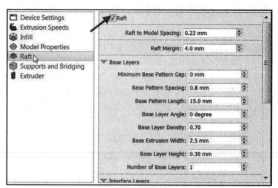

Rafts are also used to help stabilize thin tall parts with small build plate footprints.

When the print is complete, remove the part from the build plate. Peel the raft away from the part. If needed, use a scraper or spatula.

☀ The Raft Settings dialog box illustrates numerous settings and options.

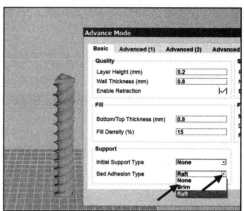

A Skirt is a layer of filament that surrounds the part with a 3-4mm offset. The layer does not connect the part directly to the build plate. The Skirt primes the extruder and establishes a smooth flow of filament. In some slicers, the skirt is added automatically when you select None for Bed Adhesion Type.

A Brim is basically like a Skirt for the part. A Brim has a zero offset from the part. It is a layer of filament that is laid down around the base of the part to increase its surface area. A Brim, however, does not extend underneath the part, which is the key difference between a brim and a raft.

☀ Proper part orientation for thin parts will make the removal of the raft easier.

Part with a Skirt on the Build plate

Part with a Raft on the Build plate

Support and Touching Buildplate

Printing with support is required when material must be deposited on a layer where there is no or insufficient material on the previous layer. This includes steep overhanging surfaces, straight overhangs, and fully suspended islands. Learning to print objects on a 3D Printer that require support structures will dramatically expand the potential of your printer and give you the confidence to undertake printing tasks that perhaps you had previously avoided.

You can remove supports after building the object, but be careful in the initial orientation of the part.

If the part has numerous holes, sharp edges, steep angles or thin bodies, additional support will be added and can make it difficult to remove cleanly.

In some slicers, there is a Touching Buildplate option. This option provide supports only where the part touches the build plate. This reduces build time, clean up and support build material. Use this option when you have overhangs and tricky angles toward the bottom of a design, but do not wish to plug up holes, hollow spaces, or arches in the rest of the design.

See the below illustration of a support material example.

Support material

My favorite tools to remove support and raft material are a good pair of needle nose pliers, angle tweezers and a small flat head screwdriver.

Slicer Engine

All 3D printers use a slicer engine. Slicing generates the G-code necessary to feed into your printer. Slicing is the process of turning your 3D model into a toolpath for your 3D printer. Most people call it slicing because the first thing the slicing engine does is cut your 3D model into thin horizontal layers. Open source slicing engines include Slic3r, Skeinforge, Netfabb, KISSkice, Cura, etc. to name a few.

G-code

There are different ways to prepare G-code for a printer. One is to use a slicer engine. These programs take a CAD model, slice it into layers, and output the G-code required for each layer. Slicers are an easy way to go from a 3D model to a printed part, but the user sacrifices some flexibility when using them. Another option for G-code generation is to use me-code, a lower level open source library. Me-code libraries give precise control over the toolpath providing a solution for a complex print that is not suitable for slicing. If you need to run a few test lines while calibrating your 3D printer, then the final option is to write your own G-code.

Infill

Infill is the internal structure of your object, which can be as sparse or as substantial as you would like it to be. A higher percentage will result in a more solid object, so 100% infill will make your object completely solid, while 0% infill will give you something completely hollow. The higher the infill percentage, the more material and longer the print time required. In general, use a 10% - 15% infill.

Infill Pattern/Shape

When using any infill percentage, a pattern is used to create a strong and durable structure inside the print. A few standard patterns are Rectilinear, Honeycomb, Circular and Triangular.

Shells/Parameters

The number of shells on the object refers to the number of times the outline of the model is retraced. Shells are the outermost layer of the object, the part of the object you see and interact with.

More shells result in a stronger object but longer printing time and more material.

Shells are also referred to as perimeters in some software and documents.

☀ Do not use additional shells on fine featured models, such as small text. It will obscure the detail.

View the different infill and number of shells between the two models.

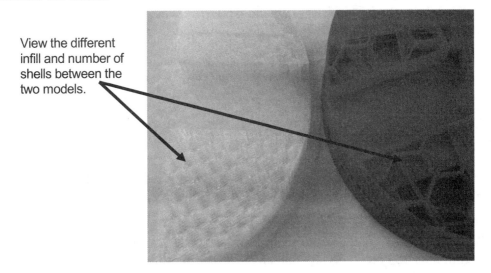

Layer Height

Traditionally, extrusion-based 3D printers have emphasized the layer height (such as 0.1mm or 0.3mm) as the main indicator of accuracy or quality. One reason for this may be that 3D prints made with this technology typically have visible ridges between different layers.

Layer height has a significant effect on the resolution of organic (curvy) parts. In general use 0.3mm for fast draft quality, 0.25mm for medium draft quality, 0.2mm for standard quality, and 0.1mm for high quality.

☀ (1micron = 1μm = 0.001mm).

Remove the Model from the Build Plate

If you have a non-heated build plate with a sheet of good quality blue painter's tape, it is not too difficult to remove the part. Utilize a flat edge tool (a thin steel spatula), gently work under the part, and lift the raft or the part directly on the tape. You may rip the tape when taking the part off. Replace the tape. Re-level your build plate after every build.

If you have a heated build plate your temperatures can range between 60 - 90C (Kapton tape) depending on the material, so be careful. Again, as above, utilize a flat edge tool (a thin steel spatula), gently work under the part, and lift the part directly from the plate. Re-level your build plate after every build.

Know the Printer's Limitations

There are features that are too small to be printed in plastic on a desktop 3D printer. An important, but often overlooked, variable in what your printer can achieve is thread width.

Thread width is determined by the diameter of your printer's nozzle. Most printers have a 0.4mm or 0.5mm nozzle. Practically, this means that a circle drawn by a 3D printer is always two thread widths deep: 0.8mm thick with a 0.4mm nozzle to 1mm thick for a 0.5mm nozzle. A good rule of thumb is "The smallest feature you can create is double the thread width."

Tolerance for Interlocking Parts

For objects with multiple interlocking parts, design in your fit tolerance. Getting tolerances correct can be difficult. Typical minimum wall thickness for a model is roughly 1mm, and printed part accuracy is ±0.2mm. It is recommended to use a ±0.2mm offset for tight fit (press fit parts, connectors) and use a ±0.4mm offset for loose fit (hinges, box lids).

Keep in mind the underlying problems with low cost 3D printers. The same 3D model will produce prints with varying part tolerances when printed on different types and brands of 3D printers. Users need to check the specifications from the 3D printer and filament manufacturer and then adjust the model geometries accordingly. Also, with any 3D printer, make sure the printer is calibrated to ensure the resolution will be the same across multiple prints.

Test the fit yourself with the particular model to determine the right tolerance for the items you are creating and material you are using.

General Printing Tips

Reduce Infill

When printing a model, you can choose to print it hollow or completely solid, or some percentage between 0 and 100. Infill is a settable variable in most Slicer engines. The material inside the part exerts a force on the entire printed part as it cools. More material increases cost of the part and build time.

Parts with a lower percentage of Infill should have a lower internal force between layers and can reduce the chance of curling, cracking, and layer delamination along with a low build cost and time.

Control build area temperature

For a consistent quality build, control your build area and environment temperature. Eliminate all drafts and control air flow that may cause a temperature gradient within the build area.

Changes in temperature during a build cycle can cause curling, cracking and layer delamination, especially on long thin parts. From 1000s of hours in 3D printing experience, having a top cover, sides and a heated build plate along with a consistent room temperature provides the best and repeatable builds.

When troubleshooting issues with your printer, it is always best to know if the nozzle and heated bed are achieving the desired temperatures. A thermocouple and a thermometer come in handy. I prefer a Type-K Thermocouple connected to a multi-meter. But a non-contact IR or Laser-based thermometer also works well.

Cover

One important thing to remember is that IR and Laser units are not 100% accurate when it comes to shiny reflective surfaces. A Type-K thermocouple can be taped to the nozzle or heated bed using Kapton tape, for a very accurate temperature measurement.

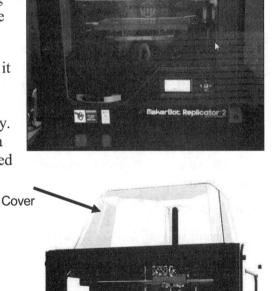

Add Pads

Sometimes, when you are printing a large flat object, such as a simple box container or a very long thin feature, you may view warping at the corners or extremities. One way to address this is to create small pads to your part during the modeling process. Create the model for the print. Think before you print and know your printer limitations. The pads can be any size and shape, but generally, diameter 10mm cylinders that are 1-2 layers thick work well. After the part is printed, remove them.

Makerbot Image

Unique Shape or a Large Part

If you need to make parts larger than your build area or create parts that have intricate projections, here are a few suggestions:

- Fuse smaller sections together using acetone (if using ABS). Glue if using PLA.

- Design smaller parts to be attached together (without hardware).

- Design smaller parts to be screwed together (with hardware).

Safe Zone Rule

Parts may have a safe zone. The safe zone is called "self-supporting" and no support material is required to build the part.

The safe zone can range between 30° to 150°. If the part's features are below 30° or greater than 150°, it should have support material during the build cycle. This is only a rule. Are there other factors to consider? Yes. They are layer thickness, extrusion speed, material type, length of the overhang along with the general model design of features.

☀ Design your part for your printer. Use various modeling techniques (ribs, fillets, pads, etc.) during the design process to eliminate or to minimize the need for supports and clean up.

Wall Thickness

In 3D printing, wall thickness refers to the distance between one surface of your model and the opposite sheer surface. A model made in stereolithography with a minimal wall thickness of 1mm provides you with a strong solid surface.

☀ If you scale your model with the 3D printer software, the wall thickness also scales proportionally. Make modifications in the CAD model to ensure the minimal wall thickness of 1mm.

Extruder Temperature

When working with a new roll of filament for the first time, I generally start out printing at about 200C - 210C (heated plate) and 225C - 230C (non-heated plate) for PLA and then adjust the temperature up or down by a few degrees until I obtain the quality of the print and the strength of the part to be in good balance with each other.

If the temperature is too high, you will see more strings between the separate parts of your print and you may notice that the extruder leaks out material while moving between separate areas of the print.

If the temperature is too cold, you will either see that the filament is not sticking to the (non-heated build plate) or the previous layer and you are getting a rough surface. You will get a part that is not strong and can be pulled apart easily.

Too cold – rough surface

The extruder temperature for PLA ranges between 200C - 215C (heated bed 60C - 65C), 225C - 230C (non-heated bed). For ABS they are 225C - 240C (heated bed 90C - 95C).

Various factors can influence the optimal extruding temperature:

- Moisture content.

- Temperature of the printing environment.

- Color.

- Glow in the dark ability.

- Elevation (from sea level) of the printing environment.

First Layer Not Sticking

One of the toughest aspects of 3D printing is to get your prints to stick to the build surface or bed platform. Investigate the following:

- Make sure the bed is level.

- Make sure the bed is hot enough. Do not use blue painter's tape with a heated plate.

- Make sure that the ambient temperature of the print environment isn't too hot or cold (or else adjust accordingly).

- Make sure you put the adhesive on the bed.

- Make sure the print head is close enough to make a nice squished first layer.

- Make sure you run the extruder enough before your print starts so there is filament going onto the bed during the entire first layer.

- Kapton/PET tape is a great way to print ABS. It makes a great shiny bottom layer and the heated bed ensures that your parts stay nice and flat.

Level Build Platform

An unleveled build platform will cause many headaches during a print. You can quickly check the platform by performing the business card test: use a single business card to judge the height of your extruder nozzle over the build platform. Achieve a consistent slight resistance when you position the business card between the tip of the extruder and the platform for all leveling positions.

Minimize Internal Support

Design your part for your printer. Use various modeling techniques (ribs, fillets, pads, etc.) during the design process to eliminate or to minimize the need for support and final clean up.

Water Tight Mesh

A water-tight mesh is achieved by having closed edges creating a solid volume. If you were to fill your geometry with water, would you see a leak? You may have to clean up any internal geometry that could have been left behind accidentally from Booleans.

Clearance

If you are creating separate or interlocking parts, make sure there is a large enough distance between tight areas. 3D Printing production, such as Selective Laser Sintering (SLS), makes moving parts without assembly a possibility that was not there before. Take advantage of this strength by creating enough clearance that the model's pieces do not fuse together or trap support material inside.

In General

- Keep your software and firmware up to date.

- Think before you print. Design your model for your printer.

- Understand the printer's limitations. Adjust one thing at a time between prints and keep notes about the settings and effect on the print. Label test prints with a Sharpie and take photographs.

- Always level and clean the build plate before a build.

- Select the correct material (filament) for the build and application. Materials are still an area of active exploration. Use ABS, PLA and Nylon, each of which has specific printing requirements.

- Select the correct part orientation on the build plate. Many of these devices require some attention when printing. 3D printers fabricate objects from thin layers of material; there is a grain to the structure of the printed parts, much like there is grain in wood. Try to print in an orientation so that the "grain" of the print is oriented to maximize the strength of the part.

- Make sure that the bottom surface of each part of the print is firmly secured to the build platform, both for the success of the print and for the surface finish on the bottom face of the object.

- Select the correct Slicing engine settings. Models go through two software processes on their way to becoming finished prints: slicing and sending. Slicing divides a model into printable layers and plots the toolpaths to fill them in. The printer client then sends these movements to the hardware and provides a control interface for its other functions.

- Control the environment for the filament and build area (temperature, humidity, etc.).

- If in doubt, create your first build with a raft and support.

- 3D printers cannot print perfectly, so there will always be a bit of variation between the model and the output. If you make a round hole that's 10mm in diameter and a 10mm diameter drive shaft to fill that hole, it won't have enough clearance to fit into the hole. The best current commercially available printers have a resolution of 0.1mm. This means there could be up to 0.2mm difference between the actual surface of your print and the 3d model. Models also shrink a little after being printed.

- The best thing to do after a print has been completed is to cool down your machine entirely before switching it off. But, if you are in a rush, make sure to at least get it under 100C before switching it off.

Summary

With 1000s of hours using multiple low cost 3D printers, learning about additive print technology is a great experience. Students face a multitude of obstacles with their first 3D prints. Understanding what went wrong and knowing the capabilities of the 3D printer produces positive results.

Never focus too much on one single issue. These machines are complex, and trouble often arises from multiple reasons. A slipping filament may not only be caused by a bad gear drive, but also by an obstructed nozzle, a wrong feed value, a too low (or too high) temperature or a combination of all these.

As printed parts cool (PLA, ABS and Nylon), various areas of the object cool at different rates. Depending on the model being printed and the filament material, this effect can lead to warping, curling and or layer delamination.

Design your part for your printer. Use various modeling techniques (ribs, fillets, pads, etc.) during the design process to eliminate or to minimize the need for supports and clean up.

Technology for 3D printing continues to advance in three key areas: **printers** and **printing methods**, **design software**, and **materials** used in printing.

Additive manufacturing, sometimes known as *rapid prototyping*, can be slower than Subtractive manufacturing. Both take skill in creating the G-code and understanding the machine limitations.

Appendix

Engineering Changer Order (ECO)

D&M Engineering Change Order				ECO # _____ Page 1 of __	
Product Line	☐ Hardware ☐ Software ☐ Quality ☐ Tech Pubs			Author Date Authorized Mgr. Date	
Change Tested By					
Reason for ECO(Describe the existing problem, symptom and impact on field)					
D&M Part No.	Rev From/To	Part Description	Description		Owner

ECO Implementation/Class		Departments	Approvals	Date	
All in Field	☐	Engineering			
All in Test	☐	Manufacturing			
All in Assembly	☐	Technical Support			
All in Stock	☐	Marketing			
All on Order	☐	DOC Control			
All Future	☐				
Material Disposition		ECO Cost			
Rework	☐	DO NOT WRITE BELOW THIS LINE (ECO BOARD ONLY)			
Scrap	☐	Effective Date			
Use as is	☐	Incorporated Date			
None	☐	Board Approval			
See Attached	☐	Board Date			

This text follows the ASME Y14 2009 Engineering Drawing and Related Documentation Practices for drawings. Display of dimensions and tolerances are as follows:

TYPES of DECIMAL DIMENSIONS (ASME Y14.5 2009)			
Description:	**UNITS: MM**	**Description:**	**UNITS: INCH**
Dimension is less than 1mm. Zero precedes the decimal point.	0.9 0.95	Dimension is less than 1 inch. Zero is not used before the decimal point.	.5 .56
Dimension is a whole number. Display no decimal point. Display no zero after decimal point.	19	Express dimension to the same number of decimal places as its tolerance. Add zeroes to the right of the decimal point. If the tolerance is expressed to 3 places, then the dimension contains 3 places to the right of the decimal point.	1.750
Dimension exceeds a whole number by a decimal fraction of a millimeter. Display no zero to the right of the decimal.	11.5 11.51		

TABLE 1 — TOLERANCE DISPLAY FOR INCH AND METRIC DIMENSIONS (ASME Y14.5 2009)		
DISPLAY:	**UNITS: INCH:**	**UNITS: METRIC:**
Dimensions less than 1	.5	0.5
Unilateral Tolerance	$1.417^{+.005}_{-.000}$	$36^{0}_{-0.5}$
Bilateral Tolerance	$1.417^{+.010}_{-.020}$	$36^{+0.25}_{-0.50}$
Limit Tolerance	.571 .463	14.50 11.50

SOLIDWORKS Keyboard Shortcuts

Listed below are some of the pre-defined keyboard shortcuts in SOLIDWORKS:

Action:	Key Combination:
Model Views	
Rotate the model horizontally or vertically	**Arrow** keys
Rotate the model horizontally or vertically 90 degrees	**Shift + Arrow** keys
Rotate the model clockwise or counterclockwise	**Alt** + left of right **Arrow** keys
Pan the model	**Ctrl + Arrow** keys
Magnifying glass	**g**
Zoom in	**Shift + z**
Zoom out	**z**
Zoom to fit	**f**
Previous view	**Ctrl + Shift + z**
View Orientation	
View Orientation menu	**Spacebar**
Front view	**Ctrl + 1**
Back view	**Ctrl + 2**
Left view	**Ctrl + 3**
Right view	**Ctrl + 4**
Top view	**Ctrl + 5**
Bottom view	**Ctrl + 6**
Isometric view	**Ctrl + 7**
NormalTo view	**Ctrl + 8**
Selection Filters	
Filter edges	**e**
Filter vertices	**v**
Filter faces	**x**
Toggle Selection Filter toolbar	**F5**
Toggle selection filters on/off	**F6**
File menu items	
New SOLIDWORKS document	**Ctrl + n**
Open document	**Ctrl + o**
Open From Web Folder	**Ctrl + w**
Make Drawing from Part	**Ctrl + d**
Make Assembly from Part	**Ctrl + a**
Save	**Ctrl +s**
Print	**Ctrl + p**
Additional shortcuts	
Access online help inside of PropertyManager or dialog box	**F1**
Rename an item in the FeatureManager design tree	**F2**
Rebuild the model	**Ctrl + b**
Force rebuild – Rebuild the model and all its features	**Ctrl + q**
Redraw the screen	**Ctrl + r**

Cycle between open SOLIDWORKS document	**Ctrl + Tab**
Line to arc/arc to line in the Sketch	**a**
Undo	**Ctrl + z**
Redo	**Ctrl + y**
Cut	**Ctrl + x**
Copy	**Ctrl + c**
Additional shortcuts	
Paste	**Ctrl + v**
Delete	**Delete**
Next window	**Ctrl + F6**
Close window	**Ctrl + F4**
View previous tools	**s**
Selects all text inside an Annotations text box	**Ctrl + a**

☀ In a sketch, the **Esc** key unselects geometry items currently selected in the Properties box and Add Relations box. In the model, the **Esc** key closes the PropertyManager and cancels the selections.

☀ Use the **g** key to activate the Magnifying glass tool. Use the Magnifying glass tool to inspect a model and make selections without changing the overall view.

☀ Use the **s** key to view/access previous command tools in the Graphics window.

Windows Shortcuts

Listed below are some of the pre-defined keyboard shortcuts in Microsoft Windows:

Action:	Keyboard Combination:
Open the Start menu	Windows Logo key
Open Windows Explorer	Windows Logo key + E
Minimize all open windows	Windows Logo key + M
Open a Search window	Windows Logo key + F
Open Windows Help	Windows Logo key + F1
Select multiple geometry items in a SOLIDWORKS document	Ctrl key (Hold the Ctrl key down. Select items.) Release the Ctrl key.

Helpful On-Line Information

The SOLIDWORKS URL
http://www.SOLIDWORKS.com contains
information on Local Resellers, Solution Partners,
Certifications, SOLIDWORKS users' groups and
more.

Access 3D ContentCentral using the Task Pane to
obtain engineering electronic catalog model and
part information.

Use the SOLIDWORKS Resources tab in the
Task Pane to obtain access to Customer Portals,
Discussion Forums, User Groups, Manufacturers,
Solution Partners, Labs and more.

Helpful on-line SOLIDWORKS information is
available from the following URLs:

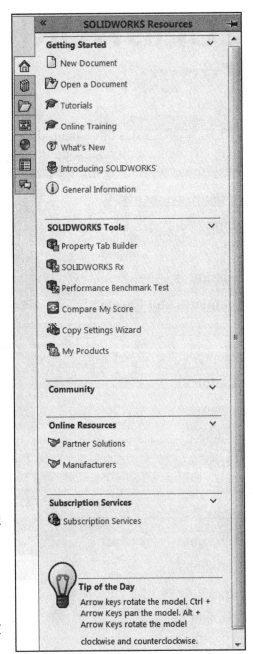

- http://www.mechengineer.com/snug/

  News group access and local user group
  information.

- http://www.swugn.org/

  List of all SOLIDWORKS User groups.

- http://www.caddedge.com/SOLIDWORKS-
  user-group-calendar-for-CT-MA-ME-NH-NJ-
  NY-PA-RI-VT/

  Updated SOLIDWORKS information and
  user group calendar for New England and
  surrounding areas.

- http://www.SOLIDWORKS.com/sw/engineer
  ing-education-software.htm

  SOLIDWORKS in Academia. Information on
  software, support, tutorials, blog and more.

*On-line tutorials are for educational purposes only.
Tutorials are copyrighted by their respective owners.

.

SOLIDWORKS DOCUMENT TYPES

SOLIDWORKS has three main document file types: Part, Assembly and Drawing, but there are many additional supporting types that you may want to know. Below is a brief list of these supporting file types:

Design Documents	**Description**
.sldprt	SOLIDWORKS Part document
.slddrw	SOLIDWORKS Drawing document
.sldasm	SOLIDWORKS Assembly document

Templates and Formats	**Description**
.asmdot	Assembly Template
.asmprp	Assembly Template Custom Properties tab
.drwdot	Drawing Template
.drwprp	Drawing Template Custom Properties tab
.prtdot	Part Template
.prtprp	Part Template Custom Properties tab
.sldtbt	General Table Template
.slddrt	Drawing Sheet Template
.sldbombt	Bill of Materials Template (Table-based)
.sldholtbt	Hole Table Template
.sldrevbt	Revision Table Template
.sldwldbt	Weldment Cutlist Template
.xls	Bill of Materials Template (Excel-based)

Library Files	**Description**
.sldlfp	Library Part file
.sldblk	Blocks

Other	**Description**
.sldstd	Drafting standard
.sldmat	Material Database
.sldclr	Color Palette File
.xls	Sheet metal gauge table

Appendix: Check your understanding Answer key

The Appendix contains the answers to the questions at the end of each chapter in the CSWA Section.

Chapter 7

1. Identify the illustrated Drawing view.

The correct answer is B: Alternative Position View.

2. Identify the illustrated Drawing view.

The correct answer is B: Break View.

3. Identify the illustrated Drawing view.

The correct answer is D: Aligned Section View.

4. Identify the view procedure. To create the following view, you need to insert a:

The correct answer is B: Closed Profile: Spline.

5. Identify the view procedure. To create the following view, you need to insert a:

The correct answer is B: Closed Spline.

6. Identify the illustrated view type.

The correct answer is A: Crop View.

7. To create View B from Drawing View A insert which View Type?

The correct answer is Aligned Section View.

8. To create View B it is necessary to sketch a closed spline on View A and insert which View type?

The correct answer is Broken out Section View.

9. To create View B it is necessary to sketch a closed spline on View A and insert which View type?

The correct answer is Horizontal Break View.

Chapter 8

1. Part 1. Calculate the overall mass of the part, volume, and locate the Center of mass with the provided illustrated information.

   - Overall mass of the part = 1280.91 grams
   - Volume of the part = 474411.54 cubic millimeters

- Center of Mass Location: X = 0.00 millimeters, Y = -29.17 millimeters, Z = 3.18 millimeters

2. Part 2. Calculate the overall mass of the part, volume, and locate the Center of mass with the provided information.

   - Overall mass of the part = 248.04 grams

   - Volume of the part = 91868.29 cubic millimeters

   - Center of Mass Location: X = -51.88 millimeters, Y = 24.70 millimeters, Z = 29.47 millimeters

3. Part 3. Calculate the overall mass of the part, volume, and locate the Center of mass with the provided information.

   - Overall mass of the part = 0.45 pounds, Volume of the part = 4.60 cubic inches and the Center of Mass Location: X = 0.17 inches, Y = 0.39 inches, Z = 0.00 inches

4. Part 4. Calculate the overall mass of the part, volume, and locate the Center of mass with the provided information.

   - Overall mass of the part = 0.28 pounds, Volume of the part = 2.86 cubic inches and the Center of Mass Location: X = 0.70 inches, Y = 0.06 inches, Z = 0.00 inches

5. Part 5. Calculate the overall mass and volume of the part with the provided information.

   - Overall mass of the part = 888.48grams. Overall volume of the part = 111059.43 cubic millimeters.

6. Part 5 Modify. Calculate the overall mass and volume of the part with the provided information.

   - Overall mass of the part = 309.75 grams. Overall volume of the part = 114721.22 cubic millimeters.

7. Part 6. Calculate the overall mass and volume of the part with the provided information.

   - Overall mass of the part = 509.92 grams. Overall volume of the part = 188860.93 cubic millimeters.

8. Part 6 modify. Calculate the overall mass and volume of the part with the provided information.

   - Overall mass of the part = 1465.70 grams. Overall volume of the part = 187910.60.

Chapter 9

1. Calculate the overall mass of the part, volume, and locate the Center of mass with the provided information.

    - Overall mass of the part = 1.99 pounds

    - Volume of the part = 6.47 cubic inches

    - Center of Mass Location: X = 0.00 inches, Y = 0.00 inches, Z = 1.49 inches

2. Calculate the overall mass of the part, volume, and locate the Center of mass with the provided information.

    - Overall mass of the part = 279.00 grams

    - Volume of the part = 103333.73 cubic millimeters

    - Center of Mass Location: X = 0.00 millimeters, Y = 0.00 millimeters, Z = 21.75 millimeters

3. Calculate the overall mass of the part, volume and locate the Center of mass with the provided information.

    - Overall mass of the part = 2040.57 grams

    - Volume of the part = 755765.04 cubic millimeters

    - Center of Mass Location: X = -0.71 millimeters, Y = 16.66 millimeters, Z = -9.31 millimeters

4. Calculate the overall mass of the part, volume and locate the Center of mass with the provided information. Create Coordinate System1 to locate the Center of mass for the model.

    - Overall mass of the part = 2040.57 grams

    - Volume of the part = 755765.04 cubic millimeters

    - Center of Mass Location: X = 49.29 millimeters, Y = 16.66 millimeters, Z = -109.31 millimeters

5. Calculate the overall mass of the part, volume and locate the Center of mass with the provided information.

    - Overall mass of the part = 37021.48 grams

    - Volume of the part = 13711657.53 cubic millimeters

    - Center of Mass Location: X = 0.00 millimeters, Y = 0.11 millimeters, Z = 0.00 millimeters

Chapter 10

1. Calculate the overall mass and volume of the assembly. Locate the Center of mass using the illustrated coordinate system.

    - Overall mass of the assembly = 843.22 grams

    - Volume of the assembly = 312304.62 cubic millimeters

    - Center of Mass Location: X = 30.00 millimeters, Y = 40.16 millimeters, Z = -53.82 millimeters

2. Calculate the overall mass and volume of the assembly. Locate the Center of mass using the illustrated coordinate system.

    - Overall mass of the assembly = 19.24 grams

    - Volume of the assembly = 6574.76 cubic millimeters

    - Center of Mass Location: X = 40.24, Y = 24.33, Z = 20.75

3. Calculate the overall mass and volume of the assembly. Locate the Center of mass using the illustrated coordinate system.

    - Overall mass of the assembly = 19.24 grams

    - Volume of the assembly = 6574.76 cubic millimeters

    - Center of Mass Location: X = 40.24, Y = -20.75, Z = 24.33

GLOSSARY

Alphabet of Lines: Each line on a technical drawing has a definite meaning and is drawn in a certain way. The line conventions recommended by the American National Standards Institute (ANSI) are presented in this text.

Alternate Position View: A drawing view superimposed in phantom lines on the original view. Utilized to show range of motion of an assembly.

Anchor Point: The origin of the Bill of Material in a sheet format.

Annotation: An annotation is a text note or a symbol that adds specific information and design intent to a part, assembly, or drawing. Annotations in a drawing include specific note, hole callout, surface finish symbol, datum feature symbol, datum target, geometric tolerance symbol, weld symbol, balloon and stacked balloon, center mark, centerline marks, area hatch and block.

ANSI: American National Standards Institute.

Area Hatch: Apply a crosshatch pattern or solid fill to a model face, to a closed sketch profile, or to a region bounded by a combination of model edges and sketch entities. Area hatch can be applied only in drawings.

ASME: American Society of Mechanical Engineering, publisher of ASME Y14 Engineering Drawing and Documentation Practices that controls drawing, dimensioning and tolerancing.

Assembly: An assembly is a document in which parts, features and other assemblies (sub-assemblies) are put together. A part in an assembly is called a component. Adding a component to an assembly creates a link between the assembly and the component. When SOLIDWORKS opens the assembly, it finds the component file to show it in the assembly. Changes in the component are automatically reflected in the assembly. The filename extension for a SOLIDWORKS assembly file name is *.sldasm.

Attachment Point: An attachment point is the end of a leader that attaches to an edge, vertex, or face in a drawing sheet.

AutoDimension: The Autodimension tool provides the ability to insert reference dimensions into drawing views such as baseline, chain, and ordinate dimensions.

Auxiliary View: An Auxiliary View is similar to a Projected View, but it is unfolded normal to a reference edge in an existing view.

AWS: American Welding Society, publisher of AWS A2.4, Standard Location of Elements of a Welding Symbol.

Axonometric Projection: A type of parallel projection, more specifically a type of orthographic projection, used to create a pictorial drawing of an object, where the object is rotated along one or more of its axes relative to the plane of projection.

Balloon: A balloon labels the parts in the assembly and relates them to item numbers on the bill of materials (BOM) added in the drawing. The balloon item number corresponds to the order in the Feature Tree. The order controls the initial BOM Item Number.

Baseline Dimensions: Dimensions referenced from the same edge or vertex in a drawing view.

Bill of Materials: A table inserted into a drawing to keep a record of the parts and materials used in an assembly.

Block: A symbol in the drawing that combines geometry into a single entity.

BOM: Abbreviation for Bill of Materials.

Broken-out Section: A broken-out section exposes inner details of a drawing view by removing material from a closed profile. In an assembly, the Broken-out Section displays multiple components.

CAD: The use of computer technology for the design of objects, real or virtual. CAD often involves more than just shapes.

Cartesian Coordinate System: Specifies each point uniquely in a plane by a pair of numerical coordinates, which are the signed distances from the point to two fixed perpendicular directed lines, measured in the same unit of length. Each reference line is called a coordinate axis or just axis of the system, and the point where they meet is its origin.

Cell: Area to enter a value in an EXCEL spreadsheet, identified by a Row and Column.

Center Mark: A cross that marks the center of a circle or arc.

Centerline: An axis of symmetry in a sketch or drawing displayed in a phantom font.

CommandManager: The CommandManager is a Context-sensitive toolbar that dynamically updates based on the toolbar you want to access. By default, it has toolbars embedded in it based on the document type. When you click a tab below the Command Manager, it updates to display that toolbar. For example, if you click the Sketch tab, the Sketch toolbar is displayed.

Component: A part or sub-assembly within an assembly.

ConfigurationManager: The ConfigurationManager is located on the left side of the SOLIDWORKS window and provides the means to create, select and view multiple configurations of parts and assemblies in an active document. You can split the

ConfigurationManager and either display two ConfigurationManager instances, or combine the ConfigurationManager with the FeatureManager design tree, PropertyManager or third party applications that use the panel.

Configurations: Variations of a part or assembly that control dimensions, display and state of a model.

Coordinate System: SOLIDWORKS uses a coordinate system with origins. A part document contains an original origin. Whenever you select a plane or face and open a sketch, an origin is created in alignment with the plane or face. An origin can be used as an anchor for the sketch entities, and it helps orient perspective of the axes. A three-dimensional reference triad orients you to the X, Y, and Z directions in part and assembly documents.

Copy and Paste: Utilize copy/paste to copy views from one sheet to another sheet in a drawing or between different drawings.

Cosmetic Thread: An annotation that represents threads.

Crosshatch: A pattern (or fill) applied to drawing views such as section views and broken-out sections.

Cursor Feedback: The system feedback symbol indicates what you are selecting or what the system is expecting you to select. As you move the mouse pointer across your model, system feedback is provided.

Datum Feature: An annotation that represents the primary, secondary and other reference planes of a model utilized in manufacturing.

Depth: The horizontal (front to back) distance between two features in frontal planes. Depth is often identified in the shop as the thickness of a part or feature.

Design Table: An Excel spreadsheet that is used to create multiple configurations in a part or assembly document.

Detail View: A portion of a larger view, usually at a larger scale than the original view. Create a detail view in a drawing to display a portion of a view, usually at an enlarged scale. This detail may be of an orthographic view, a non-planar (isometric) view, a section view, a crop view, an exploded assembly view or another detail view.

Detailing: Detailing refers to the SOLIDWORKS module used to insert, add and modify dimensions and notes in an engineering drawing.

Dimension Line: A line that references dimension text to extension lines indicating the feature being measured.

Dimension Tolerance: Controls the dimension tolerance values and the display of non-integer dimensions. The tolerance types are *None, Basic, Bilateral, Limit, Symmetric, MIN, MAX, Fit, Fit with tolerance* or *Fit (tolerance only).*

Dimension: A value indicating the size of the 2D sketch entity or 3D feature. Dimensions in a SOLIDWORKS drawing are associated with the model, and changes in the model are reflected in the drawing, if you DO NOT USE DimXpert.

Dimensioning Standard - Metric: - ASME standards for the use of metric dimensioning required all the dimensions to be expressed in millimeters (mm). The (mm) is not needed on each dimension, but it is used when a dimension is used in a notation. No trailing zeros are used. The Metric or International System of Units (S.I.) unit system in drafting is also known as the Millimeter, Gram Second (MMGS) unit system.

Dimensioning Standard - U.S: - ASME standard for U.S. dimensioning uses the decimal inch value. When the decimal inch system is used, a zero is not used to the left of the decimal point for values less than one inch, and trailing zeros are used. The U.S. unit system is also known as the Inch, Pound, Second (IPS) unit system.

DimXpert for Parts: A set of tools that applies dimensions and tolerances to parts according to the requirements of the ASME Y.14.41-2009 standard.

DimXpertManager: The DimXpertManager lists the tolerance features defined by DimXpert for a part. It also displays DimXpert tools that you use to insert dimensions and tolerances into a part. You can import these dimensions and tolerances into drawings. DimXpert is not associative.

Document: In SOLIDWORKS, each part, assembly, and drawing is referred to as a document, and each document is displayed in a separate window.

Drawing Sheet: A page in a drawing document.

Drawing Template: A document that is the foundation of a new drawing. The drawing template contains document properties and user-defined parameters such as sheet format. The extension for the drawing template filename is .DRWDOT.

Drawing: A 2D representation of a 3D part or assembly. The extension for a SOLIDWORKS drawing file name is .SLDDRW. Drawing refers to the SOLIDWORKS module used to insert, add, and modify views in an engineering drawing.

Edit Sheet Format: The drawing sheet contains two modes. Utilize the Edit Sheet Format command to add or modify notes and Title block information. Edit in the Edit Sheet Format mode.

Edit Sheet: The drawing sheet contains two modes. Utilize the Edit Sheet command to insert views and dimensions.

eDrawing: A compressed document that does not require the referenced part or assembly. eDrawings are animated to display multiple views in a drawing.

Empty View: An Empty View creates a blank view not tied to a part or assembly document.

Engineering Graphics: Translates ideas from design layouts, specifications, rough sketches, and calculations of engineers & architects into working drawings, maps, plans and illustrations which are used in making products.

Equation: Creates a mathematical relation between sketch dimensions, using dimension names as variables, or between feature parameters, such as the depth of an extruded feature or the instance count in a pattern.

Exploded view: A configuration in an assembly that displays its components separated from one another.

Export: The process to save a SOLIDWORKS document in another format for use in other CAD/CAM, rapid prototyping, web or graphics software applications.

Extension Line: The line extending from the profile line indicating the point from which a dimension is measured.

Extruded Cut Feature: Projects a sketch perpendicular to a Sketch plane to remove material from a part.

Face: A selectable area (planar or otherwise) of a model or surface with boundaries that help define the shape of the model or surface. For example, a rectangular solid has six faces.

Family Cell: A named empty cell in a Design Table that indicates the start of the evaluated parameters and configuration names. Locate Comments in a Design Table to the left or above the Family Cell.

Fasteners: Includes Bolts and nuts (threaded), Set screws (threaded), Washers, Keys, and Pins to name a few. Fasteners are not a permanent means of assembly such as welding or adhesives.

Feature: Features are geometry building blocks. Features add or remove material. Features are created from 2D or 3D sketched profiles or from edges and faces of existing geometry.

FeatureManager: The FeatureManager design tree located on the left side of the SOLIDWORKS window provides an outline view of the active part, assembly, or drawing. This makes it easy to see how the model or assembly was constructed or to examine the various sheets and views in a drawing. The FeatureManager and the Graphics window are dynamically linked. You can select features, sketches, drawing views and construction geometry in either pane.

First Angle Projection: In First Angle Projection the Top view is looking at the bottom of the part. First Angle Projection is used in Europe and most of the world. However, America and Australia use a method known as Third Angle Projection.

Fully defined: A sketch where all lines and curves in the sketch, and their positions, are described by dimensions or relations, or both, and cannot be moved. Fully defined sketch entities are shown in black.

Foreshortened radius: Helpful when the centerpoint of a radius is outside of the drawing or interferes with another drawing view: Broken Leader.

Foreshortening: The way things appear to get smaller in both height and depth as they recede into the distance.

French curve: A template made out of plastic, metal or wood composed of many different curves. It is used in manual drafting to draw smooth curves of varying radii.

Fully Defined: A sketch where all lines and curves in the sketch, and their positions, are described by dimensions or relations, or both, and cannot be moved. Fully defined sketch entities are displayed in black.

Geometric Tolerance: A set of standard symbols that specify the geometric characteristics and dimensional requirements of a feature.

Glass Box method: A traditional method of placing an object in an *imaginary glass box* to view the six principle views.

Global Coordinate System: Directional input refers by default to the Global coordinate system (X-, Y- and Z-), which is based on Plane1 with its origin located at the origin of the part or assembly.

Graphics Window: The area in the SOLIDWORKS window where the part, assembly, or drawing is displayed.

Grid: A system of fixed horizontal and vertical divisions.

Handle: An arrow, square or circle that you drag to adjust the size or position of an entity such as a view or dimension.

Heads-up View Toolbar: A transparent toolbar located at the top of the Graphic window.

Height: The vertical distance between two or more lines or surfaces (features) which are in horizontal planes.

Hidden Lines Removed (HLR): A view mode. All edges of the model that are not visible from the current view angle are removed from the display.

Hidden Lines Visible (HLV): A view mode. All edges of the model that are not visible from the current view angle are shown gray or dashed.

Hole Callouts: Hole callouts are available in drawings. If you modify a hole dimension in the model, the callout updates automatically in the drawing if you did not use DimXpert.

Hole Table: A table in a drawing document that displays the positions of selected holes from a specified origin datum. The tool labels each hole with a tag. The tag corresponds to a row in the table.

Import: The ability to open files from other software applications into a SOLIDWORKS document. The A-size sheet format was created as an AutoCAD file and imported into SOLIDWORKS.

Isometric Projection: A form of graphical projection, more specifically, a form of axonometric projection. It is a method of visually representing three-dimensional objects in two dimensions, in which the three coordinate axes appear equally foreshortened and the angles between any two of them are 120°.

Layers: Simplifies a drawing by combining dimensions, annotations, geometry and components. Properties such as display, line style and thickness are assigned to a named layer.

Leader: A solid line created from an annotation to the referenced feature.

Line Format: A series of tools that controls Line Thickness, Line Style, Color, Layer and other properties.

Local (Reference) Coordinate System: Coordinate system other than the Global coordinate system. You can specify restraints and loads in any desired direction.

Lock Sheet Focus: Adds sketch entities and annotations to the selected sheet. Double-click the sheet to activate Lock Sheet Focus. To unlock a sheet, right-click and select Unlock Sheet Focus or double click inside the sheet boundary.

Lock View Position: Secures the view at its current position in the sheet. Right-click in the drawing view to Lock View Position. To unlock a view position, right-click and select Unlock View Position.

Mass Properties: The physical properties of a model based upon geometry and material.

Menus: Menus provide access to the commands that the SOLIDWORKS software offers. Menus are Context-sensitive and can be customized through a dialog box.

Model Item: Provides the ability to insert dimensions, annotations, and reference geometry from a model document (part or assembly) into a drawing.

Model View: A specific view of a part or assembly. Standard named views are listed in the view orientation dialog box such as isometric or front. Named views can be user-defined names for a specific view.

Model: 3D solid geometry in a part or assembly document. If a part or assembly document contains multiple configurations, each configuration is a separate model.

Motion Studies: Graphical simulations of motion and visual properties with assembly models. Analogous to a configuration, they do not actually change the original assembly model or its properties. They display the model as it changes based on simulation elements you add.

Mouse Buttons: The left, middle, and right mouse buttons have distinct meanings in SOLIDWORKS. Use the middle mouse button to rotate and Zoom in/out on the part or assembly document.

Oblique Projection: A simple type of graphical projection used for producing pictorial, two-dimensional images of three-dimensional objects.

OLE (Object Linking and Embedding): A Windows file format. A company logo or EXCEL spreadsheet placed inside a SOLIDWORKS document are examples of OLE files.

Ordinate Dimensions: Chain of dimensions referenced from a zero ordinate in a drawing or sketch.

Origin: The model origin is displayed in blue and represents the (0,0,0) coordinate of the model. When a sketch is active, a sketch origin is displayed in red and represents the (0,0,0) coordinate of the sketch. Dimensions and relations can be added to the model origin but not to a sketch origin.

Orthographic Projection: A means of representing a three-dimensional object in two dimensions. It is a form of parallel projection, where the view direction is orthogonal to the projection plane, resulting in every plane of the scene appearing in affine transformation on the viewing surface.

Parametric Note: A Note annotation that links text to a feature dimension or property value.

Parent View: A Parent view is an existing view on which other views are dependent.

Part Dimension: Used in creating a part, they are sometimes called construction dimensions.

Part: A 3D object that consists of one or more features. A part inserted into an assembly is called a component. Insert part views, feature dimensions and annotations into 2D drawing. The extension for a SOLIDWORKS part filename is .SLDPRT.

Perspective Projection: The two most characteristic features of perspective are that objects are drawn: smaller as their distance from the observer increases and foreshortened: the size of an object's dimensions along the line of sight are relatively shorter than dimensions across the line of sight.

Plane: To create a sketch, choose a plane. Planes are flat and infinite. Planes are represented on the screen with visible edges.

Precedence of Line Types: When obtaining orthographic views, it is common for one type of line to overlap another type. When this occurs, drawing conventions have established an order of precedence.

Precision: Controls the number of decimal places displayed in a dimension.

Projected View: Projected views are created for Orthogonal views using one of the following tools: Standard 3 View, Model View or the Projected View tool from the View Layout toolbar.

Properties: Variables shared between documents through linked notes.

PropertyManager: Most sketch, feature, and drawing tools in SOLIDWORKS open a PropertyManager located on the left side of the SOLIDWORKS window. The PropertyManager displays the properties of the entity or feature so you specify the properties without a dialog box covering the Graphics window.

RealView: Provides a simplified way to display models in a photo-realistic setting using a library of appearances and scenes. RealView requires graphics card support and is memory intensive.

Rebuild: A tool that updates (or regenerates) the document with any changes made since the last time the model was rebuilt. Rebuild is typically used after changing a model dimension.

Reference Dimension: Dimensions added to a drawing document are called Reference dimensions and are driven; you cannot edit the value of reference dimensions to modify the model. However, the values of reference dimensions change when the model dimensions change.

Relation: A relation is a geometric constraint between sketch entities or between a sketch entity and a plane, axis, edge or vertex.

Relative view: The Relative View defines an Orthographic view based on two orthogonal faces or places in the model.

Revision Table: The Revision Table lists the Engineering Change Orders (ECO), in a table form, issued over the life of the model and the drawing. The current Revision letter or number is placed in the Title block of the Drawing.

Right-Hand Rule: Is a common mnemonic for understanding notation conventions for vectors in 3 dimensions.

Rollback: Suppresses all items below the rollback bar.

Scale: A relative term meaning "size" in relationship to some system of measurement.

Section Line: A line or centerline sketched in a drawing view to create a section view.

Section Scope: Specifies the components to be left uncut when you create an assembly drawing section view.

Section View: You create a section view in a drawing by cutting the parent view with a cutting, or section line. The section view can be a straight cut section or an offset section defined by a stepped section line. The section line can also include concentric arcs. Create a Section View in a drawing by cutting the Parent view with a section line.

Sheet Format: A document that contains the following: page size and orientation, standard text, borders, logos, and Title block information. Customize the Sheet format to save time. The extension for the Sheet format filename is .SLDDRT.

Sheet Properties: Sheet Properties display properties of the selected sheet. Sheet Properties define the following: Name of the Sheet, Sheet Scale, Type of Projection (First angle or Third angle), Sheet Format, Sheet Size, View label, and Datum label.

Sheet: A page in a drawing document.

Silhouette Edge: A curve representing the extent of a cylindrical or curved face when viewed from the side.

Sketch: The name to describe a 2D profile is called a sketch. 2D sketches are created on flat faces and planes within the model. Typical geometry types are lines, arcs, corner rectangles, circles, polygons, and ellipses.

Spline: A sketched 2D or 3D curve defined by a set of control points.

Stacked Balloon: A group of balloons with only one leader. The balloons can be stacked vertically (up or down) or horizontally (left or right).

Standard views: The three orthographic projection views, Front, Top and Right positioned on the drawing according to First angle or Third angle projection.

Suppress: Removes an entity from the display and from any calculations in which it is involved. You can suppress features, assembly components, and so on. Suppressing an entity does not delete the entity; you can unsuppress the entity to restore it.

Surface Finish: An annotation that represents the texture of a part.

System Feedback: Feedback is provided by a symbol attached to the cursor arrow indicating your selection. As the cursor floats across the model, feedback is provided in the form of symbols riding next to the cursor.

System Options: System Options are stored in the registry of the computer. System Options are not part of the document. Changes to the System Options affect all current and future documents. There are hundreds of Systems Options.

Tangent Edge: The transition edge between rounded or filleted faces in hidden lines visible or hidden lines removed modes in drawings.

Task Pane: The Task Pane is displayed when you open the SOLIDWORKS software. It contains the following tabs: SOLIDWORKS Resources, Design Library, File Explorer, Search, View Palette, Document Recovery and RealView/PhotoWorks.

Templates: Templates are part, drawing and assembly documents that include user-defined parameters and are the basis for new documents.

Third Angle Projection: In Third angle projection the Top View is looking at the Top of the part. First Angle Projection is used in Europe and most of the world. America and Australia use the Third Angle Projection method.

Thread Class or Fit: Classes of fit are tolerance standards; they set a plus or minus figure that is applied to the pitch diameter of bolts or nuts. The classes of fit used with almost all bolts sized in inches are specified by the ANSI/ASME Unified Screw Thread standards (which differ from the previous American National standards).

Thread Lead: The distance advanced parallel to the axis when the screw is turned one revolution. For a single thread, lead is equal to the pitch; for a double thread, lead is twice the pitch.

Tolerance: The permissible range of variation in a dimension of an object. Tolerance may be specified as a factor or percentage of the nominal value, a maximum deviation from a nominal value, an explicit range of allowed values, be specified by a note or published standard with this information, or be implied by the numeric accuracy of the nominal value.

Toolbars: The toolbar menus provide shortcuts enabling you to access the most frequently used commands. Toolbars are Context-sensitive and can be customized through a dialog box.

T-Square: A technical drawing instrument, primarily a guide for drawing horizontal lines on a drafting table. It is used to guide the triangle that draws vertical lines. Its name comes from the general shape of the instrument where the horizontal member of the T slides on the side of the drafting table. Common lengths are 18", 24", 30", 36" and 42".

Under-defined: A sketch is under defined when there are not enough dimensions and relations to prevent entities from moving or changing size.

Units: Used in the measurement of physical quantities. Decimal inch dimensioning and Millimeter dimensioning are the two types of common units specified for engineering parts and drawings.

Vertex: A point at which two or more lines or edges intersect. Vertices can be selected for sketching, dimensioning, and many other operations.

View Palette: Use the View Palette, located in the Task Pane, to insert drawing views. It contains images of standard views, annotation views, section views, and flat patterns (sheet metal parts) of the selected model. You can drag views onto the drawing sheet to create a drawing view.

Weld Bead: An assembly feature that represents a weld between multiple parts.

Weld Finish: A weld symbol representing the parameters you specify.

Weld Symbol: An annotation in the part or drawing that represents the parameters of the weld.

Width: The horizontal distance between surfaces in profile planes. In the machine shop, the terms length and width are used interchangeably.

Zebra Stripes: Simulate the reflection of long strips of light on a very shiny surface. They allow you to see small changes in a surface that may be hard to see with a standard display.

Index

About Us

SDC Publications specializes in creating exceptional books that are designed to seamlessly integrate into courses or help the self learner master new skills. Our commitment to meeting our customer's needs and keeping our books priced affordably are just some of the reasons our books are being used by nearly 1,200 colleges and universities across the United States and Canada.

SDC Publications is a family owned and operated company that has been creating quality books since 1985. All of our books are proudly printed in the United States.

Our technology books are updated for every new software release so you are always up to date with the newest technology. Many of our books come with video enhancements to aid students and instructor resources to aid instructors.

Take a look at all the books we have to offer you by visiting SDCpublications.com.

NEVER STOP LEARNING

Keep Going

Take the skills you learned in this book to the next level or learn something brand new. SDC Publications offers books covering a wide range of topics designed for users of all levels and experience. As you continue to improve your skills, SDC Publications will be there to provide you the tools you need to keep learning. Visit SDCpublications.com to see all our most current books.

Why SDC Publications?

- Regular and timely updates
- Priced affordably
- Designed for users of all levels
- Written by professionals and educators
- We offer a variety of learning approaches

TOPICS
3D Animation
BIM
CAD
CAM
Engineering
Engineering Graphics
FEA / CAE
Interior Design
Programming

SOFTWARE
Adams
ANSYS
AutoCAD
AutoCAD Architecture
AutoCAD Civil 3D
Autodesk 3ds Max
Autodesk Inventor
Autodesk Maya
Autodesk Revit
CATIA
Creo Parametric
Creo Simulate
Draftsight
LabVIEW
MATLAB
NX
OnShape
SketchUp
SOLIDWORKS
SOLIDWORKS Simulation